Terror and Wonder

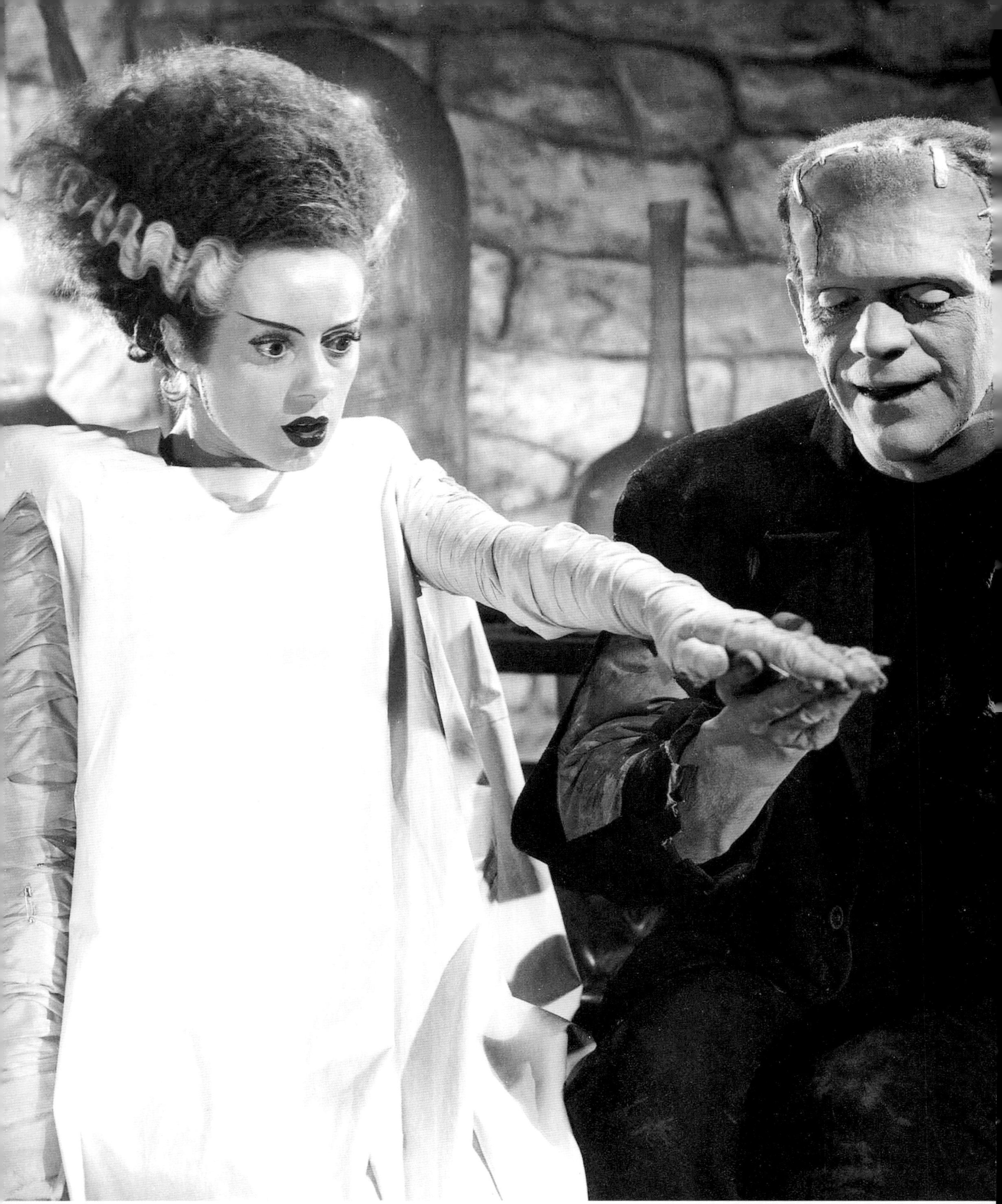

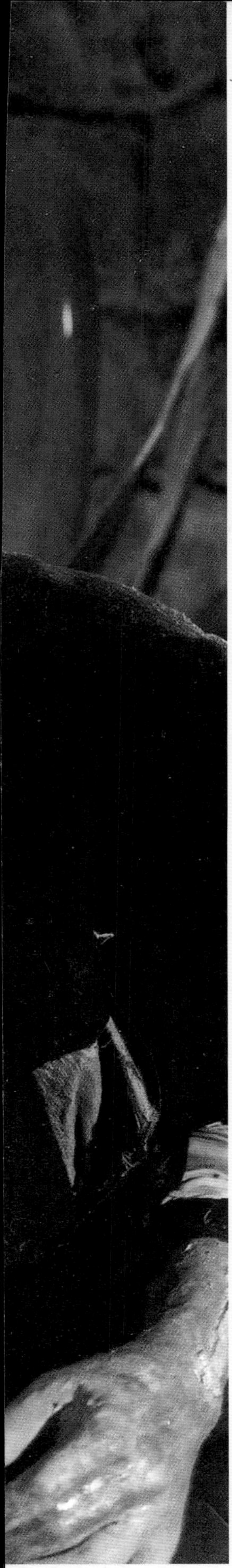

Terror and Wonder
The Gothic Imagination

Edited by Dale Townshend

The British Library

First published in 2014 by
The British Library
96 Euston Road
London NW1 2DB

On the occasion of the British Library exhibition
Terror and Wonder: The Gothic Imagination
3 October 2014–20 January 2015

British Library Cataloguing-in-Publication Data
A catalogue record for this book is available from the
British Library

ISBN 978 0 7123 5791 3 (paperback)
ISBN 978 0 7123 5755 5 (hardback)

HALF-TITLE: From the title page of *Tales of Terror*,
published 1801.
British Library 11660.e.39.
FRONTISPIECE: Elsa Lanchester and Boris Karloff
in *The Bride of Frankenstein*.

Note to the Reader
Quotations in this book follow the sometimes idiosyncratic capitalisation, punctuation and formatting of the original sources. Each chapter concludes with a section, titled 'From the Crypt', in which the curators of the British Library exhibition *Terror and Wonder* have selected key exhibits to discuss in more detail.

Designed by Andrew Shoolbred
Picture research by Sally Nicholls
Printed in Hong Kong by Great Wall Printing Co. Ltd

Contents

Preface

Ghosts and ghouls, sublime wonders and supernatural terrors, readers poring intently over ancient manuscripts and dusty tomes: there is something remarkable, to say the least, about an exhibition entitled *Terror and Wonder: The Gothic Imagination* at the British Library in the year 2014. Most significantly, it marks the 250th anniversary of the publication of Horace Walpole's *The Castle of Otranto* in late 1764 – a fiction that, while drawing upon impulses prevalent in British culture since the fifth century AD, assembled for the first time a coherent and instantly recognisable sense of a Gothic literary aesthetic.

And yet, as Walpole used the term in the second edition of *The Castle of Otranto* in 1765, here subtitling his tale of ghosts, bloodshed and villainy as 'A Gothic Story', Gothic was originally anything but a term for a distinctive literary mode of horror, terror and awe-inspiring wonder. Rather, from the time of antiquity onwards, the Gothic in British culture encompassed such divergent meanings as the name for a barbaric Teutonic tribe, a sense of the medieval period or 'Dark Ages', an anti-classical impulse in cultural life, an uncouth excess or savage wildness, a distinctive European architectural style, a native tradition of Englishness, a sense of the national British past and more.

Complementing a major exhibition at the British Library, *Terror and Wonder: The Gothic Imagination* explores these and other manifestations of the Gothic, tracing the manifold meanings, forms and expressions that the Gothic has assumed in Western culture from the eighteenth century to the present day. Consisting of seven highly illustrated chapters and an original photo-essay by the award-winning British photographer Martin Parr, *Terror and Wonder* provides an accessible and comprehensive overview of the dark and exciting world of the Gothic imagination, from Gothic history, literature, architecture and film to Goth fashion, music and beyond.

OPPOSITE:
Frontispiece to *The Southern Tower; or, Conjugal Sacrifice, and Retribution.* An abridged, unauthorised and anonymous version of *A Sicilian Romance* by Ann Radcliffe.
British Library 1578/2144.(1).

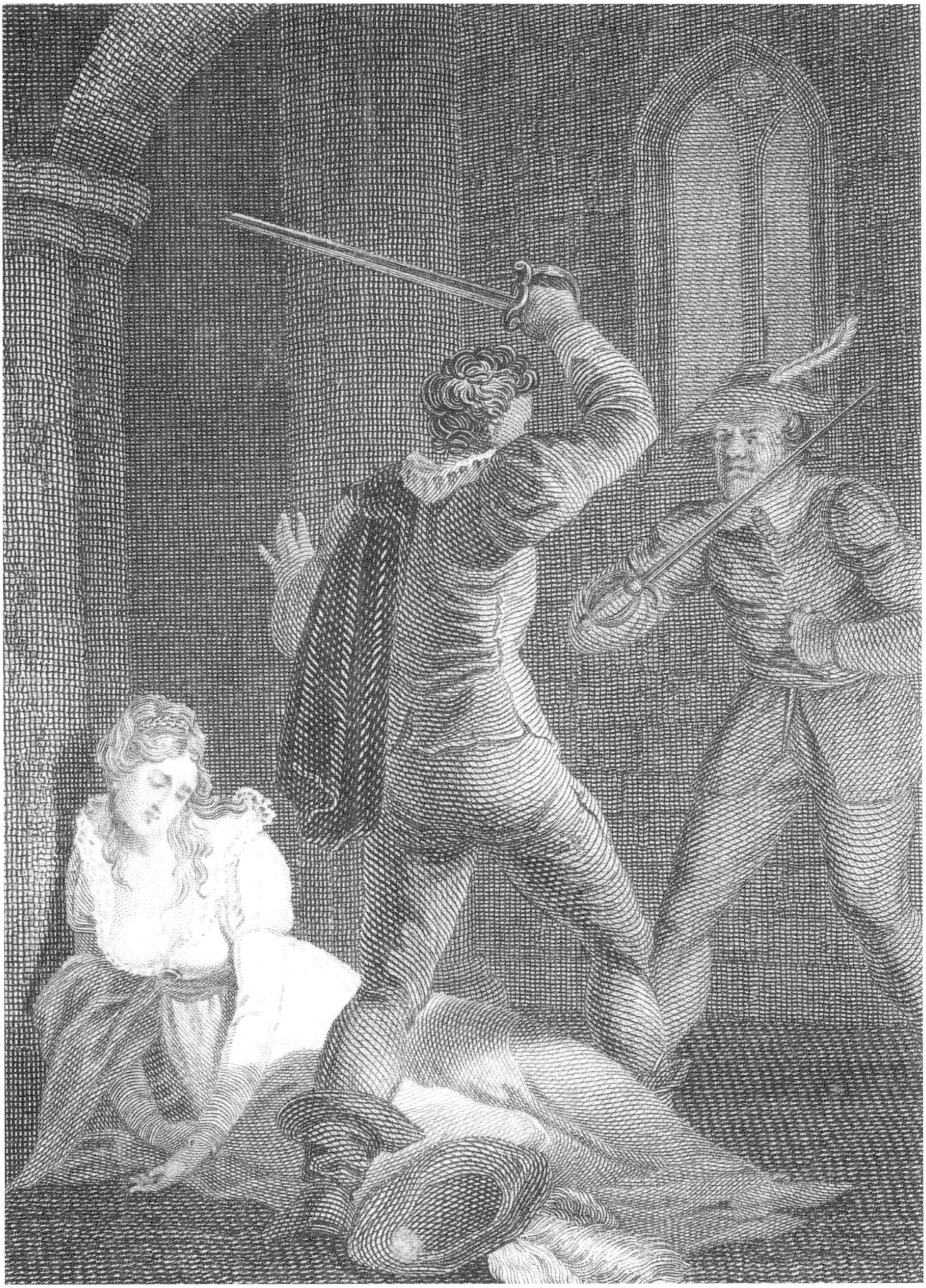

Notes on Contributors

Lucie Armitt is Professor of Contemporary English Literature at the University of Lincoln. Her principal publications include *Twentieth-Century Gothic* (University of Wales, 2011); *Fantasy Fiction* (Continuum, 2005); *Contemporary Women's Fiction and the Fantastic* (Palgrave, 2000); (ed) *George Eliot: A Reader's Essential Guide to Criticism* (Palgrave, 2000); *Theorising the Fantastic* (Arnold, 1996); (ed) *Where No Man Has Gone Before: Women and Science Fiction* (Routledge, 1991). She is currently working on a project entitled *Haunted Landscapes: Tourism and the Gothic.*

Nick Groom is Professor in English at the University of Exeter. He has written widely on literature and culture, and among his many publications are essays on eighteenth-century Gothic, on Tolkien and the literary tradition and on Nick Cave and murder ballads. He is the author of several books, including *The Gothic: A Very Short Introduction* (Oxford University Press, 2012). His anniversary edition of Horace Walpole's novel *The Castle of Otranto* is published in 2014.

Andrew Smith is Reader in Nineteenth-Century English Literature at the University of Sheffield. His 16 published books include *The Ghost Story 1840–1920: A Cultural History* (Manchester University Press, 2010), *Gothic Literature* (Edinburgh University Press, 2007, revised 2013), *Victorian Demons* (Manchester University Press, 2004) and *Gothic Radicalism* (Macmillan, 2000). He is editor, with Benjamin Fisher, of the award-winning series 'Gothic Literary Studies' and 'Gothic Authors: Critical Revisions', published by the University of Wales Press. Smith is also the series editor, with William Hughes, of the 'Edinburgh Companions to the Gothic' series, published by Edinburgh University Press. He is a past president of the International Gothic Association and is currently writing a book entitled *Gothic Death, 1740–1914.*

Catherine Spooner is Senior Lecturer in English at Lancaster University. She has published widely on Gothic in literature, film and popular culture, including the books *Fashioning Gothic Bodies* (Manchester University Press, 2004), *Contemporary Gothic* (Reaktion, 2006) and, with Emma McEvoy, *The Routledge Companion to Gothic* (Routledge, 2007). Her next book will be *Post-Millennial Gothic: Comedy, Romance and the Rise of Happy Gothic*, to be published by Bloomsbury in 2015.

Dale Townshend is Senior Lecturer in Gothic and Romantic Literature at the University of Stirling, where he is programme director for the MLitt in the Gothic imagination. In the field of Gothic studies, his most recent publications include *The Gothic World* (with Glennis Byron; Routledge, 2014) and *Ann Radcliffe, Romanticism and the Gothic* (with Angela Wright; Cambridge University Press, 2014). He is currently at work on a collection of essays entitled *Romantic Gothic: An Edinburgh Companion* (with Angela Wright; Edinburgh University Press) and a monograph entitled *Gothic Antiquity: History, Romance and the Architectural Imagination, 1760–1840.*

Alexandra Warwick is Head of the Department of English, Linguistics and Cultural Studies at the University of Westminster. Her research interests are in the field of nineteenth-century literature and culture studies and she has published on various topics including *Oscar Wilde* (Northcote House, 2007) and *Jack the Ripper: Media, Culture, History* (with Martin Willis; Manchester University Press, 2008). A two-volume edition of the works of Andrew Lang is published by Edinburgh University Press in 2014. She is currently working on archaeology and the Victorian imagination.

Angela Wright is Senior Lecturer in Romantic Literature at the University of Sheffield. She is the editor of 'Eighteenth-century Gothic', a special issue of *Gothic Studies* (14/1, May 2012). Wright is the author of *Gothic Fiction* (Palgrave, 2007), *Britain, France and the Gothic, 1764–1820: The Import of Terror* (Cambridge University Press, 2013) and *Ann Radcliffe, Romanticism and the Gothic* (with Dale Townshend; Cambridge University Press, 2014). At present she is working on a study of Mary Shelley for the University of Wales Press and *Romantic Gothic: An Edinburgh Companion* (with Dale Townshend; Edinburgh University Press).

OPPOSITE:
'The Ghost Story' from *Seymour's Humorous Sketches* by Robert Seymour, *c.* 1875.
British Library 12333.bb.21.

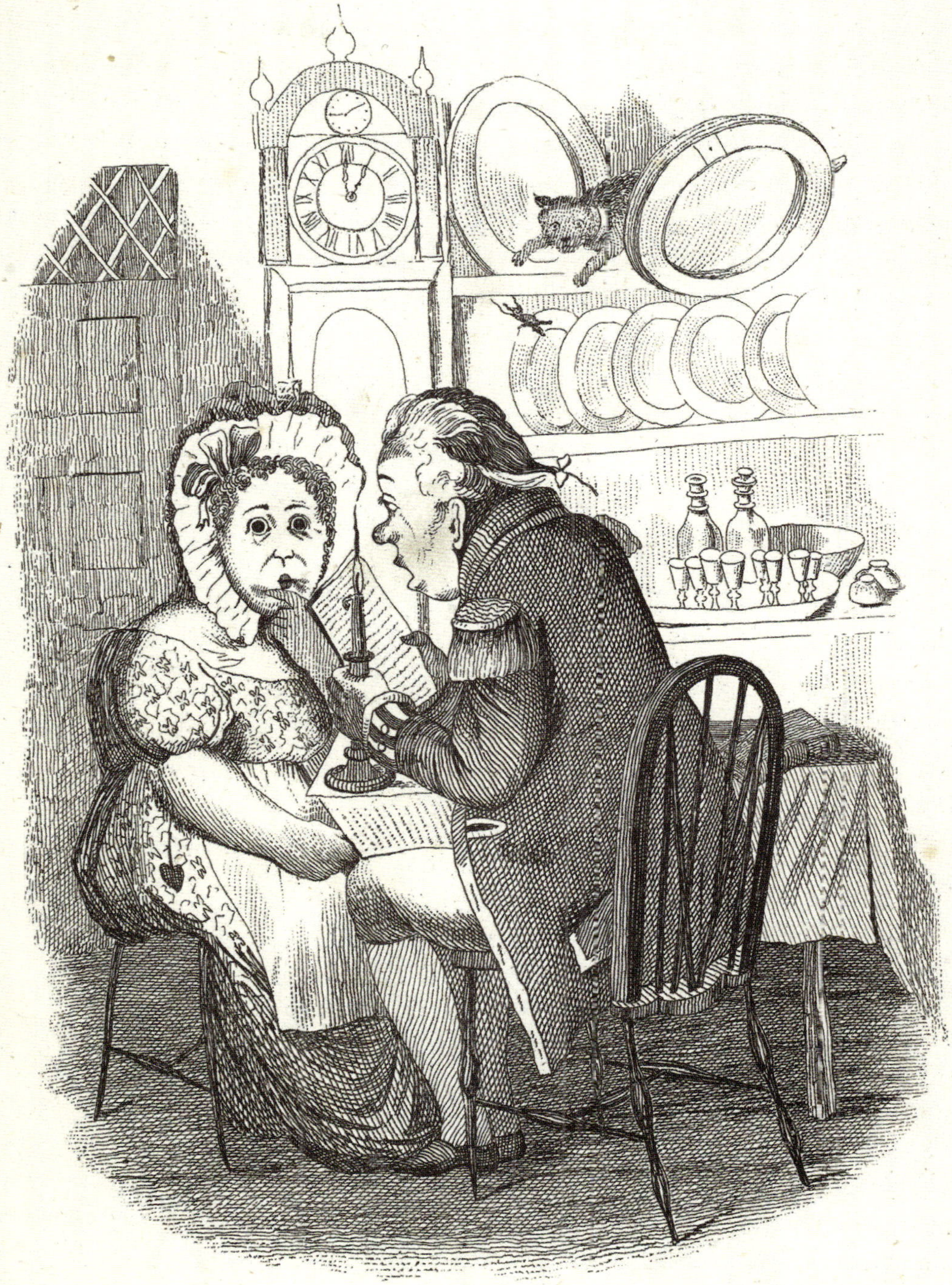

The Ghost Story.

"At this awful moment the Lady we are writing of, beheld something white glide through the desolate apartment, when all of a sudden a tremendous crash" &c.&c.

DALE TOWNSHEND

Terror and Wonder: The Gothic Imagination

OPPOSITE:
The Bleeding Nun, of the Castle of Lindenberg; or, the History of Raymond and Agnes, 1823.
British Library 1578/2144.(2).

Filled with Gothic Story

The year 2014 marks the 250th anniversary of an important literary event. On Christmas Eve 1764, the London publisher, Thomas Lowndes, published a slim novella with a somewhat cumbersome title: *The Castle of Otranto, A Story. Translated by William Marshal, Gent. From the Original Italian of Onuphrio Muralto, Canon of the Church of St. Nicholas at Otranto.* As its author, Horace Walpole, subsequently described it in a letter of 9 March 1765, written to his lifelong friend, the Reverend William Cole, *The Castle of Otranto* owed its genesis to a curious intersection of dreaming and architectural reverie, specifically in the 'Gothic' architectural space that Walpole had been intensively engaged in constructing, decorating and filling with all manner of arcane collectibles at Strawberry Hill, his 'Gothic' residence since the late 1740s:

> I waked one morning in the beginning of last June from a dream, of which all I could recover was, that I had thought myself in an ancient castle (a very natural dream for a head filled like mine with Gothic story) and that on the uppermost bannister of a great staircase I saw a gigantic hand in armour. In the evening I sat down and began to write, without knowing in the least what I intended to say or relate. The work grew on my hands, and I grew fond of it – add that I was very glad to think of anything rather than politics – In short I was so engrossed with my tale, which I completed in less than two months, that one evening I wrote from the time I had drunk my tea, about

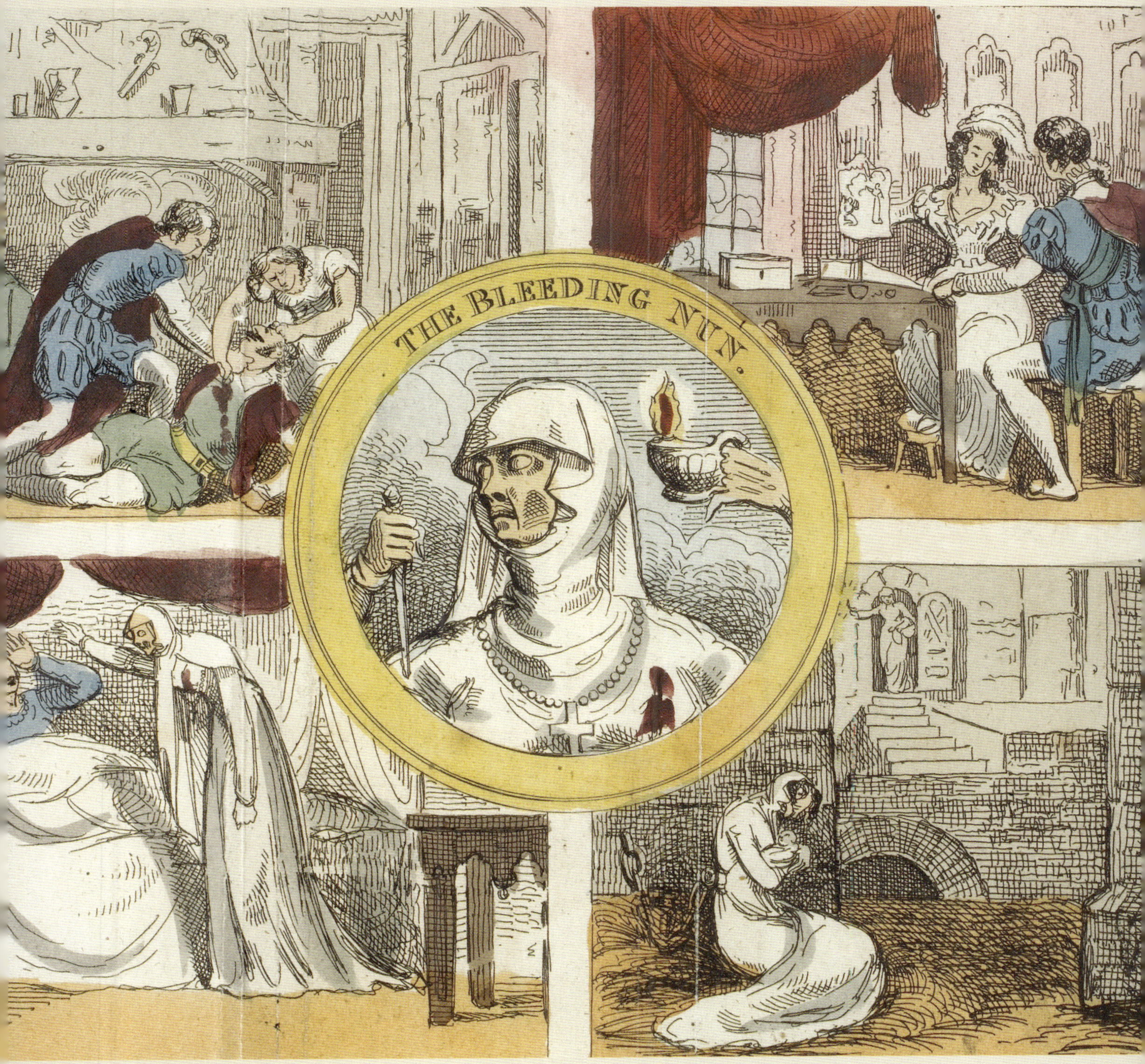
THE BLEEDING NUN.

six o'clock, till half an hour after one in the morning, when my hand and fingers were so weary, that I could not hold the pen to finish the sentence, but left Matilda and Isabella talking, in the middle of a paragraph. You will laugh at my earnestness, but if I have amused you by retracing with any fidelity the manners of ancient days, I am content, and give you leave to think me as idle as you please. (Lewis 1937–83: I.88)

Thus began one of the most extraordinary literary hoaxes of the eighteenth century, and with it the birth, in fiction, of what has become known as the 'Gothic imagination'. Though feverishly written by Horace Walpole over the summer of 1764, the first edition of *The Castle of Otranto* purported to be the reprinting of a medieval story that was 'found in the library of an ancient Catholic family in the north of England'. Originally written in Italian by one Onuphrio Muralto somewhere 'between 1095, the era of the first crusade, and 1243, the date of the last, or not long afterwards', it was supposedly translated from Italian into English by one William Marshal and had been printed in Naples in the 'black' or Gothic script in 1529 (Walpole

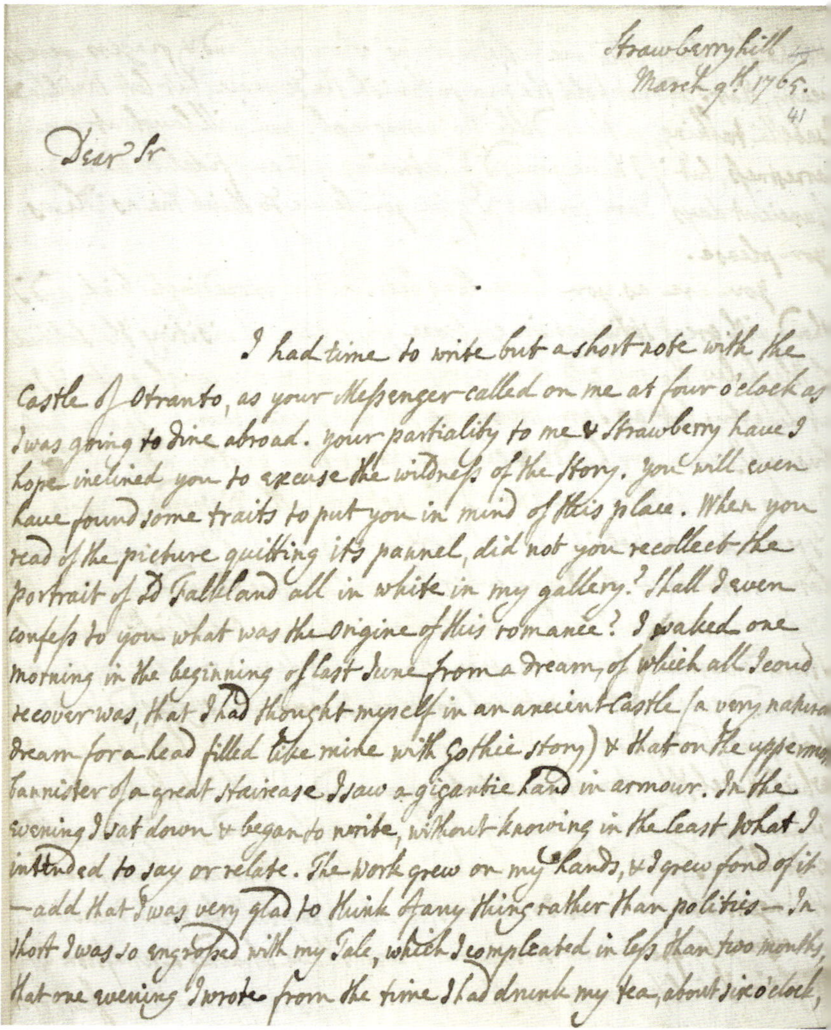

Strawberry hill
March 9th 1765.
41

Dear Sr

I had time to write but a short note with the
Castle of Otranto, as your Messenger called on me at four o'clock as
I was going to dine abroad. your partiality to me & Strawberry have I
hope inclined you to excuse the wildness of the Story. you will even
have found some traits to put you in mind of this place. When you
read of the picture quitting its pannel, did not you recollect the
portrait of Ld Falkland all in white in my gallery? Shall I even
confess to you what was the origine of this romance? I waked one
morning in the beginning of last June from a dream, of which all I could
recover was, that I had thought myself in an ancient Castle (a very natural
dream for a head filled like mine with Gothic story) & that on the uppermost
bannister of a great staircase I saw a gigantic hand in armour. In the
evening I sat down & began to write, without knowing in the least what I
intended to say or relate. The work grew on my hands, & I grew fond of it
—add that I was very glad to think of any thing rather than politics— In
short I was so engrossed with my Tale, which I compleated in less than two months,
that one evening I wrote from the time I had drunk my tea, about six o'clock,

Letter from Horace Walpole to William Cole describing the dream that inspired *The Castle of Otranto*.
British Library Add. MS 5952 f.41.

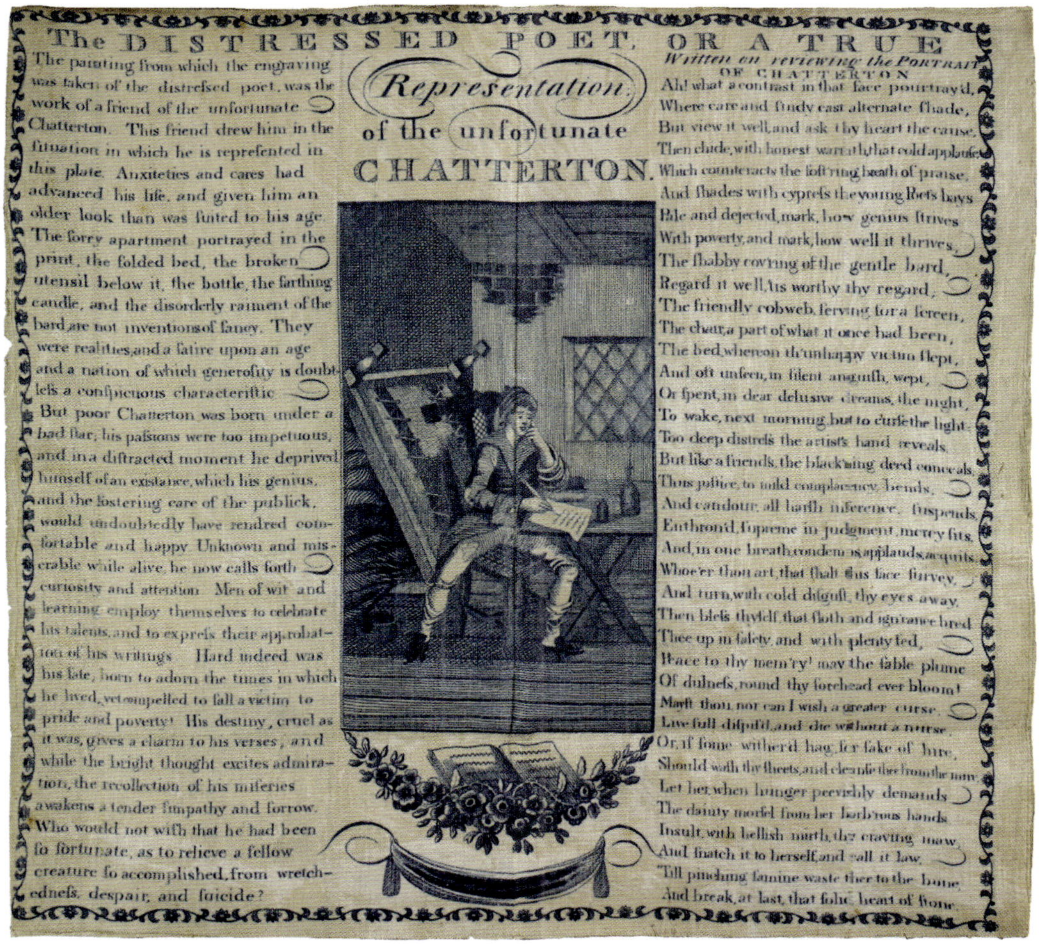

'The Distressed Poet'.
British Library C.39.h.20.
A handkerchief eulogising Thomas Chatterton, the creator of the Rowley forgeries, shortly after his death.

2003: 59). As Walpole would later famously remark, of Thomas Chatterton's forgery of ancient medieval poetry in the Rowley debacle, 'All of the house of forgery are relations' (1779: 24). In late 1764, the publication of *The Castle of Otranto* revealed Walpole himself to be a member of the forger's clan.

Though some critics were sceptical of the authenticity of this 'found' and 'translated' story from the start, the public initially responded positively to the text. Urged by what he described as the 'favourable manner' in which his 'little piece' had been received (Walpole 2003: 65), Walpole disclosed his authorship of the tale in a second edition of *The Castle of Otranto* in May 1765. He justified it as, among other things, a defence of the genius of Shakespeare and an attempt at rejuvenating the dull realism of the novel with the terrors and wonders of ancient medieval romance. More significantly, perhaps, the second edition of *Otranto* included, for the first time, the word 'Gothic' on its title page. Walpole, now choosing to subtitle the fiction 'A Gothic Story', included an epigraph taken from Horace's *Ars Poetica* that, when translated, stressed the tale's commitment to the generation of the readerly responses of terror and wonder: 'Idle fancies shall be shaped like a sick man's dream so that neither foot nor head can be assigned a single shape' (Walpole 2003: 63).

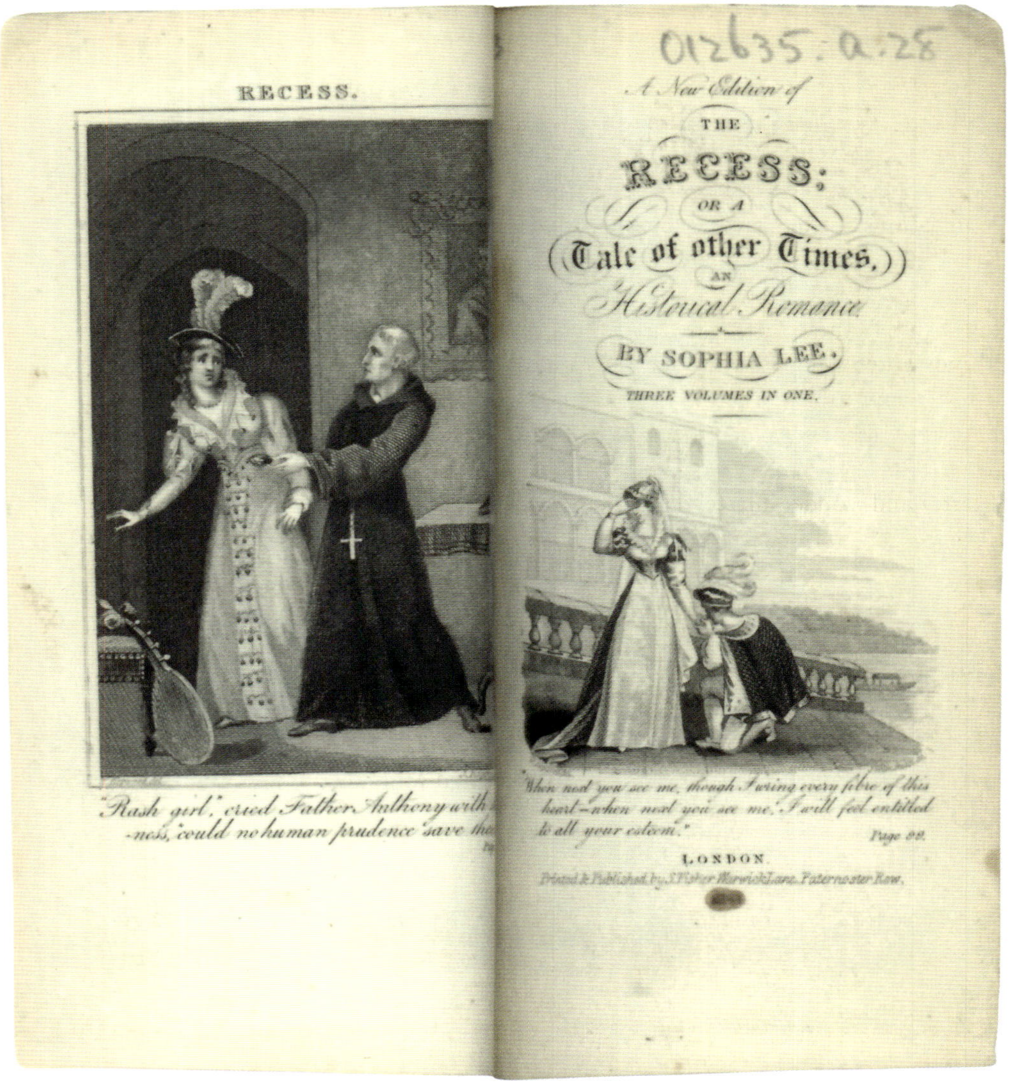

Title page and frontispiece to Sophia Lee's *The Recess*.
British Library 012635.a.25.

Walpole's frank disclosure of the text's modern origins in the second edition saw a rapid turnaround of critical opinion. For what was initially hailed by the poet and translator John Langhorne in the *Monthly Review* as promising 'considerable entertainment' to those 'who can bear the absurdities of Gothic fiction, and bear with the machinery of ghosts and goblins' was summarily dismissed by the same reviewer as a 'false tale' of 'preposterous phenomena', replete with 'the barbarous superstitions of Gothic devilism!' (Sabor 1987: 70–71). The roughness and extravagance that initially seemed entirely appropriate to the tale's medieval origins were now deemed offensive to a civilised sense of the modern present.

Preposterous fake that it undoubtedly was, *The Castle of Otranto* bequeathed a rich literary inheritance to subsequent writers in late eighteenth-century Britain. While jettisoning Walpole's initial claims to authenticity, many subsequent manifestations of what we have come to regard as the Gothic strain in late eighteenth-century fiction appropriated *Otranto*'s technique of the 'found' or 'discovered' ancient manuscript as the occasion for their narratives. In 1783, for instance, Sophia Lee would publish the first volume of her three-volume *The Recess; or, A Tale of Other Times*. This fantastical tale, set in Elizabethan times, concerned two fictional daughters of Mary, Queen of Scots; it was prefaced with an 'Advertisement' claiming that the narrative was 'extracted' from a 'manuscript' in which the 'depredations of time have left chasms' (2000: 5). In her second fiction, *A Sicilian Romance* (1790), Ann Radcliffe, undoubtedly the most admired 'Gothic' writer of the late eighteenth century, would follow suit, framing the text in the prologue as a transcription of the most interesting portions of a tale read by an unnamed narrator from a manuscript kept in the library of a nearby monastery.

And so examples proliferated throughout the 1790s, the decade in which Britain's literary marketplace seemed to be flooded by tales of terror and wonder, mystery and intrigue, spectres and sprites, all purportedly set in ancient, medieval or 'Gothic' times. When not appropriating the discovered manuscript as a narrative frame, early Gothic fictions would often detail the discovery, reading and attempted deciphering of old, only partially legible manuscripts within their own storylines. These included, in such fictions as Ann Radcliffe's *The Romance of the Forest* (1791), Mary-Anne Radcliffe's *Manfroné: or, The One-Handed Monk* (1809) and Charles Robert Maturin's *Melmoth the Wonderer* (1820), hastily figured confessions, incomplete disclosures and imperfectly preserved histories that seem to hold the keys to personal identity, narrative truth and the resolution of all enigmas.

Indeed, the act of reading is a task that is fraught with particular difficulty in early Gothic romance, one subject to all manner of horrid presentiments and fanciful mispresumptions. The heroine of a Gothic fiction perhaps grapples with nothing so much as her shortcomings as a reader, most famously, of course, in the case of Catherine Morland in Jane Austen's playful Gothic parody *Northanger Abbey* (written 1798–99; published late 1817; dated 1818 on title page). Libraries and ancient manuscripts, books and their susceptible, overly imaginative readers have been staple ingredients of the Gothic imagination ever since its inception.

However, to note the Gothic's intimate connection with libraries, manuscripts and acts of reading and interpretation is not necessarily to take us any closer to an understanding of what the 'Gothic imagination' actually is. Recourse to the *Oxford English Dictionary* (*OED*), that standard source of authority whenever matters of definition are at stake, only seems to complicate matters further. Rather than giving a simple and univocal account of the term, the *OED* lists no fewer than seven different meanings, supplementing these with two draft additions dated 1993 and 2007. These include 'Of, pertaining to, or concerned with the Goths or their language' (1.a.); an extended use of the term to include a sense of the Teutonic or the Germanic (2.); 'Belonging to, or characteristic of, the Middle Ages', or 'medieval' and 'romantic', as opposed to classical, and chiefly used with reprobation in early instances, signifying that which belongs to the 'dark ages' (3.a.); 'A term for the style of architecture

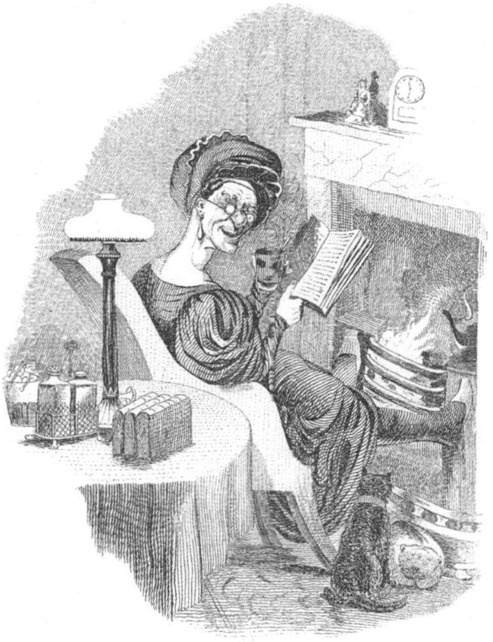

'Kitty, take these books to the library and get Mrs Brown to change them, tell her I'm fond of the rumantic', from *Seymour's Humorous Sketches* by Robert Seymour, *c.* 1875. British Library 12333.bb.21.

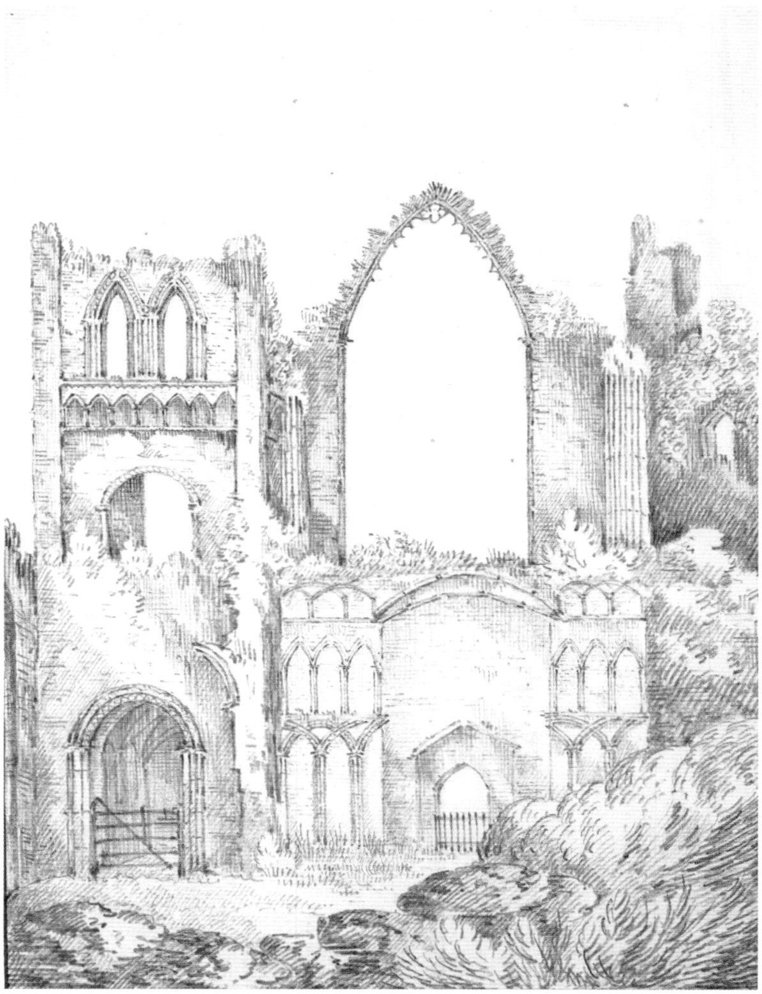

Castle Acre, Norfolk.
Pencil drawing, 1805.
British Library K.Top XXXI 48g.

The magnificent Gothic ruins of Castle Acre Priory, Norfolk. Like many of the ruins that would inspire Gothic authors, these are the result of Henry VIII's dissolution of the monasteries.

prevalent in Western Europe from the twelfth to the sixteenth century, of which the chief characteristic is the pointed arch' (3.b); a reference to the 'Gothic Revival', or the reintroduction of a Gothic style of architecture towards the middle of the nineteenth century (3.d); 'Barbarous, rude, uncouth, unpolished, in bad taste' or 'Savage' (4); the name of the type commonly used for printing German in England, as distinguished from roman and italic characters (5.b); 'Gothic architecture or ornamentation' (6.c); 'Of or pertaining to goth music or its followers' (a draft addition that was added to the *OED* in 1993); and 'Of or designating a genre of fiction characterized by suspenseful, sensational plots involving supernatural or macabre elements and often (esp. in early use) having a medieval theme or setting' (a draft addition added in December 2007).

How, though, might these divergent implications relate to one another, and how, if at all, may they be reconciled? Although this is not the place to embark upon a searching etymological analysis of the word 'Gothic', it is nonetheless necessary to explore, gloss and elaborate upon some of these meanings. If no more, this will provide us with a clearer sense of the remit, ambit and coverage of this exhibition, devoted, as it is, to showcasing the various facets of the Gothic imagination as it has manifested itself in Western culture since at least the end of the seventeenth century.

Suspense, Sensation and Supernaturalism: Gothic as a Literary Mode

The task is best approached through a consideration of the final *OED* entry listed above. Gothic as a term is used in both popular and academic circles to describe a particular mode in modern fiction, one initiated in *The Castle of Otranto* in 1764 and self-consciously described as 'Gothic' in the second edition of 1765. It has continued to be characterised, from that moment onwards, by a predilection for suspense and sensation, the supernatural and macabre, and the generation in its readers of horror, terror and wonder. That the seemingly unpleasant experiences of terror and wonder could be harnessed to an aesthetic of pleasure was a claim persuasively advanced by eighteenth-century theorists of the sublime, most notably Edmund Burke in his *Philosophical Enquiry into the Origin of Our Ideas of the Sublime and the Beautiful* (1757). It had also been explored, in terms more immediately applicable to Gothic fiction, by John and Anna Laetitia Aikin in 'On the Pleasure Derived from Objects of Terror' (1773) and Ann Radcliffe in her posthumously published essay, 'On the Supernatural in Poetry' (1826).

Of this particular literary mode, there is no better illustration than that called to mind by the title of this exhibition itself. *Tales of Terror and Wonder*, a successful compendium of Gothic ballads, was published in both London and New York by George Routledge and Sons as part of Henry Morley's 'Universal Library' series in 1887. Although erroneously attributed on the title page to Matthew Gregory Lewis, the author of, among other fictions, translations and dramas, the scandalous Gothic fiction *The Monk: A Romance* in 1796, *Tales of Terror and Wonder* was in fact a late nineteenth-century anthologising of two earlier publications: Lewis's own two-volume *Tales of Wonder*, first published (despite the title page's date of 1801) in London by W Bulmer and J Bell in late 1800, and the anonymous *Tales of Terror*, published by the same collaboration between Bulmer the printer and Bell the bookseller in May 1801.

Even beyond the success of the volumes suggested by Morley's decision to reprint both of them in a composite edition over 80 years later, these two anthologies seem, quite independently of one another, to have been extremely successful in their own day. Not only had Bulmer and Bell, presumably spurred on by rising sales figures, seen fit to follow up the publication of Lewis's *Tales of Wonder* with the rather lavishly illustrated companion volume, *Tales of Terror*, a few months later, but they had also, presumably in response to criticisms concerning the expense of the two-volume *Tales of Wonder*, published a slimmer, single-volume edition of the collection in November 1801 (Thomson 2010). Later, an anthology of similar Gothic ballads, poems and prose pieces, published by Sherwood, Gilbert and Piper in London in 1826, would pay homage to the success of the two earlier publications through the title *Legends of Terror! And Tales of the Wonderful and the Wild*. So popular, in fact, had

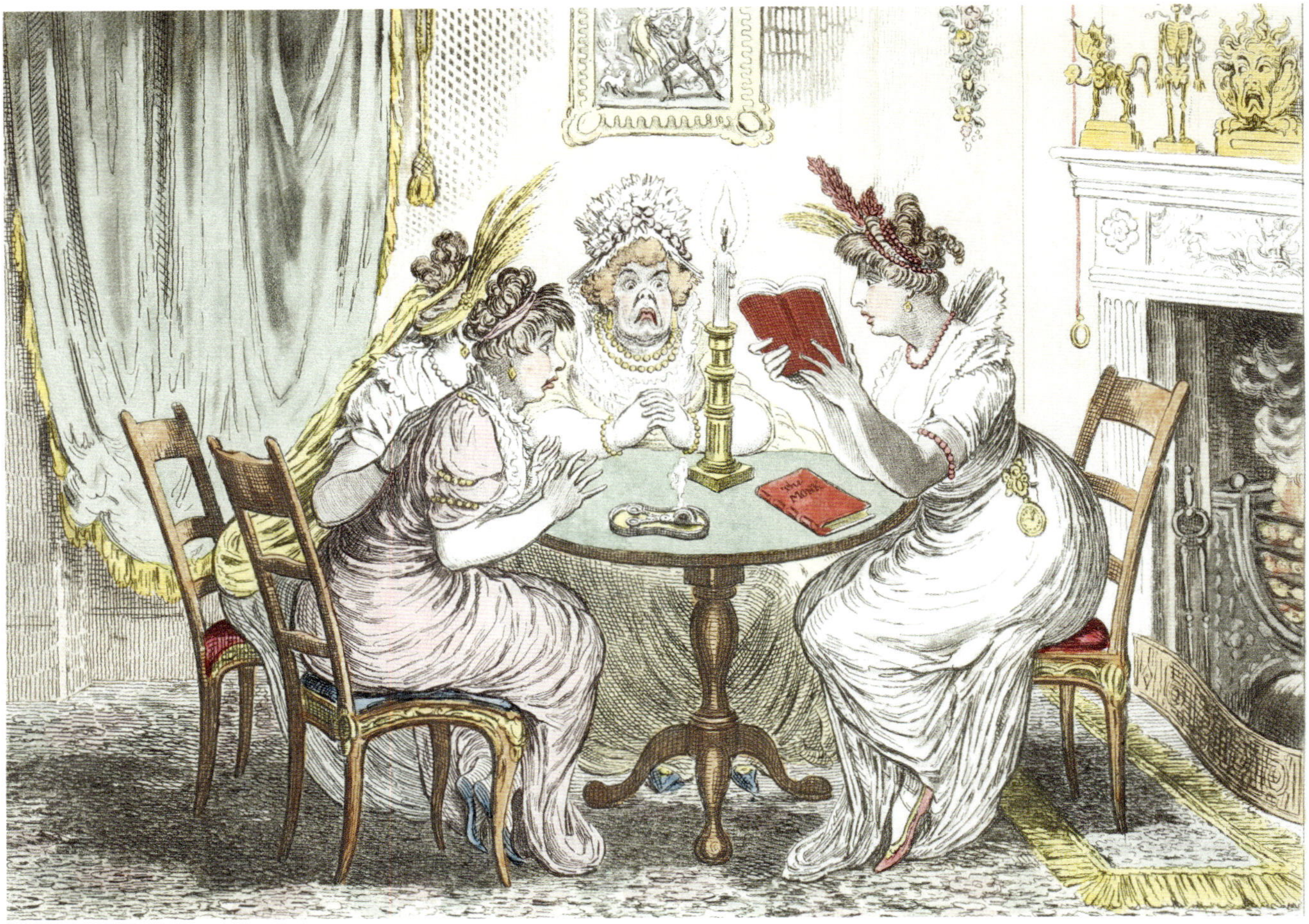

James Gillray,
'Tales of Wonder!', 1802.
British Library 745.a.6.

these publications become that the printmaker and caricaturist James Gillray would subsequently appropriate the title of Lewis's collection for his well-known hand-coloured etching, 'Tales of Wonder!' in February 1802.

As the inscription to the etching reads, '*This attempt to describe the effects of the Sublime & Wonderful is dedicated to M.G. Lewis Esq. M.P.*'. This image, in its depiction of four spellbound women poring over a copy of Lewis's collection in a bourgeois parlour room, with a copy of *The Monk* placed on the table, soon became iconic of the lurid, sensational tastes of many a female reader of Gothic romance. The scene moved beyond immediate reference to Lewis's fictions to become a cultural shorthand for more general Gothic reading habits in the early nineteenth century. Almost in confirmation of Gillray's satirical sense that the popular 'taste' for literary horrors and terrors is a debased 'appetite' tantamount to a form of addiction – witness, for example, the figure in the foreground's tense, physical anticipation of the next gory instalment to fall from the reader's lips – a second edition of *Tales of Terror* was published by a broad consortium of London-based booksellers in 1808. As in the final decade of the eighteenth century, it would seem, the reading public's demand for Gothic at the turn of the new century was a veritable 'craving' that writers and publishers found difficult, at times, to satisfy.

Tales of Terror and Wonder consists of a broad selection of supernatural ballads or ghostly narrative verses, some the anonymous transcriptions from the oral tradition in storytelling, others translations from Danish and German originals, some by lesser-known writers such as John Leyden and Henry William Bunbury, and others by such well-known Romantic authors as Robert Southey, Matthew Lewis and even the young Walter Scott. Reverberating throughout the collection are plots, character names and fictional scenarios drawn from a few of the most successful Gothic romances of the late eighteenth century, including William Beckford's *Vathek* (1786), Ann Radcliffe's *The Castles of Athlin and Dunbayne* (1789) and *The Romance of the Forest* (1791), as well as Lewis's notorious *The Monk*. Each was a manifestation of the veritable 'thirst' and 'hunger' for Gothic that characterised British culture in the period, particularly in the post-French Revolutionary decade of the 1790s.

Though scant use is made of the term 'Gothic' throughout, *Tales of Terror and Wonder* neatly displays some of the conventions of the 'Gothic imagination'. Paramount among them is a concern with architectural space, with action that, as in *The Castle of Otranto*, takes place in a ruined Gothic architectural pile such as a castle, a monastery, an abbey, an underground catacomb or a labyrinth-like recess. Indeed, it was through this consistent coupling of a

Netley Abbey. Aquatint, 1814.

British Library K.top.14.83.i.

The overgrown remains of Netley Abbey provide a quintessentially Gothic setting. These famous ruins were inspirational to writers and artists in the eighteenth century, including Thomas Gray and Jane Austen.

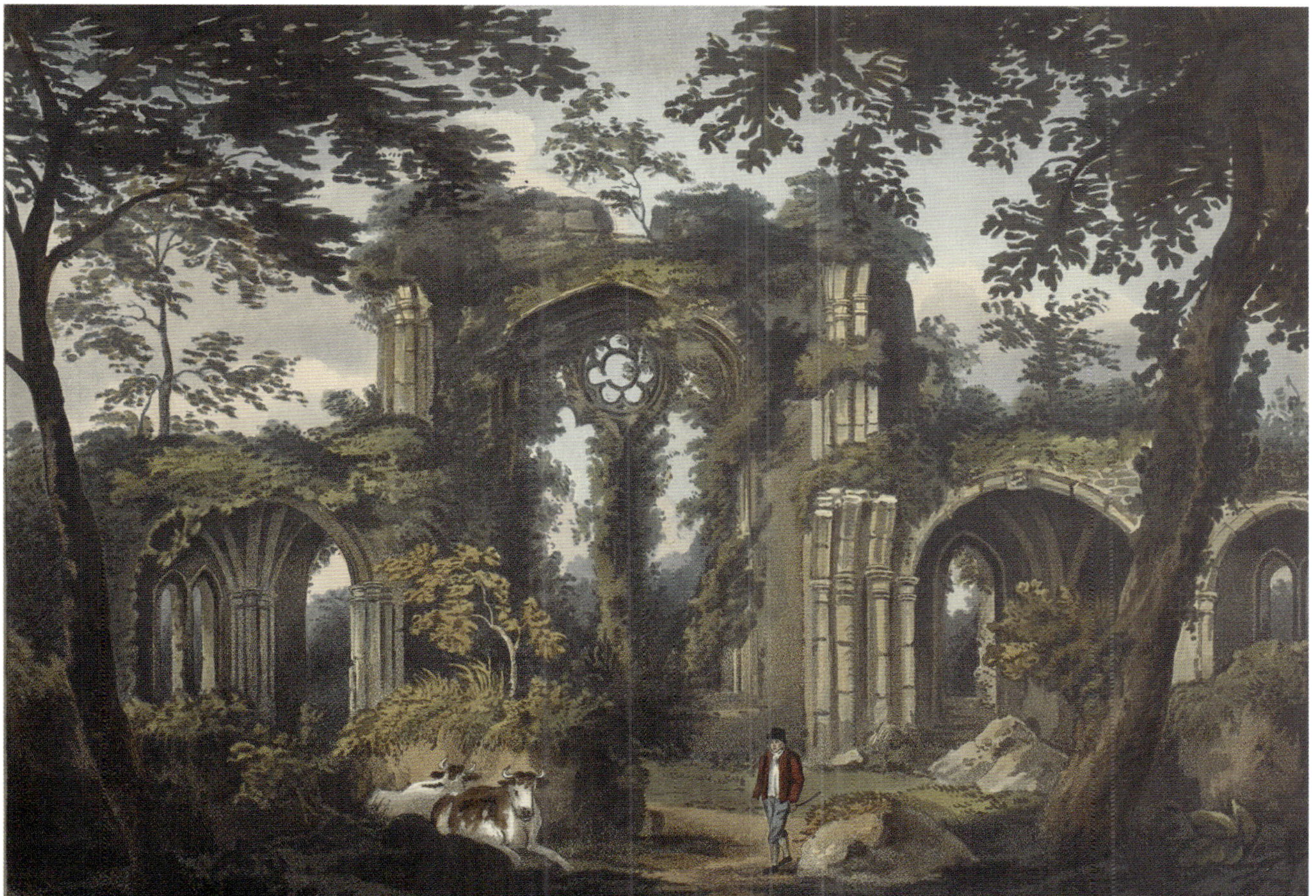

distinct set of literary conventions with representations of ruined architectural space in numerous late eighteenth-century romances that the term 'Gothic' (though primarily a word used to describe medieval architectural form and style in the eighteenth century) eventually came to signify a particular impulse, strand or mode in modern fiction, poetry and drama.

Like many earlier, full-length Gothic fictions, for instance, 'The Pilgrim of Valencia: A Spanish Romance' from *Tales of Terror* situates its action in the 'dreary old pile' that is a Gothic ruin. It exploits the location's potential for generating sublime terror and suspense through a description of the uncanny sounds that reverberate throughout: 'The clock now struck midnight, with thundering sound, / Echo roars through the high Gothic arches around' (Morley 1887: 45). 'The House upon the Heath: A Welsh Tale' similarly features a ruined Gothic building – one that, in characteristic fashion, has the potential to conjure up foreboding presentiments of horror and melancholy in the sable-cloaked stranger who stumbles upon it:

Fast by the moor a lonely mansion stood;
Cheerless it stood! a melancholy shade
Its mouldering front, and rifted walls arrayed;
Barred were the gates, the shattered casements closed.
And brooding horror on its site reposed;
No tree o'erhung the uncultivated ground,
No trace of labour, nor of life around. (Morley 1887: 96)

Watercolour by Charles Reuben Ryley depicting a scene from *The Monk*, c. 1796.

Lewis Walpole Library, Yale University.

Ambrosio, the eponymous character in Matthew Lewis's *The Monk*, is arguably the most famous example of anti-Catholic sentiment in Gothic fiction. Here he sees Matilda's breast and 'a thousand wild wishes bewilder his imagination'.

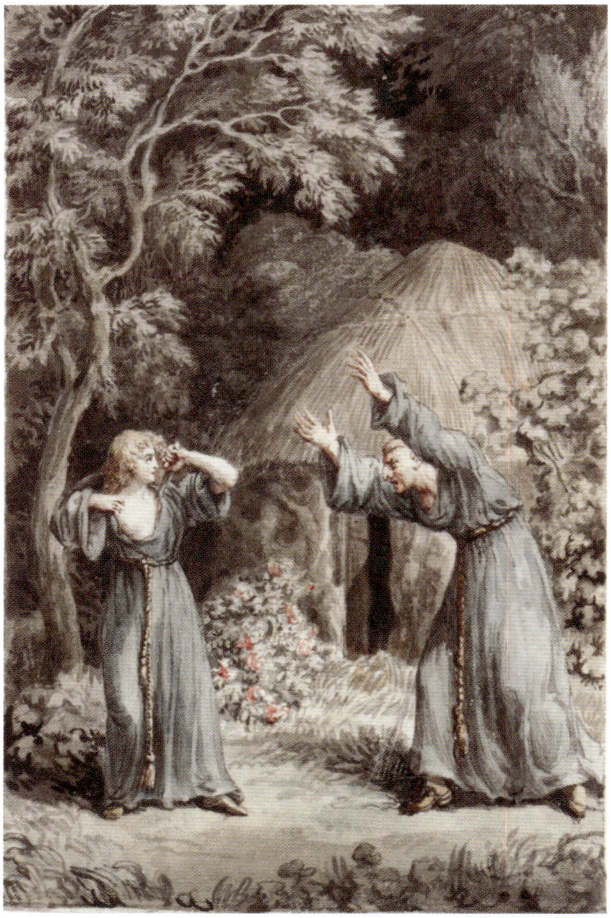

Squatting ominously on a landscape ravaged by the blasts of wind and rain, these Gothic ruins feature more as the objects of Edmund Burke's sublime terror than the pleasing forms of William Gilpin's Picturesque contemplation. The architectural rapidly gives way to the anti-Catholic for, built in the medieval past and demolished with the onset of the Reformation, the ruin in early Gothic writing is, perhaps unsurprisingly, often peopled with the spectral remains of Catholic history. In the ballad 'The Black Canon of Elmham: or, Saint Edmond's Eve', for instance, the architectural space of the abbey simultaneously serves as the site of a ghostly haunting and the eponymous Black Canon's attempts at laying the restless spirit to rest:

He goeth to sing the burial chaunt,
And to lay the wandering sprite,
Whose shadowy form doth restless haunt
The abbey's drear aisle this night. (Morley 1887: 76)

Issuing from an eighteenth-century Britain that, as Linda Colley (1992) has argued, had self-consciously defined itself as Protestant ever since the Act of Union in 1707, much early Gothic writing was vehemently anti-Catholic in its ideological bias and import. The mode thus served to define and constitute a sense of British nationhood, clearly distinct from an alien, predominantly Catholic Europe. Consequently, eighteenth-century Gothic tales are replete with nefarious monks and libidinous nuns. Brooding abbots, shrouded beneath their cowls, conceal their past crimes and injustices, while pernicious abbesses exact the most torturous of punishments on the novices in their care.

Several of the ballads in *Tales of Terror and Wonder* draw strongly upon these anti-Catholic sentiments. 'The Stranger: A Norman Tale', for example, conjures up a sense of craftily concealed Catholic indiscretion in the lines 'Why move the slow monks through the cloisters' thick gloom? / Whose corse do they bear to the deep-vaulted tomb?' (Morley 1887: 14). When not trafficking in the outmoded superstitions of the Catholic faith, the shadowy, mysterious outsiders who stalk these ballads dabble in the dark arts of magic, witchcraft, necromancy and sorcery. Other stock characters that feature throughout include grim strangers who interminably wander and traverse the world, brigands, pirates, robbers and black-masked assassins. Some of them are guilty of the 'primal crime' of fratricide, while others assume in their criminality the monstrous proportions of the ferryman in Lewis's 'Bothwell's Bonny Jane', the ballad that opens *Tales of Wonder*:

> With burning steel his temples bound
> Throbbed quick and high with fiery pangs;
> He rolled his blood-shot eyeballs round,
> And furious gnashed his iron fangs. (Morley 1887: 114)

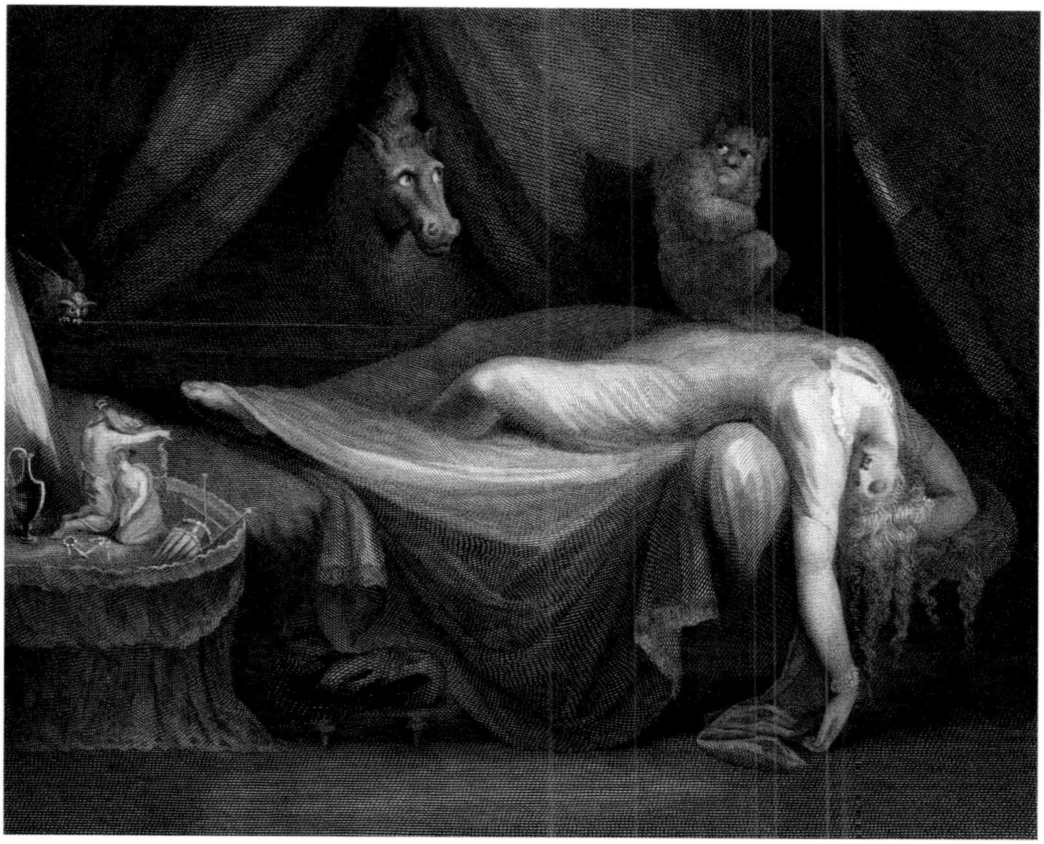

Print of Henry Fuseli's *The Nightmare*.
British Museum.

The Gothic preoccupation with demon lovers is clearly encapsulated in Henry Fuseli's iconic image. The prone position of the female suggests an ambiguity between love and death.

Love, Death and Superstition

Romantic love features prominently in these verse narratives, as it does throughout much early Gothic fiction. Often in a self-conscious attempt to cultivate a fashionable sense of medievalism, several of the ballads in *Tales of Terror and Wonder* recount tales of chivalrous action, of knights, maidens and heroic quests, of battles, crusades and tournaments, each set in some mystical, far-off land and vaguely medieval or 'ancient' time. Prohibited free expression by a series of tyrannous fathers, the lovers of the younger generation that feature in many of these poems either elope, invariably to disastrous ends, or become permanently separated from one another, and consequently locked into a painful, morbid existence in which love and mourning become indistinguishable. Lovers who pine interminably for their objects of desire recur repeatedly, as do demon lovers, spurned lovers, lovers who are betrayed or who themselves betray. In 'Alonzo the Brave and Fair Imogene', for example, a ballad originally published in Lewis's *The Monk* but extracted later in *Tales of Wonder*, the spurned lover returns in the form of a ghastly death's head. This horrid, uninvited guest plagues the wedding feast of the treacherous Imogen:

> The lady is silent: the stranger complies,
> His visor he slowly unclosed;

Frontispiece to *Tales of Terror*, 1801.
British Library 11660.e.39.

The frontispiece of *Tales of Terror* (often misattributed to Matthew Lewis) is an early graphic example of the Gothic fascination with death and the decaying human body.

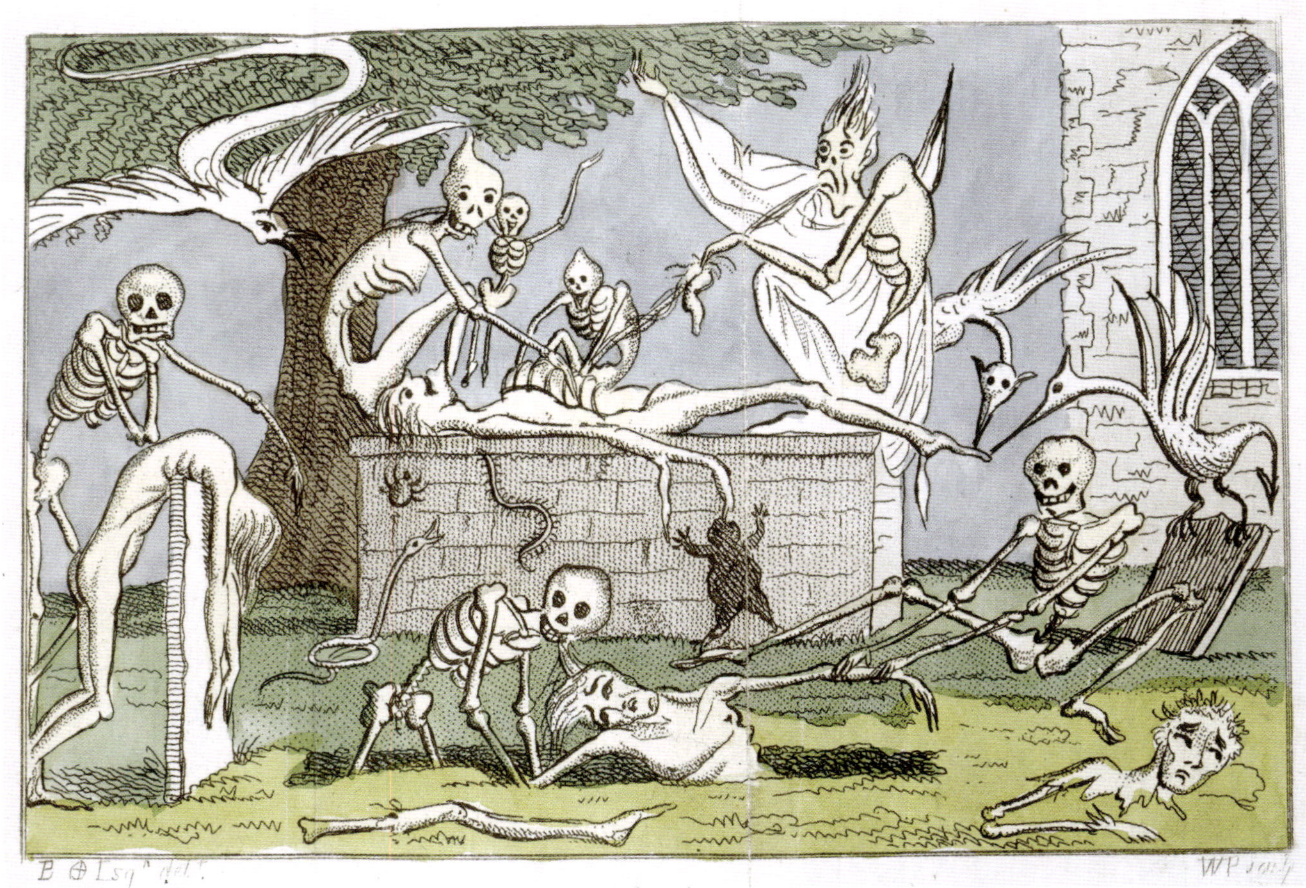

Oh! then what a sight met Fair Imogene's eyes!
What words can express her dismay and surprise,
When a skeleton's head was exposed! (Morley 1887: 126)

In another reworking of the famous inset narrative from Lewis's *The Monk*, the ghost of the bleeding nun discloses, in a moment of absolute, spine-chilling terror, her treacherous, spectral identity to her recently wed groom, Raymond. In Lewis's translation of Johann Wolfgang von Goethe's 'The Fisherman', the lover is a siren-like *femme fatale* who tempts her suitor to a watery grave, while in 'The House upon the Heath, A Welsh Tale' it is suggested that the lovers are incestuously related. The infant fruit of this monstrous union of brother and sister is found lying dead upon its mother's breast.

Preoccupied then, as now, with abuse, incest, sexual transgression and other taboo subjects, the Gothic imagination is nothing if not sensationalist. Love and death are continuously interwoven throughout the ballads, rendering *Tales of Terror and Wonder* somewhat littered with the corpses of once beautiful women. The gruesome example below is from 'Albert of Werdendorff, or The Midnight Embrace: A German Romance':

All shrouded she was in the garb of the tomb!
Her lips they were livid, her face it was wan!
A death the most horrid had rifled her bloom,
And each charm of beauty was faded and gone! (Morley 1887: 38)

Indeed, death and its paraphernalia loom particularly large in Morley's anthology, with several of the ballads referring to tombs, graves, winding cloths, shrouds, churchyards, coffins and taper-lit funeral processions. Beyond mortality, the very fact of the human body itself – corporeality in all its ghastly, material immediacy – is one of the primary preoccupations in both volumes. Here, bodies continuously bleed and haemorrhage, to the extent that 'gore' becomes the anthology's most frequently repeated word. Fresh corpses and skeletons drained of all vitality rattle throughout its pages, and towards the end of Leyden's 'The Elfin-King', skulls of mangled heads in a burial ground let out blood-curdling screams whenever they are trodden on. Corporeal horror resides at other moments in *Tales of Terror and Wonder* in the figure of ghastly metamorphosis, perhaps none more powerfully than at the end of the translation of Gottfried August Bürger's well-known and extremely influential ballad 'Lenora':

His head became a naked skull,
Nor haire nor eyen had hee;
His body grew a skeleton,
Whilome so blythe of blee. (Morley 1887: 282)

Perhaps what is most characteristic of the 'Gothic imagination' in these ballads, though, is their collective preoccupation with the supernatural. Such a feature places them clearly within the fictional

Drawing by Bertie Greatheed from an extra-illustrated copy of *The Castle of Otranto*, 1781–1804.

Lewis Walpole Library, Yale University.

The spectre of a hermit, with 'fleshless jaws and empty sockets of a skeleton', is one of several ghosts that feature in *The Castle of Otranto*.

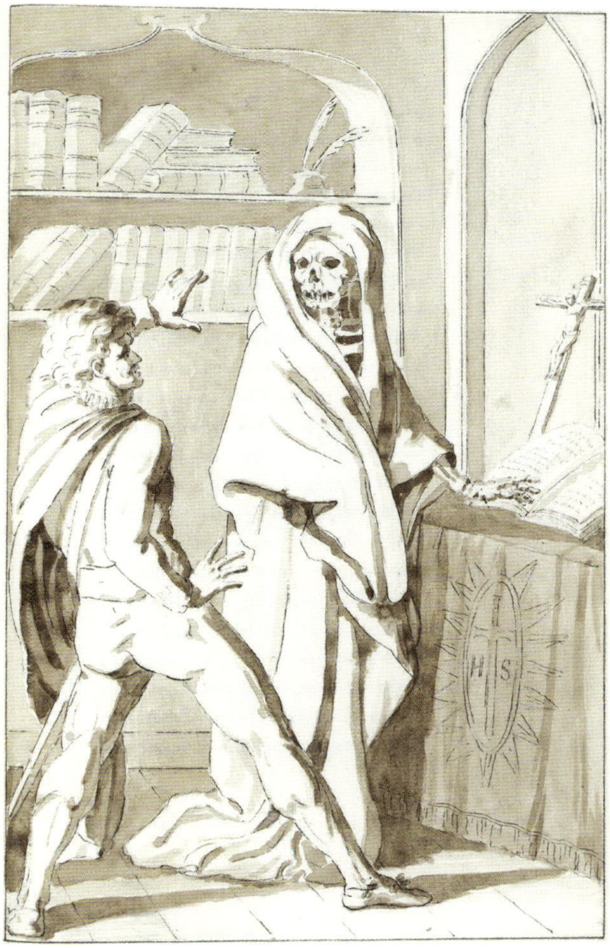

line initiated by Walpole's introduction of a ghost to the pages of *The Castle of Otranto*. *Tales of Terror and Wonder* is replete with 'grim spectres', 'shrouded ghosts' and 'pale spectres' that glide forth from the tomb. Spectre-brides and spirits dance, cavort and make merry, drinking, as towards the end of 'Alonzo the Brave and Fair Imogene', from skulls newly torn from graves. Issuing forth from unquiet tombs, these shroud-covered spirits are said to 'swarm' the churchyard in 'Grim, King of the Ghosts; Or, The Dance of Death: A Churchyard Tale' (Morley 1887: 54). When the eponymous King of Ghosts makes his appearance in this ballad, the effect is particularly gruesome:

> No flesh had the spectre, his skeleton skull
>   Was loosely wrapped round with a brown shrivelled skin
> His bones, 'stead of marrow, of maggots were full,
>   And the worms they crawled out, and the worms they crawled in.
>
> His shoes they were coffins, his dim eye revealed
>   The gleam of a grave-lamp with vapours oppressed;
> And a dark crimson necklace of blood drops congealed,
>   Reflected each bone that jagged out of his breast. (Morley 1887: 56)

When the two constituent volumes were published in 1801, the figure of the vampire was still to take cultural root as the nineteenth century's most distinctive Gothic trope. Yet many of the ghouls in both *Tales of Wonder* and *Tales of Terror* are drinkers of their victims' blood, such as those in 'Grim, King of the Ghosts' that threaten to 'feast on thy flesh' and 'drink of thy blood', or the tale of the flesh-hungry creatures 'all dropping with gore, / In visage so grim, and so monstrous in height' (Morley 1887: 119) in Lewis's 'Osric the Lion'. In 'The Grim White Woman' Lewis figures the eponymous character as a monster who feasts hungrily on the blood of her victims, while 'Courteous King Jamie' features a ravenous female ghost who appears in the guise of a Medusa-like virago (Morley 1887: 262).

Though they are by no means lacking in moments of humour – a playful, self-parodic impulse, for instance, runs through lines such as 'The worms they crept in, and the worms they crept out, / And sported his eyes and his temples about' in Lewis's 'Alonzo the Brave and Fair Imogene' (Morley 1887: 126) – these ballads, brought into dialogue with one another in Morley's *Tales of Terror and Wonder* in 1887, clearly epitomise what for us today is the Gothic imagination: an aesthetic of the ghostly, the ghastly and the gruesome, a popular mode of cultural production that seeks to instil in participants the revulsions of horror and the chills of terror in 'each nerve and bone' (Morley 1887: 233).

As E J Clery has pointed out, the term 'Gothic novel' is largely a twentieth-century coinage. The fictions of Ann Radcliffe, Matthew Lewis and countless other late eighteenth-century writers whom we designate today as 'Gothic' were not necessarily conceived, named or marketed as such in their day (2002: 22). For Alfred E Longueil, similarly, the term 'Gothic' only assumed its current literary-critical functions in the late 1790s, after the publishing endeavours of Radcliffe, Lewis and their contemporaries. Before then, Longueil continues, usages of the term 'Gothic' had grouped around two primary sets of meanings, the first being 'barbaric' and the second 'medieval'. It was only as a consequence of the fact that so many late eighteenth-century tales set, in the fashion of *The Castle of Otranto*, in ancient 'Gothic' or medieval times happened to contain elements of the supernatural that the term eventually began to reflect these elements, substituting a sense of the 'medieval' with reference to these fictions' ghastly and ghostly contents (1923: 459). The *OED* confirms the relative belatedness of the literary associations of 'Gothic', citing Walter Scott's use of the phrase 'gothic romance' in his account of Ann Radcliffe in *Lives of the Novelists* (1825) as the earliest instance.

And yet several such usages of the word seem to predate this moment. Prior to describing Ann Radcliffe as 'the Shakspeare [*sic*] of Romance Writers' (1798: 249), Nathan Drake delineated a distinct strain of 'Gothic superstition' in his *Literary Hours: or, Sketches Critical and Narrative* (1798), one in which the ghost occupied a central position, and over which Shakespeare, in distinction from the Italian poets Ariosto and Tasso, was magisterially said to preside:

> When well conducted, a grateful astonishment, a welcome sensation of fear, will alike creep through the bosom of the Sage and of the Savage, and it is, perhaps, to the introduction of such well-imagined agency, or when not introduced upon the scene, to a very frequent allusion to it, that Shakespeare, beyond any other poet, owes the capability of raising the most awful, yet the most delightful species of terror. No poet, adopting a machinery of a similar kind, has wielded it with equal effect. Among the Italians it is too frequently addressed solely to the imagination, Ariosto in general, and Tasso sometimes, descending to all the extravagance of oriental fiction; conducted, as by Shakespeare, it powerfully moves the strongest passions of the heart. (1798: 90)

As this indicates, 'Gothic' in the mid-to-late years of the eighteenth century also served as a synonym for a national English tradition of ghostliness, one which was said to originate in the oral tradition of storytelling, flourish throughout medieval romance, inform the work of Shakespeare and his contemporary playwrights, and manifest itself most recently in the supernatural romances of Ann Radcliffe during the 1790s. Consequently, in 1804 Nathan Drake, in a third volume of *Literary Hours*, articulated in an essay on the seventeenth-century English poet Robert Herrick a definite sense of what he described as a 'Gothic mythology', a category that, at least with regards to its supernaturalism, comes remarkably close to modern-day interpretations of the term 'Gothic':

> That species of poetry which is employed in painting the imaginary existence and manners of fairies, elves and goblins,

> and which Shakspeare [*sic*] and Jonson delighted to indulge in, is frequently to be found in the volume of Herrick. He appears, indeed, to have been alive to all the superstitions of his age, and his Collection abounds with amulets and charms against the fiends and spectres of gothic mythology. (Drake 1804: 81–2)

In fact, if there is an origin for modern understandings of 'the Gothic imagination' at all, it appears to lie in the third volume of Nathan Drake's *Literary Hours* of 1804. Here Drake employs the term as a category to describe what he took to be the superiority of Scottish literary renditions of the supernatural over those of their English counterparts:

> but what heroic ballad of the eighteenth century, shall be put in competition with the *Hardyknute* of SIR JOHN BRUCE, or what legend of gothic imagination with the *Tam O'Shanter* of BURNS? To these let us add *The Harp* of MACNEIL, the *Eve of Saint John*, *Glenfinlas*, and the *Grey Brother*, by SCOTT, and the *Mermaid* of LEYDEN. (1804: 262)

At least two of Scott's poems cited here, 'The Eve of Saint John' and 'Glenfinlas', had been published in Lewis's anthology, *Tales of Wonder*. Drake elsewhere discloses his familiarity with Lewis's collection in his claim that these Scottish poems are only rivalled in the English tradition by, inter alia, 'two or three ballads of the terrific kind by LEWIS' (1804: 262).

By the early nineteenth century, a strong cultural, even literary-critical sense of a 'Gothic imagination' was thus already in place. Examples of it had appeared in the two anthologies, Lewis's *Tales of Wonder* and the anonymous *Tales of Terror*, revealing a discrete imaginative predilection towards the ghastly, the ghostly and the supernatural that had manifested itself in British culture since medieval times. As Nick Groom's essay in this collection points out, its origins stretch as far back as the ancient Gothic tribe itself.

Gothic and the Gothic Tribes

As the *OED* notes, by far the earliest recorded instances of the word 'Gothic' in English signify not the literary taste outlined above, but rather a sense of the Gothic as being 'of', 'pertaining to' or 'concerned with' the ancient tribe of the Goths. Groom's essay offers a thorough account of the Goths and their perceived place in ancient British and European history. Suffice it for the moment, however, to say that, amidst a plethora of different accounts of their origins, the only common claims that persist are that the Goths were a barbarian, Christian tribe. Forced out of their central and eastern European territories by the migration of the Huns into the area, they crossed the River Danube into the Roman Empire in AD 376, eventually engaging in a bloody, full-scale sacking of Rome in AD 410.

The Gothic tribe was given a shared point of origin in the work of Jordanes, a historian writing in Constantinople in the sixth century who traced his descent from the Goths. In his influential

Getica (AD 551), Jordanes claimed that the Goths had originated from Scandza, apparently a great 'island' situated around the region today known as southern Scandinavia. From there, he maintained, the Goths migrated to Scythia – a region in classical geography that encompassed the areas known today as central and eastern Europe – prior to their later subdivision into the Visigothic and Ostrogothic tribes. Whatever the precise details, the perception of the Goths as a northern people who eventually settled in and around Germany and other parts of eastern Europe was a historiographic assumption that Jordanes' *Getica* influentially set in place for at least the next thousand years (Groom 2012: 12).

In any event, more than the precise details of their passage, it was the symbolic value with which the Goths were charged that became increasingly significant as the centuries wore on. If the effect of Jordanes' work had been to provide the barbarian Gothic tribe with a detailed history and a complex genealogy at least rivalling that of Rome, it also did much to galvanise the symbolic values and connotations that had been accreting around the term 'Gothic' since its earliest usages. For, given the Goths' role in the Roman Empire's downfall, Gothic was a term associated from the outset with a strongly anti-classical spirit. It came to epitomise a solid set of hardy, northern, Christian values, in sharp contrast to the decadent paganism of the Romans they conquered. In place of the tyranny of Roman leaders, moreover, the Goths were perceived as the harbingers of democratic systems of government in Europe. Such a set of values became particularly significant for historiographers in Britain, who, from the end of the seventeenth century onwards, consistently looked to the ancient Gothic tribe as the source of their own political ideals.

The story of how the Goths, or conceptions of the Gothic, ever came to be so closely intertwined with the history of Britain is in fact an interesting one. As Samuel Kliger (1952) has argued, from around the end of the seventeenth century onwards, progressive Whig historians in Britain – intent, as they were, upon justifying William of Orange's vanquishing of the Stuart line of Kings with the Glorious Revolution of 1688 – made frequent recourse to a powerful political ideology in which notions of the 'Gothic' played a vital role.

If the more liberal Protestant Whigs, in marked contrast to the absolutism of the Catholic Stuart line, favoured a delicate system of power-sharing between the monarch and Parliament, this political structure could be strategically projected back on to certain Gothic antecedents. The nascent system of democracy, the argument went, originated with the ancient Gothic tribe in the 'woods of Germany'. Sources such as the Venerable Bede's *An Ecclesiastical History of the English People* (*c.* 731) and the *Anglo-Saxon Chronicle* were cited to describe how it was felicitously transplanted into England with the arrival of the Angles, Saxons and Jutes in Britain in or around 449. Jordanes' *Getica* had unwittingly implied that all German tribesmen were genetically of Gothic extraction: having originated in Scandza in the north, they eventually inhabited much of central Europe,

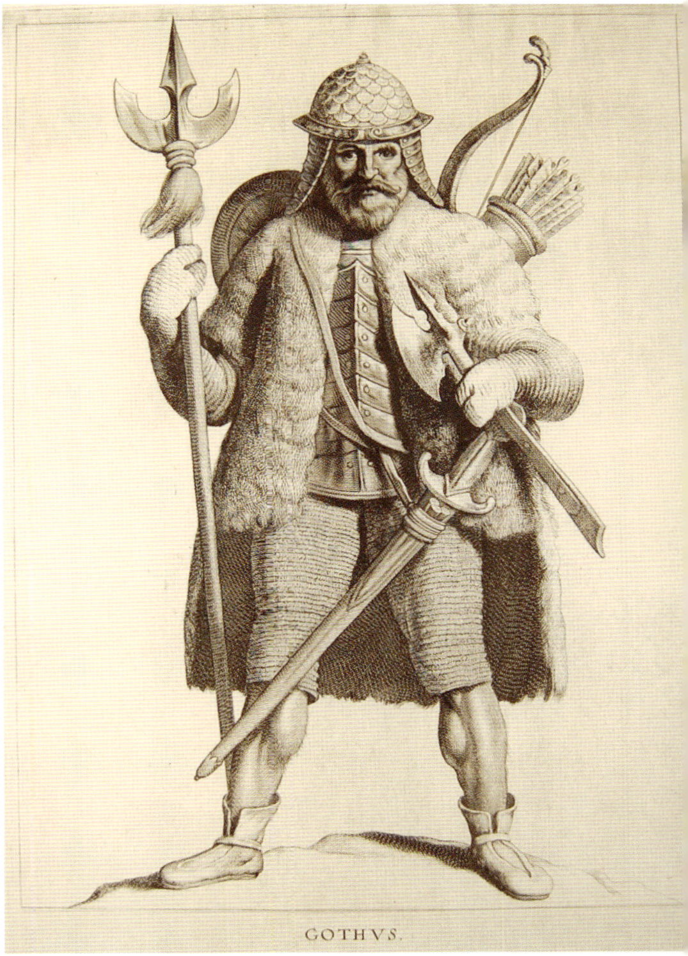

Engraving of a Goth by Cornelis Visscher, 1650.
British Museum.

colonising much of the known, civilised world, including England, as they did so. Given that the Angles, Saxons and Jutes hailed from similar northern European territories, it did not require too great a leap of historical logic to render them, too, as 'Gothic' tribes.

The work of the Roman historian Cornelius Tacitus in *Germania* (*c.* AD 98) became particularly influential in this regard. As John Aikin, in the preface to his translation of Tacitus into English in 1777, put it, the 'manners of the most civilized parts of the globe' were thought 'to originate from the woods and desarts [*sic*] of Germany' (1777: vii). According to this line of reasoning, Britain, or, somewhat more narrowly, England, was a nation that derived originally from the Goths: a country in which the original Gothic values of liberty, equality, democracy, virtue, proto-Protestantism, the adulation of women and a respect for the institution of monogamous marriage had persisted to the late seventeenth-century present, despite the challenges posed to Anglo-Saxon culture by William the Conqueror's Norman invasion in 1066. It was commonly believed that Hengist and Horsa, the brothers who by repute led the conquering armies of the Angles, Saxons and Jutes, had been invited into England by Vortigern, king of the Britons, as much-needed reinforcement against the violence and aggression of Scots and Picts to the north of Hadrian's Wall.

The name of the same Germanic people that had invaded Rome, then, was seen to have a direct relation to the ancient history of England. As a result, the terms 'German' or 'Germanic', 'Gothic', 'English' and 'Anglo-Saxon' were often used interchangeably when British historians of the late seventeenth and eighteenth centuries turned to account for the nation's ancient origins. In the hands of writers such as James Thomson, Charles-Louis de Secondat Montesquieu, John Pinkerton, Paul-Henri Mallet and countless others, this 'myth of Gothic origins' was particularly powerful, serving, as it did, both to ground the nation in a noble, valiant past and provide historical anchorage and legitimacy to political values cherished by the present. According to a particular strand in post-Renaissance thought known as the '*translatio imperii ad Teutonicos*', an enduring analogy was to be drawn between the Goths' sacking of Rome, on the one hand, and the Reformation in Europe on the other. Both involved the emancipation of original liberties from the yoke of Roman or Roman-Catholic oppression (Kliger 1952: 33–4), and so Gothic became, in some seventeenth- and eighteenth-century circles, a byword for Enlightenment. It represented a native tradition in British culture that celebrated moral purity, liberty, vigour and non-absolutist forms of kingship over the depravity, indolence and luxury of the Roman Empire.

From Medieval Barbarism to Gothic Revival

And yet, despite these positive, salutary connotations to the term, notions of the 'Gothic' in the seventeenth and eighteenth centuries remained dogged by the negative associations the term had held ever since the Renaissance. The architect Donato Bramante and the painter Giorgio Vasari, for example, both used 'Gothic' pejoratively to denounce the cultural production of the medieval period (Groom 2012: 13). Active during the height of the Italian Renaissance, these writers regarded medieval architecture, variously referred to as 'barbaric', 'German' or 'Gothic', as a somewhat monstrous style, utterly devoid of Greek- and Roman-derived ideals of proportion, beauty, balance and symmetry. If the Renaissance marked the rebirth of classical Greek and Roman art, knowledge and philosophy, so the medieval past, in all its perceived savagery and darkness, was to be discarded as 'Gothic', an age wholly at odds with the modern Renaissance present. As the *OED* reveals, 'Gothic' also denoted that which belonged to, or was characteristic of, the middle or 'dark' ages, and could be used pejoratively to signify its difference from classical values.

In Britain, such implications would persist alongside more positive historiographic usages well into the eighteenth century, despite the fact that Gothic, for some, marked an original, British political system of liberty and enlightenment. For many, it still remained the name for a rude and benighted medieval past, at once Catholic, feudal and tyrannous. During the eighteenth century, the traces of a Gothic or medieval past in both literary and architectural remains – the oral traditions of many medieval ballads, the manuscripts of many Old English poems, the ruined and dilapidated cathedrals, abbeys and monasteries that had squatted so ominously on the landscape ever since Henry VIII's dissolution of the monasteries in the sixteenth century – fell short of the aesthetic standards of neoclassicism, all derived from ancient Greek and Roman precedents.

Indeed, had it not been for the cultural impulses of what has subsequently been identified as the 'Gothic Revival' in British culture from around 1740 onwards, Gothic or medieval art, literature and architecture – the cultural products of the so-called 'dark ages' – would have remained in relative obscurity, either relegated to the dusty preserve of the myopic antiquary or permanently consigned to the embarrassing annals of bad national taste. The reasons for a revival of interest in the medieval past, and a profound reassessment of its virtues, during the Gothic Revival in British culture of the early-to-mid eighteenth century are difficult to determine. They may reside in a combination of factors, including a growing sense of national identity, increasing dissatisfaction with the preponderance of 'imported' classical Roman and Greek aesthetic ideals, international conflicts with Britain's European neighbours, particularly France, and the growing need to re-read, and re-interpret, aspects of national history.

Whatever the precise causes, artists, antiquaries, aestheticians, poets and architects of the mid-eighteenth century became engaged in a widespread reappraisal of the British Gothic past and its material remains. The endeavour coincided neatly with the political appeals to the ancient Gothic constitution that were being made by the progressive historiographers of the period. Graveyard poets such as Thomas Parnell, Thomas Warton, Thomas Gray, Robert Blair and Edward Young began to use the ruins of Gothic buildings as the settings for their reflections on life, death and the afterlife. Batty Langley and other architects began to produce style guides for a fashion-conscious bourgeoisie who sought to restyle their houses with architectural additions and finishings inspired by ancient Gothic buildings. In a more sober and scholarly mode, a tradition of antiquarian scholarship, represented, for example, by Charles Lyttelton, Richard Gough, John Pinkteron, John Carter, William Stukeley, James Bentham and Francis Grose, turned away from the classical interests of their antiquarian forebears to study, trace, collect, sketch and write about Britain's own domestic, Gothic past – ostensibly 'inventing' a national historical past and people in each apparent gesture of 'discovery'.

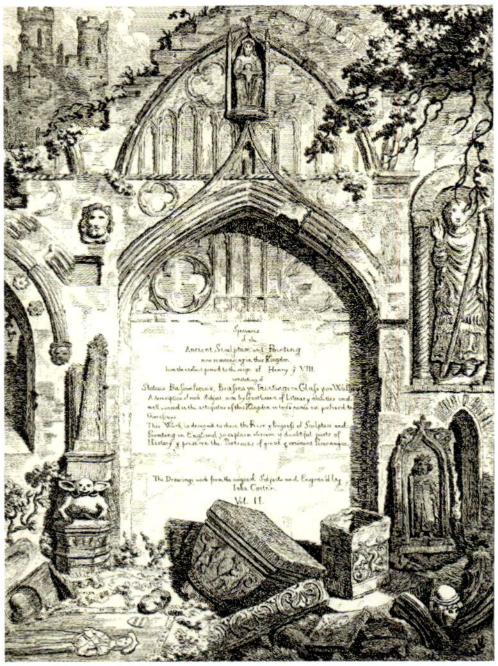

Drawing for *Views of Ancient Buildings in England Drawn in Different Tours and Engrav'd by John Carter Commencing 1764*.
British Museum.

John Carter's exquisitely detailed drawings of British medieval buildings were an attempt to enhance the status of Gothic architecture.

Arguing against the neoclassical, Palladian biases of architects such as Sir Christopher Wren, who in his *Parentalia*, compiled and published by his son in 1750, had used 'Gothick' as a synonym for barbarity and untamed wildness, such architects and antiquaries stressed the beauty and significance of England's Gothic architectural ruins. They mapped the country in countless local histories, topographies and illustrated guides with increasing insistence as the eighteenth century wore on. For an architect and Gothic antiquarian such as John Carter, a considerable aspect of this endeavour involved combatting and revising the implications of 'Gothic', invested for many late eighteenth-century Britons with associations of the crude artefacts of the 'dark ages'. For Carter, the term 'Gothic' was to be used only reluctantly, and alongside such similes for the medieval architectural style as 'English', Norman, or 'the pointed style of architecture'. The revival of interest in Gothic antiquities, in other words, was driven in part by a nationalist agenda – a conviction that, while manifestations of similar architectural styles could be identified abroad, a more accurate interpretation of Gothic meant something quintessentially English in nature, and so worthy of veneration and respect.

This architectural antiquarianism had its literary equivalents too. Thomas Warton's *Observations on the Faerie Queene of Spenser* (1754), for instance, drew positive and influential parallels between the form of Edmund Spenser's poetic romance and Gothic architectural structure. As he did so, Warton articulated a new set of standards by which both Spenserian romance and ancient Gothic piles could be appreciated, evaluated and understood. Similarly, in his *Letters on Chivalry and Romance* (1762), the Reverend Richard Hurd set about a large-scale recovery of the medieval past. In the medieval romance in particular Hurd found a literary form worthy of both preservation and emulation.

In 1765 Thomas Percy published his *Reliques of Ancient English Poetry*, for the most part an anthology of old English ballads. In addition to providing material for Lewis's *Tales of Wonder*, these were also to have a considerable impact on later Romantic poets such as William Wordsworth and Samuel Taylor Coleridge. In *The Minstrelsy of the Scottish Border* (1802–3), Walter Scott, effecting what he termed his 'escape' from the critical furore occasioned by *Tales of Wonder*, would attempt to do the same for his native Scotland, here

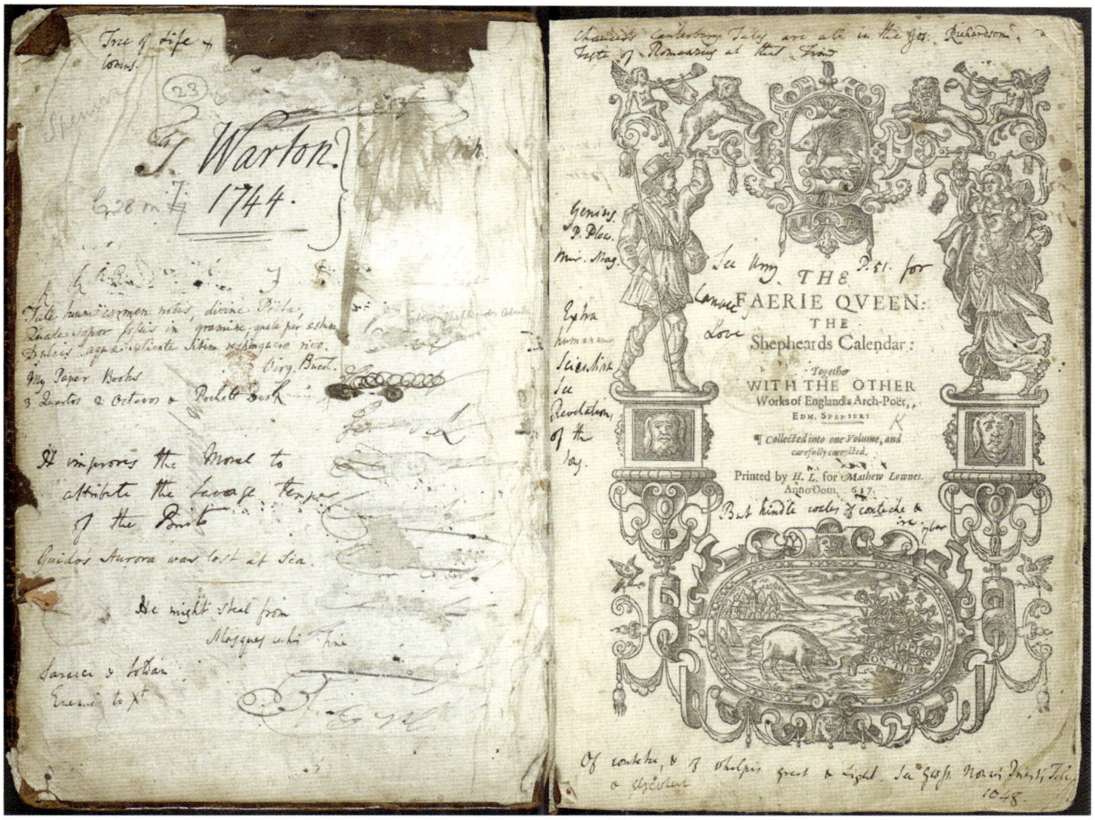

Thomas Warton's copy of *The Faerie Queene* with heavily annotated flyleaf and title page.
British Library C.28.m.7.

returning Lewis's adaptations of old Scottish ballads to their more 'authentic' forms (Thomson 2010: 25). Perhaps predictably, however, it was Shakespeare who became particularly central to this recovery of, and reinvigorated interest in, a national literary heritage in the eighteenth century.

As early as 1725 Alexander Pope had drawn a comparison between the plays of Shakespeare and 'an ancient majestic piece of *Gothick* architecture' (1725: xxiii). His analogy expressed a kind of reluctant admiration for the dramatist and his works: though as transgressive of the Aristotelian unities of time, space and action as the Gothic pile was of neoclassical architectural ideals, Shakespeare and his plays were nonetheless worthy of praise and admiration. In the preface to his edition of Shakespeare's plays in 1765, Samuel Johnson described *A Midsummer Night's Dream* as being 'replete with the *Gothick* mythology of fairies' (1765: xx), while in 1769 Elizabeth Montagu embraced Shakespeare as 'our Gothic bard' in *An Essay on the Writings and Genius of Shakespear* [*sic*] (1769: 147). In all of these instances, the coupling of Shakespeare and the term 'Gothic' served to situate the Bard in a national English or 'Gothic' line of literature that, for all its apparent indifference to neoclassical strictures, was still legitimate and worthy of national recognition. As the example of Drake cited above indicates, though, the term also contained at least some reference to supernatural wonders and terrors. The English literary canon, said to begin with Chaucer, and, despite the prevailing neoclassicism of the Renaissance, to continue as strongly in the works of Spenser and Shakespeare, was one in which ghostliness was thought to play a central role.

These considerations bring us ever closer to the cultural terrain both opened up and exploited by Horace Walpole in *The Castle of Otranto*. As it appears on the title page of the second edition of the text, the word 'Gothic' serves several functions. Most saliently, it is a marker of the story's historical provenance, at least as it was described in the preface to the first edition, purportedly written by one Onuphrio Muralto, translated from the Italian by William Marshal and printed in Naples in Gothic or 'black' script in 1529, but originally written somewhere between 1095 and 1243. Walpole's sense of the Gothic as a historical term suggestive of a malevolent and superstitious medieval past is borne out by the events of the story itself. A tale of political tyranny, incestuous sexuality, wondrous occurrences and spectral terrors, *The Castle of Otranto* exploits several of the meanings of 'Gothic' – unenlightened, Catholic, medieval, barbaric – that were current in mid-to-late eighteenth-century Britain.

In 1777, some 13 years later, Clara Reeve followed Walpole's lead by subtitling her romance *The Champion of Virtue* as 'A Gothic Story'. In 1778, revising and reissuing the fiction under its more familiar title, *The Old English Baron*, Reeve described her 'Gothic Story' in a preface as 'a picture of Gothic times and manners' (2003: 2). Within the context of Reeve's narrative, however, Gothic, while continuing to describe the medieval period, appears to have been divested of its connotations of savagery, barbarism and darkness. Although supernatural, and despite being characterised by wonders and terrors arguably more sublime than those of Walpole's text, the medieval past in *The Old English Baron* is far less negatively rendered.

The Castle of Otranto also remains fundamentally 'Gothic' in a recuperated, more positive sense of that term. For insofar as the story, as Walpole concedes in the second preface, was intended as a rigorous defence of the 'genius' of Shakespeare against the tide of neoclassical criticism directed by the French Enlightenment philosopher Voltaire towards England's national bard, *The Castle of Otranto* is 'Gothic' because it defiantly asserts a native Englishness in at least two ways: formally, through suturing the ancient romance to the modern novel and so creating a new hybrid literary mode, and thematically, through pitting the sublime terrors of a native 'Gothic' tradition of supernaturalism against the dull, prosaic turns of realist narrative.

The Haunted Library

As noted at the outset of this introduction, the year 2014 marks the 250th anniversary of *The Castle of Otranto*'s publication. By a strange coincidence, it also marks the 250th birthday of Ann Radcliffe, acclaimed by Nathan Drake as the 'Shakspeare [*sic*] of Romance Writers' (1798: 249), Walter Scott as the 'first poetess of Romantic fiction' (1824: iv) and Thomas De Quincey as the 'great enchantress' (2000: 147). In recognising these and other important cultural moments, the British Library's exhibition *Terror and Wonder: The*

Gothic Imagination showcases the Gothic imagination in its manifold aspects. It explores the architectural and antiquarian interests of the seventeenth and eighteenth centuries, and how they continued through the Victorian period, and reveals the various forms, both literary and otherwise, that the Gothic has assumed to the present day. In doing so, this exhibition brings to the Gothic an important institutional recognition, celebrating a mode of cultural expression that, at least at its origins, was considered to be more a source of national embarrassment than pride.

The Introductory Dialogue that opens Morley's *Tales of Terror and Wonder* succinctly captures some of the critical biases that prevailed against the Gothic imagination at the turn of the nineteenth century. In staging an imaginary exchange between an 'Author' of ghostly balladry and a concerned 'Friend', it ventriloquises the voice of Gothic's numerous detractors. As the Friend, having learned of the Author's intentions to pen a collection of supernatural fictions, somewhat incredulously enquires,

> WHAT, scribble tales? Oh, cease to play the fool!
> Christmas is past, and children gone to school;
> E'en active Harlequin abashed retires,
> Neglected witches quench the cauldron's fires,
> Whilst fairy phantoms vanish swift away,
> And sense and nature reassume their sway.
> What gain, what pleasure, can your labours crown?
> A nursery's praise shall be your best renown;
> Each feeble tale ingloriously expire,
> A gossip's story at a winter's fire. (Morley 1887: 9)

Encapsulated in this short passage are many of the criticisms levelled against the Gothic mode in the late eighteenth century. These views were repetitively peddled in the scathing reviews of romances and dramas published in the periodicals of the day, and expressed by dismissive members of the Romantic literati, such as William Wordsworth and Samuel Taylor Coleridge, both of whom regarded the Gothic as the puerile and immature fancy of the nursery, the evanescent stuff of old wives' tales and gossipy servant girls rather than the worthwhile aesthetic creation of a writer of 'genius' or originality.

Commenting on Lewis's over-reliance upon the work of others in *Tales of Wonder*, for instance, Wordsworth dismissively referred to the anthology as 'Tales of Plunder' (Thomson 2010: 26). As the Friend in this Introductory Dialogue continues, supernatural ballads, the likes of which the reader is about to encounter in *Tales of Terror and Wonder*, are both the 'Prepost'rous births' of a 'monstrous mind' (Morley 1887: 9) and the sign of a 'perverted taste' (Morley 1887: 10), examples of a debased literary appetite that, in its aims 'To freeze some silly female breast with fear' (Morley 1887: 10), becomes ultimately associated with foolish, impressionable female readers such as those satirically pictured in Gillray's etching of 1802. Indeed, denigrations of the Gothic were often expressed in highly gendered

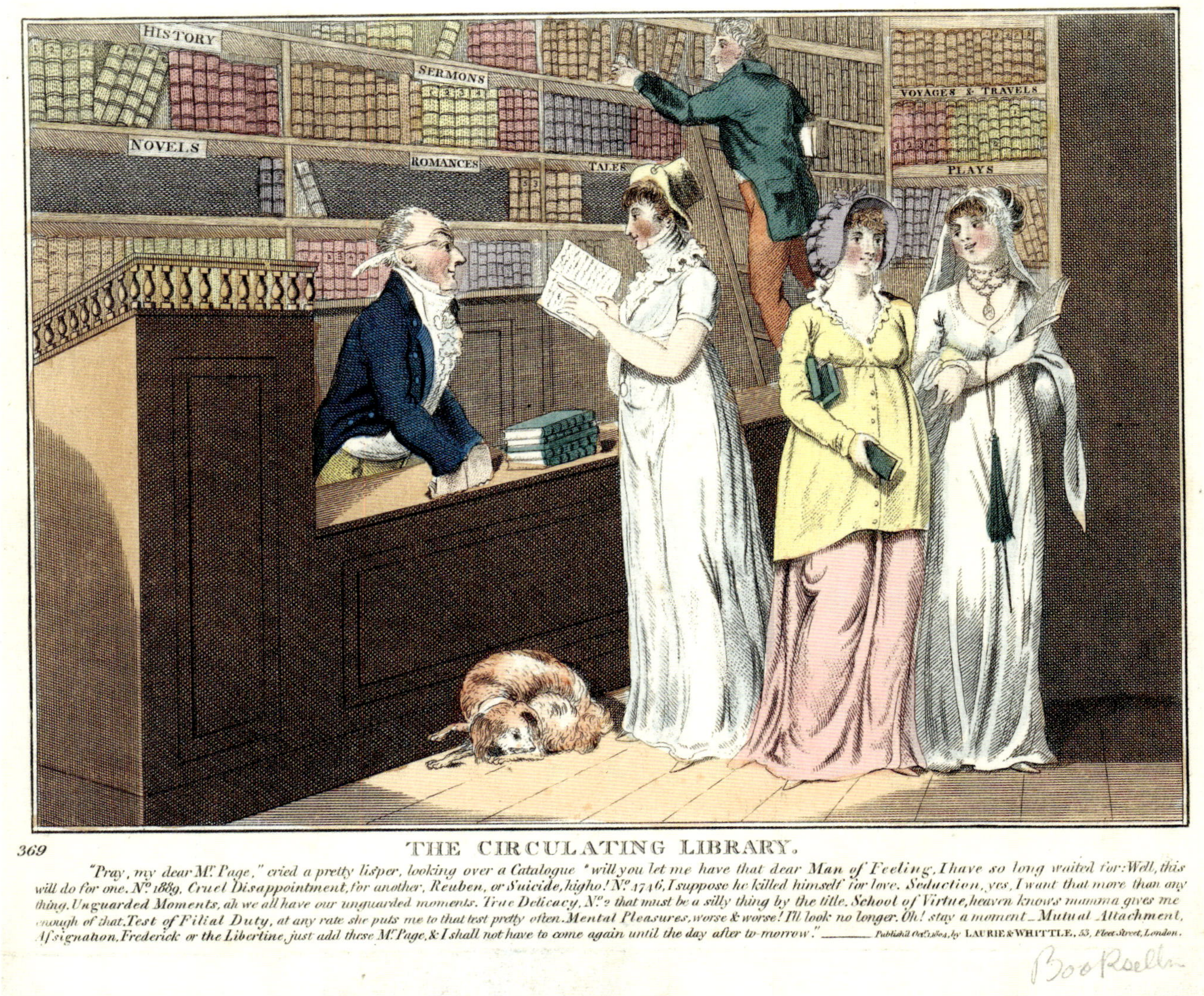

'The Circulating Library', satirical print, 1804.
British Museum.

Although satirical, this representation of a circulating library highlights the popularity of fiction among women readers during Gothic literature's 'Golden Age'.

terms, to the extent that the female reader, overly absorbed in the perusal of these lurid fictions, became a frequently rehearsed cultural trope. Evanescent and impermanent, such works leave no lasting trace behind them, but rather 'Like brilliant bubbles, glitter for a day, / Till, swoln too big, they burst, and pass away' (Morley 1887: 10). In short, the idea that the Gothic imagination could ever merit the commemoration, celebration and display it is receiving in the year 2014 at the British Library was inconceivable 250 years ago. Be it due to the exceptional versatility of the form, the continued appeal of the Gothic since the eighteenth century, its profound and global resurgence in our own day and age, or the academic re-evaluation of previously marginalised forms of literary production since the 1970s, the Gothic has become the object of considerable popular and scholarly interest.

Indeed, the very notion of a library in the eighteenth century lent itself to the opponents of Gothic not as place for the display, preservation and conservation of Gothic fictions, but rather as a metaphorical shorthand through which Gothic romance could be further derided and critiqued. Given that books were not affordable for most sectors of the population in the eighteenth century, the majority of the Gothic's early readers obtained copies of the latest Gothic fictions through the circulating library, a lending facility that allowed patrons to borrow books volume by volume for the price of a nominal subscription. In the fashion of Catherine Morland and Isabella Thorpe in Jane Austen's *Northanger Abbey*, it was through the circulating library that most eighteenth-century readers gained access to such attention-grabbing titles as *The Castle of Wolfenbach*, *Clermont*, *Mysterious Warnings*, *Necromancer of the Black Forest*, *The Midnight Bell*, *The Orphan of the Rhine*, and *Horrid Mysteries*. Some of the publishing houses most renowned for their production of Gothic fictions in the 1790s, such as William Lane's Minerva Press in Leadenhall Street, London, stocked the particular circulating libraries with which they were affiliated, thus ensuring that readers and patrons had almost immediate access to the sentimental and Gothic romances that they produced. In the hands of the Gothic's detractors, though, the circulating library was a dangerous source of a contagion, the site at which female readers, in particular, gained dangerous access to what one correspondent in the *Monthly Magazine and British Register* in 1797 described as 'hobgoblin-romances'. Gothic fiction, this writer made clear, belonged among 'all the trash of a circulating library' (Anon. 1797: 347–9). While the morally instructive novels of such writers as Henry Fielding, Samuel Richardson, John Moore and Frances Burney, this correspondent continued, ought to occasion a sense of national pride, these cheap, tawdry thrillers 'disgrace our public libraries, under the same general denomination of novels' (Anon. 1797: 348). In his *Biographia Literaria* of 1817, Coleridge, too, drew upon the associations of the circulating library to criticise what he took to be the idle, all-too-passive consumers of the Gothic aesthetic: 'For as to the devotees of the circulating libraries, I dare not compliment their pass-time, or rather kill-time, with the name of reading. Call it rather a sort of beggarly day-dreaming during which the mind of the dreamer furnishes for itself nothing but laziness and a little mawkish sensibility' (Clery and Miles 2000: 276). From cultural 'trash' and detritus to a major exhibition at the British Library: since the eighteenth century the Gothic imagination has come a long way.

Such a venue is in many ways entirely appropriate. For the Gothic, in its preoccupation with ancient discovered manuscripts, documentary fragments and charmed books, has always been concerned with the stuff of libraries. Beyond that, the library itself has often proven to be, in Gothic writing, a particularly haunted space: the library of the northern English Catholic family mentioned in the preface to the first edition of *The Castle of Otranto*; the mysterious reading room in the College Library of the University of St Andrews that is inhabited by a ghostly scholar in Margaret Oliphant's 'The Library Window' (1896); the appearance of a monstrous shape in the thinly disguised Cambridge University Library in M R James's 'The Tractate Middoth' (1911); and, most appropriately, the setting of the British Museum conjured up at the beginning of James's eerie tale 'Casting the Runes' (1911). Similar preoccupations with manuscripts, books, libraries and the readers who use them persist in modern and contemporary Gothic works too, from the labyrinthine medieval library in Umberto Eco's *The Name of the Rose* (1980), through the ghostly Cemetery of Forgotten Books in Carlos Ruiz Zafón's *The Shadow of the Wind* (2001), to the library of the narrator's father, where she first stumbles upon a cache of Dracula-related letters, in Elizabeth Kostova's *The Historian* (2005). The return of the Gothic to the British Library tacitly acknowledges the mode's enduring love affair with books.

Though firmly consolidated by the early nineteenth century, the Gothic imagination has by no means remained stable, consistent or monolithic. As the essays in this collection indicate, the Gothic has shifted, altered and mutated considerably since its inception. It is best conceived of today as a protean, ever-changing mode rather than a fixed generic category – an imaginative tendency able, perhaps like no other, to infuse a variety of forms, mediums and technologies across historical time and cultural space. Angela Wright's essay on eighteenth-century Gothic in this collection gives some sense of its mutability. Permeating romance, drama, chapbooks and poetry alike during the 1790s, the Gothic imagination was swift to reinvent itself in the Promethean narratives of writers such as Lord Byron, Mary Shelley and Percy Bysshe Shelley.

Crossing the Atlantic with the work of Charles Brocken Brown in the late 1790s, the Gothic would develop into a prominent strand in nineteenth-century American fiction. Edgar Allan Poe, Nathaniel Hawthorne, Herman Melville and others established a rich Gothic tradition that continues to inform much American fiction and horror cinema to this day. In nineteenth-century Britain, the Gothic had not long been cast as a term to evoke a dark and gruesome literary strain when it was absorbed and re-appropriated by the major exponents of the Gothic Revival in Victorian architecture, notably in Charles Barry and Augustus W N Pugin's designs for the rebuilding of the Houses of Parliament in the late 1830s, George Gilbert Scott's work on the Midland Grand Hotel, St Pancras, and John Ruskin's commentaries on the Gothic architectural style in *The Seven Lamps of Architecture* (1849) and *The Stones of Venice* (1851–3).

In the hands of these and other Revivalists, the Gothic imagination was, for the most part, divested of its connotations of darkness, barbarism and superstition. Instead, it signified a faded, noble and somewhat sanitised medieval past, portraying an age of supreme cultural, political, religious and artistic achievement. This Victorian interest in what we might term the 'white' Gothic had its counterparts in the age's literature and fine art, too, informing the work of Alfred Lord Tennyson, William Morris and other poets and painters of the Pre-Raphaelite Brotherhood. Nonetheless, and as Alexandra Warwick's essay in this collection reveals, the mode's more unsettling aspects would continue to plague and disrupt the niceties of the bourgeois Victorian world in many of the period's novels, shadowing the soaring arches of Revivalist architecture with dark forms.

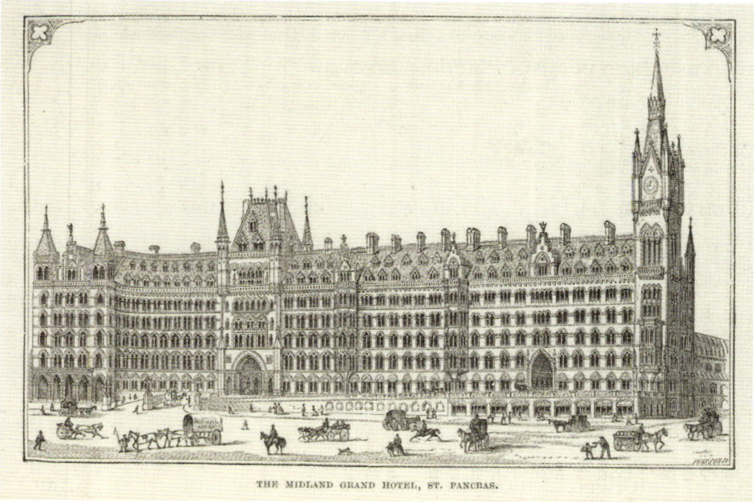

Midland Grand Hotel, St Pancras, from *The Midland Railway: Its Rise and Progress*, 1876.
British Library 08235.k.7.

The Midland Grand Hotel was Sir George Gilbert Scott's masterpiece of Gothic Revival architecture.

As Andrew Smith's essay points out, the Gothic underwent a vivid, full-scale renaissance during the *fin de siècle* of the 1880s and 1890s. Consolidating the tendencies initiated in earlier fictions such as James Hogg's *The Private Memoirs and Confessions of a Justified Sinner* (1824), the mode manifested itself most characteristically in the uncanny doubling of self and other in the fictions of Oscar Wilde, Robert Louis Stevenson and others. With the advent of the twentieth century, the Gothic mutates thematically and technically on to the silver screen, infiltrating the new technologies of first the cinema and later the more domestic reaches of the television. Even so, and as Lucie Armitt's essay observes, several of the tropes and conventions of the earlier Gothic tradition continue to haunt much literary production of the twentieth century, inevitably returning, vampire-like, to feed off the bodies that sustain them.

Spreading, like a virus, from page to screen to a sub-cultural look forged on the aesthetics of early horror film, Gothic became 'Goth' in the post-Punk decade of the 1980s, thereby incorporating reference to a particular taste in music, fashion and lifestyle. As Catherine Spooner's reading of the Gothic in contemporary culture indicates, some of the most recent manifestations of the Gothic imagination seem to have come full circle. Current Gothic fiction and film consistently probe the perilous uncertainty of textuality and reading, returning, in some respects, to eighteenth-century origins and reflecting contemporary anxieties about the future of the book and the library in an increasingly digital age. No longer tied into a specifically British national and cultural tradition, the Gothic has become a global force, permeating literature, film, music, fashion, the internet and other forms of cultural production around the world. It is our hope that *Terror and Wonder: The Gothic Imagination* will provide a useful and informative point of entry into this dark and fascinating universe.

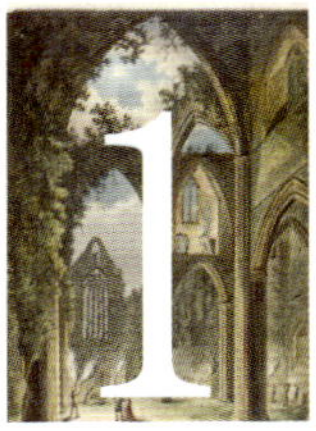

NICK GROOM

Gothic Antiquity: From the Sack of Rome to *The Castle of Otranto*

A Haunted Past

From earliest times, the mysterious Germanic tribes of the Goths were perceived as agents of both terror and wonder. They claimed to have migrated from the northern isle of 'Scandza' to settle in Scythia, the lands on the western shores of the Black Sea, but in AD 376 they were driven from their homelands by the Huns – a tribe that, according to the Roman historian Marcellinus Ammianus, 'had appeared from some remote corner of the earth, uprooting and destroying everything in its path like a whirlwind descending from high mountains' (1986: 416). The Goths crossed the Danube, the natural border of the Roman Empire, at the invitation of the Emperor Valens. But relations were tense, and within a short time fighting broke out.

The ensuing Romano-Gothic war was a catastrophe for the Romans: in AD 378 the Emperor Valens was slain in battle (his body was never recovered) and the Goths overran the empire. In *De Bello Gothico*, the poet Claudian (*c.* 370–*c.* 404) dwells on the supernatural menace of this sinister new enemy:

> Then – for fear is by nature a babbler and allows all sorts of tales to be invented and believed – dreams, portents and omens of ill were discussed on all sides. What, men asked, did that flight of birds portend, what message would heaven fain deliver to mortals by the thunderbolt, what did those prophetic books demand that guard the destiny of Rome? Constant eclipses of the moon alarmed us and night after night throughout the

OPPOSITE:
Tintern Abbey.
British Library K. Top. 31.16.f.
The wild beauty of Tintern Abbey as seen by moonlight.

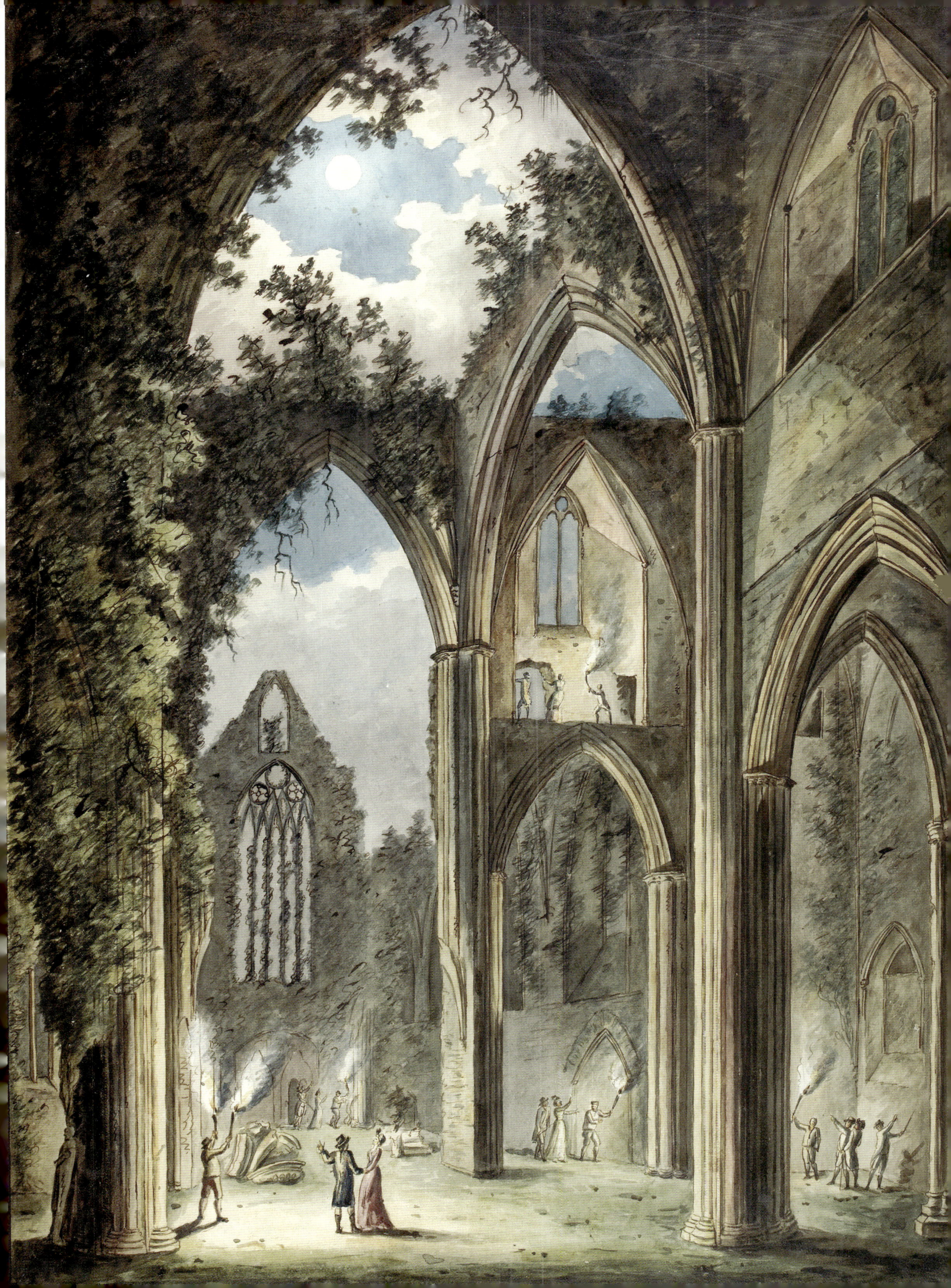

> cities of Italy sounded wailings and the beating of brazen gongs to scare the shadow from off her darkened face. Men would not believe that the moon had been defrauded of her brother the sun, forbidden to give light by the interposition of the earth; they thought that Thessalian witches, accompanying the barbarian armies, were darkening her rays with their country's magic spells. Then with these new portents their troubled minds link the signs of the past year and any omens that perchance peaceful days had neglected – showers of stones, bees swarming in strange places, furious fires destroying houses from no known cause, a comet – ne'er seen in heaven without disaster [...]. (1963: 142–4)

The Goths preyed on the Roman imagination like a nightmare. In 410 an army led by Alaric sacked Rome. As Edward Gibbon later observed, history has never forgiven the Goths for despoiling the Eternal City, and their name became a byword for destructive savagery: 'So memorable was the part that they acted in the subversion of the Western empire, that the name of Goths is frequently but improperly used as a general appellation of rude and warlike barbarism' (1994: I.255).

As for the Huns, they were, in the striking phrase of the fifth-century Gothic historian Jordanes, 'fiercer than ferocity itself' (1915: 85). The Goths considered them to be 'scarcely human', the result of unnatural union between Gothic witches expelled from Scythia and 'unclean spirits' of the wilderness: 'Though they live in the form of men, they have the cruelty of wild beasts' (1915: 85, 87). St Jerome (*c.* 347–419/20) described their ruthless onslaught against civilised Christianity in 391 in comparable terms:

> Behold, the wolves, not of Arabia, but of the North, were let loose upon us last year from the far-off rocks of Caucasus, and in a little while overran great provinces. How many monasteries were captured, how many streams were reddened with human blood! [...]
>
> No, not if I had a hundred tongues, a hundred mouths
> And a voice of iron, could I describe all the shapes of
> wickedness. (Virgil 1998: VI, 625–6)
>
> [...] They filled the whole earth with slaughter and panic as they flitted hither and thither on their swift horses [...] They were at hand everywhere before they were expected: by their speed they outstripped rumour, and they took pity neither upon religion nor rank nor age nor wailing childhood. Those who had just begun to live were compelled to die and, in ignorance of their plight, would smile amid the drawn swords of the enemy. (Thompson 1948: 27)

Perhaps inevitably the Goths were conflated with the Huns by later chroniclers and epic poets, with the Hunnish chieftain Attila, for example, appearing in later Teutonic poems. But there were in any case deep connections between the two tribes. Some Goths practised the weird Hunnish tradition of cranial deformation (elongating the head for ritualistic or aesthetic reasons), while the name Attila means 'little father' in Gothic. Nor is it a coincidence that Attila also became the ancestor from whom Count Dracula would later trace his lineage.

Empires of the Goths

Not surprisingly these early associations of the Goths with fear and horror, carnage and the supernatural tended to eclipse their social and political achievements. After the Sack of Rome the Goths settled in Europe, establishing kingdoms in Italy and Spain (the Ostrogothic and Visigothic strains respectively) that rested on the foundations of Roman civic structures. The Goths became the earliest Germanic tribe to develop a literate culture, their alphabet being devised by Bishop Ulfila in the fourth century for his biblical translations, and among their leading thinkers were the poet and rhetorician Ennodius (later Bishop of Pavia), the historian Cassiodorus and the philosopher Boethius. In the opinion of the French historian Lucien Musset, the Goths built the 'earliest barbarian intellectual culture' (1975: 144), and the northeast Italian city of Ravenna, capital of the Kingdom of the Ostrogoths, appears to have been a seat of learning and scriptoria. The Goths were also staunchly Christian (if adherents of the Arian heresy, which denied the divinity of Christ), and according to theologians such as Orosius and Augustine of Hippo they had been instruments of God's own vengeance. Rome had been sacked as a

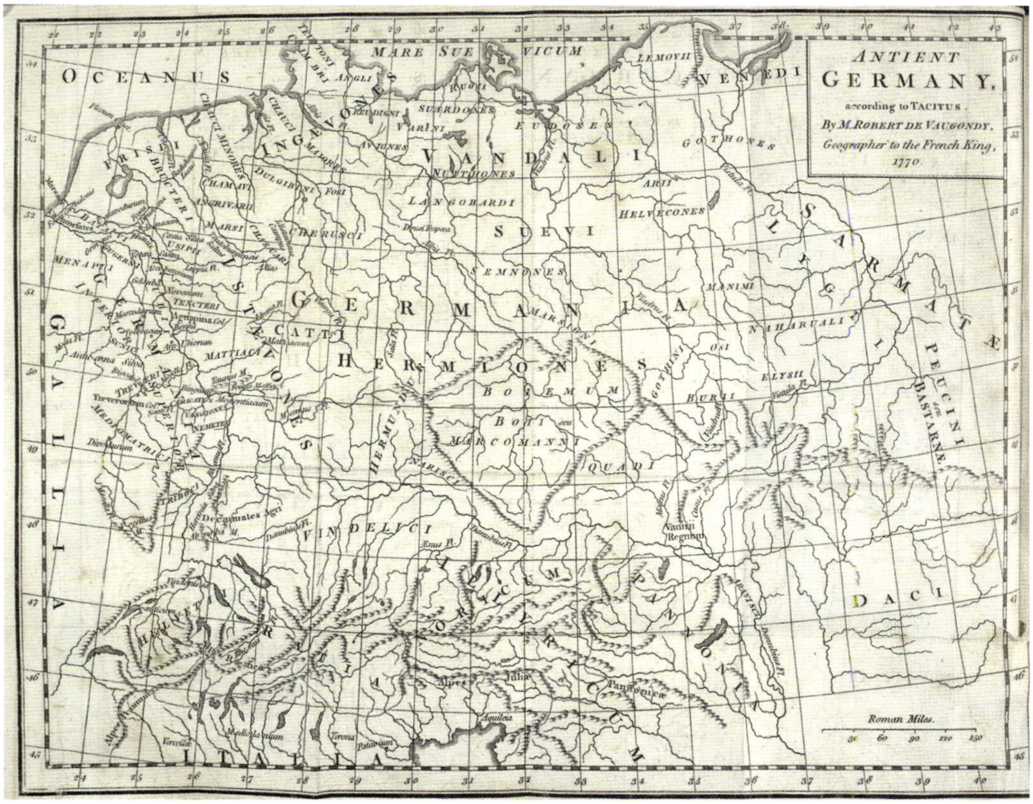

Map showing early Gothic settlement, 1777.

A map of ancient Germany from John Aikin's translation of Tacitus's *Germania*, including an area marked 'Gothones'.

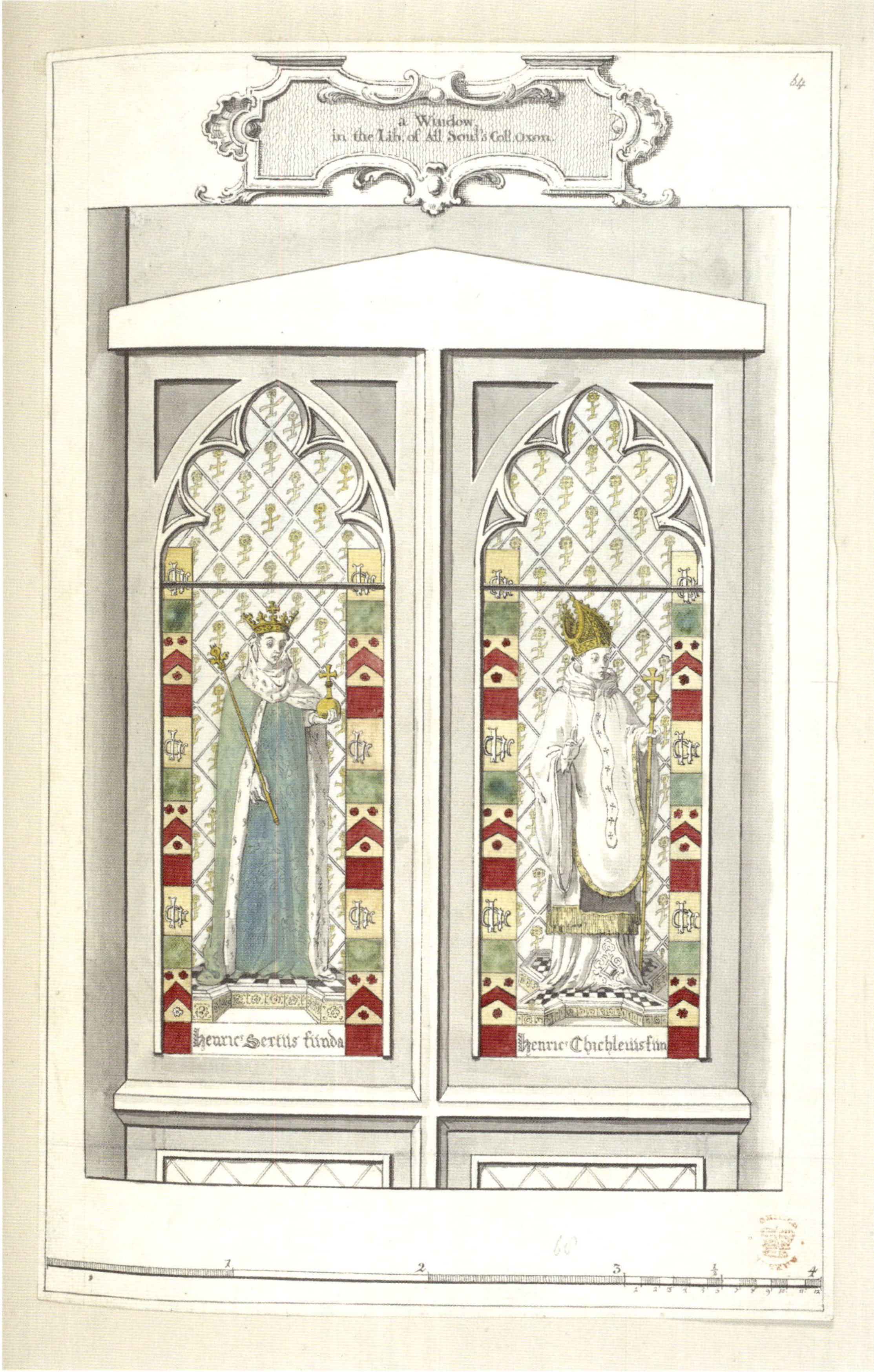
a Window
in the Lib. of All Soul's Coll. Oxon.
64
Henric. Sextus funda
Henric. Chichleius fun
60
1
2
3
4

warning to the empire against returning to paganism. Indeed, the marauding Goths were so devout that they pillaged no Christian temples and even paused in their destruction to pray.

More significantly, perhaps, the Goths had been praised by Roman historians such as Tacitus, who in his anthropological history *Germania* (AD 98) contrasted the vigour and morality of the Teutonic tribes with the decadence and enervation of Rome. In doing so he detailed their distinctively democratic political system, as well as their martial values. This favourable account was subsequently developed by Gothic historians such as Cassiodorus and Jordanes; they chronicled the mythic origins of their people in northern climes and described the oral culture of 'ancient songs' that dramatised their tribal migrations and shared history. The Goths, far from being figured as the destroyers of classical civilisation, could potentially be regarded as offering an alternative to the Mediterranean domain and all its arts and intrigues: one that was focused on the north.

Such was the split personality of the Gothic that successive European epochs inherited. One the one hand, the Goths were synonymous with destruction, causing the collapse of the classical world, and bringing about a thousand years of degeneration and superstition – the Dark Ages. On the other, however, they were imagined to be the primal northern race – robust and dynamic, and characterised by a natural love of liberty and freedom of imagination that had instinctively rebelled against the cruel might of the tyrannical Roman Empire. Accordingly the Gothic came to constitute the ground on which the major cultural, intellectual and political debates of later centuries took place.

The Italian Renaissance, for instance, deplored the advent of the Goths and the decline and fall of classical grandeur. In 1510 Donato Bramante dismissed all non-classical and non-Mediterranean architecture as 'Germanic', condemning all the 'squat little figures, badly carved, which are used as corbels to hold up the roof beams, along with bizarre animals and figures and crude foliage, all unnatural and irrational' (Brooks 1999: 9). Giorgio Vasari agreed: the 'German' style was 'monstrous and barbaric, wholly ignorant of any accepted ideas of sense and order'. These buildings were 'confused and disordered [...] there are portals with flimsy columns twisted like corkscrews [...] façades made up of one damned tabernacle on top of the other [...] and lots of pinnacles, gables and foliage'. For Vasari, 'This manner of building was invented by the Goths, who put up structures in this way after all the ancient buildings had been destroyed and all the architects killed in the wars. It was they who made vaults with pointed arches [...] and then filled the whole of Italy with their accursed buildings' (Brooks 1999: 10). The Goths of late antiquity were therefore perceived as being responsible for the art and architecture of the Middle Ages – from the dizzying majesty of medieval cathedrals to the grotesque imagery of the cult of the macabre: from pointed arches, ribbed vaulting and flying buttresses to emaciated cadavers, putrid corpses and animated skeletons.

OPPOSITE:
Stained glass window, All Souls College Library, Oxford. From a collection of antiquarian drawings owned by Walpole.
British Library Add. MS 27350, f. 64.

Shaping the Gothic Myth

The reception of the Gothic in Britain reflected the Renaissance denunciation of all non-classical styles and the extension of the term to cover medieval culture, but it also became entangled in questions of national identity and contemporary political debate. Foremost among those antiquarians who became entranced by the Gothic myth was William Camden, whose era-defining work *Britannia* was published in Latin in 1586 (an English version followed in 1607). Camden especially drew on Tacitus and Jordanes, describing how the '*Gothick* Nations' swarmed 'from the Northern Hive' to the Black Sea. They embodied the spirit of liberty, resisting all attempts at invasion and subjugation, and being 'a most ancient people [...] invincible themselves, and free from any foreign yoke' (1722: I. xlvii–xlix). The Angles, Saxons and Jutes ('*Getes*') all descended from the Goths; the forms of governance they established were therefore versions of Gothic institutions, exemplifying democratic rule.

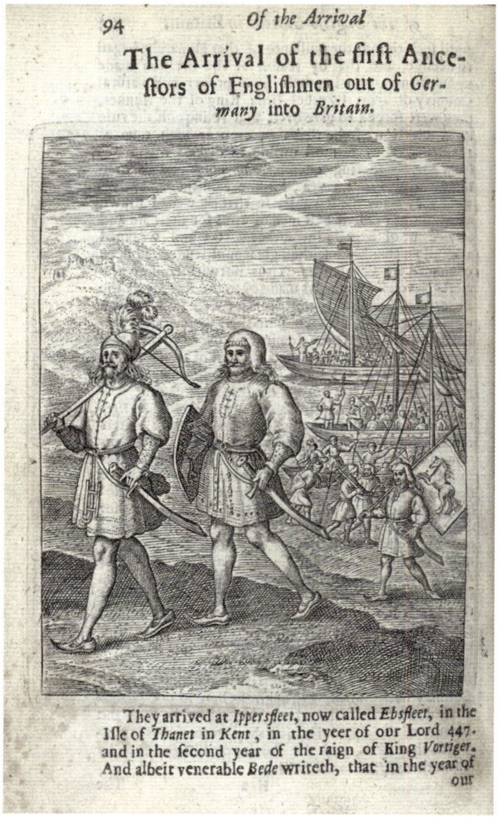

Plate from Richard Verstegan, *A Restitution of Decayed Intelligence*, 1605.
British Library 1489.p.47.
The arrival of Hengist and Horsa, the mythical first Germanic settlers in Britain.

Moreover, Camden drew on the fifth-century Gallic poet Sidonius Apollinaris to argue that the Gothic was as much a sartorial fashion as it was a racial heritage. Clothes symbolised identity, and were therefore a manifestation of the history and values of a people:

> They shine (*says he*) with yellow; and cover their Feet as high as their Ancle [*sic*], with hairy Leather. Their Knees, Legs, and Calves are all bare. Their Garment is high, close, and particolour'd, hardly reaching down to their Hams. Their Sleeves cover only the upper parts of their Arm. Their inner Coat is green, and edg'd with red Fringes. Their Belts hang down from the Shoulder. The lappets of their Ears are cover'd with locks of Hair hanging over them. Their Arms are hooked Spears, and Hatchets to fling. (1701: I.45)

The account concludes by describing how widely and deeply Gothic blood ran in the dynasties of Europe, from 'the most Potent Kings of Spain' to 'the Noblest Italian Families'; indeed 'the Emperor *Charles* V was wont to say, in good earnest, That all the Nobility of *Europe* were deriv'd from *Scandia* and the Goths' (1701: I.45). The Goths, far from simply being a barbaric disruption of classical history, had established themselves as the fountainhead of European aristocracy and the primal non-classical race.

In *A Restitution of Decayed Intelligence* (1605) Richard Verstegan similarly argued that Gothicism was inherent throughout the nationalities of Europe, proposing, for example, that the Danes and Normans were really Germans. Verstegan's *Restitution*, which went through five editions in the century, has been described by the historian Colin Kidd as 'the foundational text of English Gothicism' (1999: 218). Drawing on Tacitus, Verstegan emphasised the Goths' morality, particularly their respect for women, and the principle of *dux bellorum* – the legal convention of electing a leader in times of war, a position that was neither hereditary nor above the law, with the leader returning to the ranks of the nobility after the conflict had ended.

The Goths therefore had particular, distinguishing and, most significantly, non-Roman forms of governance, and these had been incorporated into the English constitution. The political economist Charles Davenant, in his 'Essay upon Peace, War and Alliances', claimed that the Goths 'did not make their hazardous Migrations and blindly follow Cheifs [*sic*] and Leaders without any Conditions'. On the contrary, he argued:

> 'tis evident from History, that they who accompany'd the Princes that made those Expeditions from the North assisted with Men and Mony in the Enterprize and were to participate both as to Property in the Land, and as to Authority in Governing the Territories and Dominions which with their joint Forces they purposed to Invade. There was, what we now call, an Original Compact among 'em. (1701: 236)

Northern European forms of government were originally Gothic and subsequently developed under similar conditions of climate, temper and inclination. All were alike in being anti-tyrannical, and this 'Original Compact' of land and government contrasted sharply with Roman forms of political order. 'Gothick polity' was epitomised by a constitutional monarchy and feudal land management: land tenure was granted by a superior and held 'in feu' by vassals, who were required to make some reciprocal payment or service. Such rule of the land by a sovereign, an assembly of barons and an assembly of commoners was a 'Government of Freemen', a system of government shared by all the northern nations as well as Poland, Hungary and parts of Spain and Portugal. As the writer and diplomat Sir William Temple put it, 'This Constitution has been celebrated, as framed with great Wisdom and Equity, and as the truest and justest Temper that has been ever found out between Dominion and Liberty' (Temple 1720: I.219–20).

The poet and historian Samuel Daniel concurred in his *Collection of the History of England* (1621), stating that English laws were Gothic in their origin – an opinion apparently borne out by the publication in 1642 of *The Mirror of Justices* (*c.* 1285–90). Written in Latin by Andrew Horn, a thirteenth-century lawyer and legal scholar, it was translated into English in 1646. Horn comprehends the arrival of Gothic tribes in Britain as a divine mission, led by the democratic and virtuous Saxons and expressed in their institution of parliament. As Temple later put it, 'The *Saxons* were one Branch of those *Gothick* Nations which swarming from the Northern Hive, had under the Conduct of *Odin*, possessed themselves of all those mighty Tracts of Land that surround the Baltick Sea' (1720: II.557). Moreover, trial by a jury of twelve of one's peers was also Gothic in origin, established by the Saxons and adopted by the Normans, and therefore evidence of their shared Gothic ancestry.

The antiquarian researches in tracing the descent of the English from the Goths therefore had profound political implications in ascertaining the foundation and history of parliament. The concept of *dux bellorum* in particular was championed by seventeenth-

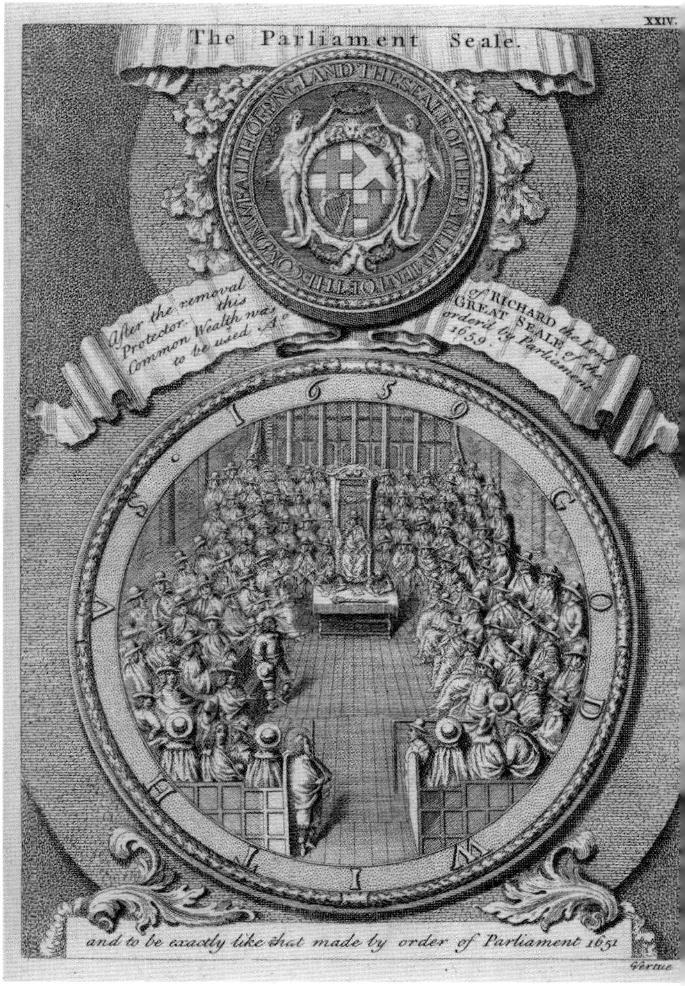

The Seal of the Parliament of the Commonwealth, from *Medals, Coins, Great-Seals, Impressions* by George Vertue, second edition, 1780.
British Library 603.i.29.

An engraving of the Great Seal of the Commonwealth showing parliament in session. According to some antiquarians, Parliament, and the overthrow of Charles I, were founded on Gothic principles.

century Parliamentarians to justify rebellion against the king – a leader who ruled not by divine right but by the will of the people, and who was consequently subject to their restrictions. Furthermore, in the 1640s commentators such as John Hare and Nathaniel Bacon advanced an uncompromising theory of anti-Normanism. This directly challenged the notion that William the Bastard had ever conquered the English in 1066 and had thereafter governed as an absolute king; rather, it was asserted, he had ruled in accordance with the Saxon *Witenagemot*, an early form of parliament.

Among the Ruins

The 1640s, the decade of fiercest political debate about the Gothic, also proved the most bloodthirsty in English history. The Civil Wars culminated in the regicide of Charles I, who was brought to the block by arguments framed by Gothicist antiquarians. Hence Royalists developed very real fears that Gothicism was akin to the more extreme ideas of the New Model Army and radical republicanism. The staggering political events of the seventeenth century – the internecine strife, the execution of the king, the turbulent Commonwealth, the restoration of the monarchy, the invasion by William of Orange and the overthrow of James II (commonly called the 'Glorious Revolution') – were apparently the price to be paid for social progress. In other words, the roots of modern English society lay not only in the thorny confusions of a semi-mythical race implicated in the fall of the Roman Empire and in the rise of the medieval; they were also soaked in blood – and, it transpired, lay in ruins.

The English countryside was strewn with architectural ruins. Some were the remains of baronial castles fallen into disrepair or plundered for building materials, but most were of a far more recent vintage: the evidence of the Protestant Reformation. Henry VIII began the dissolution of the monasteries in the 1530s to break with Roman Catholicism; by the seventeenth century this split from Rome had been incorporated into national myth as another rebellion against tyranny, parallel to the Gothic resistance to Imperial Rome and the Parliamentarian revolt against the absolutist pretensions of the king. For the Gothicists, then, the Reformation was interpreted as a rebellion against despotic papal jurisdiction; for others it was the barbaric overthrow of a millennium and a half of culture and civilisation. In the popular topographical poem *Coopers-Hill* (1642), the Royalist Sir John Denham assessed the ruinous behaviour of Henry VIII:

> Who sees these dismal Heaps, but would demand
> What barbarous Invader sack'd the Land?
> But when he hears, no Goth, no Turk did bring
> This desolation, but a Christian King;
> When nothing but the Name of Zeal, appears
> 'Twixt our best actions, and the worst of theirs,
> What does he think our Sacrilege would spare,
> When such th' effects of our Devotion are? (1709: 10)

Likewise the Roman Catholic priest Thomas Innes compared the Scottish Reformation with the Sack of Rome in his attack on the leading reformer, John Knox: 'It is *Knox* himself who hounded out, or led on the furious mobb [*sic*] in this wretched expedition, that hath thought fit to record it, with many other such noble exploits, more becoming the *Goths* or *Vandals*, than an apostolical man, as he pretended to be' (1729: 569).

The Reformation was, according to Chris Brooks in *The Gothic Revival*, essentially 'ideological warfare, battles about meaning': he indicates that Catholic abbeys and priories were 'semantic structures – structures of meaning – as well as architectural structures' (1999: 19). Hence the Protestant Reformers could attack both the spiritual values and worldly status, indeed the entire theology of the Catholic Church, by destroying the fabric of its buildings. And as iconoclasts they let the debris of their devastations remain in the defaced images of saints and decapitated statuary amid the remnants of architectural wreckage: the point was to leave perpetual reminders of the fall of Catholicism. Thus ruins, fragments and the ghosts of the past became woven into both the English countryside and the national imagination as another example of the raging progress of history.

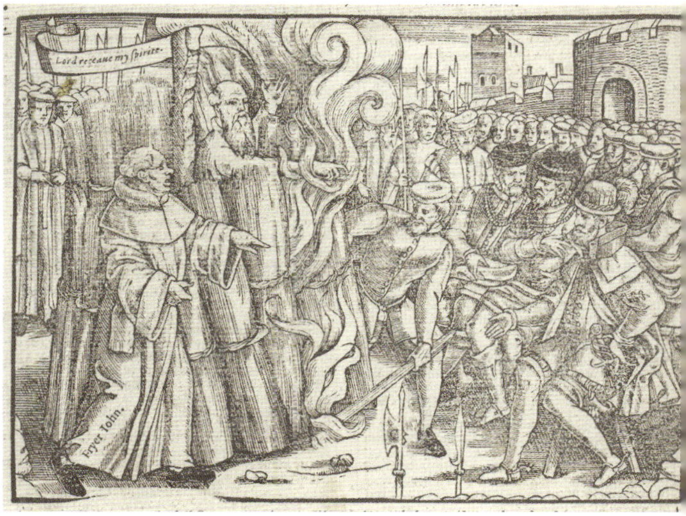

Execution of Thomas Cranmer from Foxe's *Book of Martyrs*.
British Library 4705.h.4.

Within a few years, however, Queen Mary returned the country to Catholicism for the duration of her reign (1553–8). In this brief period of Counter-Reformation, 'Bloody' Mary executed hundreds of Protestants, victims subsequently commemorated in John Foxe's *Actes and Monuments*, first published in 1563. Foxe's anthology of Protestant martyrdoms, popularly known as Foxe's *Book of Martyrs*, was second only to the Bible in the Protestant canon, and the fourth edition of 1583 was four times as long as the first. Copies were kept in churches and it was reprinted in portable formats. The regular reading of the faithful, Foxe's *Book of Martyrs* is also a punishing compendium of human ingenuity in torture and execution. Moreover, for those who could not read, the book was illustrated. The edition of 1570 included a large, fold-out woodcut featuring dozens of examples of suffering:

> ...being cast from a cliff, stoning and mattocking, disembowelling, inverse crucifixion, roasting on a griddle or a spit, immolation, being hanged by the hair, being torn apart by horses, various forms of suspension, being devoured by beasts, flagellation, extreme dentistry, having strips of flesh removed, branding and searing, boiling alive and eye-drilling, as well as the more usual stabbings, dismemberments and beheadings. (Groom 2012: 32)

The legacy of Foxe's *Book of Martyrs* was that the Protestant imagination was filled with graphic images of torture and Catholic devilry. If the antiquarianism of William Camden and John Leland is pervaded by a fascination with ruins, the popular culture of ballads and later revenge tragedy is obsessed by the carnality of the body. Both deathly tendencies fleshed out the Gothic imagination with an uncanniness that haunted its more theoretical leanings, and also afforded a perpetual reminder of the worldly consequences of a theological politics that moved between wonder and terror.

Whig Historiography

By the end of the seventeenth century the '*Gothick* Constitution' was recognised as a form of governance that allegedly embodied natural rights of freedom, one that was inimical to tyranny and absolutism. English history could therefore be read as being predicated on the Gothic myth: a series of rebellions against oppression, from Magna Carta to the execution of Charles I. This version of events appealed particularly to progressive Whigs and Nonconformists; indeed, it eventually became known as the 'Whig' theory of history, depicting the triumph of Protestantism and Parliamentarianism as the destiny of the nation – a destiny that continued into the present with the Act of Settlement (1701) and the Act of Union (1707). For Daniel Defoe in *Jure Divino* (1706), the '*Gothick* rules of Government' were a manifestation of natural order and human rights over absolutism:

> Nature first taught Men Schemes of Life to draw,
> In Order live, and call'd that Order LAW:
> Nature directed Men to understand,
> And State Subjection, when they State-Command:
> As Nature taught, they Nature still obey,
> And struggle hard for Native Liberty.
> In vain assuming Tyrants have opprest;
> In vain deny the craving Nation's rest:
> The subjugated injur'd People rise,
> And guilty Tyranny from Justice flies. (1706: VIII, 186–7)

Within a generation, the claim that the British political system had Gothic foundations was a commonplace, frequently alluded to: 'It is to the *Gothick* Constitution that we owe our Parliaments, which are the Guardians of our Rights and Liberties' (MacDowall 1747: 28). England was considered to be a natural home for the Goths. Weather and the environment were believed to be primary determinants of national character, and thus the irrepressible Gothic vigour was nurtured by wet and wild regions, by mist and moor. Everyone felt qualified to pronounce on the topic. Even quack treatises such as *Wholesome Advice against the Abuse of Hot Liquors, Particularly of Coffee, Chocolate, Tea, Brandy, and Strong Waters* (1706) passed comment on the meteorological efficacy of northern climes:

> The cool Bowels of the North are more prolifick than those of the South. We can scarce instance in the latter, such Colonies and numerous Armies as have sprung from time to time from the former, and over-run the whole Universe: of this the *Goths*, *Visigoths*, *Allemains*, and *Gauls* are numerous Instances. (Duncan 1706: 75)

In such contexts it was inevitable that the influence of the Gothic imagination on the arts would arrest the attention.

From the late seventeenth century a great deal of ink was spilt in pondering the cultural achievements of the ancient Goths themselves, notably in architecture and in literature. Following the disparaging remarks of Renaissance writers, the first recorded architectural use of the word 'Gothic' in English was in John Evelyn's diary for 29 July 1641, in which he used the term to describe Utrecht Cathedral. This identification of Gothicist ideology with the architecture of the Middle Ages drew attention to one of the contradictions of the Gothic. Despite the Reformist and Parliamentarian rhetoric that had mobilised the Gothic myth, no-one could pretend that the medieval period, typified by its ecclesiastical architecture, had been anything but intensely Catholic. Evelyn was implying that to claim a Gothic, or more precisely an Anglo-Saxon, national and cultural identity was therefore to flirt with Rome. The earliest revivals of Gothic architecture in the early seventeenth century thus tended to be conservative, even Catholic-tinged, responses to the Puritanical extremism of Protestantism. Yet if the renewal of interest in medieval theology consciously united sacred with secular power, identifying the authority of the church with that of the king was not only politically dangerous – within a few years it was to prove fatal to Charles I.

Georgian Gothic

The year 1716 marks the beginning proper of the Gothic Revival in architecture. Work started on All Souls College, Oxford, following Nicholas Hawksmoor's designs, while a few miles away the first Gothic edifice was erected in Shotover Park, on the estate of the Whig constitutional historian James Tyrrell. Although plenty of Whig party grandees still favoured classical styles – none more so than the prime minister, Robert Walpole, who built the Palladian mansion Houghton Hall in 1735 – Gothic buildings were landmarks in the history of England: reminders of a medieval past, the struggle for rights, and the emergence of a distinctive, non-classical style and culture. Thus Gothic as a cultural form first entered the national consciousness in landscape gardening, through what the historian of the picturesque Malcolm Andrews identifies as 'the aesthetic appeal of the ruins of native antiquities' (1989: 36). As Joseph Holden Pott claimed towards the end of the century in *An Essay on Landscape Painting* (1782):

> Although the refined in taste may prefer the chaste and noble proportions of Grecian art, to the more irregular and wild ideas of northern climes [...] yet, in the venerable state of ruin, there is an awful romantic wildness in the Gothic remains, that moves the mind very powerfully. (1782: 58–9)

To have the post-Reformation remains of an abbey on one's estate was, then, to be a guardian of the Protestant heritage. But if no authentic ruin around which a garden could be planned was available, then one could be built. The vogue for sham ruins is highly suggestive of the desire to historicise the land, to make it speak to a particular political credo. It also enabled ruins, with all their atmosphere of decay and menace, to be sentimentalised as picturesque sites for fashionably melancholic ruminations on the passage of time. In this way historical ruins, and all their associations

The Great South Front of All Souls College, Oxford, designed by Nicholas Hawksmoor.
British Library 1899.n.42.

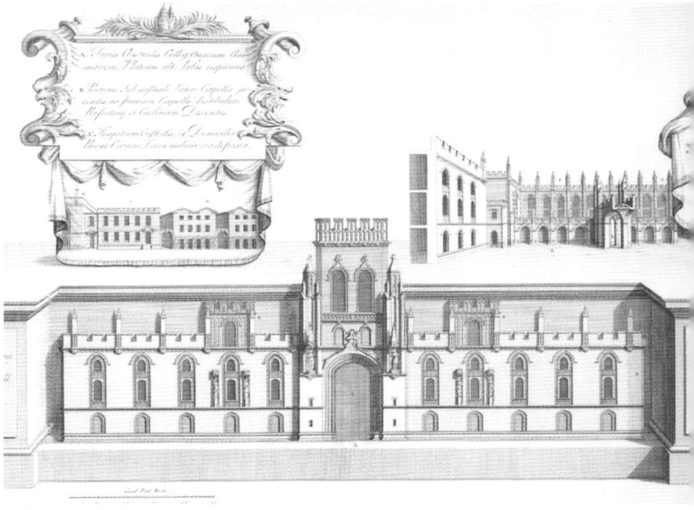

of Whiggism, were naturalised and presented as essentially English – a symbol of national pride.

Although these ruins were celebrated as clear evidence of the Protestant zeal of the Reformation, the inherent irony of this was not lost on contemporaries. The ancient Goths had toppled the Romans and demolished their buildings, before turning to architectural projects themselves. Yet these medieval Gothic buildings were destined to fall by the very principles – of rebellion against tyranny – that had erected them. Was, then, the Gothic wilfully self-destructive, only able to renew itself by destroying its own monuments? In the poem *Masonry* (1739), the Jacobite ballad-singer Charles Leslie deplored the destruction of:

> HUGE piles, 'tis true, even then were seen to rise,
> With lofty turrets, aiming at the skies:
> Great work of Kings, which scarce an age could raise!
> And the just wonder of preceding days! [...]
> With skill adorn'd, and science unconfin'd;
> The best, the noblest of the *Gothic* kind. (1739: 9)

He takes no delight in the downfall of these great edifices; they yet retain a ghost of their former splendour despite the false taste that attempts to glorify the ruins:

> Behold the awful relick! see how bare
> The shatter'd roofs and lofty walls appear!
> Illustrious monuments of former Art,
> Domes, Pillars, Arches, Figures, every part
> Now mangl'd, with their last remains, upbraid
> The spite and fury of hot zeal run mad. [. . .]
> Still wild disorder shapes the vast design,
> The whole's a blunder, tho' each part is fine;
> Grov'ling conceits with noble figures plac'd,
> A motley mixture, speak the *Gothic* taste:
> And tho' its beauties we with wonder view,
> Yet almost still the false eclipse the true. (1739: 9–10)

Leslie was, however, a voice in the wilderness. Ruins were the new craze. The excavation of the Roman town of Herculaneum began in 1738 and *Ruins of Rome*, a Miltonic work by the painter and poet John Dyer, appeared in 1740. Both were strong reminders of the passing of classical culture. In the latter year the antiquarian and mystic William Stukeley published his survey of Stonehenge; his account of Avebury followed three years later. Together these treatises demonstrated the apparent sophistication of British antiquities. Five years later, in 1748, the ruins of Pompeii were discovered. The past was inescapable.

Stukeley's fascination with the prehistoric monuments of the ancient Britons was again pitched as an indigenous alternative to imported classical culture. His work revived interest in megaliths and stone circles, and reasserted the ostensible connections between

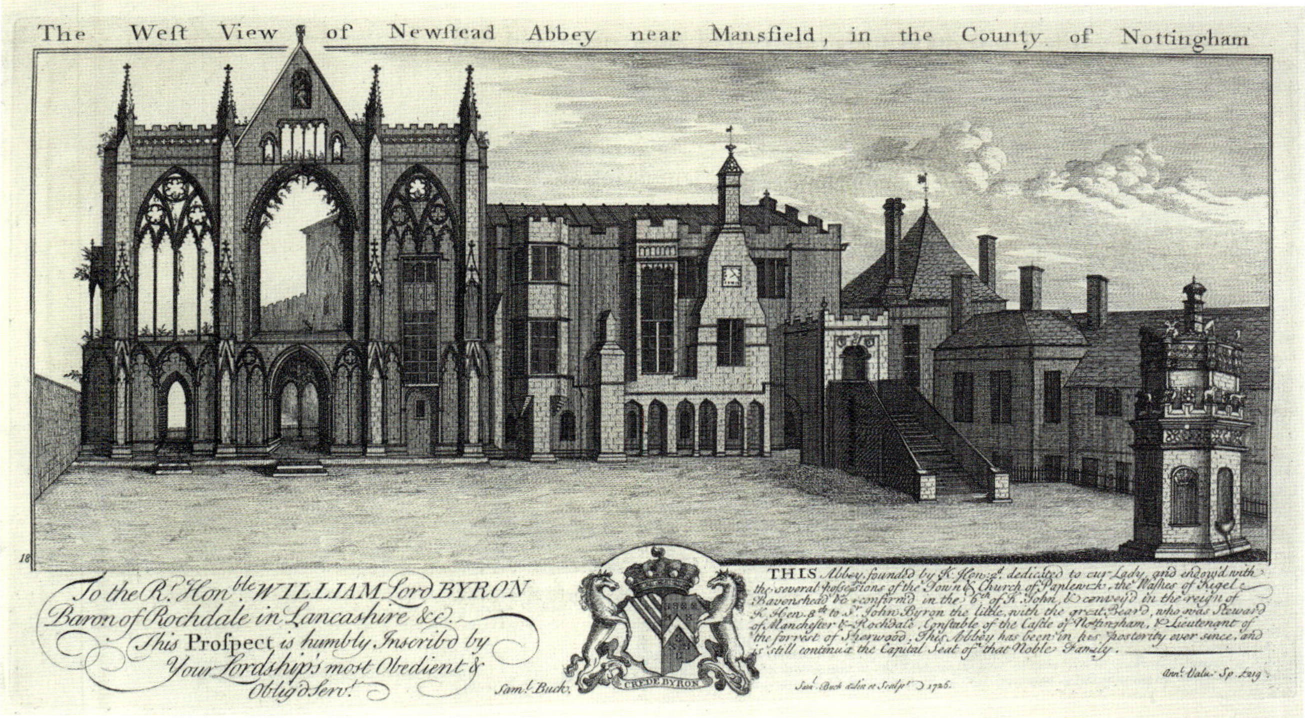

Newstead Abbey. Engraving by S. Buck, 1720–45.

British Library G.2255-9.

The ruins of the genuinely medieval Newstead Abbey were converted into a country residence owned by the ancestral family of Lord Byron.

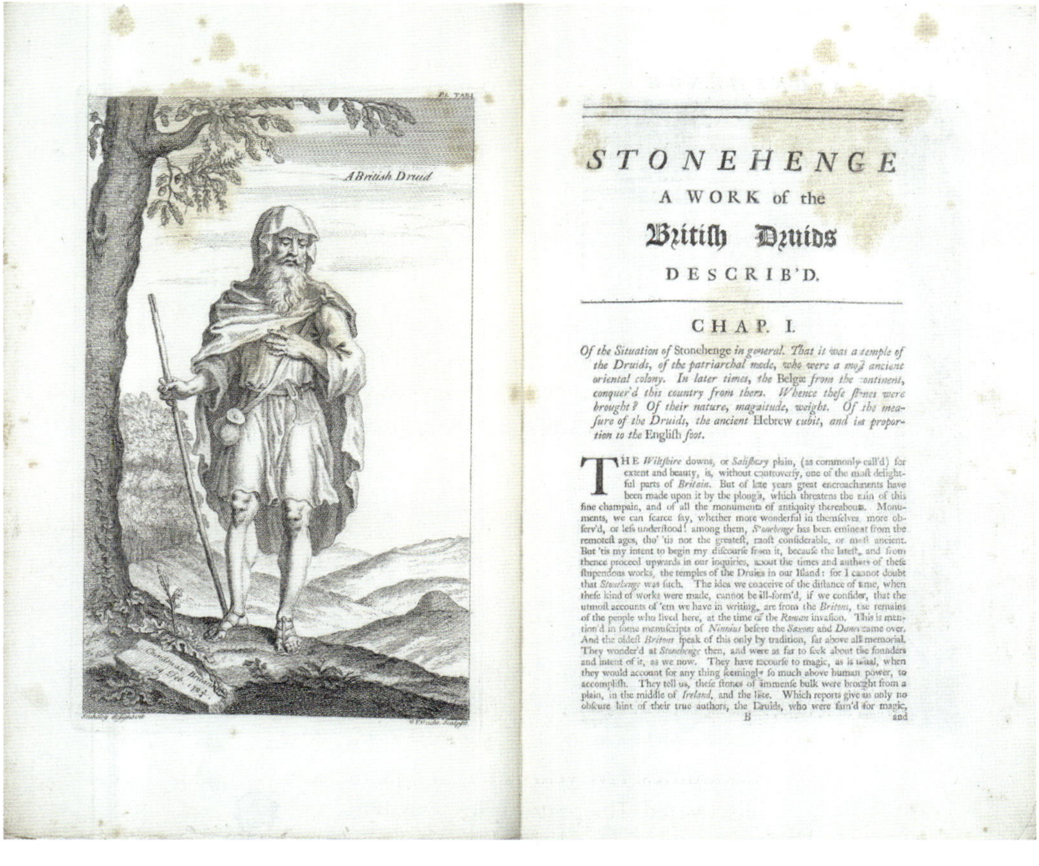

STONEHENGE
A WORK of the
British Druids
DESCRIB'D.

CHAP. I.

Of the Situation of Stonehenge *in general. That it was a temple of the Druids, of the patriarchal mode, who were a most ancient oriental colony. In later times, the* Belgæ *from the continent, conquer'd this country from them. Whence these stones were brought? Of their nature, magnitude, weight. Of the measure of the Druids, the ancient* Hebrew *cubit, and its proportion to the* English *foot.*

THE *Wiltshire* downs, or *Salisbury* plain, (as commonly call'd) for extent and beauty, is, without controversy, one of the most delightful parts of *Britain*. But of late years great encroachments have been made upon it by the plough, which threatens the ruin of this fine champain, and of all the monuments of antiquity thereabouts. Monuments, we can scarce say, whether more wonderful in themselves, more observ'd, or less understood! among them, *Stonehenge* has been eminent from the remotest ages, tho' 'tis not the greatest, most considerable, or most ancient. But 'tis my intent to begin my discourse from it, because the latest, and from thence proceed upwards in our inquiries, about the times and authors of these stupendous works, the temples of the Druids in our Island: for I cannot doubt that *Stonehenge* was such. The idea we conceive of the distance of time, when these kind of works were made, cannot be ill-form'd, if we consider, that the utmost accounts of 'em we have in writing, are from the *Britons*, the remains of the people who lived here, at the time of the *Roman* invasion. This is mention'd in some manuscripts of *Ninnius* before the *Saxons* and *Danes* came over. And the oldest *Britons* speak of this only by tradition, far above all memorial. They wonder'd at *Stonehenge* then, and were as far to seek about the founders and intent of it, as we now. They have recourse to magic, as is usual, when they would account for any thing seemingly so much above human power, to accomplish. They tell us, these stones of immense bulk were brought from a plain, in the middle of *Ireland*, and the like. Which reports give us only no obscure hint of their true authors, the Druids, who were fam'd for magic,

B and

Title page and frontispiece to *Stonehenge, A Temple Restor'd to the British Druids*, London, 1740.

British Library G.6042.(1).

the ancient Goths and later history. It therefore represents a further strand in the reception and invention of Gothic antiquity, knitting together more firmly the seemingly continuous architectural history of the nation, running from megaliths to cathedrals. Alexander Pope was initially rather arch in his analysis of this link, seeing in the Middle Ages an epoch almost wholly bereft of classical learning. His poem 'An Essay on Criticism' deplores a dismal reprise of the ignorance of the Gothic hordes: 'A *second* Deluge Learning thus o'er-run, / And the *Monks* finish'd what the *Goths* begun' (1984: ll. 691–2). However, he later found his own inspiration in the dark wonder of northern lore and legend. In 'Temple of Fame', Pope explored the architectural dynamics of the Gothic in an allegorical building. Each façade of the symbolic temple is aligned to a point of the compass, and each represents a different cradle of civilisation: the western classical, the eastern Arabian and Asian, the southern Egyptian and the northern Gothic. The Gothic elevation draws emphatically on the fables of the Goths of antiquity to conjure up a vision of terror, bloody and hallucinatory:

> Of *Gothic* Structure was the Northern Side,
> O'er-wrought with Ornaments of barb'rous Pride.
> There huge Colosses rose, with Trophies crown'd,
> And *Runic* Characters were grav'd around:
> There sat *Zamolxis* with erected Eyes,
> And *Odin* here in mimick Trances dies.
> There, on rude Iron Columns smear'd with Blood,
> The horrid Forms of *Scythian* Heroes stood,
> *Druids* and *Bards* (their once loud Harps unstrung)
> And Youths that dy'd to be by Poets sung.
> These and a Thousand more of doubtful Fame,
> To whom old Fables gave a lasting Name,
> In Ranks adorn'd the Temple's outward Face;
> The Wall in Lustre and Effect like Glass,
> Which o'er each Object casting various Dies,
> Enlarges some, and others multiplies.
> Nor void of Emblem was the mystic Wall,
> For thus Romantick Fame increases all. (1984: ll.119–36)

The intoxicating distortions caused by the warped and gleaming wall anticipate the delirium and dislocation of psychological disturbance so enticing to later Gothic writers: dreams, delusions and the fear of impending death. The doomed poet William Collins too felt his way through the viscera of the past towards the governance of the present in his 'Ode on the Popular Superstitions of the Highlands of Scotland' (written 1749–50; published 1788). Not only do 'Old Runic bards [...] seem to rise around', but small vaults are discovered on the Flannan Islands containing the bones of pygmies, and burial mounds contain the secrets of power: 'The rifted mounds their yawning cells unfold, / And forth the monarchs stalk with sovereign power' (Lonsdale 1969: l.41, ll.151–2).

Ancient Gothic, Modern Gothic

Thus it was that two strands of Gothic architecture were proposed: ancient and modern. Ancient Gothic was 'massive, heavy and coarse' – in effect everything non-classical, from megaliths and stone circles to Norman churches and castles; modern Gothic, however, was 'light, delicate, and rich to Excess' and referred to medieval architecture – key examples being Westminster Abbey and Lichfield Cathedral. Modern Gothic, moreover, was differentiated by an 'Abundance of little, whimsical, wild, and chimerical Ornaments' (*Builder's Dictionary* 1734: I.[439]). This decorative excess in which 'Every Thing is cramm'd with Windows, Roses, Crosses, Figures, &c.' was in stark contrast not to enigmatic standing stones or heavy Norman churches, but to the chilly grandeur of classical styles. Indeed, this opposition between the Gothic and the classical was repeatedly stressed in the most minute ways:

> There are two Kinds of the Plant *Acanthus*; the one wild, and full of Prickles; and the other of the Garden, without Prickles. The *Greek* Masons adorn'd their Works with the Garden *Acanthus*, and the *Gothic* Masons with that of the wild [...].
>
> (*Builder's Dictionary*, 1734: I.[14])

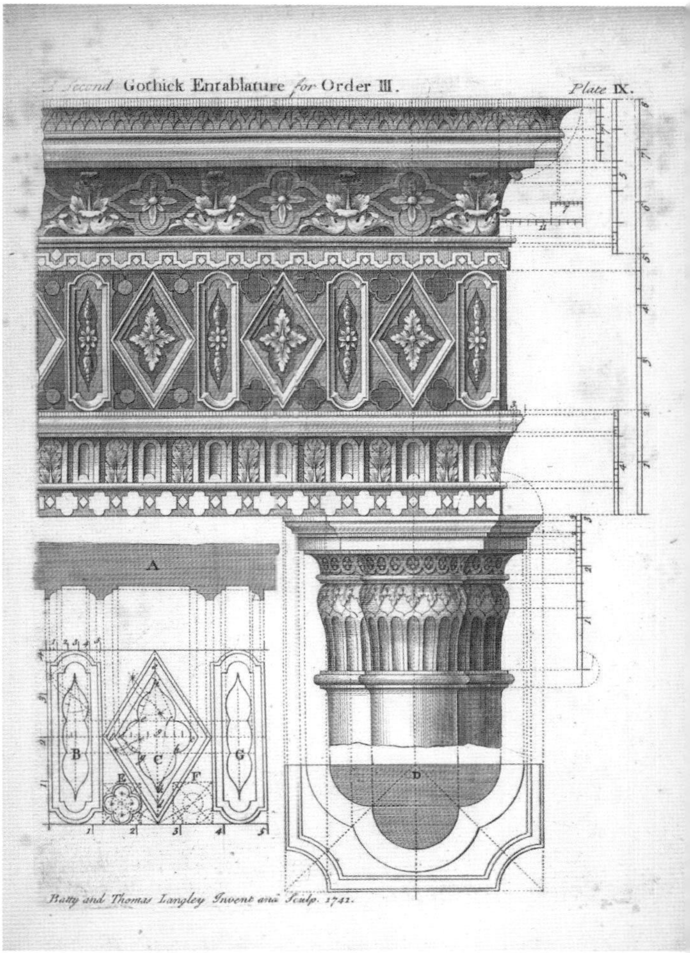

Plate from *Gothic Architecture* by Batty Langley, 1807.
British Library C.175.dd.26.

Batty Langley's instructive book full of detailed engravings proved invaluable for anyone wanting to introduce Gothic architectural features into their home.

In the eighteenth century the Gothic evidently had influence in some unexpected areas – from the design of gazebos to the excavation of prehistoric barrows, from inspiring ecclesiastical interior décor to boosting local tourism. The antiquarian Richard Gough claimed that the trend for taking the Grand Tour had eclipsed the attractions of native antiquities – 'Temples and palaces of the polite nations of antiquity engross our attention, while the works and memorials of our own priests and heroes have no effect on our curiosity' (1768: xxi) – but by the middle of the century there was a growing taste for investigating local historical remains. In 1726 Nathanael and Samuel Buck began publishing their engravings of the castles and abbeys of England, a magnificent series that included the first image of the ruins of 'Tyntern Abby'. In 1745 the Fourth Duke of Beaufort inherited Tintern, and in the same year began to clear and level the grounds in the expectation of visitors to the monument. A steady stream of sightseers have arrived there ever since, the most renowned among them William Wordsworth. His famous 'Lines Written a Few Miles above Tintern Abbey' was published in *Lyrical Ballads* in 1798.

The theologian Gilbert Burnet explicitly associated the Gothic style with the Goths and Vandals, Normans and medieval cathedrals: in short, with non-classical taste, and, by extension, the taste of the northern nations. In 1762 the literary historian and later poet laureate Thomas Warton traced English architecture from the Saxons to the Reformation, identifying the Saracenic influence on the 'Gothic' and dividing it into four different orders: Saxon Gothic, Absolute Gothic, Ornamental Gothic and Florid Gothic (1762: II.185–98). By this time architectural entrepreneurs such as Batty Langley had published *Gothic Architecture Improved* (1742), the first of a series of handbooks

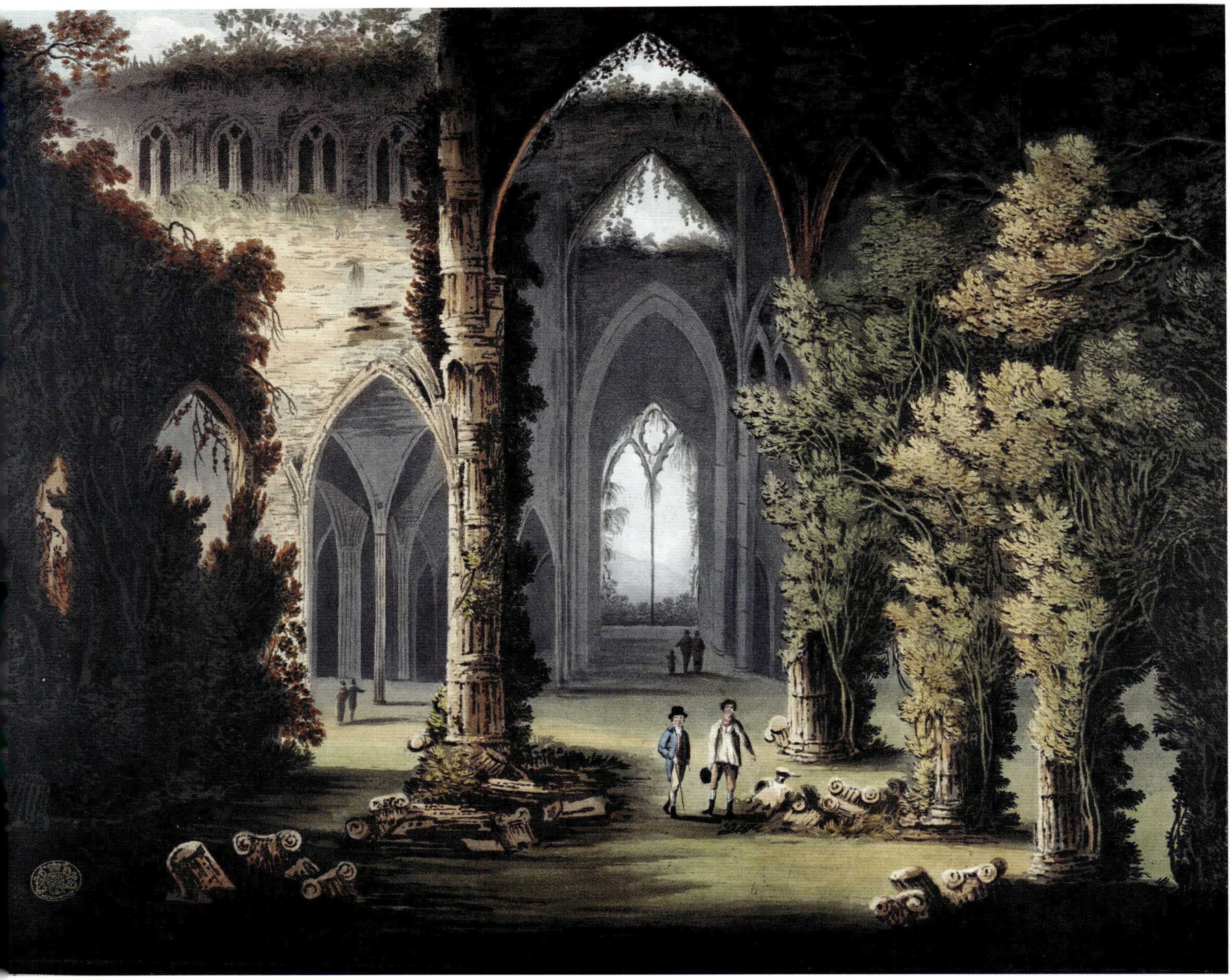

Tintern Abbey.
British Library K. Top. 31.

on how to Gothicise houses. Langley too identified the medieval with the Goths of late antiquity and the origins of the English nation, writing in 1747, 'And 'tis very reasonable to believe, that as in all ages of the Saxon monarchy there was no distinction of Goths from Saxons, but in general all were called Saxons' (1747: 1). The market for the Gothic proved to be buoyant in interior decoration, and the master cabinetmaker Thomas Chippendale specialised in household Gothic-ware, from Gothic tables and chairs to Gothic beds.

The unrivalled example of such Georgian 'Gothickry' was undoubtedly Strawberry Hill, Horace Walpole's 'little cottage' in Twickenham. This prime example of speculative architecture began life as a Thameside villa. Over the course of nearly 30 years it was transformed into one of the wonders of the Gothic world, its style a hybrid of the most extravagant Gothic relics that had survived:

a spectacular apparition composed of pointed arches, cloisters, battlements and towers, and fabulously arrayed within with fake pillars and faux vaulting. Walpole, the son of the prime minster Robert Walpole and a Whig politician and historian himself, had an abiding influence on the adaptation of the Gothic for domestic settings, again naturalising the style and thereby Whig thinking. The house itself became a tourist attraction and its guidebook a manual for Gothic taste. Writing at the beginning of the nineteenth century, Edmund Bartell declared that

> Different parts of Gothic buildings, tombs, and shrines, frequently apply very happily to Gothic houses, as chimney-pieces, book-cases, doors, windows, and cielings [*sic*]. I mention these, not as ornaments that could perhaps be made to coincide properly with the simplicity of the cottage: in a larger fabric, as the adorned farm, or professed Gothic mansion, such imitations are the most in character. Of this, Strawberry Hill, the seat of the late Earl of Orford, is an example of the first kind; designs of the principle parts of which have been published by Mr. Bentley. (1804: 49)

With Horace Walpole, who literally, he claimed, dreamt up *The Castle of Otranto* (1764) in Strawberry Hill, we approach the synthesis of the various strands of eighteenth-century Gothicism and antiquity, the final element being of course the Goths and literature. If the Goths could be condemned as desecrators wherever they went, it followed that even the way in which they spoke was contagiously 'barbarous': coarse, harsh, repetitive and infectious. Thus according to Roger Ascham's *The Scholemaster* (1570), rhyme or 'rude beggarly ryming [*sic*]' was introduced by Goths and Huns (1570: f.60r). The anonymous author of *The Comical Pilgrim* (1722) shares the sentiment: 'The Purity of the *Latin* was debauch'd by the *Vandals*, and hunn'd into Corruption by that barbarous People [...] *Latin* was barbarously *Goth'd* out of *Italy*' (anon. 1722: 47–8).

Yet the Goths were also notoriously *literate* barbarians. In the development of written language the importance of Gothic runes (written runic characters) could be compared with the hieroglyphs of ancient Egypt. For some historians, therefore, the *Runæ* (Runers), supposedly the intellectual caste of the Goths, were equal to the Egyptian *Heliopolitani*, Roman *Philosophi* and British Druids. John Webb, for instance, in his study of Stonehenge, declares that the Runers:

> studied Nature, Astronomy and Magick, and without their Advice nothing of publick Importance was transacted; thus highly were they reverenced for their Familiarity with Devils, whom with supream Veneration they adored: These they took with them to the Wars, by whose prying into the Bowels of Captives, they presaged the Event: These were the Executioners of their impious Rites and Ceremonies, their barbarous Monument-makers, and Extollers of those by Epitaphs, that in Fight died for their Country. (1725: 86)

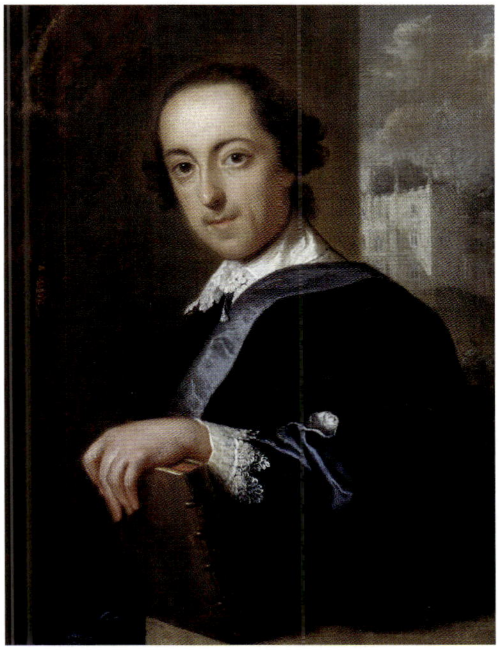

Horace Walpole. Portrait by John Giles Eccardt, 1754.

National Portrait Gallery, London.

Horace Walpole in 1754 with his hand on a volume from his library and the Gothicised Strawberry Hill in the background.

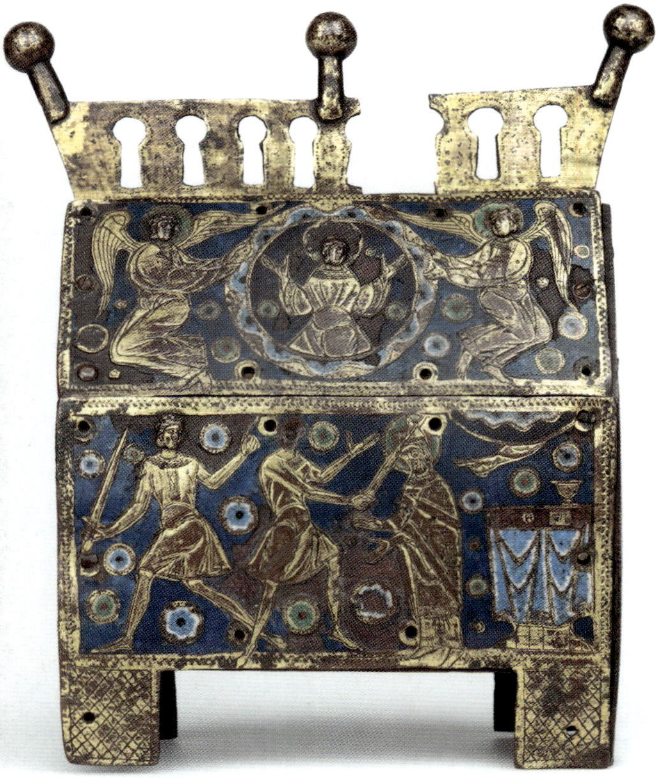

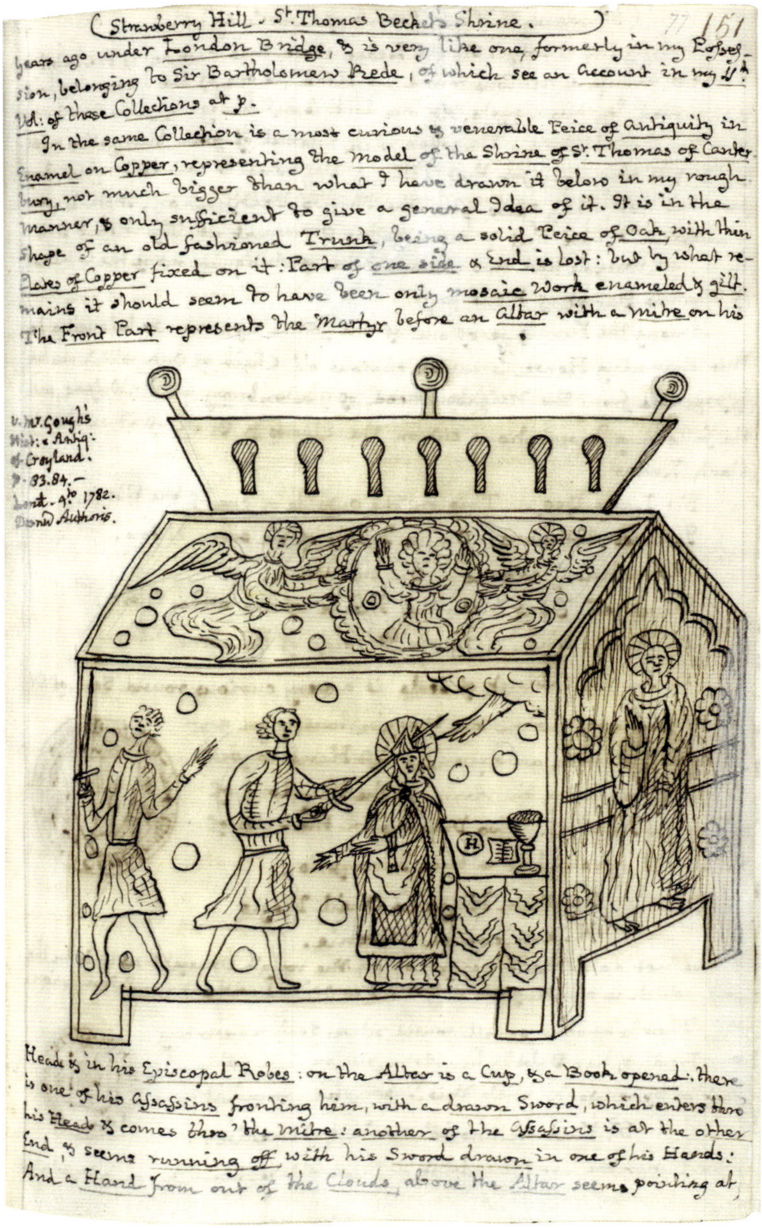

(Strawberry Hill - St. Thomas Becket's Shrine.) 77 151
years ago under London Bridge, & is very like one, formerly in my Posses-
sion, belonging to Sir Bartholomew Rede, of which see an Account in my 4th
Vol: of these Collections at p.
In the same Collection is a most curious & venerable Peice of Antiquity in
Enamel on Copper, representing the Model of the Shrine of St. Thomas of Canter-
bury, not much bigger than what I have drawn it below in my rough
manner, & only sufficient to give a general Idea of it. It is in the
Shape of an old fashioned Trunk, being a solid Peice of Oak, with thin
Plates of Copper fixed on it: Part of one side & End is lost: but by what re-
mains it should seem to have been only mosaic Work enameled & gilt.
The Front Part represents the Martyr before an Altar with a Mitre on his

v. Mr. Gough's Hist: & Antiq: of Croyland. p. 83.84.— Lond. 4to 1782. Donor Authoris.

Head, & in his Episcopal Robes: on the Altar is a Cup, & a Book opened: there
is one of his Assassins fronting him, with a drawn Sword, which enters thro'
his Head & comes thro' the Mitre: another of the Assassins is at the other
End, & seems running off with his Sword drawn in one of his Hands:
And a Hand from out of the Clouds, above the Altar seems pointing at

ABOVE:
St Thomas Becket's reliquary from Strawberry Hill.
Glasgow Museums.

RIGHT:
St Thomas Becket's reliquary from Strawberry Hill. Drawing by William Cole.
British Library Add. MS 5841, f.77.

This Thomas Becket casket – housed in the Tribune, the main chamber for art treasures at Strawberry Hill – was one of the artefacts that William Cole particularly noticed (and drew) during his visit to Walpole's home on 3 September 1762.

The central position afforded to the Runers meant that laws, governance and literature were embodied in the same figure, one whose writing was a magical force that harnessed the power of demons and could foretell the future by anthropomancy, or reading entrails: a figure of terror and wonder.

Gothic Culture and the Age of Reason

Webb's work draws on the model of Gothic society and culture developed by Sir William Temple in his essay 'Of Poetry'. For Temple, Runic poetry was characterised by unrestrained flights of fancy, the sorcery of the Runers:

> But as the true Flame of Poetry was rare among them, and the rest was but Wild-fire that sparkled or rather crackled a

while, and soon went out with little Pleasure or Gazing of the Beholders; those *Runers* who could not raise Admiration by the Spirit of their Poetry, endeavoured to do it by another, which was that of Enchantments: This came in to supply the Defect of that Sublime and Marvellous, which has been found both in Poetry and Prose among the learned Ancients. The *Gothick Runers,* to gain and establish the Credit and Admiration of their Rhymes, turned the use of them very much to Incantation and Charms, pretending by them to raise Storms, to calm the Seas, to cause Terror in their Enemies, to transport themselves in the Air, to conjure Spirits, to cure Diseases, and stanch bleeding Wounds, to make Women kind or easy, and Men hard or invulnerable; as one of their most ancient *Runers* affirms of himself and his own Atchievements, by Force of these Magical Arms: The Men or Women, who were thought to perform such Wonders or Enchantments, were from *Viises* or *Wises,* the Name of those Verses wherein their Charms were conceived, called *Wizards* or *Witches.* (1720: I.243–4)

Such was the force of poetry: their verses were bewitching. And Temple particularly relishes these supernatural elements:

Mara in old *Runick* was a *Goblin* that seized upon Men asleep in their Beds, and took from them all Speech and Motion. Old *Nicka* was a Sprite that came to strangle People who fell into the Water: *Bo* was a fierce *Gothick* Captain, Son of *Odin,* whose name was used by his Soldiers when they would fright or surprize their Enemies. (1720: I.244)

Thus the frightful exclamation 'boo!' has its roots in a Gothic warcry. Temple's ultimate argument is that the Gothic imagination ('*Gothick* Wit') laid the enchanted ground of folklore traditions and later medieval romance, from which 'may be derived, all the visionary Tribe of *Fairies, Elves,* and *Goblins,* of *Sprites* and of *Bulbeggars*' (1720: I.244). Temple argued that medieval Spanish Romances were likewise the product of 'the *Gothick* Wit' (via the Visigoths), thereby identifying the tradition with the eerie Catholicism of the Middle Ages.

The culture of the Goths that was promulgated in the eighteenth century was one of supernatural and fantastic quests (their migrations south had led them into Oriental realms that had fired their imagination), a code of chivalry based on martial prowess and honour (duelling, for example, is described in Tacitus's *Germania*) and a reverence for women and monogamy, effectively translated into manners and decorum. As the ballad collector and literary antiquarian Thomas Percy put it in 1765:

That fondness of going in quest of adventures, that spirit of challenging to single combat, and that respectful complaisance shewn to the fair sex, (so different from the manners of the Greeks and Romans) all are of Gothic origin, and may be traced up to the earliest times among all the northern nations. (1765: III.iii–iv)

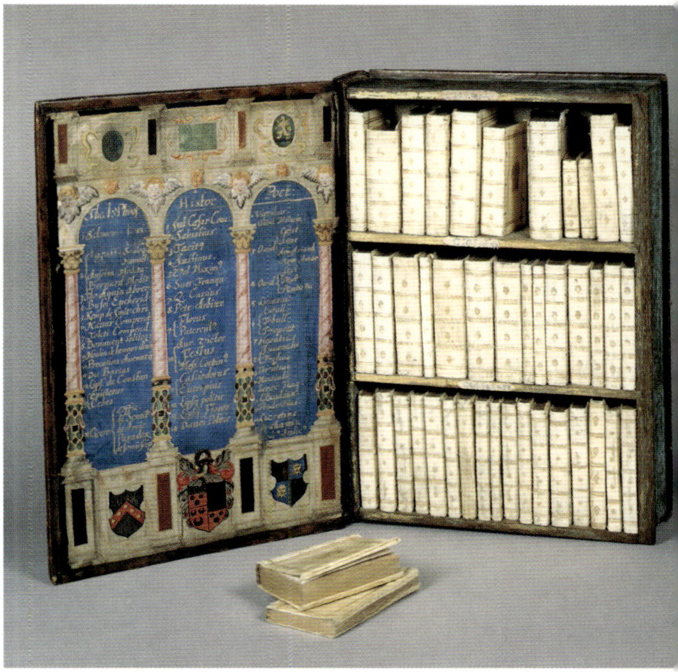

ABOVE:
Travelling Library from Strawberry Hill.
British Library C.20.f.15–58.
The travelling library of Sir Julius Caesar (*c.* 1558–1636), an example from Walpole's vast, eclectic collection at Strawberry Hill.

All of these elements seemed self-evident in medieval romance, and all could be equally condemned by sceptical neoclassicists. By 1762 the publisher John Newbery, for instance, had already poured scorn on the '*Gothic* ignorance and superstition' of 'the barbarous and uncultivated nations of the North' – what he derided as 'absurd and unmeaning tales of giants, champions, inchanted [*sic*] knights, witches, goblins, and such other monstrous fictions and reveries, as could only proceed from the grossest ignorance, of a distempered brain' (1762: II.154).

The Cult of Gothic Literature

Yet by the time of Newbery's denunciation there was already a growing canon of contemporary Gothic literature that blended Whig history with medievalism, the supernatural and anti-classicism. The more politically explicit of these include Gilbert West's poem on Viscount Cobham's gardens at Stowe (1732) and James Thomson's blank-verse work *Liberty* (1735–6). West describes how Whig politics were becoming acclimatised in country estates, using his uncle Richard Temple, Viscount Cobham as a salient example (Cobham formed the focal point of Whig opposition to Robert Walpole). The garden included a 'Temple of Liberty' populated by Saxon deities:

> Hail! Gods of our renown'd Fore-Fathers, hail!
> Ador'd Protectors once of *England*'s Weal.
> Gods, of a Nation, valiant, wise, and free,
> Who conquer'd to establish *Liberty*! (1732: 24)

Thomson similarly focuses on the word 'liberty' in *Liberty*, an ambitious poem that offered a historical perspective on the word by describing the progress and breakdown of civic freedom in the classical world and medieval era before it finds its ultimate expression in England in the Glorious Revolution of 1688:

> Of *Gothic* Nations This the final Burst;
> And, mix'd the Genius of these People all,
> Their Virtues mix'd in one exalted Stream,
> Here the rich Tide of *English* Blood grew full. (1736: Pt I, ll.742–5)

Thomson subsequently wrote the imperial anthem 'Rule, Britannia' (1740), later included in the patriotic oratorio *Alfred the Great* by David Mallet (1754), as well as *Tancred and Sigismunda, A Tragedy* (1745) set in twelfth-century Sicily. Indeed, Gothic antiquity provided the setting for several mid-eighteenth-century stage plays, including Henry Brooke's politically controversial plays *Gustavus Vasa* (1737) and *Jack the Giant-Queller* (1748; both suppressed), Richard Glover's *Boadicea* (1753), John Brown's *Athelstan* (1756) and William Mason's dramatic poems *Elfrida* (1752) and *Caractacus* (1759). The dramas of William Shakespeare remained popular in performance, particularly supernatural and northern European thrillers such as *Hamlet* and *Macbeth*. In fiction, Tobias Smollett produced the parodic novel *The Adventures of Sir Launcelot Greaves* (1761), adapting *Don*

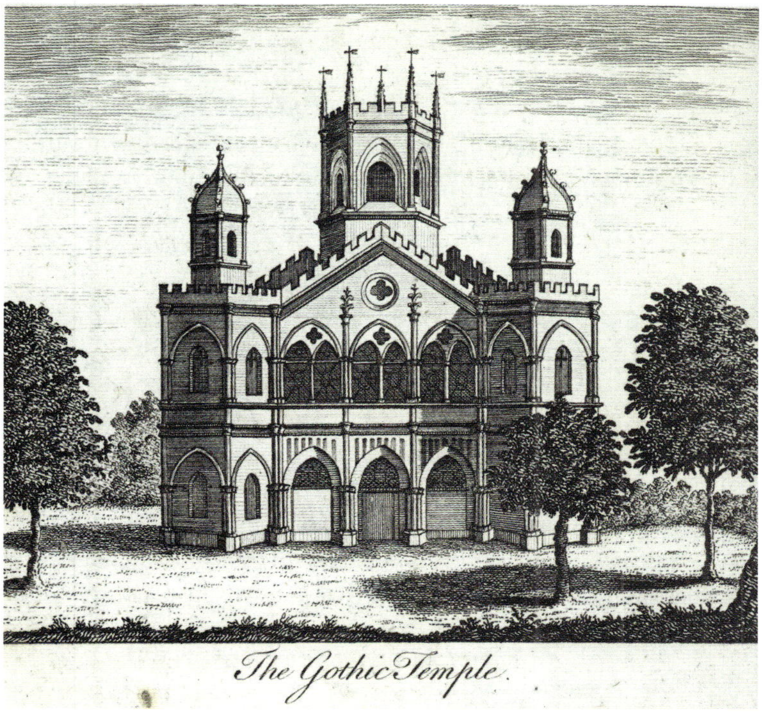

Temple of Liberty in the gardens at Stowe, Buckinghamshire. Engraving from *Stowe: A Description of the House and Gardens*, 1788.
British Library 10360.c.15.

This Gothic temple in the grounds of Stowe House, designed by James Gibbs, demonstrated the Whiggish pride in Britain's Gothic past of the owner, Viscount Cobham.

Quixote to an eighteenth-century English setting, while Thomas Leland's ground-breaking narrative *Longsword, Earl of Salisbury: An Historical Romance*, published in 1762, is arguably the first eighteenth-century Gothic novel. Set in the thirteenth century, it has a plot that pits chivalry, honour and good governance against perfidy, betrayal and conspiracy, all against a vivid backdrop of medieval manners and incident.

The year of *Longsword*, 1762, proved a watershed for Gothic medievalism. Richard Hurd published his *Letters on Chivalry and Romance*, in part a defence of Edmund Spenser's *Faerie Queene*, arguing contextually that sixteenth- and seventeenth-century writers had been heavily influenced by medieval romance and that the institution of chivalry 'seems to have sprung immediately out of the FEUDAL CONSTITUTION' (1762: 7). Hurd dwells on the familiar qualities of knight errantry, proficiency in arms, battlefield honour and the veneration of women. *Longsword* exemplifies such archaic values through the medium of a sentimental novel, providing in effect a conduct book of the Gothic virtues. Thomas Warton likewise defended Spenser in the second edition of his *Observations on The Faerie Queene of Spenser*, which also included his orders of Gothic architecture, and Horace Walpole advocated a theory of Gothic taste in his *Anecdotes of Painting in England*, considering Gothic architecture as 'a species of modern elegance' (1762–3: I.107). Like Hurd, Walpole maintained that the Gothic should not be judged anachronistically by classical standards: 'One must have taste to be sensible of the beauties of Grecian architecture; one only wants passions to feel Gothic' (1762–3: I.107–8). Neither could he resist invoking the supernatural that haunted the Gothic aesthetic: 'Gothic churches infuse superstition' and so display the 'magic hardiness' of their craftsmen's imaginations (1762–3: I.108).

Gothic history also provided the raw material for more contemplative literary pursuits. The stony remains that littered the British countryside, from ancient megaliths to the ruins left in the wake of the Reformation, became sites of poetic meditation – not only to lament the unavoidable devastation that had accompanied the advancement of liberty, but also to reflect in a more personal way on one's own mortality and transience. Hence they became associated with the literary cult of melancholia, a historical condition of Gothic futility.

Melancholic poetry, morbidly introspective and self-absorbed, caught the mood of a country in the grip of an evangelical revival. Edward Young's *The Complaint, or, Night-Thoughts on Life, Death, and Immortality* (1742–5), Mark Akenside's *The Pleasures of Imagination* (1744) and Robert Blair's *The Grave* (1743) were all runaway bestsellers and inaugurated the 'graveyard' or 'mortuary' school in eighteenth-century verse, which in Blair's lines verges on a revival of the medieval cult of the macabre. The scene is ghastly, riven with the supernatural horror of howling wind, creaking doors, ominous cries of birds and cavernously echoing churches. Even the weather conspires against reason:

> The Wind is up: Hark! How it howls! Methinks
> Till now, I never heard a Sound so dreary:
> Doors creak, and Windows clap, and Night's foul Bird
> Rook'd in the Spire screams loud: The gloomy Isles [aisles]
> Black-plaster'd, and hung round with Shreds of 'Scutcheons
> And tatter'd Coats of Arms, send back the Sound
> Laden with heavier Airs, from the low Vaults
> The mansions of the Dead. (1743: ll.32–9)

The mood evoked is one of sheer terror as the dead rise from their tombs to walk again, soundlessly pacing:

> Rous'd from their Slumbers
> In grim Array the grizly Spectres rise,
> Grin horrible, and obstinately sullen
> Pass and repass, hush'd as the Foot of Night. (1743: ll.39–42)

The horror of the grave is visceral ('it makes one's Blood run chill') and inspires primal fears born of grim folklore and occult wisdom:

> Strange Things, the Neighbours say, have happen'd here:
> Wild Shrieks have issu'd from the hollow Tombs,
> Dead men have come again, and walk'd about,
> And the Great Bell has toll'd, unrung, untouch'd. (1743: l.44, ll.50–3)

Such revenants and spectral manifestations appear in early ballads in the form of demon lovers, and in Jacobean drama as spirits

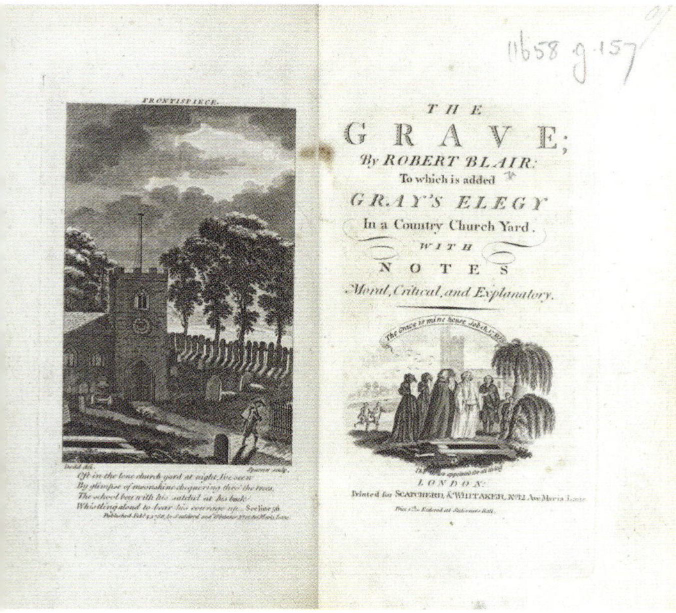

Title page and frontispiece to Robert Blair's *The Grave*, 1787.
British Library 11658.g.157.

prefiguring vengeance; they even appear in idiosyncratic love poetry of the 1730s. Eighteenth-century rationality often appears to be ill-disposed to any suggestion of supernatural activity. Daniel Defoe wrote a prosaic account of the supposed post-mortem apparition of one Mrs Veal (1706) and Samuel Johnson debunked the Cock-Lane ghost (1762). Yet Blair's popularity was such that it ensured that the phantasmic aesthetic went mainstream. The ghosts were here to stay.

Thomas Gray's *Elegy Written in a Country Churchyard* (1751) dealt with mortality and the weight of the past in a far less sensational, more moderate way, though the poem still resonates with some of the unnerving aspects of the 'graveyard school': tolling bells, night falling, owls hooting, the incarceration of the grave and the despair of forgotten and unfulfilled dreams. Gray is, moreover, haunted by history, particularly the Civil Wars of the previous century. This burden becomes heavier in later poems such as 'The Bard' (1757), which recounts with grim fascination the cost of English progress and the gradual genesis of British identity, achieved in this case (in the reign of Edward I) through the liquidation of Welsh culture. Such policies of extermination were fresh in living memory: the Battle of Culloden, fought only in 1746, had been followed by the mass execution of the Jacobite leaders and subsequent oppressive

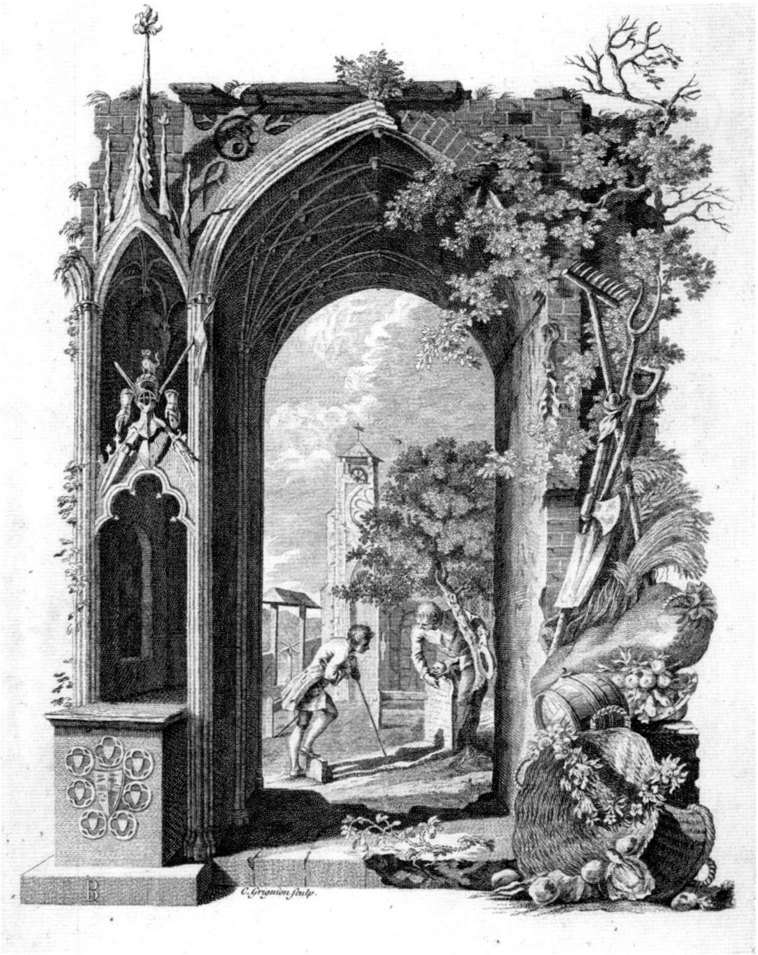

Illustration by Richard Bentley to an edition of Thomas Gray's *Elegy Written in a Country Churchyard*, 1753.
British Library C.57.h.5.

anti-Gaelic legislation. 'The Bard' enlarges elegy into something apocalyptic.

Gray's proto-Gothic experiments were informed by the attention given to the sublime in the period, itself strongly associated with melancholia and the 'graveyard school', as well as with Whig aesthetics of individualism and even republicanism. In Edmund Burke's *Philosophical Enquiry into [...] the Sublime and Beautiful*, published in the same year as 'The Bard', the sublime was theorised as an effect triggered by the imagination encountering terror and power, especially when somehow obscured and hinting at the infinite. For Burke, Milton's portrayal of Death in *Paradise Lost* was utterly sublime: 'all is dark, uncertain, confused, terrible, and sublime to the last degree':

> ...that shape had none
> Distinguishable in member, joint, or limb,
> Or substance might be called that shadow seemed,
> For each seemed either; black it stood as night [...]. (1990: 55)

He was also impressed by the unfathomable remoteness of Stonehenge and the extraordinary power required to erect such a monument:

> ...those huge rude masses of stone, set on end, and piled on each other, turn the mind on the immense force necessary for such a work. Nay, the rudeness of the work increases this cause of grandeur, as it excludes the idea of art, and contrivance. (1990: 71)

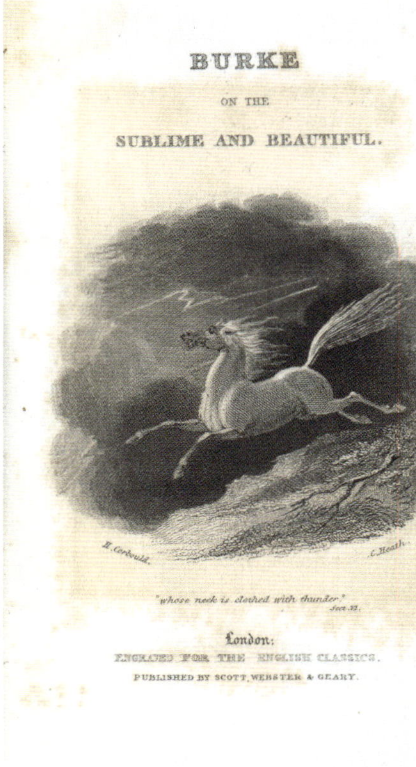

Title page to Edmund Burke's *Philosophical Enquiry into [...] the Sublime and Beautiful*, 1839 edition.
British Library RB.23.a.18100.

For Burke unintelligibility, or obscurity of perception, marked the extent of reason and dilated the mind into previously unimagined intensities; this suspension in the wonder of terror would come to be the Gothic imagination incarnate.

'Enter Ghost'

Come the end of the eighteenth century, the pioneering Anglo-Saxon scholar Sharon Turner could sum up the Gothic bequest as follows: 'Our language, our government and our laws, display our Gothic ancestors in every part: they live not merely in our annals and traditions, but in our civil institutions and perpetual discourse' (1799–1805: I.52). The Gothic also lived in literature. Horace Walpole's novel, *The Castle of Otranto*, was published on Christmas Eve 1764: an odd, antiquarian tale that was not simply an unnerving ghost story for the season, but something far more daring. Walpole synthesised the prevailing Gothic appetite for medievalism and the sublime with the powerful political credos of liberty and progress; his novel consequently arose as much from a prevailing and deepening mood of Gothicism as from its author's idiosyncratic medievalist taste.

Yet Walpole was not merely the aspiring architect of a new social code of chivalry, any more than Strawberry Hill simply purported to offer a novel lexicon of exterior and interior decoration. Rather, he was preternaturally alive to the more sinister aspects of

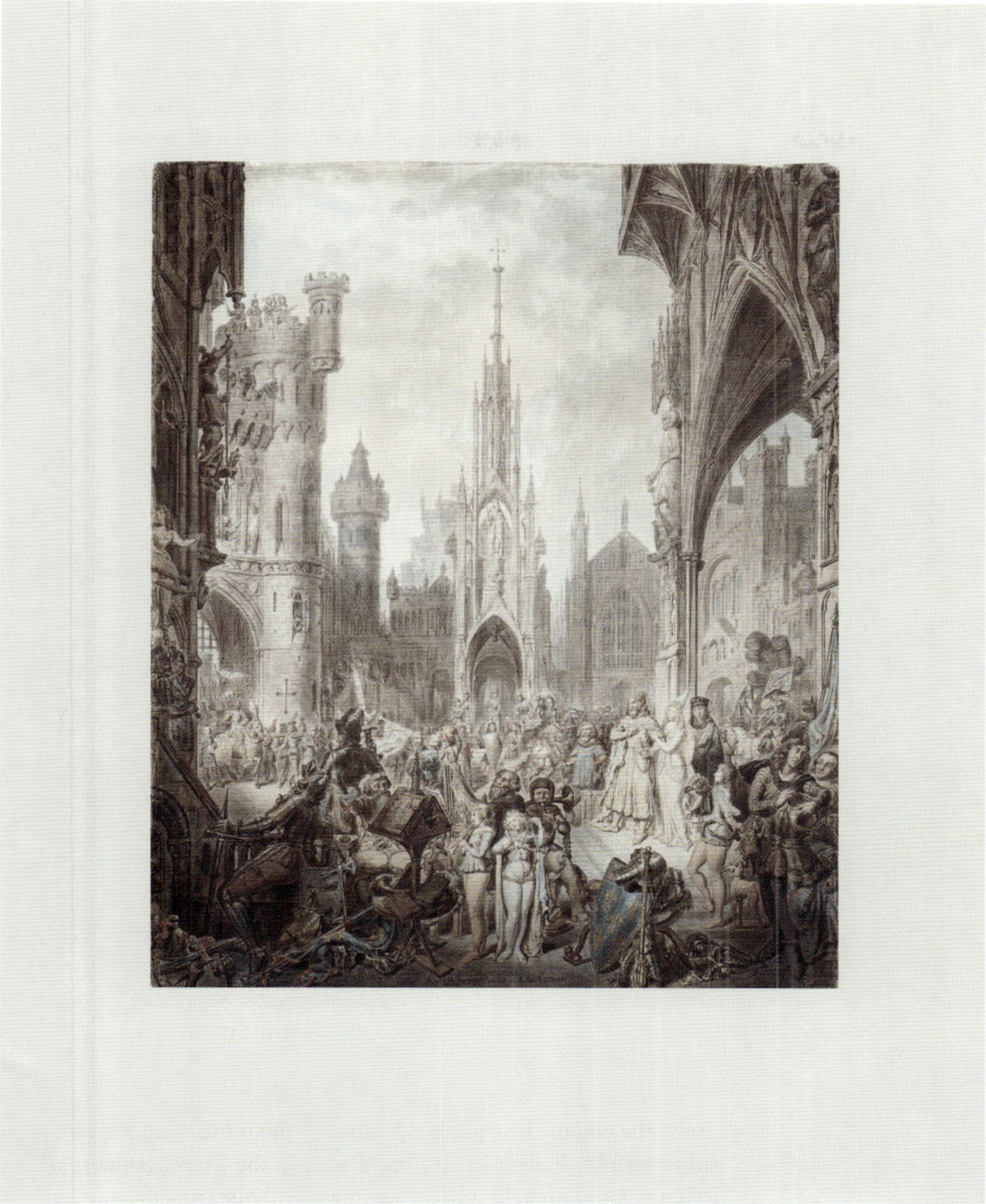

The procession in *The Castle of Otranto*. Watercolour by John Carter, 1790.
Lewis Walpole Library, Yale University.

both aesthetic and Whiggish Gothicism, a sensibility that was to define his literary impact. *Otranto* was accordingly infused with the cult of the macabre: ghosts, an animated cadaver, haunted funerary monuments and the carnal horror and desire of the body. Furthermore, the plot of the novel, which was presented in the first edition as if it were an ancient text discovered in a northern Catholic library, is an obsessive study of legitimacy, inheritance and dynastic will. Its twists and turns expose the political machinations of a tyrant king and the struggle for individual freedom and self-determination. It is perhaps no surprise that copies of both the Magna Carta and the execution order for Charles I were above Walpole's bed – the very bed in which he dreamt the opening scene of *The Castle of Otranto*.

As Walpole's infamous letter to William Cole on 9 March 1765 described it, the book was inspired, daemonic, driven by the passion of an unfettered imagination that sought some release from the claustrophobic arena of 1760s politics. While writing it, Walpole admitted, 'I was very glad to think of anything rather than politics' (Lewis 1937–83: I.88), and it was indeed a particularly troubled period. At the time of *Otranto*'s composition, Walpole become entangled in the political furore surrounding his cousin, Henry Seymour Conway. He had urged Conway to take a principled stand on attempts to stifle the radical firebrand John Wilkes; that had promptly resulted in Conway being stripped of his rank and offices. Walpole had decently (or rashly) offered to sacrifice his own inheritance, including Strawberry Hill, to save Conway, and had become embroiled in a bitter pamphlet war. The situation was desperate, and *Otranto*, despite disclaimers of topical reference in his letter to Cole, reflects this political turmoil, even if, as with all legendary history, it was twisted by dream and fantasy, prophecy and the supernatural – as well as the uncanny literary conventions of a distant age.

Although *Otranto* was undoubtedly medievalist, Walpole's great model was Shakespeare, who mingled styles and genres in an emphatically anti-classicist way, effectively offering a new, romantic

Henry Fuseli, 'Hamlet and the Ghost', plate from Boydell's *Collection of Prints, from pictures painted for the purpose of illustrating the Dramatic Works of Shakespeare*, 1803. British Library Tab.599.c.

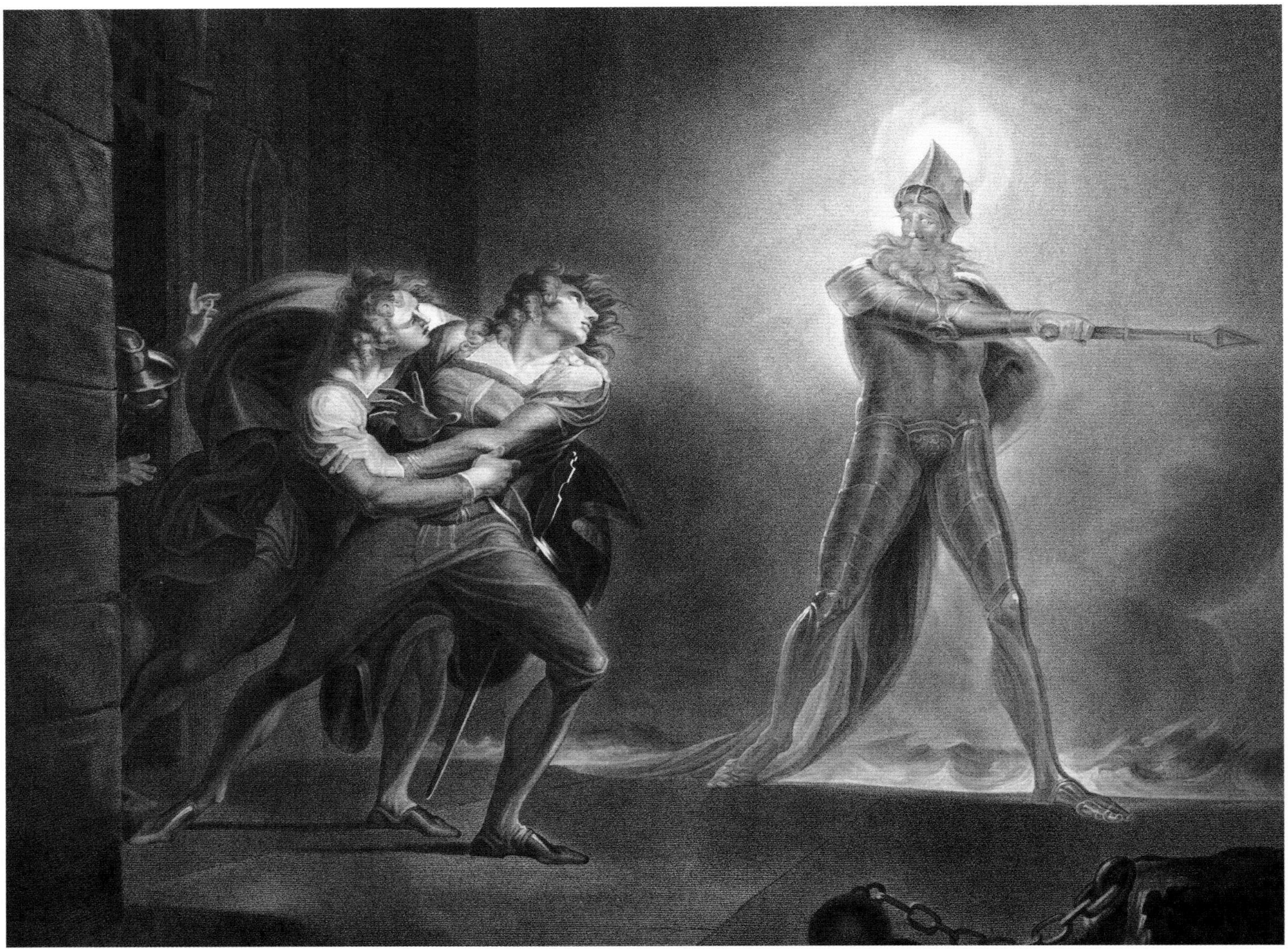

and essentially English genealogy for literature. Samuel Johnson had cited Shakespeare more than any other writer in his *Dictionary of the English Language* (1755–6) – a dictionary that explicitly identified English as being of Teutonic, or Gothic, origin. Shakespeare, supposedly born on St George's Day, was considered the archetypal English writer: a natural genius, free from the classical restraint of unity of place, time and plot, who promiscuously mingled genres and mixed high and low characters. Shakespeare wrote more English history plays than any of his contemporaries, and, with the exception of the pageant of spirits in Christopher Marlowe's *Tragical History of Dr Faustus* (1588–92), introduced more ghosts into his dramas. As Johnson put it in the preface to his edition of Shakespeare (published just months after *Otranto* in 1765), Shakespeare's use of supernatural folkloric elements was Gothic, as exemplified in *A Midsummer Night's Dream*, which displayed 'the *Gothick* mythology of fairies' (1765: I.xxi) and recalled Sir William Temple's early invocation of 'all the visionary Tribe'. Ghosts haunt Shakespeare's plays, and they terrified his audiences and readers. Samuel Johnson's friend and confidante Hester (Thrale) Piozzi related how 'when he was about nine years old, having got the play of Hamlet in his hand, and reading it quietly in his father's kitchen, he kept on steadily enough, till coming to the Ghost scene, he suddenly hurried up stairs to the street door that he might see people about him' (1786: 20). Indeed, *Hamlet, Prince of Denmark* (*c.* 1600–01) haunts the Gothic imagination to this day, and the whole literary tradition of terror and wonder could be seen as trying to answer the short, existential question that opens the play: 'Who's there?'

'Who's there?' This question haunts *Otranto*, beset as it is by fantastical and baffling events. Generations of readers have sought answers as stealthy figures materialise out of dreams, rise from the grave and emerge from the very fabric of the castle; this is also the question that assails the novel's malevolent Prince Manfred. 'Who's there?' The answer is already given in the Bible: 'My name is Legion: for we are many' (Mark 5: 9), and it resounds down the centuries to *The Exorcist* (1973), the notorious horror movie of diabolical possession. *The Castle of Otranto* thus unleashes a multitude of demons and makes manifest the Gothic. Abandon hope, all ye who enter here...

Further Reading

Brooks, Chris 1999. *The Gothic Revival* (London: Phaidon). A searching account of all aspects of the Gothic Revival across Europe in the eighteenth and nineteenth centuries.

Clark, Kenneth 1962. *The Gothic Revival: An Essay in the History of Taste* (Harmondsworth: Penguin). An early but still influential study of the Gothic Revival in eighteenth- and nineteenth-century Britain, with a particular emphasis upon literature and architecture.

Heather, Peter 1996. *The Goths* (Oxford: Blackwell). Standard account of the ancient Goths, synthesising sources from ancient history, archaeology, anthropology and the history of religion.

Kliger, Samuel 1952. *The Goths in England: A Study in Seventeenth and Eighteenth Century Thought* (Cambridge, Mass.: Harvard University Press). Excellent sourcebook on the Gothic myth in constitutional history, including material on climate theory, the Levellers and the Rabbinical tradition.

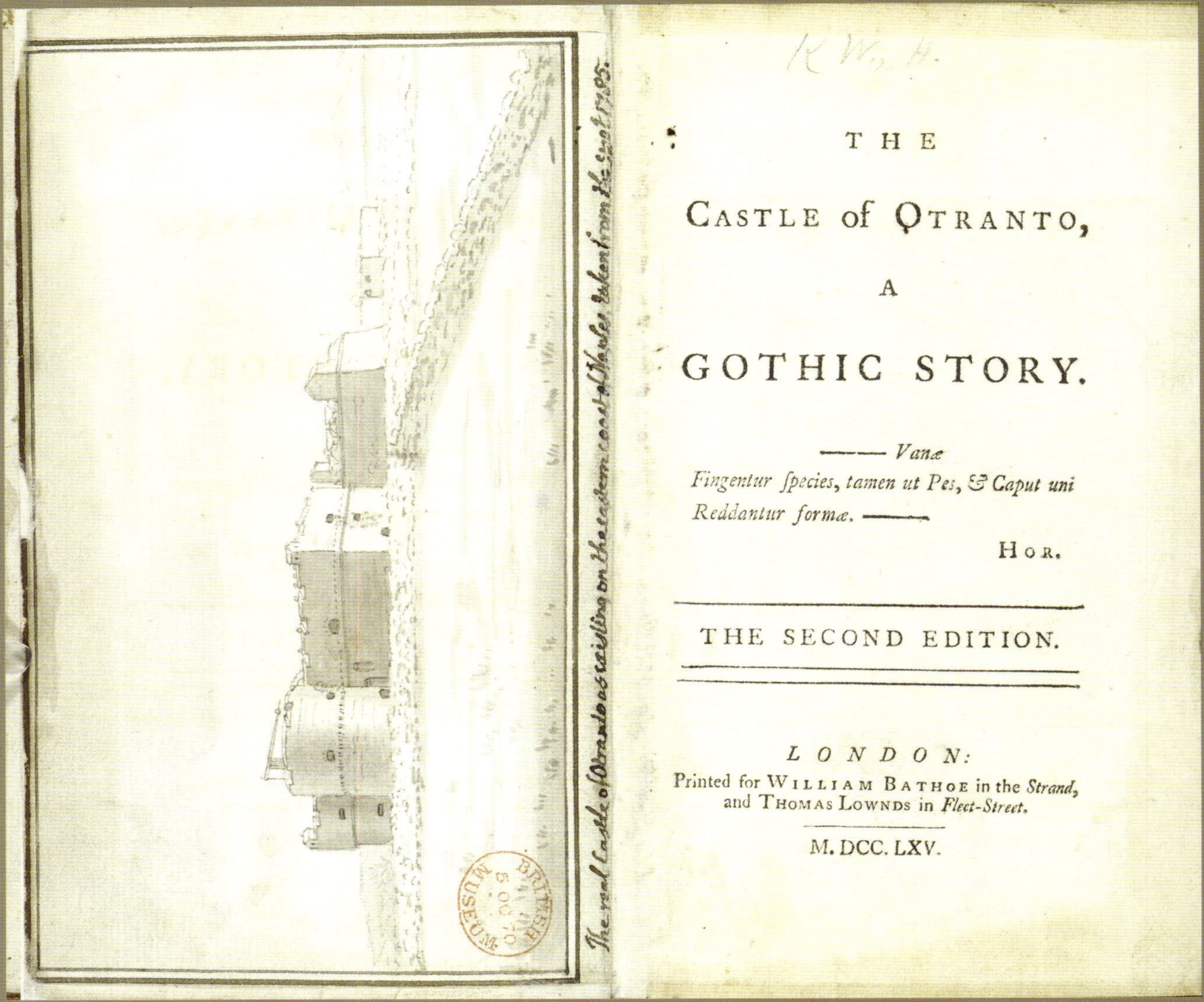

THE

CASTLE of OTRANTO,

A

GOTHIC STORY.

—— *Vanæ*
Fingentur species, tamen ut Pes, & Caput uni
Reddantur formæ. ——

HOR.

THE SECOND EDITION.

LONDON:
Printed for WILLIAM BATHOE in the *Strand*,
and THOMAS LOWNDS in *Fleet-Street*.

M.DCC.LXV.

Title page and frontispiece to Horace Walpole's copy of *The Castle of Otranto*.
British Library C.40.c.24.

From the Crypt: *The Castle of Otranto*

Horace Walpole's *Otranto*

Waking from a vivid dream in the summer of 1764, Horace Walpole put pen to paper and wrote solidly for just short of two months. The end result was the novel *The Castle of Otranto*, which was published on Christmas Eve of the same year. The importance of Walpole's fictional creation in the history of Gothic literature cannot be over-emphasised. By situating his story of mistaken identity, supernatural happenings, tense pursuits and heightened sexuality in the dark, labyrinthine corridors of a medieval Italian castle, Walpole laid the blueprint for countless other writers, from the eighteenth century through to the present day. By subtitling his fictional experiment 'A Gothic Story' in a second edition a few months later, he inadvertently coined a literary movement that, some 250 years later, is still going strong.

In the months following its publication Walpole was justifiably pleased with *Otranto* and its favourable reception. All 500 copies of the anonymous first edition quickly sold out, and a new edition, identifying Walpole as the author for the first time, was issued in April 1765. However, there is some suggestion from Walpole's vast correspondence that in later years he came to regard *Otranto* as something of a trifling novel. In 1785, for instance, he admonished Hannah More (1745–1833) for sharing her copy, describing his work in seemingly embarrassed terms as 'a frantic thing'. No such embarrassment, though, is apparent in Walpole's personal copy of the second edition of *Otranto*. On the contrary, this little volume offers many clues to the pride that Walpole took in his one and only fictional narrative. Its physical placement is the first indicator of this. Of the thousands of books and manuscripts housed in Walpole's library at Strawberry Hill, only a select number of the most special volumes were kept behind lock and key in the 'Glass Closet'. This copy was one such volume.

The book itself is bound in leather, with Walpole's coat of arms stamped in gold on the front and back cover; the prominent helmet in the crest of the Walpole arms even seems uncannily to foreshadow the action contained within. Inside the front cover, Walpole pasted a poem by a Mr Birch, which describes the 'ingenious author of the Castle of Otranto' as a 'sweet enchanter'. On a blank page at the back of the book, Walpole proudly compiled a list of the various stage adaptations and printed editions of *Otranto* that appeared up to 1795, two years before his death in 1797.

The most obvious addition to this copy is the watercolour drawing bound opposite the title page. This is a depiction of the real castle in Otranto, Italy, drawn by Willey Reveley and sent to Walpole some twenty-two years after he wrote his novel. Writing to Sir William Hamilton (1731–1803) on 17 January 1788, Walpole described his reaction to learning of his eponymous castle's real-life namesake: 'When I wrote my fantastic tale, I did not know that there existed, or ever had existed, a castle at that place, but looked into the map of Naples for a name, and adopted Otranto as well-sounding'. As he continued, 'the drawing corresponds so very well with the circumstances of the narrative, that I cannot help suspecting the idea was conceived, or at least adapted to flatter the vanity of the author; and I do wish you would be so kind as to inform yourself, and then me, whether there is in fact such an actual castle'. Sir William soon verified the existence of the castle at Otranto, and Walpole, immensely pleased with the similarity between the real castle and his imagined one, had the drawing engraved for use in later editions of his novel. That the text has never been out of print since 1764, and that it stands as the origin of a Gothic strain in literature and cultural production more generally that is as popular today as it was in the eighteenth century, indicates that Walpole's pride in *The Castle of Otranto* was not misplaced.

TIM PYE

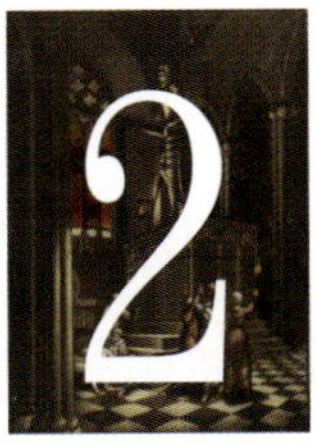

ANGELA WRIGHT

Gothic, 1764–1820

OPPOSITE:
Mistaken identity and murder in *The Castle of Otranto*.
British Museum.

Creating *The Castle of Otranto*

'It was fit for nothing but the age in which it was written, an age in which much was known; that required only to be amused', protested the author, architect, antiquarian and Member of Parliament Horace Walpole to his friend Hannah More on 13 November 1784 (Lewis 1937–83: XXXI.221). He was referring, of course, to his literary creation *The Castle of Otranto*, first published on Christmas Eve in 1764. The work is frequently hailed, though not without controversy, as the first 'Gothic' novel to appear in Britain. Yet in 1784 Walpole nonetheless appeared keen to downplay the significance of his 'Gothic' story to More, suggesting that it was written only to entertain the readers of a specific moment in an age 'that required only to be amused, nor cared whether its amusements were conformable to truth and the models of good sense' (Lewis 1937–83: XXXI.221).

Horace Walpole's tone of self-deprecation was not without precedent. On the day of its publication he had heralded *The Castle of Otranto* in a similarly understated manner to George Montagu, his close friend and long-time correspondent. It is only in the fifth paragraph of the letter, dated 24 December 1764, that Walpole chooses to mention *Otranto*, and even that comes only at the end of a list of items that he includes with his letter to Montagu: 'This comes with your muff, my *Anecdotes of Painting*, the fine pamphlet on libels, and *The Castle of Otranto*, which lost its maidenhead today' (Lewis 1937–83: X.145). His casual, brief reference to the work, and the feminised reference to its loss of 'maidenhead', suggests that Montagu may

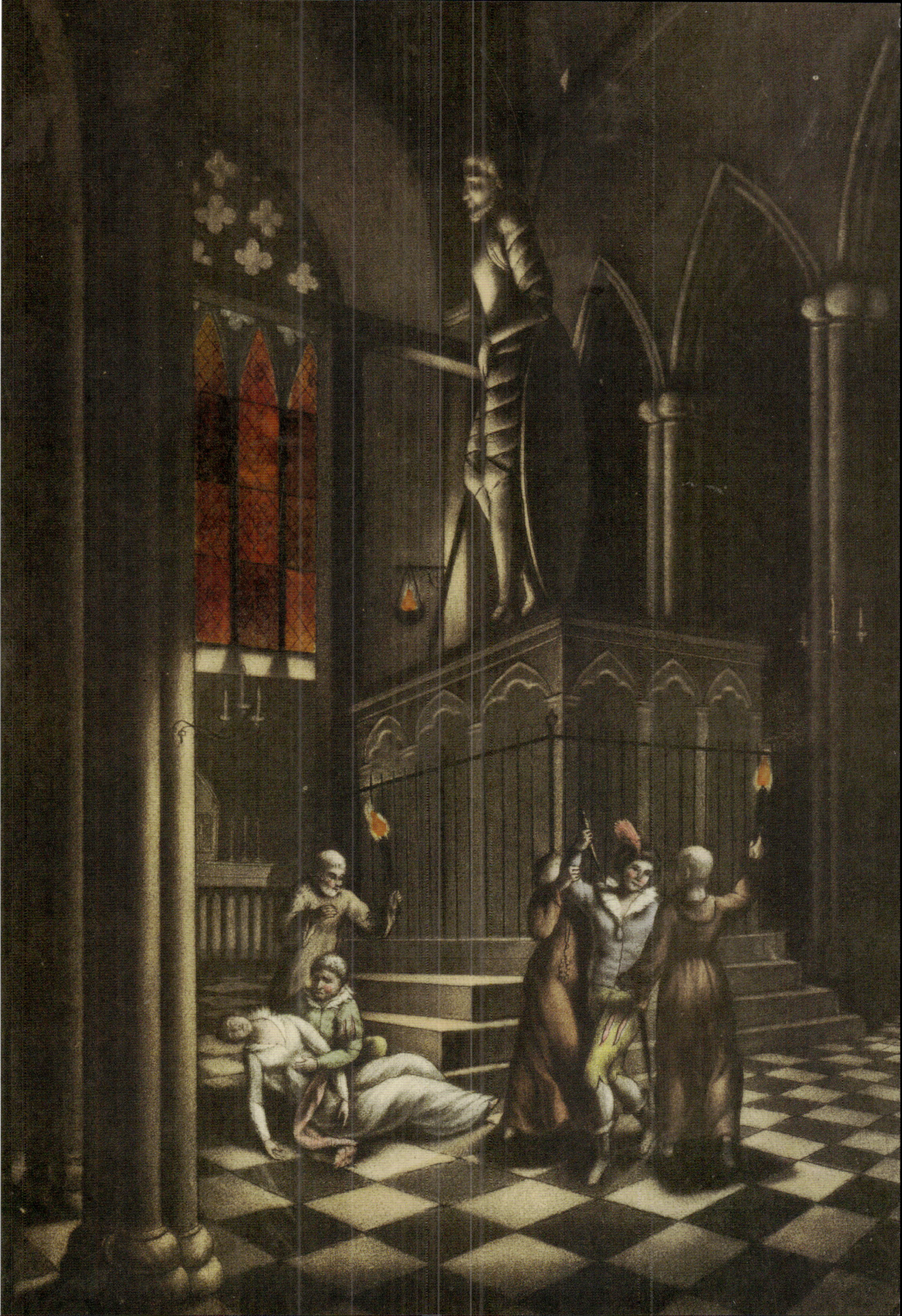

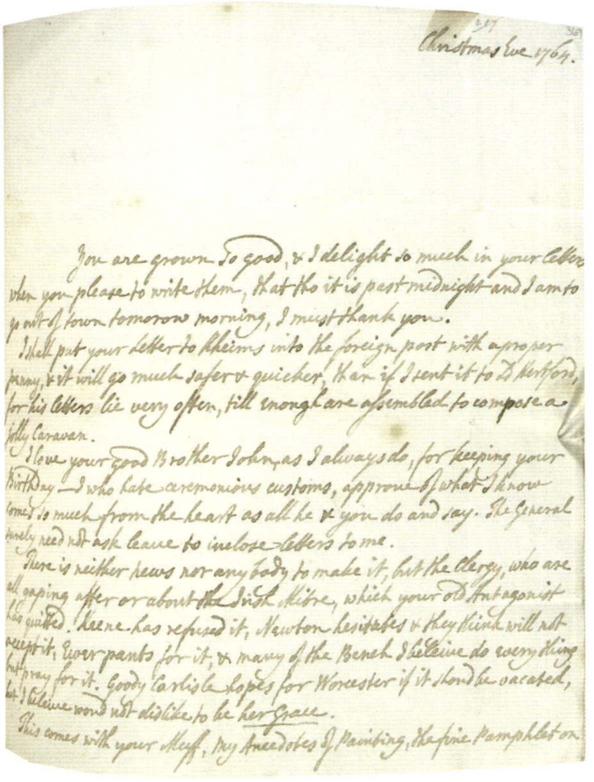

Christmas Eve 1764.

You are grown so good, & I delight so much in your letters when you please to write them, that tho it is past midnight and I am to go out of town tomorrow morning, I must thank you.

I shall put your letter to Rheims into the foreign post with a proper penny, & it will go much safer & quicker, than if I sent it to Ld Hertford, for his letters lie very often, till enough are assembled to compose a jolly Caravan.

I love your good Brother John, as I always do, for keeping your Birthday – I who hate ceremonious customs, approve of what I know comes so much from the heart as all he & you do and say. The General surely need not ask leave to inclose letters to me.

There is neither news nor any body to make it, but the Clergy, who are all gaping after or about the Irish Mitre, which your old Antagonist has quitted. Keene has refused it, Newton hesitates & they think will not accept it, Ewer pants for it, & many of the Bench I believe do every thing but pray for it. Goody Carlisle hopes for Worcester if it should be vacated, but I believe would not dislike to be her Grace.

This comes with your Mess, my Anecdotes of Painting, the fine Pamphlet on

Walpole announcing the loss of of *Otranto*'s maidenhead, Christmas Eve, 1764.
British Library Add. MS 70987, f.369.

well have already been aware of *The Castle of Otranto* before its publication. This impression is strengthened by Montagu's brief acknowledgement of it in his return letter: 'Let me hear what is said of it; it will puzzle and must please' (Lewis 1937–83: X.146).

George Montagu's prediction of a warm reception for *The Castle of Otranto* was not wide of the mark. The veneers of feudalism, Catholicism and accidental rediscovery that covered the true source of the tale contributed to its positive reception in the periodical press. Reviewing the novel for the *Monthly Review*, John Langhorne pronounced it a 'work of genius, evincing great dramatic powers', concluding that it was clearly written by 'no common pen' (Sabor 1987: 71). From this we can deduce that neither Langhorne, nor many other early readers and critics, guessed whose pen had composed *Otranto*. The first edition was published anonymously, with the conceit of an antiquarian – one 'William Marshal, Gent.' – claiming to have discovered the printed text of a tale from the original Italian source of a Catholic priest. This 'William Marshal' records in the preface to the first edition that:

> The following work was found in the library of an ancient Catholic family in the north of England. It was printed at Naples, in the black letter, in the year 1529. How much sooner it was written does not appear. The principal incidents are such as were believed in the darkest ages of Christianity; but the language and conduct have nothing that savors of that barbarism. The style is the purest Italian. If the story was written near the time when it was supposed to have happened, it must have been between 1095, the era of the first crusade, and 1243, the date of the last, or not long afterwards [. . .] It is not unlikely, that an artful priest might endeavour to turn their own arms on the innovators; and might avail himself of his abilities as an author to confirm the populace in their ancient errors and superstitions. (Walpole 2003: 59)

The conceits of this opening paragraph to William Marshal's preface lay down some important markers to what we have come to understand about Gothic fiction. The text is discovered by chance in a library that even in England is described as remote: it is no less than the library 'of an ancient Catholic family in the north of England'. At a safe remove from cosmopolitan, enlightened London, the tale's chance discovery inaugurates a series of Gothic tropes that were to become the staples of subsequent Gothic fiction during this period. It is an 'ancient Catholic family' that has preserved the tale and protected it in the north of England, presumably, one imagines, from the violent desecrations of the Protestant Reformation in which England's northern Catholic strongholds were sacked and destroyed.

This opening sentence to the preface is therefore of supreme importance, touching as it does upon England and its troubled relationship with Catholicism – from the Protestant Reformation of the sixteenth century, through the Glorious Revolution of the seventeenth century and the establishment of a Hanoverian

Protestant succession, and so into the eighteenth century. To a contemporary readership in 1765, these opening words about an 'ancient Catholic family in the north of England' would suggest something as equally remote, pushed to the fringes of the Protestant conscience, as the narrative that follows. The tale, Marshal informs us, was printed in Naples, in the 'black letter' in the year 1529. Why 1529? This was the year in which Cardinal Thomas Wolsey debated the legality of Henry VIII's marriage to Catherine of Aragon, as the Tudor king's endeavours to rid himself of his first Catholic wife became more concerted and desperate. That year, and the court over which Wolsey presided, is crucial to the history of England's Protestant Reformation. Thus, although the date and location of the publication of the work that 'William Marshal' discovers is seemingly arbitrary – 'How much sooner it was written does not appear', Marshal confesses – the implications are less so. Naples may be geographically remote from Britain, but the temporal remoteness of this 'black letter' or 'Gothic' text is more questionable. From the date of 1529, a further conundrum is opened up by Marshal's speculation that the story must have been written between 1095, the 'era of the first crusade, and 1243, the date of the last'.

We proceed through a series of portals in this first paragraph of Walpole's preface from one religious trauma to the next. However, Marshal alludes to the manuscript's original author as an 'artful priest' who may have used his powers as an author to manipulate his readership, and confirm them 'in their ancient errors and superstitions'. The present readership, implies William Marshal, is not so easily duped; it can only engage with such a tale of terror and wonder as one to read for mere amusement.

> Whatever [the author's] views were, or whatever effects the execution of them might have, his work can only be laid before the public at present as a matter of entertainment. Even as such, some apology for it might be necessary. Miracles, visions, necromancy, dreams, and other preternatural events, are exploded even now from romances. That was not the case when our author wrote; much less when the story itself was supposed to have happened. (Walpole 2003: 60)

William Marshal is at pains to suggest that the novel to follow 'can only be' a matter of entertainment – much as his creator Walpole was in his correspondence on *Otranto*. The protests of both Walpole and his fictional counterpart insist rather too much upon this point, flattering and pandering to the tastes of the rational, enlightened and predominantly Protestant credentials of their late eighteenth-century readership. 'Miracles, visions, necromancy, dreams and other preternatural events', an exhausting list even to read, are presented here for the sake of amusement only.

Characters and Context

To what extent can we take this self-conscious distancing from the supernatural at face value? Walpole himself claimed to have dreamt

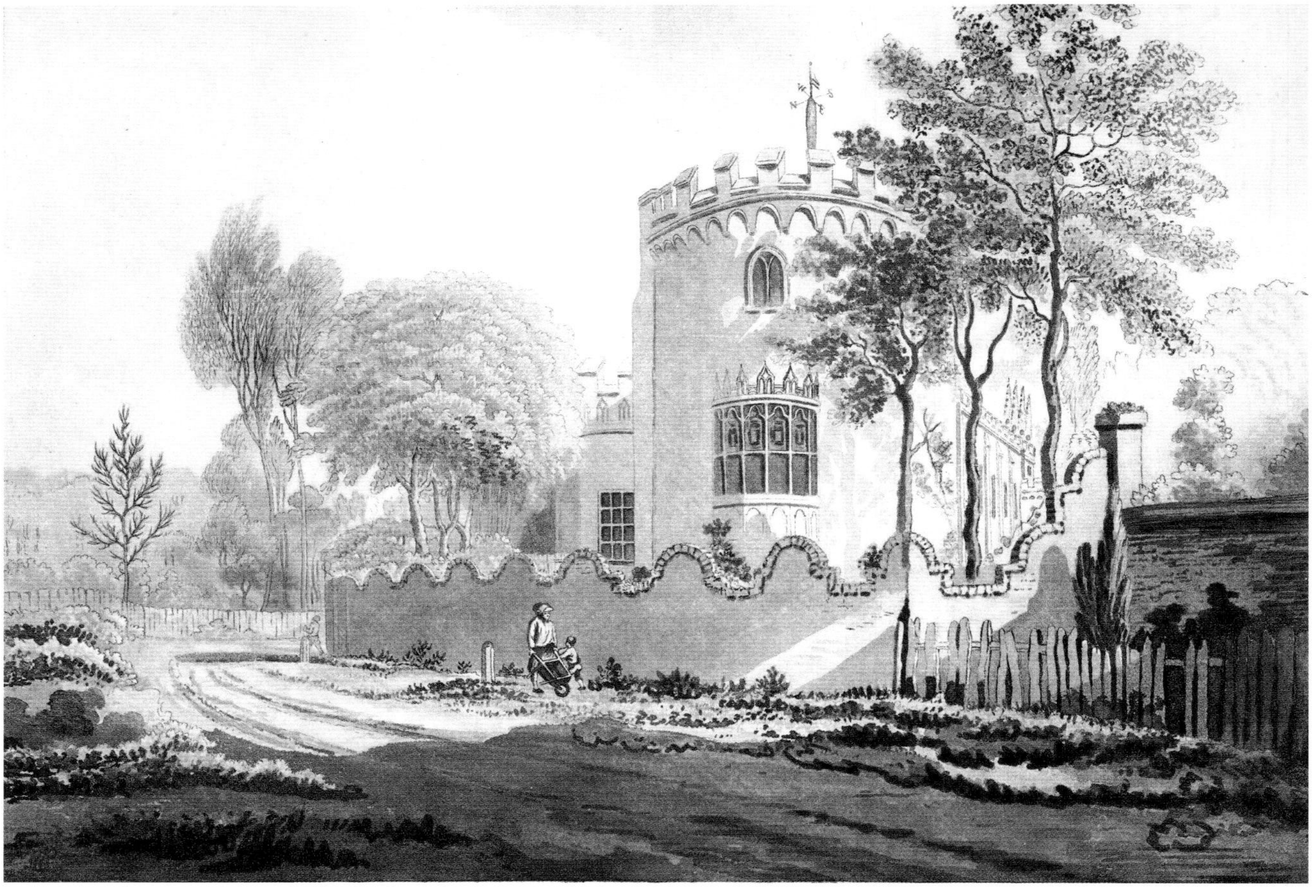

Strawberry Hill. Pen and ink on paper, 1797.
British Library Maps K. Top.30.36.b.
The west front of Strawberry Hill, showing the Beauclerk Tower.

up the story one night in his own 'Gothick castle' of Strawberry Hill. Originally a small house in Twickenham, purchased by Walpole in 1748 from the London toyshop owner Mrs Elizabeth Chevenix, Strawberry Hill was transformed over the course of some fifty years into a faux-medieval castle replete with turrets, suits of armour and Gothic battlements. Walpole took considerable pride in this achievement, later boasting to his friend Mary Berry that such modern, domestic manifestations of the ancient Gothic architectural style as Lee Priory in Kent and Strawberry Hill in Surrey were little more than an exercise in imaginative expression: 'every true Goth must perceive that they are more the works of fancy than of imitation' (Lewis 1937–83: XII.137). No less fanciful and original was the curious hybrid of ancient romance and modern novel that he offered to the public in 1764. Of the merits of his literary creation, however, Walpole remained more reserved.

The Castle of Otranto certainly entertains, as Walpole insisted that it should, with the staging of particularly amusing arguments between the servants and their superstitious master Prince Manfred. The tale commences with preparations for the marriage of Conrad, the son of Manfred – but this is to be no happy family occasion:

> Manfred, Prince of Otranto, had one son and one daughter: The latter a most beautiful virgin, aged eighteen, was called Matilda.

> Conrad, the son, was three years younger, a homely youth, sickly, and of no promising disposition; yet he was the darling of his father, who never showed any symptoms of affection to Matilda. Manfred had contracted a marriage for his son with the Marquis of Vicenza's daughter, Isabella; and she had already been delivered by her guardians into the hands of Manfred, that he might celebrate the wedding as soon as Conrad's infirm state of health would permit. (Walpole 1765: 1–2)

A sickly son 'of no promising disposition', Conrad has just as little agency in this marriage as his betrothed, Isabella: the marriage, we are told, has been 'contracted' by the respective fathers, with Isabella summarily 'delivered' 'into the hands of Manfred'. This is a business arrangement intended to secure Manfred's blood-line. His impatience to secure this lineage, the servants speculate, is due to Manfred's anxiety about an ancient prophecy, namely that 'the Castle and Lordship of Otranto should pass from the present family, whenever the real owner should be grown too large to inhabit it.' (1765: 2–3). Predictably, with such an omen presented as early as the second page of the novel, Manfred's plans are frustrated: just as the nuptials are about to take place, Conrad is discovered 'dashed to pieces, and almost buried under an enormous helmet, an hundred times more large than any casque ever made for human being, and shaded with a proportionable quantity of black feathers' (1765: 5). Momentarily mesmerised by this omen, Manfred rapidly puts aside any shock to pursue the young bride-to-be, Isabella, for himself.

Thus begins a rip-roaring narrative that features many supernatural occurrences, the most memorable of which are the appearance of a skeleton in a hermit's cowl and the portrait of Alphonso, Otranto's long-dead owner, coming off a wall to pursue Manfred. The story assumes a frantic pace, punctuated with humorous interludes between Manfred and his servants. Manfred insists that his servants are the gulls of superstition, as they attempt to articulate the ghostly occurrences that they have witnessed. In truth, however, it is Manfred himself who is superstitious: he knows that he is not the rightful heir of Otranto, but still clings with increasing desperation to his illegitimate claim to the castle. The tale oscillates rather unevenly between terror and the humour of the comic exchanges provided by the servants.

In his second preface to the novel in 1765, where Walpole somewhat anxiously admitted his authorship, the author would defend his inclusion of servants and humour, claiming that he had 'copied' this intermingling of 'high' and 'low' life, tragedy and comedy, from William Shakespeare himself. He went to some lengths to prove this provenance, citing in particular the interlude of the grave diggers in *Hamlet* – that moment in Shakespeare's play in which the tension of impending tragedy is both deflated and intensified through the somewhat earthy humour of the labourers. Walpole's gesture here was partly a riposte to Voltaire. In the 1760s the French critic had launched a strong invective against Shakespeare, arguing that he was 'barbaric' because of his 'inappropriate' use of humour.

Ink drawing of the giant ghost of Alfonso destroying the Castle of Otranto.
Lewis Walpole Library, Yale University.

This illustration, by a teenager, Bertie Greatheed, was described as 'astonishing' by Horace Walpole.

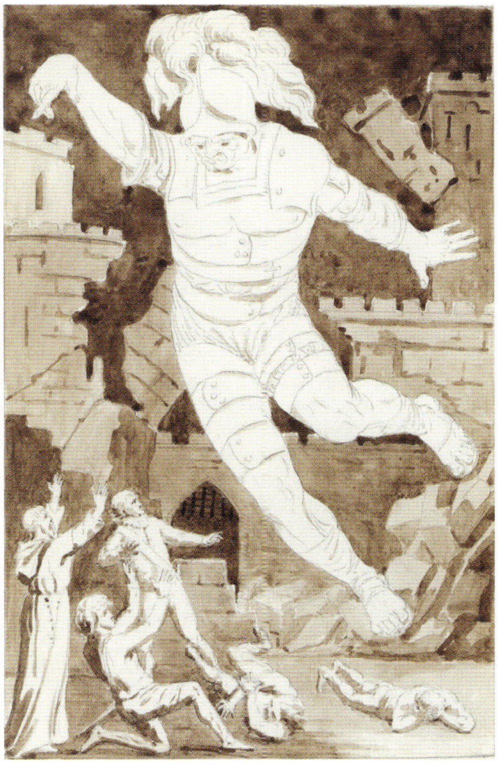

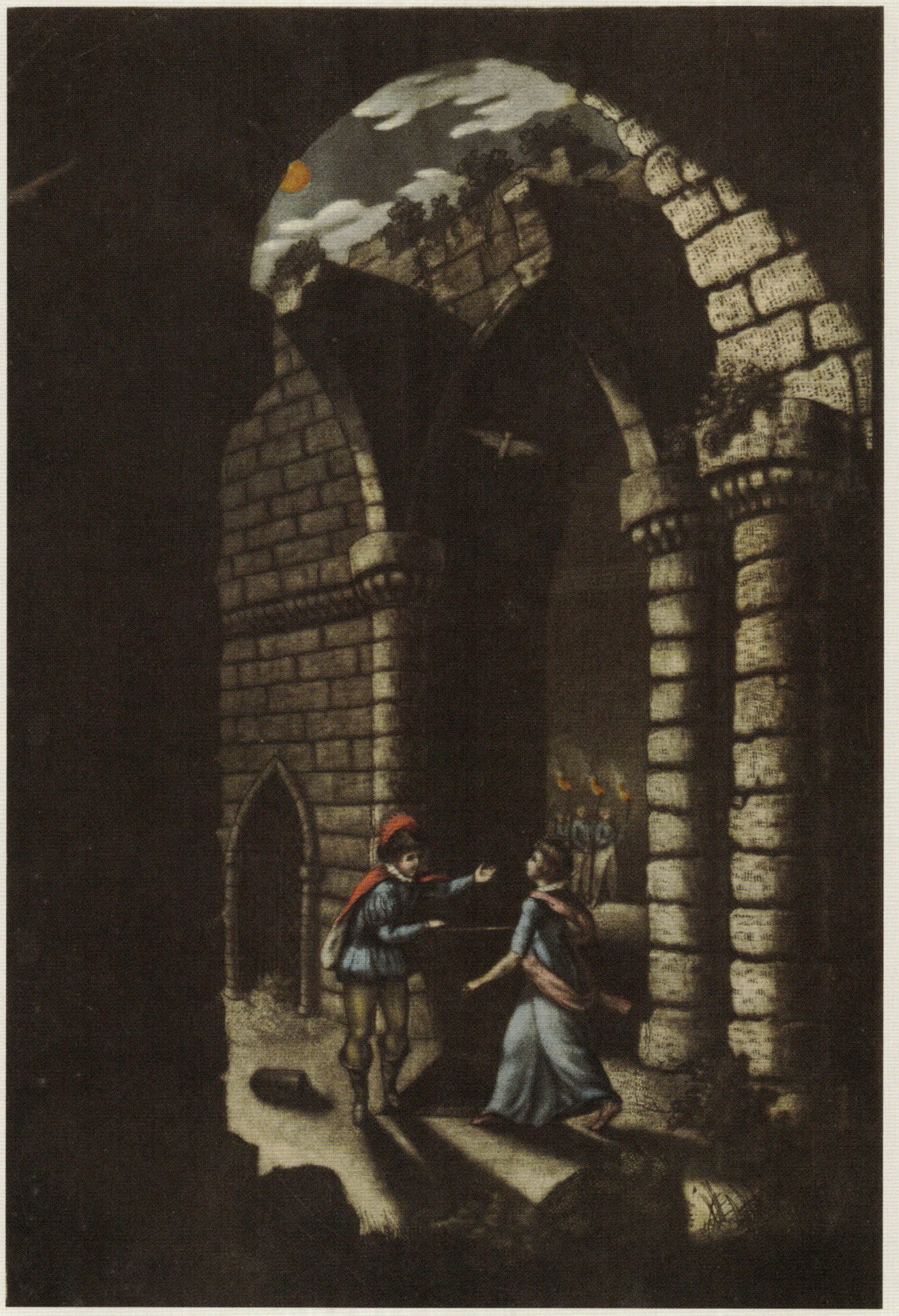

'A Gothic Story', the subtitle that Walpole appended to this second edition of his fiction, thus became irrevocably associated with a defence of Shakespeare, and by extension, a patriotic defence of English literary history more generally.

As we have seen, in both his correspondence and the two prefaces, Walpole was at pains to emphasise his tale as, primarily, a source of popular entertainment; the humorous element, provided by the servants and the impetuous usurper Manfred, was important to him. When Walpole confessed his translation hoax in the preface to the second edition of *Otranto*, the critic John Langhorne, who had initially reviewed the novel so positively (as no less than a work of 'genius') in the *Monthly Review*, recanted his position. He now called the tale 'preposterous', acceptable only when taken to be a 'translation' from a 'gross and unenlightened age' (Sabor 1987: 72).

Where then, if at all, might we locate 'terror and wonder' in the stakes of 'nonsense' and 'credibility' that soon began to plague and mute this first Gothic story? The tone of *Otranto* is more often light than serious, its supernatural manifestations more amusing than terrifying, so perhaps John Langhorne was right to deem it 'preposterous'. After all, the author himself did not seem insistent upon defending it as a serious work of literature. Once we acknowledge this levity, however, we can observe that *The Castle of Otranto* explores, in a deliberately light-hearted fashion, serious issues around gender, marriage and property. The tone of the novel becomes particularly urgent in relation to the plight of its young heroine Isabella. She is pursued through the labyrinthine passages beneath the castle by a frantic aristocrat who, believing that she is at his disposal, intends to impregnate her with his heir. The stoic, resigned counsel of Manfred's spurned wife Hippolita, namely that 'It is not ours to make election for ourselves; heaven, our fathers and our husbands must decide for us', rings hollow to the ears of the young, defenceless heroine (1765: 152).

Isabella, in fact, is the closest that we come to a heroine in the text, for Manfred's daughter Matilda is accidentally stabbed by her father in the course of the narrative. Walpole's fiction invites us to participate in the unprotected Isabella's fear, telling us at one point that 'her dread of Manfred soon outweighed every terror' (1765: 24). As the following extract makes clear, dread is linked inextricably with the terror of the ancient castle. *Otranto* thus sets in place a linking of psychological terror with architectural space that will come to characterise Gothic writing from this moment onwards:

> An awful silence reigned throughout those subterraneous regions, except now and then some blasts of wind that shook the doors she had passed, and which grated on the rusty hinges, were re-echoed through that long labyrinth of darkness. Every murmur struck her with new terror; – yet more she dreaded to hear the wrathful voice of *Manfred* urging his domestics to pursue her. She tried as softly as impatience would give her leave. – yet frequently stopped and listened to hear if she was followed. In one of those moments she thought she heard a sigh. She shuddered, and recoiled a few paces. (1765: 23)

OPPOSITE:
Isabella fleeing the oppressive Castle of Otranto.
British Museum.

The urgency of Isabella's terror is transmitted through the story's shift to the present tense, offering its readership the chance of experiencing Isabella's alarm as she attempts to outrun her determined pursuer. Her terror of Manfred becomes linked to the terror of the ancient building; the obscure, labyrinthine passages of Otranto, to her imagination, offer up a multitude of secret places out of which Manfred or his minions might leap and capture her.

The Pleasure of Terror

The curious pleasures that readers were to gain in reading of the experiences of Walpole's Isabella is what John and Anna Laetitia Aikin would later analyse in their essay 'On the Pleasure Derived from Objects of Terror' (1773). Here they investigated the 'paradox of the heart' that was pleasurable terror, or 'The apparent delight with which we dwell upon objects of pure terror, where our moral feelings are not in the least concerned, and no passion seems to be excited but the depressing one of fear' (1773: 57). As the Aikin siblings acknowledged, the paradoxical enjoyment of terror was somewhat 'difficult of solution' (1773: 57). For an enlightened, eighteenth-century Britain, this paradox constituted an uncomfortable truth.

It is one for which they had been prepared, however, by the earlier publication in 1757 of Edmund Burke's *A Philosophical Enquiry into the Origin of Our Ideas of the Sublime and Beautiful*. Here Burke had argued that the uncomfortable straining of our imaginations was both desirable and necessary. Juxtaposed with the milder form of pleasure to be derived from the beautiful, Burke's definition of the sublime revolved around a 'state of the soul, in which all its motions are suspended, with some degree of horror', the mind thus being rendered incapable of entertaining any other object (1757: 41). The imagination, for Burke, becomes so engrossed with the object of sublime contemplation that it cannot set it aside. The relevance of Burke's definitions of the sublime to Horace Walpole's first 'Gothic story' is clear. Walpole's first pseudonymous preface acknowledged that 'Terror, the author's principal engine, prevents the story from every languishing' (2003: 60); frantic pace, witty dialogue and frequent changes of tense in *The Castle of Otranto* are crucial factors in Walpole's creation of terror, and the imagination of the reader is not allowed to languish for a moment.

If Walpole's 'Gothic story' entertained with its ludicrous use of the supernatural and its insubordinate exchanges between Manfred and his servants, it also gripped its enlightened readership in the uncomfortable terrors of Isabella. Her fears, as it turns out, were not so far removed from eighteenth-century England as 'William Marshal' and Horace Walpole would have us believe. The marital law of 'coverture', according to which a woman and her property were ceded over to her husband at the time of marriage, was defined by William Blackstone in his famous *Commentaries on the Laws of England* in 1765 as that condition in which 'the very being or legal existence of the woman is suspended during marriage' (Blackstone 1765–9: I.442). This legal definition of marriage as a kind of living death, one in which a married woman's legal existence is 'suspended' or rendered

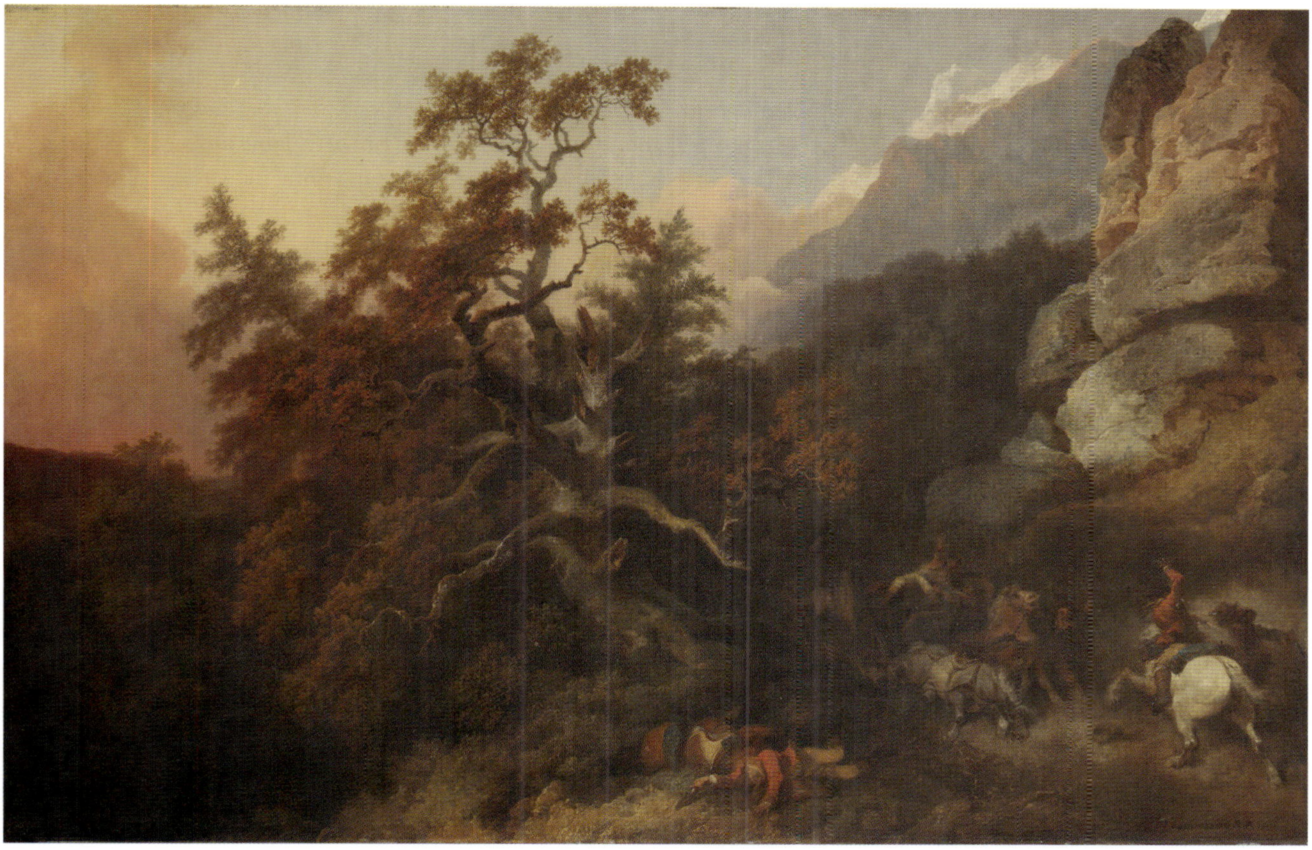

ABOVE:
Travellers Attacked by Banditti, Philip James de Loutherbourg, 1781.
Tate.
The rugged landscape and the dramatic attack combine to inspire a delicious sensation of terror.

inconsequential, would send shivers down the spine of many an eighteenth-century woman. Walpole's curiously modern heroine Isabella was no exception to this rule. Property, in the form of wives and usurped territories, lies at the heart of *The Castle of Otranto*. The story ends with the destruction of the castle, and the surrounding territories passed to the rightful heir Theodore, who dutifully marries the relieved Isabella at the narrative's end.

The Castle of Otranto may use the subtitle 'A Gothic Story' for a range of self-interested motives on the part of its author, but its blueprint slowly launched a crescendo of 'Gothic' tales that invested more firmly in the castle as the locus of terror. In 1777, for example, Clara Reeve acknowledged the inspiration of Horace Walpole when she published *The Champion of Virtue*, later to be commercially rebranded as *The Old English Baron: A Gothic Story* in 1778. A multi-talented author, Reeve variously turned her hand to translation, literary criticism and novel-writing. Her own foray into the new territory of the 'Gothic story' was cautious, with her use of the supernatural excused in her preface as remaining 'within the utmost *verge* of probability' (Reeve 1778: vi). At heart, though, Reeve's tale is close to Walpole's, both structurally and thematically. It is a tale of usurpation in which the young hero, Edmund, has been dispossessed of his rightful inheritance by a malevolent uncle who has murdered his father and destroyed a will. If anything, the terror of Reeve's Gothic story is more muted than that of Walpole, as it focuses more

BELOW:
Title page and frontispiece to Clara Reeve, *The Old English Baron*, sixth edition, 1799.
British Library 1608/4717.

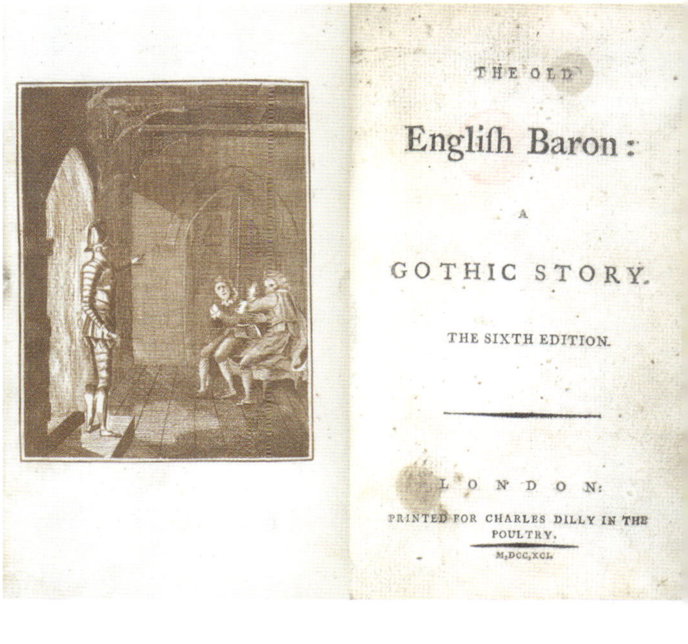
THE OLD

Englifh Baron:

A

GOTHIC STORY.

THE SIXTH EDITION.

LONDON:

PRINTED FOR CHARLES DILLY IN THE POULTRY.

M,DCC,XCI.

upon masculine battles of authority, with jousting, knights and chivalric feats absorbing the space that Walpole had devoted to the terrors of Isabella.

The heroine as the most compelling conduit for terror was developed cautiously and gradually in the final decades of the eighteenth century. Energised in equal measure by the epistolary sentimental tradition of earlier eighteenth-century fiction – Samuel Richardson's *Pamela* (1740) and *Clarissa* (1747–8), Jean-Jacques Rousseau's *Julie, ou la Nouvelle Héloïse* (1761) and Frances Burney's *Evelina* (1778) immediately spring to mind – the 1780s witnessed a number of young authors experimenting with the potent combinations of heroine-centred romance.

Sophia Lee's three-volume novel *The Recess: or, A Tale of Other Times* (1783–5), for instance, offered a tale of terror involving two imagined daughters of Mary, Queen of Scots, who are persecuted by a jealous and vigilant Queen Elizabeth I. History, romance and terror were fused together in Lee's well-received work. This historical romance, itself a reworking of an earlier historical French tale by the Abbé Prévost, capitalised upon the considerable literary resources of Britain and France during the eighteenth century. In so doing, it produced something entirely new in the history of British literature. The sense of paranoia and persecution experienced and narrated by Lee's heroines Matilda and Eleanor were not so far removed from the terrors of Isabella in which Walpole forces his readership to participate in *Otranto*.

Charlotte Smith's *Emmeline, the Orphan of the Castle* (1788) also explores the potent links between gender and property that were to become a staple of the Gothic novel in the 1790s. 'Gothic', however, is only one of many modern critical terms that can be used to describe the fictional excursions of Sophia Lee and Charlotte Smith in the 1780s. And yet, as their titles suggest, their focus upon an architectural structure – the castle or the recess – as the governing source of terror and authority links their work to *The Castle of Otranto*. It also provided a platform from which 'the great enchantress', Ann Radcliffe, was to launch her fiction from 1789 onwards.

William Beckford, *Vathek* and the Oriental Tale

Before we move on to examine the works of Ann Radcliffe, the celebrated 'Mistress of Udolpho', it is important to pause on a work of fiction initially composed in French in 1786. William Beckford's Oriental tale *Vathek*, which first appeared in June 1786 as *An Arabian Tale, from an Unpublished Manuscript: With Notes Critical and Explanatory*, is too often sidelined in accounts of the rise of late eighteenth-century Gothic. This supernatural tale of sorcery and over-arching ambition does not easily correspond with other texts of a more recognisably 'Gothic' nature that were being published during the 1780s. And yet the parallels between Horace Walpole and William Beckford, for one thing, are too striking to ignore. Both were Members of Parliament, collectors of curiosities, francophiles, architects and linguists. As John Rutter's 1823 *Delineations of Fonthill*

Abbey illustrates, Beckford's own Gothic fantasy, Fonthill Abbey, rivalled Walpole's Strawberry Hill for extravagant colour, artefacts and overall exuberance, at least until its spectacular collapse in 1825.

Beckford's fiction is as fascinating as his taste in property. Like Walpole's novel, *Vathek* adopts the conceit of a translated manuscript: the tale, so the first page of the preface tells us, was 'collected in the East by a Man of letters' and subsequently 'communicated to the Editor above three years ago' (1786: iii). The 'Editor' labours first to transcribe, and then to translate, the narrative. The various distancing devices, then, are crucial to the tale's participation within what we now recognise as a 'Gothic' tradition, and to that tale's transmission from the East.

Taking the second claim first, it is worth noting that only a year before *Vathek*'s appearance, Clara Reeve, author of *The Old English Baron*, had published an exercise in literary criticism entitled *The Progress of Romance* (1785). In this, through the mouthpiece of Euphrasia, one of her three characters, Reeve advised that the fictional form of 'romance' had been transmitted to us not only through Europe, but also, more importantly, from the East, via the Saracens. Beckford's tale was situated in a growing contemporary consensus about the Eastern origins of romance – a view that gained considerable momentum and praise from the popularity of the *Arabian Nights Entertainments*. These tales appeared in Britain as early as 1706 through the translation of the Frenchman Antoine Galland, and were enhanced, supplemented and republished at least once in every ensuing decade of the eighteenth century. First and foremost,

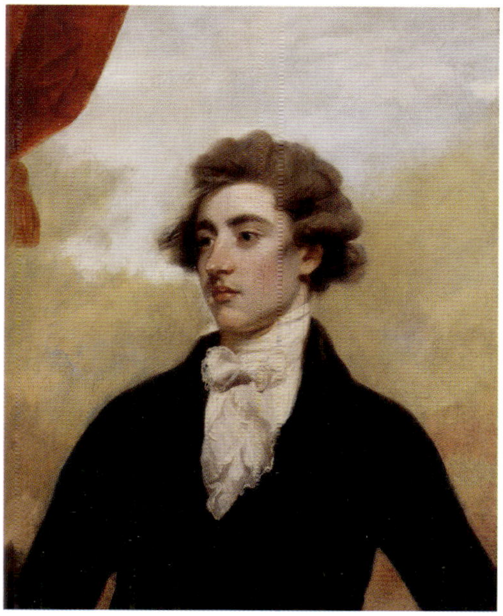

William Beckford, portrait by Joshua Reynolds, 1782.
National Portrait Gallery, London.

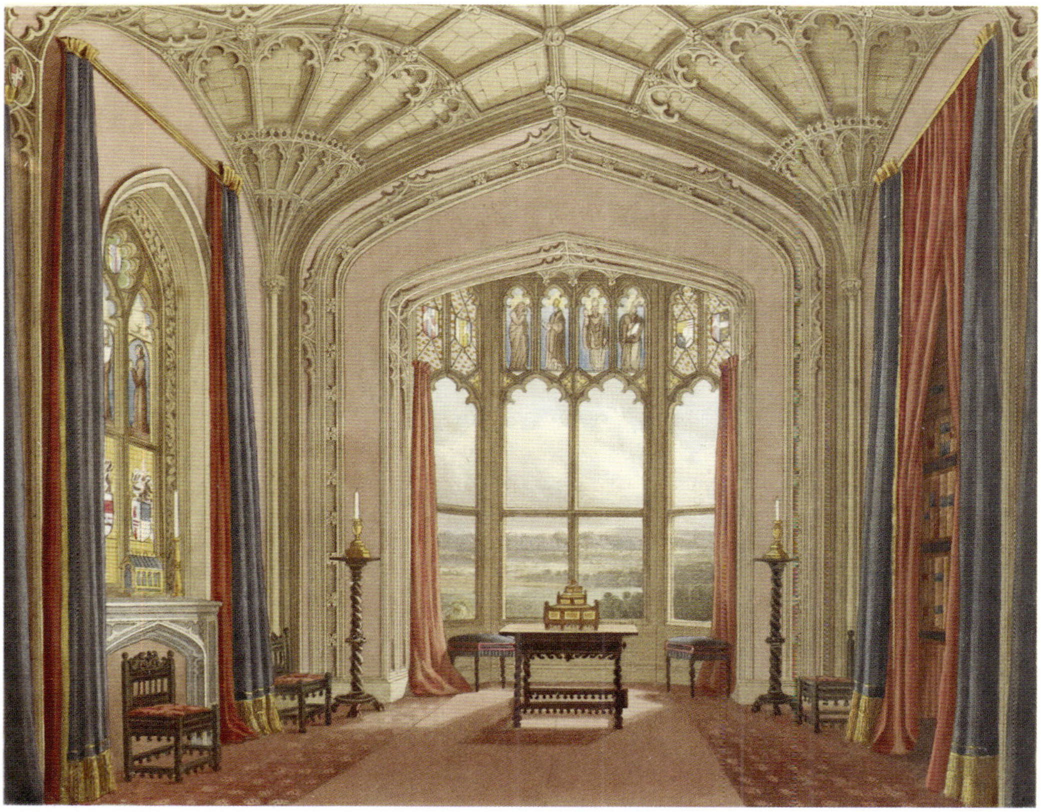

Illustration from *Delineations of Fonthill Abbey* by John Rutter, 1823.
British Library G.3067.(1.).

then, *Vathek* participates in the Oriental tradition of romance, catering to an established appetite and vogue for that particular form of fiction.

The eponymous hero of *Vathek,* however, has more than a little in common with Horace Walpole's Prince Manfred. A spoiled and easily bored Caliph, Vathek harbours dormant superstitions that are exploited by an ugly Giaour who mysteriously appears and offers him supernatural powers. The parallels with the more mortal Manfred of *Otranto* come in the form of the Caliph's reaction to his servants, mother and wives, all of whom are treated and disposed of as freely as Manfred casts off his wife, daughter and servants. Terror, capable of arousing the imaginative faculties, is the only mechanism that can raise the Caliph from his selfish torpor. He fears the Giaour, and relishes the supernatural powers that the latter awards him. Yet although terror may pique the curiosity of Vathek, it makes him no more sympathetic towards his inferiors.

Beckford's narrative pays close attention to the atmospheric conditions of terror that accompany the Giaour's appearance. Such detailed descriptions of setting and weather contribute significantly to subsequent Gothic authors' treatment of atmospheric terror. During the journey undertaken by the Caliph and his entourage, for instance, the Giaour's arrival is signalled by a change in the weather:

> Before they could reach the ascent of the steepest rock, night overtook them; and a boisterous tempest arose. [. . .] The dark clouds that overcast the face of the sky, deepened the horrors of this disastrous night insomuch that nothing could be heard distinctly, but the mewling of pages, and lamentations of Sultanas. (1786: 81)

As in *Otranto,* it is the servants and the wives who heed the 'horrors' of the tempest. Vathek, by contrast, becomes increasingly immune to both the horrors of the Giaour's presence and to the effects that he has on his kingdom and his people. Later in the novel he is urged to exorcise the supernatural presence by a delegation of old men:

> 'O heaven! Is it then by these phantoms that we have been, for six months, tormented! Alas! It was from the terror of these spectres and the noise beneath the mountains, that our people have fled; and left us, at the mercy of maleficent spirits!' The Caliph, to whom these complaints were but unpromising auguries, drove over the bodies of these wretched old men. (1786: 187)

At the opening of the narrative, Vathek's regard for his subjects was dismissive at best, but in his epicurean pursuit of sensation he becomes increasingly heedless of the warnings he receives. He drives over the 'wretched old men' so as to experience better the 'apprehensive shudder' with which he impatiently awaits the Giaour's arrival. Beckford's Oriental tale undoubtedly inspired Lord Byron's poem of 1813, *The Giaour, A Fragment of a Turkish Tale*. Besides this most obvious connection, what we gain from *Vathek* is an increasingly focused prototype of a Gothic villain – one obsessively driven in pursuit of his desires and ambitions, to the exclusion of all those around him. Vathek is more terrifyingly single-minded in pursuit of his goals than Walpole's Manfred. In his quest to stimulate his imagination by experiencing terror, he also unwittingly becomes a locus of terror, and an early model for subsequent Gothic villains.

Ann Radcliffe and the School of Terror

The dangerously exhilarating potion of terror and power that Beckford's Vathek consumes inevitably leads to the abrogation of all moral authority. He is portrayed as selfish, single-minded and increasingly immune to the warnings of nature, and to the admonishing effects of terror itself. In fact Vathek bears many affinities with the later villains of Ann Radcliffe. Eventually the most celebrated (and the best remunerated) author of this period, Radcliffe began her career as a Gothic author tentatively, with the publication in 1789 of *The Castles of Athlin and Dunbayne*. As its title suggests, Radcliffe based her feudal tale of two warring clans in the Scottish Highlands around two castles, each reflecting the respective qualities of their inhabitants. The hero Osbert inhabits the castle of Athlin, which is open, welcoming and easily explored, whereas the villain Baron Malcolm's abode is an impenetrable fortress replete with moats, ramparts and drawbridges. Osbert, in fact, spends the largest part of the narrative imprisoned in Baron Malcolm's castle, after an impetuous decision to avenge his father's death at the hands of Malcolm.

Although Malcolm's castle, with its labyrinthine passages, impenetrable ramparts and cells for imprisonment, provides spaces of potential terror, it did not entirely convince early critics. Instead they viewed its exploitation of the 'marvellous' solely as a source of 'amusement' (Becket 1789: 91). Five years and two novels later, Ann Radcliffe had proudly acknowledged authorship of her novels and struck gold with her recalibration of terror and wonder in her fiction. In her most famous novel, *The Mysteries of Udolpho* (1794), she built upon both the successes and perceived aesthetic failures of the two works that preceded it, *A Sicilian Romance* (1790) and *The Romance of the Forest* (1792).

The Mysteries of Udolpho begins in rural Gascony, France, where the young heroine Emily St Aubert receives a sentimental education from her father. St Aubert teaches his daughter Latin and English, literature and science, and warns her against the follies of idleness: 'The vacant mind is ever on the watch for relief, and ready to plunge into error, to escape from the languor of idleness. Store it with ideas, teach it the pleasure of thinking; and the temptations of the world without, will be counteracted by the gratifications derived from the world within' (1794: I.15). Trouble is anticipated, then, even at this early stage of the narrative, in the form of 'the temptations of the world without', and this undercurrent continues, with Emily's education taking the form of a series of protective warnings. She must not indulge in sensibility or exercise her imagination too much, she is told, as it will not stand her well in life.

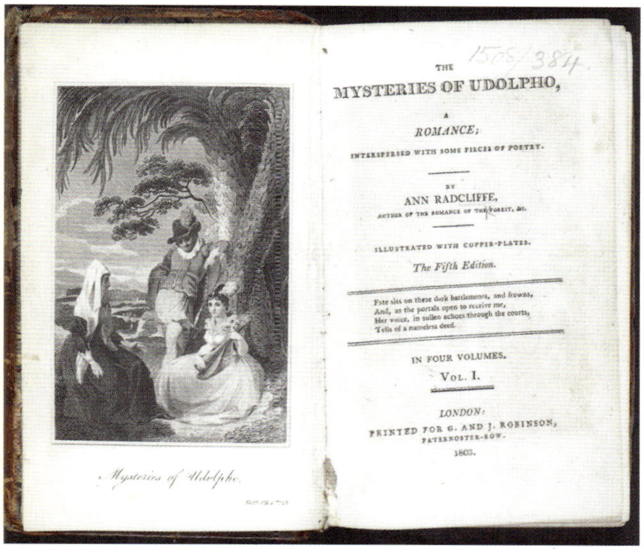

Frontispiece and title page to Ann Radcliffe, *The Mysteries of Udolpho*, fifth edition, 1803.
British Library 1508/384.

With the premature deaths of both Emily's mother and father, the anticipated trouble is realised. The vulnerable heroine is left in the guardianship of an aunt, Madame Cheron, who is imprudent enough to marry an Italian named Montoni. It does not bode well that Montoni's first spousal act is to whisk Emily and the new Madame Montoni off to Italy without any forewarning. And thus begins the reversal, in many ways, of Emily's sentimental education in France. It is in Italy, and most particularly at the Castle of Udolpho in the Apennines, that Emily's over-active imagination serves her well in many respects, alerting her to the dangers that await both her and her aunt. As she first approaches the Castle of Udolpho, Emily looks up at the ancient Gothic architectural edifice and construes it in tyrannical terms:

> The sun had just sunk below the top of the mountains she was descending, whose long shadow stretched athwart the valley, but his sloping rays, shooting through an opening of the cliffs, touched with a yellow gleam the summits of the forest, that hung upon the opposite steeps, and streamed in full splendour upon the towers and battlements of a castle, that spread its extensive ramparts along the brow of a precipice above. The splendour of these illumined objects was heightened by the contrasted shade, which involved the valley below.
>
> 'There,' said Montoni, speaking for the first time in several hours, 'is Udolpho'.
>
> Emily gazed with melancholy awe upon the castle, which she understood to be Montoni's; for, though it was now lighted up by the setting sun, the gothic greatness of its features, and its mouldering walls of dark grey stone, rendered it a gloomy and sublime object. As she gazed, the light died away on its walls, leaving a melancholy purple tint, which spread deeper and deeper, as the thin vapour crept up the mountain, while the battlements above were still tipped with splendour. From those too, the rays soon faded, and the whole edifice was invested with the solemn duskiness of evening. Silent, lonely and sublime, it seemed to stand the sovereign of the scene, and to frown defiance on all, who dared to invade its solitary reign.
>
> (1794: II.170–1)

Haddon Hall, Derbyshire.
Aquatint, 1744.
British Library K. Top.11.14.

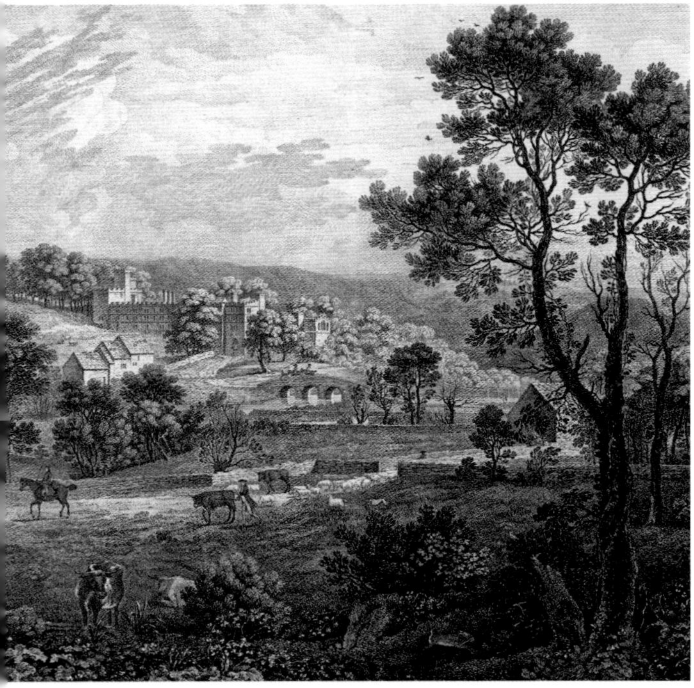

The term 'sublime' is twice invoked here in order to describe the castle, indicating to a late eighteenth-century readership conversant with Burke's treatise that Udolpho, to Emily's eye, is already a location of terror – a sensation intricately connected to the 'gothic greatness of its features'. What is of importance here is what Emily, the beholder, sees in the castle. This is no objective description of it, but one that characterises it as 'the sovereign of the scene' who 'frown[s] defiance on all, who dared to invade its solitary reign'.

Ebenezer Rhodes, in his *Peak Scenery; or, the Derbyshire Tourist* of 1824, claimed that 'Mrs. Ann Radcliffe, who was a native of Derbyshire, often visited Haddon Hall, for the purpose of storing her imagination with those romantic ideas, and impressing upon it those sublime and awful pictures which she so much delighted to pourtray [*sic*]: some of the most gloomy scenery of her "Mysteries of Udolpho" was studied within the walls of this ancient structure' (Rhodes 1824: 147). An examination of the engravings of Haddon Hall, or, even better, a visit to this august country manor in the Peak District, Derbyshire, reveals that there are indeed striking similarities between the descriptions of the battlements, great hall and terraces at Haddon Hall and the imagined castle of Udolpho.

Nonetheless, it would be hard to assemble or paint an accurate picture of Udolpho from the fragmented descriptions of battlements, passages, halls and chambers that appear in the novel. Spatial accuracy and consistency, though, are somewhat incidental to the narrative, for, as in *The Castle of Otranto*, Gothic architectural structure is ultimately charged with the generation of certain emotional effects. Radcliffe makes her heroine and her readers alike experience a frisson of terror as Emily enters Udolpho for the first time, in a pleasurable anticipation of terrors yet to come.

Emily's active imagination and anticipation of terrors is not entirely misplaced. In *The Mysteries of Udolpho*, Radcliffe sets up a correlation between the terrors of the castle and the potential malevolence of its owner. Of course, this was something that Walpole had exploited earlier, but in *Udolpho* Radcliffe allows her heroine Emily to scrutinise the connections between character and buildings more closely. At one point, Emily observes of Montoni that:

> The deep workings of his mind entirely abstracted him from surrounding objects, and threw a gloom over his visage that rendered it terrible; at others, his eyes seemed almost to flash fire, and all the energies of his soul appeared to be roused for some great enterprise. Emily observed these written characters of his thoughts with deep interest, and not without some degree of awe, when she considered that she was entirely in his power; but forbore even to hint her fears, or her observations, to Madame Montoni, who discerned nothing in her husband, at these times, but his usual sternness. (1794: II.78)

Emily reads character, as she does buildings, with considerably more nuance than her aunt. Although she over-interprets the Promethean potential of Montoni's villainy here – for, as it transpires, he is but a mercenary soldier, and roused for no 'great enterprise' at all – she remains ever more alert to danger than her aunt, who later is murdered after refusing to sign her fortune over to Montoni. Danger lurks in every shadow of the castle for Emily. In her chamber at night, she leaves a lamp burning while going to bed, 'but its gloomy light, instead of dispelling her fears, assisted it; for, by its uncertain rays, she almost fancied she saw shapes flit past her curtains and glide into the remote obscurity of her chamber' (1794: II.209). Emily's over-active imagination may play tricks on her this time, but

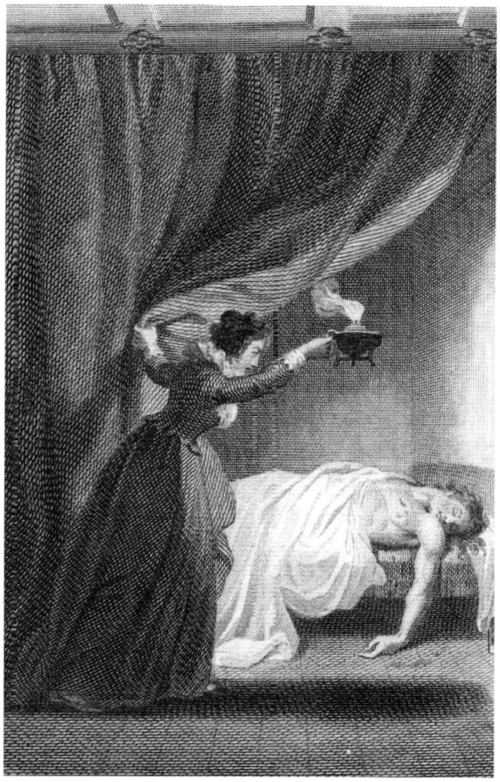

Illustration from Ann Radcliffe, *The Mysteries of Udolpho*, fifth edition, 1803.
British Library 1508/384.
Emily St Aubert, exploring an abandoned chamber within the castle, glimpses the horror that lies behind the black veil.

followers of Montoni do, indeed, penetrate her chamber. Her aunt is murdered and Montoni does try to force Emily too to sign away her property rights in France.

Terror versus Horror

'Terror', then, is viewed predominantly as a positive, salutary emotion in *The Mysteries of Udolpho*, an emotion which alerts the young heroine to the dangers, both imagined and real, by which she is surrounded. In *Literary Hours: or, Sketches Critical and Narrative* (1798), the critic Nathan Drake would praise Ann Radcliffe's careful manipulation of terror, observing that 'it is necessary either to interpose picturesque description, or sublime and pathetic sentiment, or so to stimulate curiosity by the artful texture of the fable' in order to prevent a narrative operating on the principle

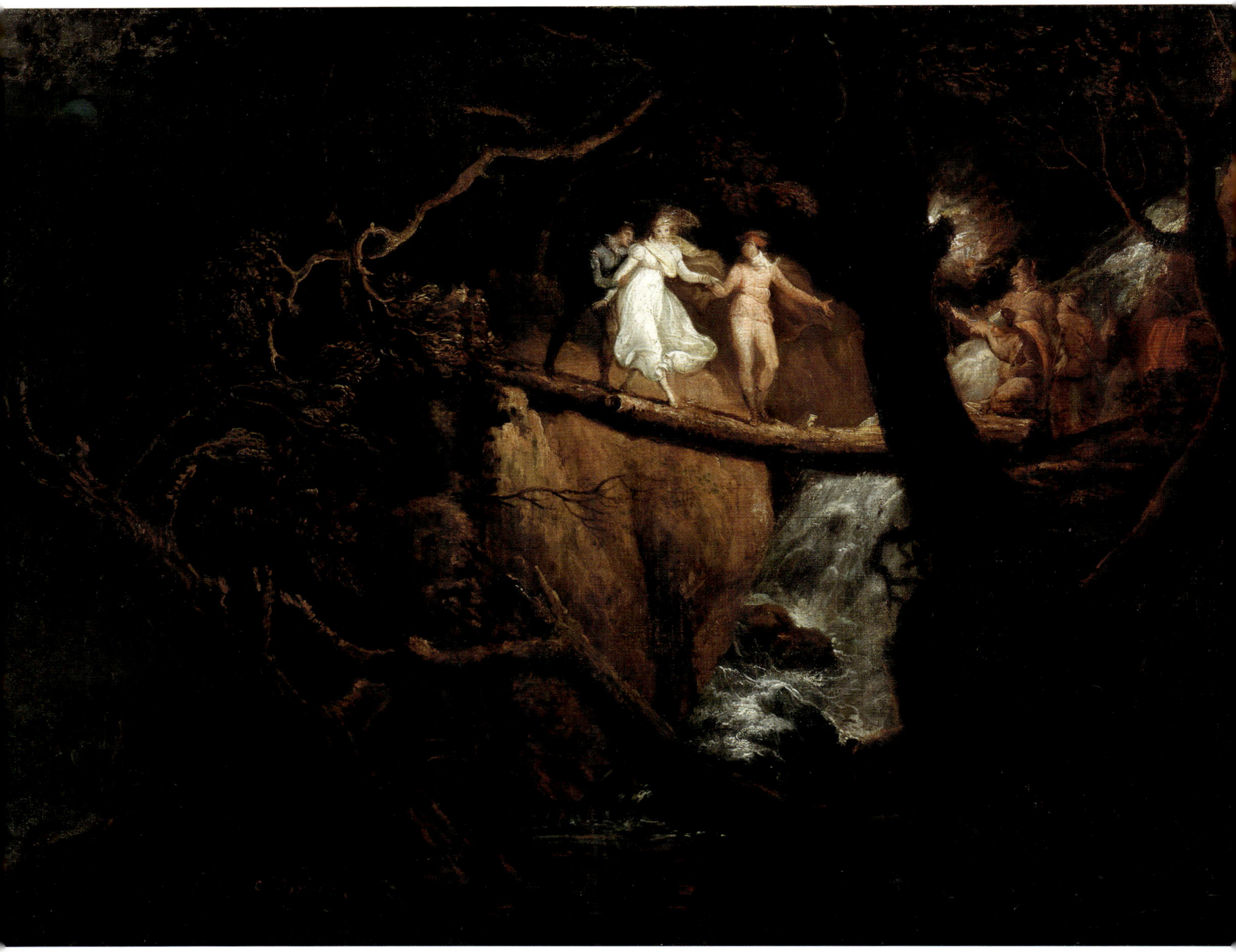

Nathaniel Grogan, *Lady Blanche Crosses the Ravine Guided by the Count and Saint Foix*, late 1790s. Oil on canvas. National Gallery of Ireland.

This scene, taken directly from *The Mysteries of Udolpho*, highlights the importance of landscape as a source of terror and wonder in Radcliffe's work.

of pain rather than pleasure (1798: I.354). So powerful were Ann Radcliffe's evocations of terror thought to be that her novels became blueprints for countless rewritings, reworkings, appropriations and even direct plagiarisms in the 1790s. For many, her name became synonymous with the numerous Gothic romances, dramas and chapbook retellings that flooded the literary marketplace in the late eighteenth century.

Drake made his observation concerning Radcliffe's deft manipulation of terror specifically in relation to the writer's penultimate novel *The Italian: or, The Confessional of the Black Penitents* (1796–7). In this work Radcliffe's command of terror was at its height, especially in her figuring of the villainous monk Schedoni poised ominously over the breast of the sleeping heroine, Ellena, during one particularly tense and climactic moment. Indeed, Radcliffe was at particular pains in *The Italian* to counteract the vogue for horror, galvanised by the earlier publication of Matthew Lewis's sensationalist novel *The Monk: A Romance* in 1796. The young Lewis claimed in a letter to his mother to have been inspired by the model of Ann Radcliffe's fiction, but Radcliffe appears to have been horrified by any possible comparison between her careful negotiations of virtue and sensibility and the lustful and ultimately victorious appetites of the licentious monk Ambrosio, who is presented in lurid detail throughout Lewis's narrative.

Radcliffe succeeded in both answering and counteracting Lewis's scandalous fiction in her portrait of Schedoni, a villainous monk who, in a former life, murdered his brother and raped his sister-in-law. He haunts the steps of the young heroine, Ellena, only stopping short of murdering her when he erroneously believes her to be his daughter. No murders or rapes take place within *The Italian*, enabling Radcliffe's novel to act as corrective, as she viewed it, to the excesses of *The Monk*.

In the wake of Edmund Burke's *Enquiry*, Radcliffe would further theorise about the superior values of terror over those of horror in a posthumously published essay, probably composed at some point between 1802 and 1803. 'On the Supernatural in Poetry' (1826) imagines a debate on horror and terror between two travellers, one of whom is eventually led to define the differences between the two aesthetic modes: 'Terror and horror are so far opposite, that the first expands the soul, and awakens the faculties to a high degree of life; the other contracts, freezes, and nearly annihilates them' (1826: 149). Radcliffe clearly viewed Lewis's *The Monk* as falling into the latter category, 'annihilating' the senses with a surplus of horror in such figures as the bleeding nun, incestuous rape, matricide, public immolation and decaying corpses.

Certainly Lewis's *The Monk* caused a scandal upon publication. Samuel Taylor Coleridge, reviewing it for the *Critical Review*, opined that 'the Monk is a romance, which if a parent saw in the hands of a son or daughter, he might reasonably turn pale', a sentiment that was echoed by many caricaturists and reviewers of the time (1797: 199). The Reverend Thomas James Mathias, in fact, went so far as to accuse Matthew Lewis, then a young Member of Parliament, of

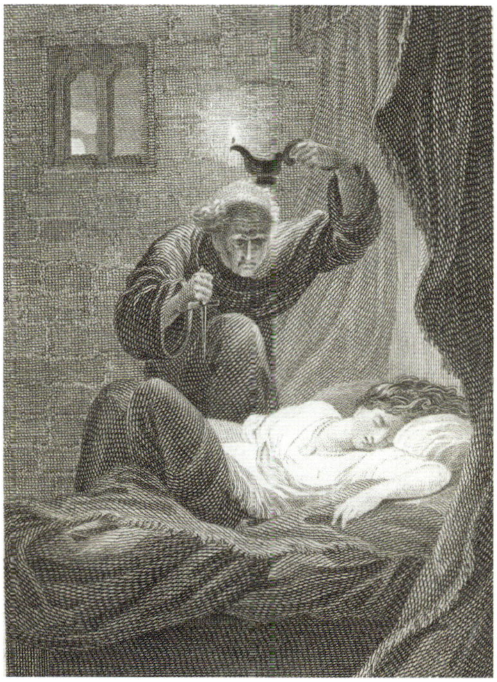

ABOVE:
Frontispiece to *The Midnight Assassin*, 1802. A pirated edition of Ann Radcliffe's *The Italian*, 1796–7.
British Library 1578/2144.(2).

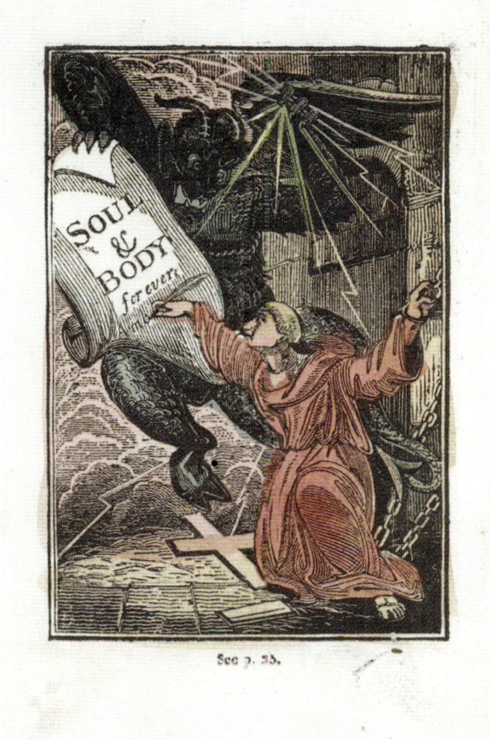

BELOW:
Frontispiece to an edition of Matthew Lewis's *The Monk*, 1818.
British Library RB.23.a.23548.

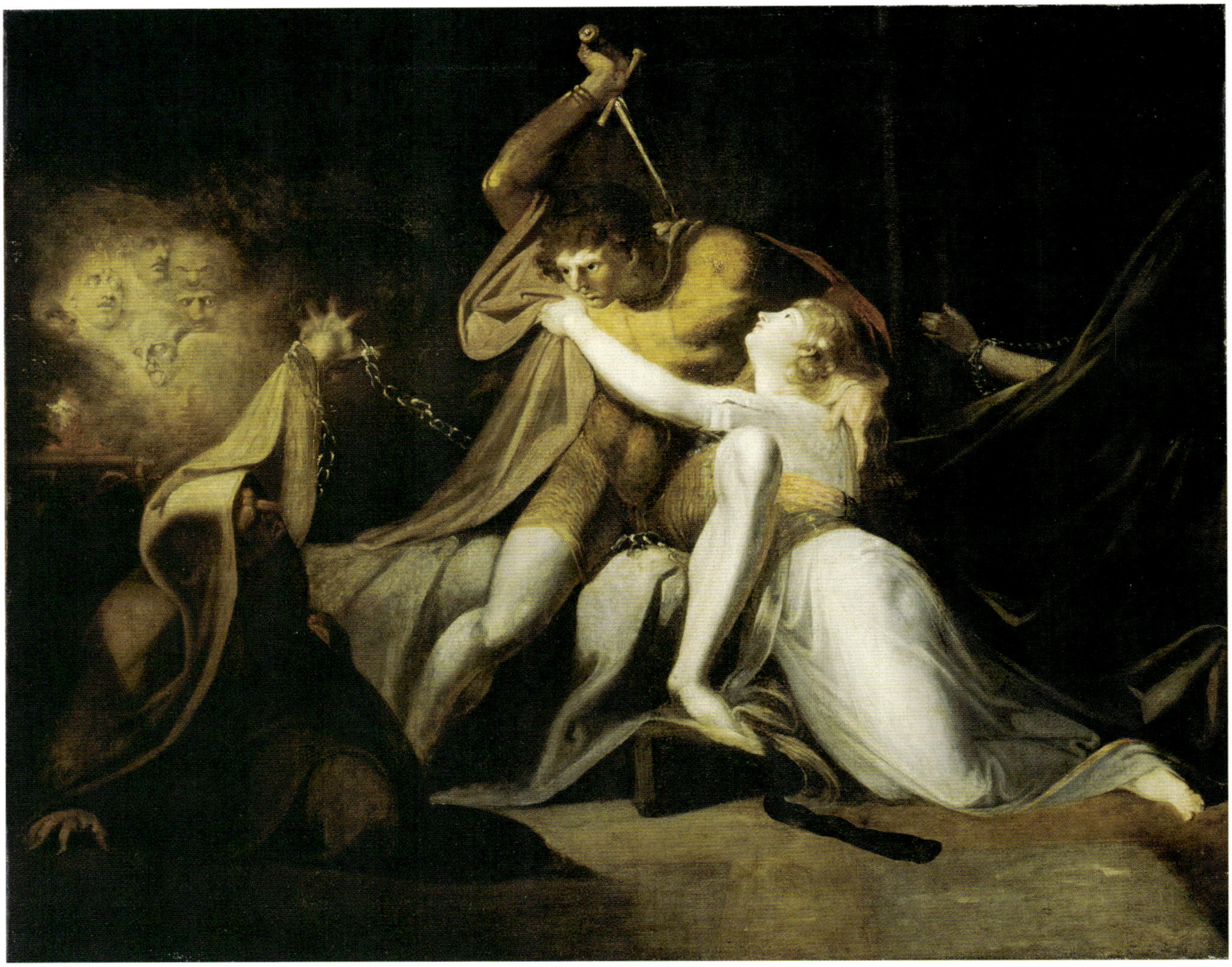

Henry Fuseli, *Percival Delivering Belisane from the Enchantment of Urma*, 1783. Oil on canvas.
Tate.

'state parricide' in his four-volume poem *The Pursuits of Literature* (1794–7). He argued that the corruption of Britain's youth, who were consuming *The Monk* with such avidity, was tantamount to treasonable practices on the part of the author. Lewis's own annotations to the third edition bitterly record his feelings, regretfully observing of his novel that 'Neglected it has not been, but criticised enough of all conscience' (Lewis 1796: iv).

The fervour surrounding the horror of *The Monk*, which, after all, portrays murder, sexual transgression and mob violence at every turn, linked it directly to the preservation of a British constitution deemed to be under threat in 1796–7 by the tumultuous consequences of the French Revolution. Fears that a revolution would engulf Britain did not abate in the wake of the execution of Louis XVI in 1793; indeed, the British monarchy and government became increasingly paranoid after a landing by the French at Fishguard. They suspended *habeas corpus* on a number of occasions, most notably in 1797. William Godwin's quasi-Gothic novel, *Things As They Are; or, The Adventures of Caleb Williams* (1794), tapped into the growing unease over the suspension of *habeas corpus*, in the constant surveillance and tyranny experienced by its revolutionary working-class protagonist. Critics of *The Monk*, published only three years after *Caleb Williams*, continue to debate its questionable revolutionary credentials. What we can say for sure, however, is that the novel's attacks upon institutional hypocrisy, its lurid demonstration of the consequences of an abbot breaking free of institutional constraints and its gruesome account of Ambrosio's death at the end all combine to suggest a climate of insurrectionary potential, if not outright revolution.

The Monk spawned many imitations. Some were in the form of drama, others chapbook redactions of the novel, and yet others novelistic homages, such as Charlotte Dacre's *Zofloya* (1806) and the young Percy Bysshe Shelley's *Zastrozzi, A Romance* (1810). Indeed by the end of the eighteenth century the Gothic aesthetic in Britain seems to have permeated almost every cultural form imaginable. By no means confined to the three-volume novel or prose romance, the Gothic infused several literary forms, from chapbooks and broadsides to popular dramas, operas and theatrical spectacles.

The Gothic imagination also provided the subject matter for much Romantic-era popular visual entertainment in the form of the magic lantern or phantasmagoric show. Manifested in such paintings as Philip James de Loutherbourg's *A Philosopher in a Moonlit Churchyard* (1790), Joseph Wright of Derby's *A Philosopher by Lamplight* (1769), William Blake's *The Ghost of a Flea* (*c.* 1819–20), and, especially, Henry Fuseli's *Percival Delivering Belisane from the Enchantment of Urma* (1783) and *The Nightmare* (1783), the Gothic was an intensely visual phenomenon, and an important strand in Romantic visual art.

A great deal of mainstream Romantic poetry, too, seems to have been influenced and inspired by popular Gothic fictions, not least *The Monk*. While Samuel Taylor Coleridge, for example, denounced Lewis's novel with such fervour in the *Critical Review*, he also began to write *Christabel* around 1797. Composed in accentual metre, this unfinished ballad concerns the temptation of a young, virginal heroine by an older woman, Geraldine, who, it later transpires, is a serpent-like being. The poem's themes of thresholds, sexual temptation and the supernatural in the form of a female demon shared much common ground with *The Monk*. In its wake, *Christabel* inspired *The Eve of St Agnes* and *Lamia* by John Keats (1820), as well as tales by the later nineteenth-century Gothic authors Edgar Allan Poe and J Sheridan Le Fanu. Lewis, who had considerable facility with foreign languages, also translated Goethe on the spot for Byron and Shelley in Italy. Byron described him as 'Wonder-working Lewis, Monk or Bard' in *English Bards and Scotch Reviewers* (1809), while Shelley would record some of the ghost stories that Matthew Lewis recounted to him and Mary Shelley during his visit to them in Geneva in 1816.

Promethean Horrors

As the Gothic grew increasingly popular in the 1790s, so too did parodies of the form. Gothic fictions, set as they then were in castles or abbeys, came to be viewed with increasing levity in such essays

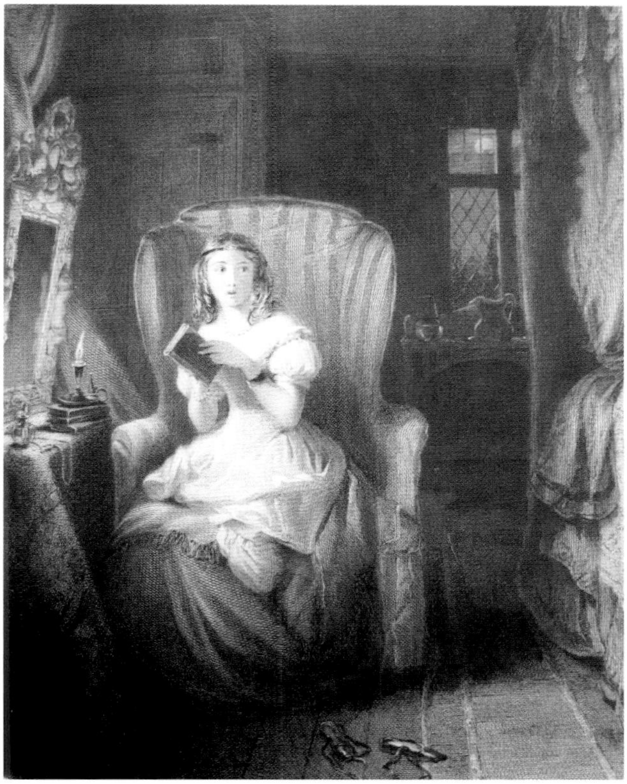

'The Ghost Story', engraving by R. Graves, *c.* 1874.
British Library P.P.1931.pc.

as 'Terrorist Novel Writing' (1797), which proposed following a Gothic 'recipe' consisting of such 'ingredients' as castles, tapestries and virgins. Jane Austen's and Thomas Love Peacock's respective spoof abbeys in *Northanger Abbey* (published late 1817; dated 1818) and *Nightmare Abbey* (1818), also poked fun at the genre. The terror of castles, abduction and incest was largely neutralised by the weight of these imitations. Writers could no longer guarantee a shudder from the proven and increasingly parodied formulas of Gothic romance. During the second decade of the nineteenth century, the Gothic was thought to be a somewhat tired and overworked style.

Reinvention, then, was necessary, and it was precisely in such innovative fictions as Thomas De Quincey's *Confessions of an English Opium-Eater* (1821) and James Hogg's *The Private Memoirs and Confessions of a Justified Sinner* (1824) that Gothic rejuvenation would occur. Yet the tributaries of the new form of Gothic most famously realised by Mary Shelley lay in the 1790s, especially in the death of Lewis's villain Ambrosio at the end of *The Monk*: 'The eagles of the rock tore his flesh piecemeal, with their crooked beaks. A burning thirst tormented him; he heard the river's murmur as it rolled beside him, but strove in vain to drag himself towards the sound' (Lewis 1796: III.314–15). The ending meted out to Lewis's anti-hero Ambrosio is undoubtedly gruesome, but it does offer some form of redemption through the implicit comparison of Ambrosio with Prometheus, the Titan of Greek myth. Denied water, his liver torn apart every day by eagles, Ambrosio has revolutionary credentials that are derived directly from Ovid's account in the *Metamorphoses*.

Without a doubt, there is much thematic material to be discerned in the very different forms of Gothic authored by Matthew Lewis and Mary Shelley. Part of this shared heritage comes through the way in which Gothic texts migrate through various

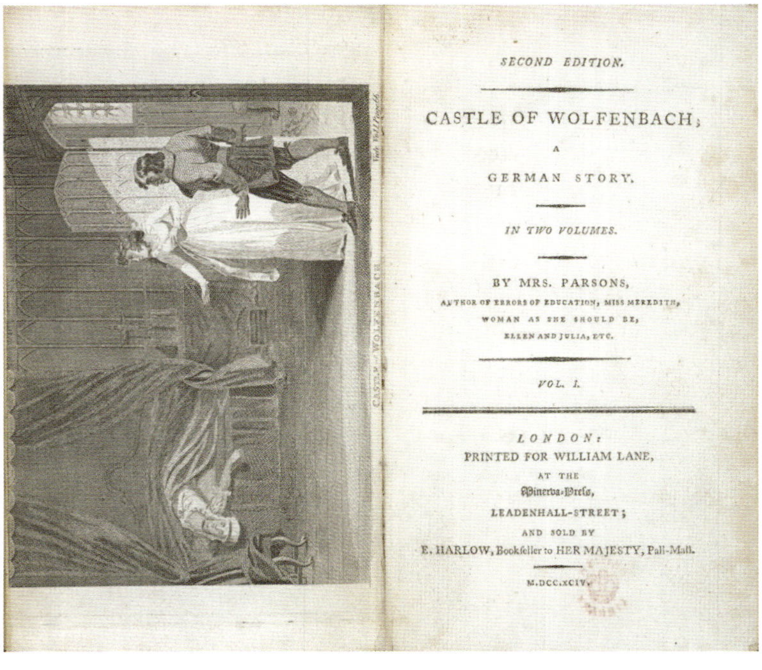

SECOND EDITION.

CASTLE OF WOLFENBACH;

A

GERMAN STORY.

IN TWO VOLUMES.

BY MRS. PARSONS,

AUTHOR OF ERRORS OF EDUCATION, MISS MEREDITH, WOMAN AS SHE SHOULD BE, ELLEN AND JULIA, ETC.

VOL. I.

LONDON:
PRINTED FOR WILLIAM LANE,
AT THE
Minerva-Press,
LEADENHALL-STREET;
AND SOLD BY
E. HARLOW, Bookseller to HER MAJESTY, Pall-Mall.

M.DCC.XCIV.

Frontispiece and title page from Eliza Parsons, *The Castle of Wolfenbach*, second edition, 1794.
British Library C.192.a.187.

The Castle of Wolfenbach is one of the 'horrid' novels recommended to Catherine Morland by her friend Isabella Thorpe in *Northanger Abbey*.

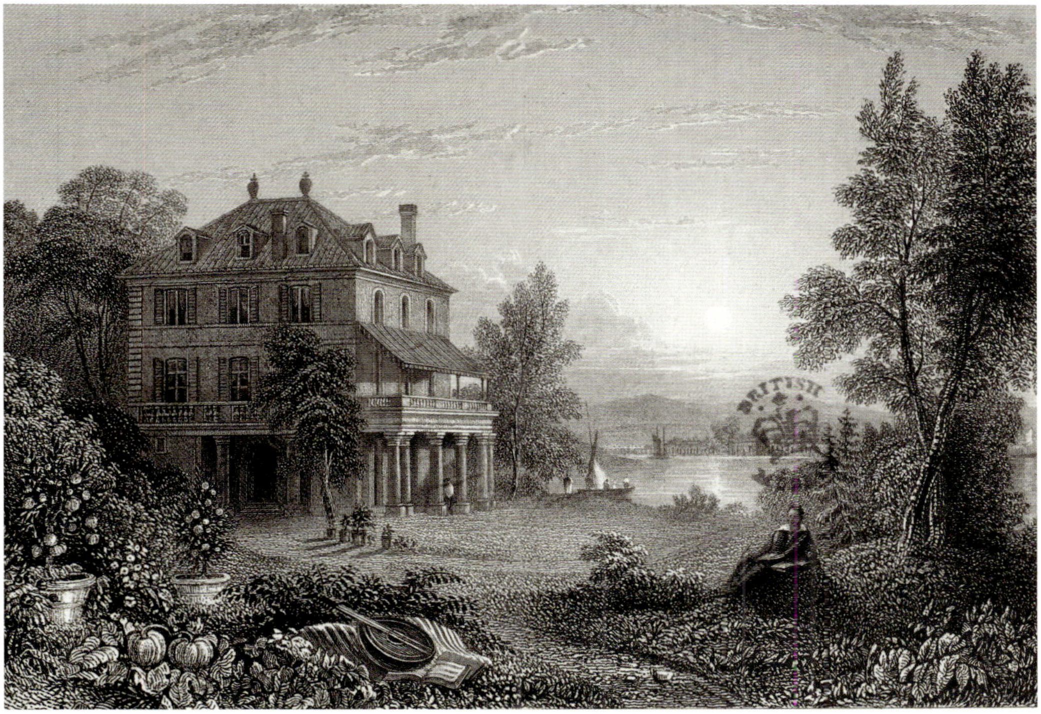

Villa Diodati, engraving from *Finden's Illustrations of the Life and Works of Lord Byron*, 1833.
British Library 841.m.18–20.

Scene of the ghost-story competition that resulted in Mary Shelley's *Frankenstein* and John Polidori's *The Vampyre*.

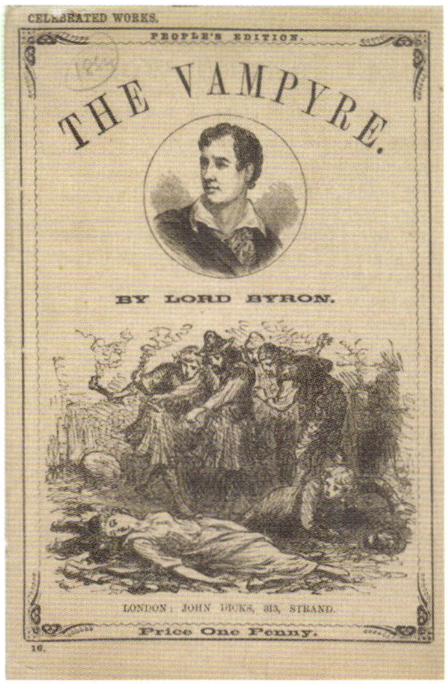

Front cover of an edition of *The Vampyre*, 1884, with the erroneous attribution to Byron still in place.
British Library 12655.b.27.

literary forms; plays, poetry, adaptations, translations and chapbook versions of longer Gothic romances were all consumed as avidly as the original novels. Despite Ann Radcliffe's rejection in *The Italian* of the mode of 'horror' employed by Lewis in *The Monk*, that mode undoubtedly proved as equally fertile to the Gothic imagination as Radcliffe's school of terror did. The Promethean end that Lewis gives to Ambrosio foregrounds torment, dismemberment and punishment quite viscerally, in ways that would later inform Mary Shelley's *Frankenstein: or, The Modern Prometheus* in 1818.

As the story goes, *Frankenstein* was conceived in a competition of ghost story-telling initiated by Lord Byron on the shore of Lake Geneva in the summer of 1816. Participants included Percy Bysshe Shelley, Byron, Mary Shelley and John Polidori, Byron's doctor. Polidori is best known today for his authorship of *The Vampyre*, although when this vampire narrative first appeared in the *New Monthly Magazine* in 1819, it was misattributed to Byron. Despite that, the influence of Polidori's text has been considerable. While it capitalised on a number of earlier British and European sources, it also spawned and galvanised the taste for such important vampire fictions as James Malcolm Rymer's *Varney the Vampire; or, the Feast of Blood* (1845–7), Sheridan Le Fanu's *Carmilla* (1872) and Bram Stoker's *Dracula* (1897) later in the nineteenth century.

Perhaps, though, the afterlife of Mary Shelley's *Frankenstein* has been even more enduring. In a deprecating fashion that we can trace back to Horace Walpole, Percy Bysshe Shelley, in the preface to the 1818 edition of *Frankenstein*, claimed that Mary's tale was conceived primarily for the sake of 'amusement'. And yet the framing narrative, involving the explorer Robert Walton who comes across

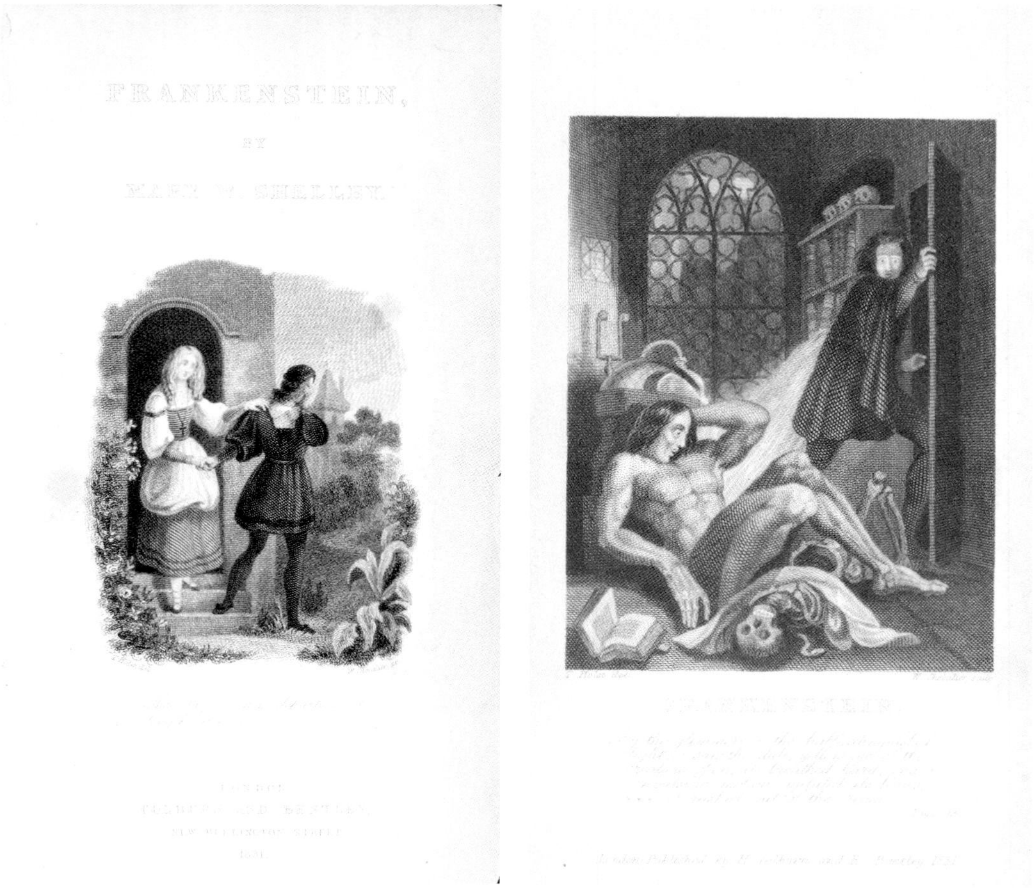

Frontispiece and title page to an edition of *Frankenstein*, 1831.
British Library 1153.a.9. (1).

Victor Frankenstein in the arctic wastes, instantly recalls Coleridge's 'The Rime of the Ancient Mariner' (1798), and invokes the weighty and portentous theme of Promethean transgression in a devastating portrayal of unrealistic ambitions. It paves the way for the inset narrative, recounted and 'augmented' by Victor Frankenstein himself, of how he plunders charnel houses with the aim of creating a new species of human being.

This is a tale of true horror; and yet at its heart lies the extremely eloquent and touching demand from Frankenstein's creation for his master/father to realise his quest for a female companion. This particular part of the narrative bears little, if any relation to what we have come to appreciate as Gothic. The creature tells a story of sympathy, learning, assistance and then rejection, drawing, from among a number of other sources, upon the writings of Jean-Jacques Rousseau, John Locke, John Milton and Plutarch. It reveals to its readers the frailties of a classical education, particularly if fellow human sympathy is found wanting. The creature is unable to persuade Frankenstein to make him a companion, and so sets about wreaking havoc upon its creator and all those whom he loves.

The identity of the 'modern Prometheus', then, seems ultimately to lie with Victor Frankenstein; he, like his mythological namesake, has sought to arrogate to himself a capacity usually reserved for the Divine. But so flexible is the novel's mythic core that it is also entirely possible to read that Promethean figure within the reassembled fragments of the creature's body. Sutured from various human and animal corpses, this is a creature assembled, an inversion of Lewis's Ambrosio's dismembered body. If the nameless creation, reincarnated so frequently ever since upon the silver screen, represents Promethean defiance in its actions, then it also serves as metaphor, in its process of composition and appearance, for the Gothic tradition itself. For a stable 'Gothic' tradition in the late eighteenth and early nineteenth centuries is hard to account for, encompassing as it does prose fiction, poetry, drama, chapbooks, bluebooks and more.

As we have seen, 'Gothic' as a literary form, in fact, began almost accidentally. Horace Walpole's appendage of 'A Gothic Story' to the second edition of *The Castle of Otranto* served, at best, as a patriotic, convenient excuse for creating something so outlandish as a supernatural tale in eighteenth-century enlightened Britain. Between the years of 1764 and 1820, however, that literary 'something' proliferates with such velocity that it comes to be appreciated as 'Gothic'. What then links these works together? 'Terror and Wonder', a composite phrase taken from the titles of Matthew Lewis's *Tales of Wonder* (1800) and the anonymous anthology *Tales of Terror* (1801), are good, supple terms to apply to the Gothic as a genre or literary mode. From its eighteenth-century origins, and even, in some senses, before that, we can view the Gothic as an 'anthology' – a veritable Frankenstein's laboratory – of the forces of terror and wonder. Linked by common but by no means identical themes, the Gothic could ask of its readership, as did John Milton's Adam and Mary Shelley's creature, 'Did I solicit thee / From darkness to promote me?'

Further Reading

Clery, E J 1995. *The Rise of Supernatural Fiction, 1762–1800* (Cambridge: Cambridge University Press). An influential account of the rise of eighteenth-century Gothic fiction that charts the links between fiction, ghostly entertainment and economic change in the period.

Davison, Carol Margaret 2009. *Gothic Literature, 1764–1824* (Cardiff: University of Wales Press). A rigorous account of early Gothic writing, from Horace Walpole onwards, that also provides an interesting overview of contemporary critical approaches to the Gothic.

Gamer, Michael 2000. *Romanticism and the Gothic: Genre, Reception and Canon Formation* (Cambridge: Cambridge University Press). An influential account of the complex relationship between the popular Gothic mode and 'high' Romantic aesthetics.

Townshend, Dale and Angela Wright (eds) 2014. *Ann Radcliffe, Romanticism and the Gothic* (Cambridge: Cambridge University Press). A collection of essays that provides coverage of Ann Radcliffe's entire oeuvre, with a particular focus upon her relationship to mainstream Romanticism.

Wright, Angela 2013. *Britain, France and the Gothic: The Import of Terror, 1764–1820* (Cambridge: Cambridge University Press). An account of the role played by translation in the genesis of early Gothic writing, covering Horace Walpole, Ann Radcliffe, Matthew Lewis and other major authors of the period.

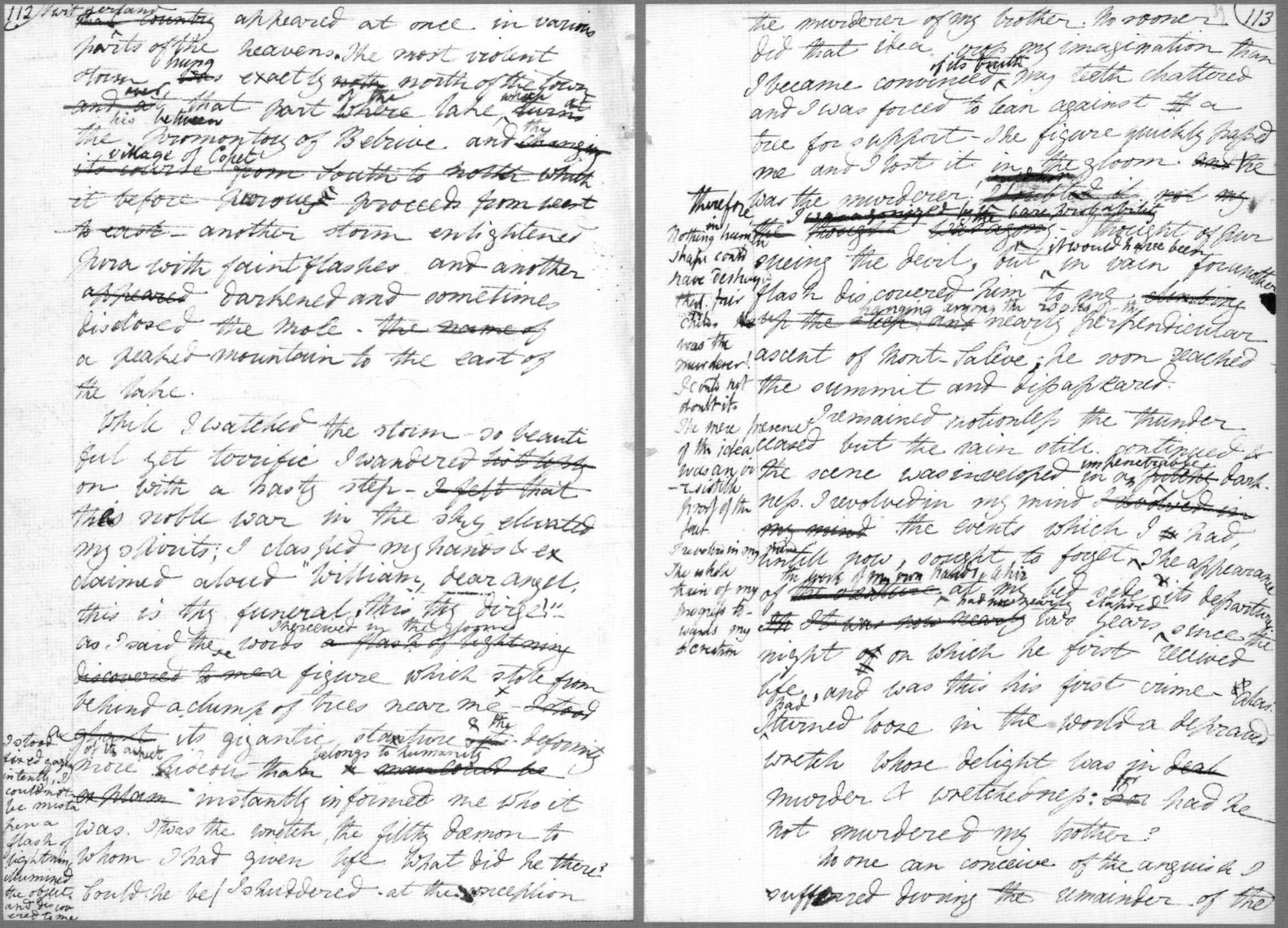

Pages from Mary Shelley's manuscript of *Frankenstein*.

Bodleian Library, Oxford University, MS Abinger C.56 ff.38v-39r.

From the Crypt: *Frankenstein*

The genesis of Mary Shelley's novel *Frankenstein* reads like a Gothic story in itself. In the summer of 1816, Lord Byron, fleeing England to escape the scandal of a failed marriage and allegations of incest, travelled with his physician, John Polidori, to Switzerland, where he took up residence at t he Villa Diodati, near Lake Geneva. The poet Percy Bysshe Shelley, together with the then Mary Godwin (she and Percy married later that year) and Mary's half-sister Claire Clairmont, one of Byron's many lovers, were staying nearby. The two parties met and spent their evenings at the Villa Diodati, reading and telling each other ghost stories by candlelight while thunder and lightning rolled across the lake. They also discussed the latest experiments in medicine and science, including those in which corpses had been made to twitch in a ghastly semblance of life by the application of galvanic batteries. Given this claustrophobic and fervid atmosphere, it seems unsurprising that, when Byron suggested a competition in which each of those present would write a ghost story, Mary Shelley would respond with *Frankenstein*, arguably the most influential Gothic novel ever written.

Frankenstein: or The Modern Prometheus was first published anonymously in 1818, with a preface penned by the author's husband, Percy Bysshe Shelley. When Mary Shelley wrote a preface to a second, revised edition of the novel in 1831, she recalled the nightmare, triggered by events at the Villa Diodati, that inspired the book:

> I saw the pale student of unhallowed arts kneeling beside the thing he had put together. I saw the hideous phantasm of a man stretched out, and then, on the working of some powerful engine, show signs of life, and stir with an uneasy, half-vital motion.

The manuscript of *Frankenstein* provides fascinating insights into the writing of the novel. Shown here are two pages, the text of which eventually became part of Volume I, Chapter 6 of the 1818 edition. Having abandoned his creation, Victor Frankenstein falls ill. When he recovers, he learns that his brother, William, has been murdered. Returning home in despair, Frankenstein finds himself among the mountains while a storm rages and lightning flashes across the lake below. The scene is reminiscent of the setting at the Villa Diodati in the summer of 1816, in which the story had its origins. However, in its evocation of a sublime landscape illuminated by a storm, 'so beautiful yet terrific', the scene also contains echoes of novels by Ann Radcliffe, whose descriptions of awe-inspiring landscapes inspired terror and wonder in fictions such as *The Mysteries of Udolpho* (1794) and *The Italian* (1797).

As Frankenstein continues his journey through the mountains, he glimpses the monster:

> A flash of lightning illuminated the object, and discovered its shape plainly to me; its gigantic stature, and the deformity of its aspect, more hideous than belongs to humanity, instantly informed me that it was the wretch, the filthy daemon to whom I had given life.

Simultaneously, Frankenstein is struck by the revelation that it is his own creation who has murdered his brother William. Throughout the manuscript, Percy Bysshe Shelley has added annotations in the margins, making suggestions to render the narrative more convincing and dramatic. The text in the margin of the right-hand page seen here is in Percy's hand, and provides the rationale for Frankenstein's sudden insight into the murderous intentions of the creature to which he has given life.

GREG BUZWELL

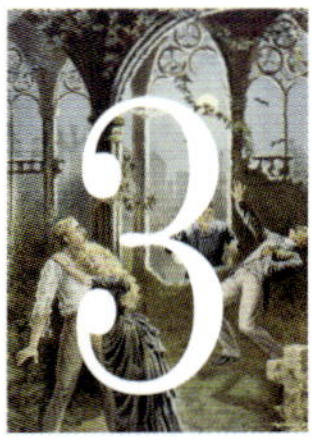

ALEXANDRA WARWICK

Gothic, 1820–1880

OPPOSITE:
Poster for the play *Manhood*, performed at the Elephant and Castle Theatre in July 1890.
British Library, Evanion 248.

A Tale of Two Abbeys

In the late 1790s work began on two abbeys, both of which were to take more than a decade to complete and both of which mark, in their different ways, one of the many 'ends' of Gothic. Jane Austen began writing *Northanger Abbey* in about 1798 and worked on it until her death in 1817. It was published in late 1817, but dated 1818 on its title page. William Beckford started work on the building of Fonthill Abbey, Wiltshire, in 1796, and continued, despite a number of setbacks, until it was announced to be complete in 1822. In the same year Beckford's debts obliged him to sell the house, and in 1825 the 300ft tower collapsed for the third and final time. Northanger and Fonthill can be seen as closing brackets that mirror another house–novel pairing, Horace Walpole's *The Castle of Otranto* (1764) and his home Strawberry Hill (completed 1776), that signals the Gothic Revival of the late eighteenth century.

Austen's novel comprehensively satirises the Gothic style. Despite the desire of the heroine, Catherine Morland, to experience the sublime views and delicious terrors of the abbey she encounters, she enters having been hardly able to notice its exterior and 'without feeling one awful foreboding of future misery to herself, or one moment's suspicion of any past scenes of horror being acted within the solemn edifice. The breeze had not seemed to waft the sighs of the murdered to her; it had wafted nothing but a thick mizzling rain' (1995: 141). The rain (thoroughly undramatic in its 'mizzling') throws cold water on the overheated passions of the reader of 'Castle of Wolfenbach, Clermont, Mysterious Warnings, Necromancer of

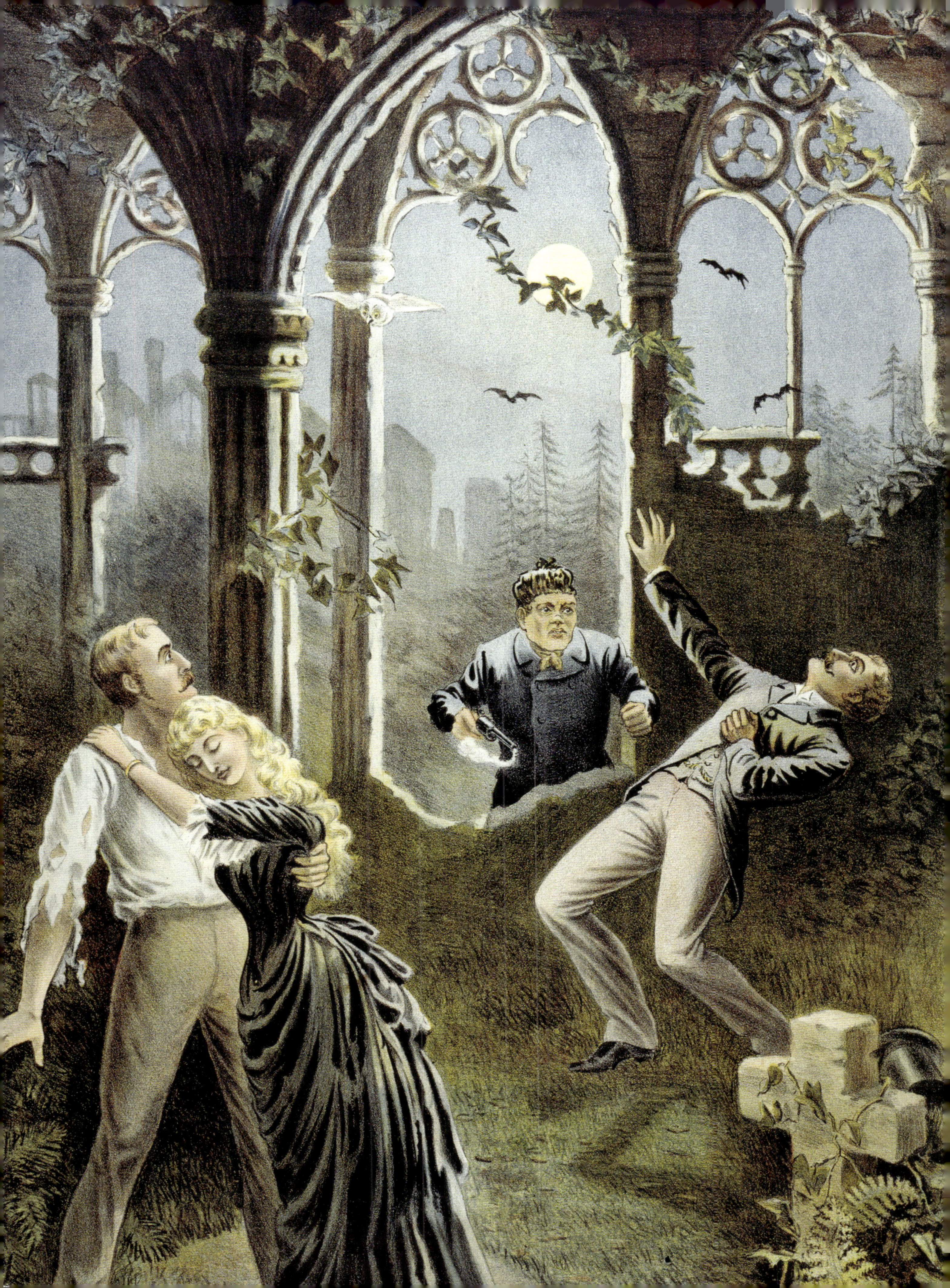

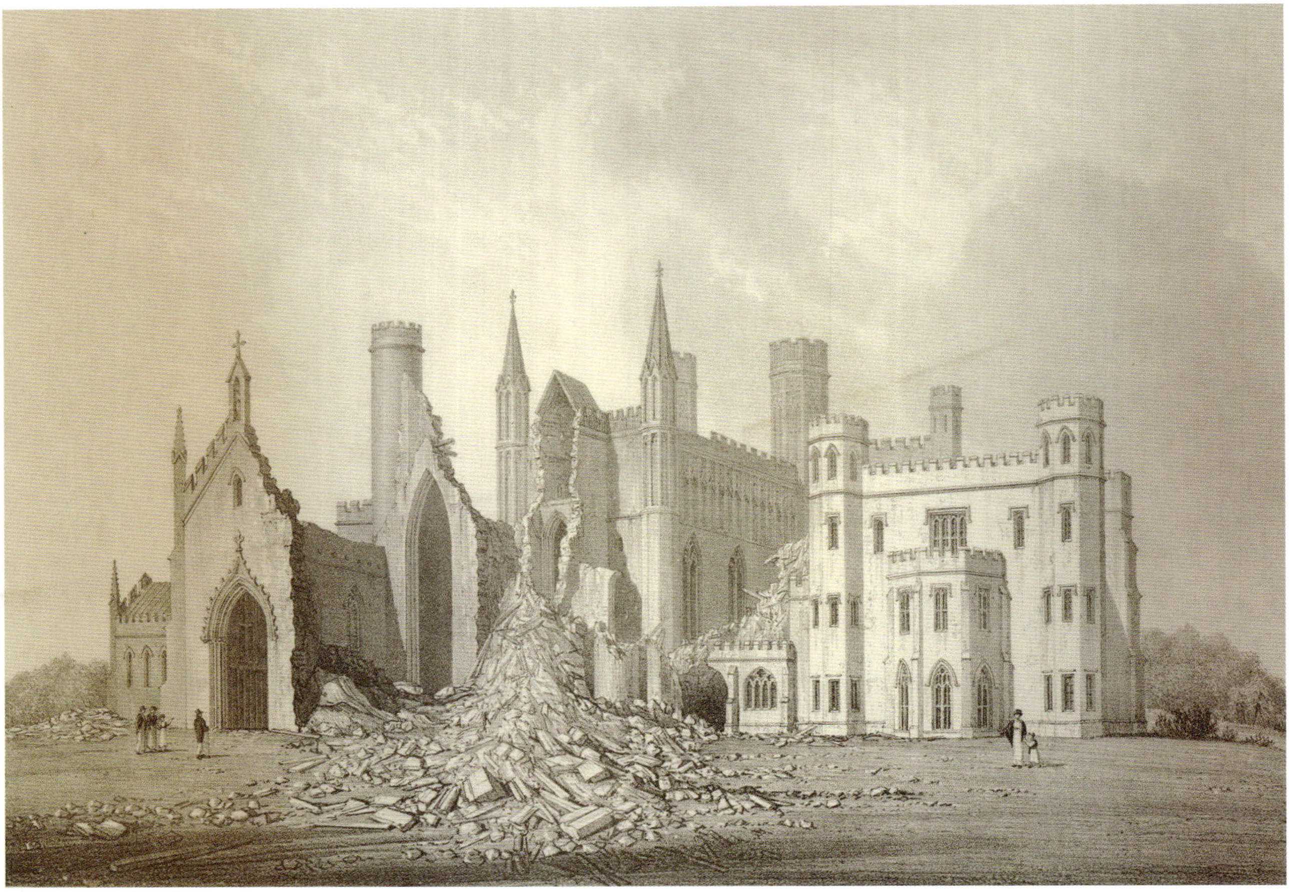

Fonthill Abbey in ruins.
British Museum.

the Black Forest, Midnight Bell, Orphan of the Rhine, and Horrid Mysteries' (1995: 37). Catherine comes to realise that true feeling comes from rational contemplation of the world as it is, rather than from the delusionary thrills encouraged by 'horrid' novels.

The tale of Fonthill is altogether darker. Built on the ruins of the family home destroyed by fire, it was begun by Beckford only on his return from a long exile necessitated by homosexual scandal. Beckford's wife had died in childbirth during his exile, and he lived alone (except for numerous servants) in the dozens of rooms of Fonthill. His fortune derived from sugar plantations in Jamaica, but their declining profitability, combined with the vast sums spent on the house, meant that Beckford fell into debt and put the abbey and its contents up for sale. It was bought by another man grown rich on the profits of blood, the arms manufacturer John Farquhar, but lasted only another three years. Although parts of Fonthill had collapsed several times during its building, the fall of the tower in 1825 proved to be its end; the ruin was never inhabited again.

The tale of these two abbeys illuminates what might be thought of as the first 'end' of Gothic. The peak moment of Gothic literary production had been reached in the 1790s, when it has been estimated that more than a third of literary output was Gothic in style (Miles 2002: 42). Many of the notable writers from the earlier tradition too were gone: Walpole had died in 1797, Clara Reeve in

1807, Matthew Lewis in 1818, Ann Radcliffe in 1823, Charles Maturin in 1824 and the painter Henry Fuseli in 1825. Austen's satire speaks of the comic over-familiarity of the tropes of the 'horrid' novel, and it is hard not to see Fonthill's collapse as emblematic of the unsustainability of the Gothic pastiche of the eighteenth century: expanded and elaborated as gestural decoration without any adequate material or theoretical support, and finally collapsing under the sheer weight of quotation.

This analogy points to another important aspect of nineteenth-century Gothic: the presence of architecture. If, as Andrew Smith elaborates in the following essay, thinking about the Victorian *fin de siècle* requires us to think about bodies, then Gothic between 1820 and 1880 requires us to think about buildings. However, these buildings are not the feudal castles or religious foundations of *Otranto* or *The Monk*, but rather the material fabric of the here and now: the contemporary built environment.

The Napoleonic Wars had ended in 1815, bringing to a close the long period of conflicts arising from the French Revolution of 1789. The end of the wars saw the states and nations of Europe reconfigured and the balance of European influence in other parts of the globe changed. Europe was opened up to travel again, as were the routes through it to further afield; an expanded Grand Tour was made possible for those with the money and leisure to undertake it. Military requirements had pushed forward some of the early industrial innovation of the late eighteenth century, and the defeat of the French meant that Britain had both a large navy and a colonial network that could be turned to facilitate trade. And in Britain it was clear by the 1820s that the Industrial Revolution constituted a permanent change, as traditions and practices that had remained almost unaltered in the preceding centuries were passing away. As the rural landscape changed so too did the towns and cities, shifting in turn the structures of human society.

Thomas Carlyle described the situation in 1829:

> Were we required to characterise this age of ours by any single epithet, we should be tempted to call it, not an Heroical, Devotional, Philosophical, or Moral Age, but, above all others, the Mechanical Age. It is the Age of Machinery, in every outward and inward sense of that word. (1829: 441–2)

Carlyle notes the passing of older forms of thought associated with the medieval, chivalric and contemplative past and the substitution both of modern industrial practices and a changed mental and social organisation. He also demonstrates a self-consciousness about the present that was to become characteristic of the Victorian age. The Victorians were intensely aware that they were living in a new age, and they expended much energy in thinking about the nature of the 'present' that they occupied. This also entailed reflection upon the past and its relationship to that present. The Victorians inherited an older antiquarianism, manifested in cabinets of curiosities and idiosyncratic private collections, many of which came to form the basis of the great museums that opened during the course of the century.

In fiction we can recognise a similar current of the systematising of curiosity about the past into forms of knowledge. Walter Scott, during his long career from the 1790s to 1832, invented the modern historical novel, giving purpose to the choices of his settings rather than selecting merely picturesque periods or locations. Like Walpole and Beckford, Scott too constructed a fantasy home, Abbotsford, in the Scottish Borders, which housed collections of historical objects and included actual pieces of the past embedded in its fabric, in the form of stones and features from old Scottish

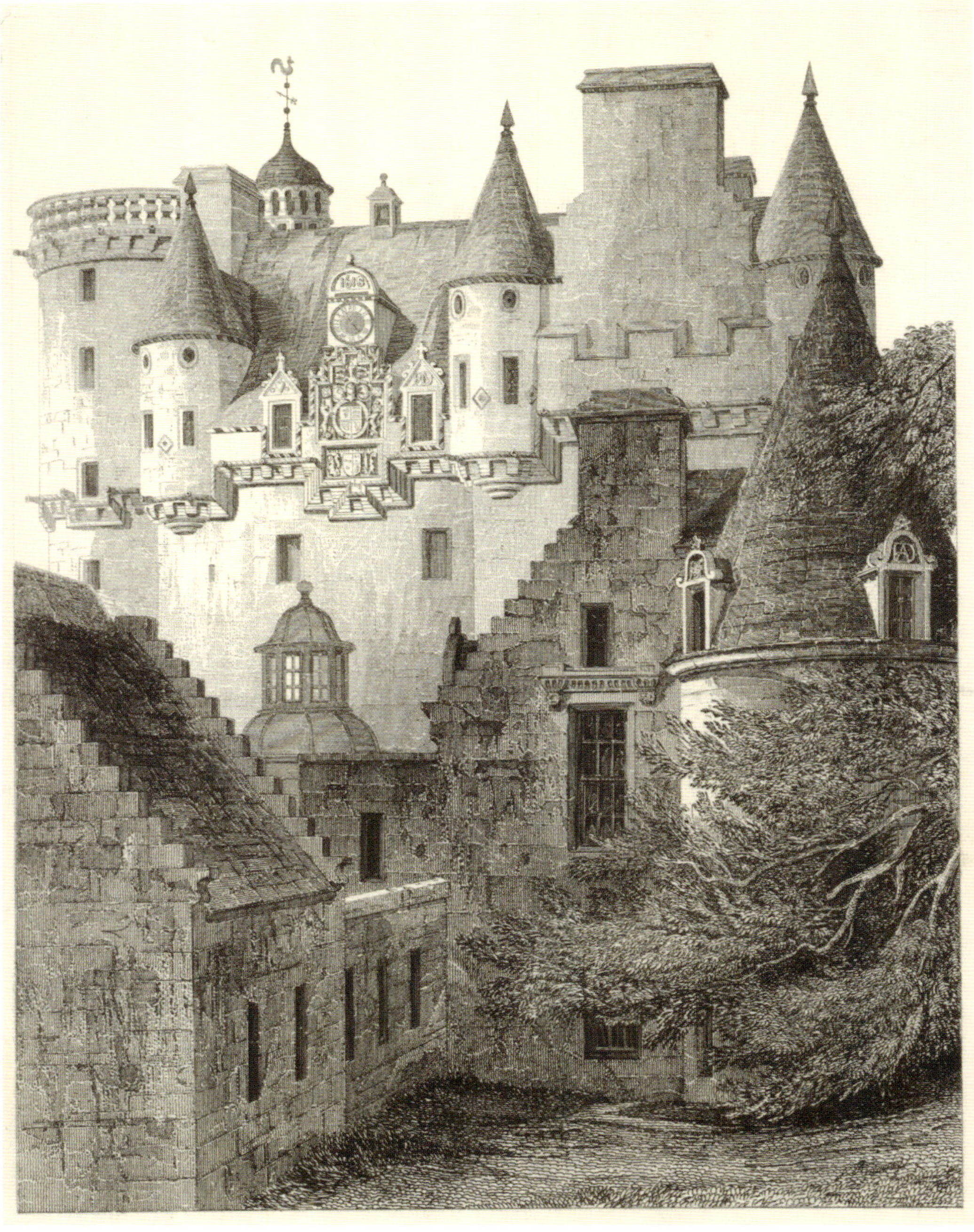

Walter Scott's Abbotsford, print after Robert William Billings, *c.* 1849.
British Museum.

castles and abbeys. The historical novel and the Gothic novel develop alongside each other, each differently using the past to speak about its complex relationship to the present. Yet whereas in the historical novel the past is shown to be continuous with the present, and a crucial means of understanding modern national consciousness, the past in Gothic returns as destructive nightmare.

Changing Times

The sense of time beyond written history was also changing. The publication of Charles Lyell's capacious work *The Principles of Geology* (1830–3) aimed to consolidate the study of geology as a proper scientific discipline, based on empirical observation of cause and effect. However, it also opened up 'deep time' in its suggestion that observation of existing conditions must lead the observer to conclude that the age of the earth is vastly greater than previously believed. Although positioned as a manifesto for the establishment of a systematic science, *The Principles of Geology*, like so many nineteenth-century scientific texts, contains lyrical passages that owe more to fictional forms than to philosophy. In Lyell, a group of chapters is headed 'How the Remains of Man and his Works are Becoming Fossil beneath the Waters' and becomes a meditation on the passing of time that would not be out of place in one of the so-called Graveyard poets of the eighteenth century. As well as seeing the ruins of the past, he imagines how 'many edifices of human workmanship, and the skeletons of men, and casts of the human form, will continue to exist when a great part of the present mountains, continents and seas have disappeared' (1997: 332). From a geological perspective, deep time reveals the present to be a precarious moment, existing on the ruins of the past and poised to become the ruins of the future.

If the collapse of Fonthill and the undermining of the foundations of the Gothic novel in *Northanger Abbey* represent an end of sorts, it is the end of a particular version of the past. The shift that takes place between the 1820s and 1840s is one in which Gothic becomes less visible in its conventional forms, but appears again, not so obviously and not separated by a clear generic boundary, with its tropes now embedded in the most contemporary forms of fictional and material expression. Much cultural production in the Victorian period is concerned with representing the present, confronting and negotiating the modern world in all its frenetic chaos. The Gothic mode, characteristically drawn to the contemplation of the past, would at first glance seem to be at odds with modernity. Yet just as the Gothic of the eighteenth century does not arise in opposition to, or reaction against, the dominant philosophies of the period, but actually from the heart of those philosophies, so too does nineteenth-century Gothic emerge from the very conditions of the time. It is not a simple 'other' to the Victorian culture in which it circulated, but a more complex expression of the material and mental conditions of the new world.

Although the real terrors of the aftermath of the French Revolution and the turbulence of the Napoleonic Wars were over by the 1820s, the third and fourth decades of the nineteenth century were by no means a politically or socially settled time. Fear of radicalism remained, but the reactionary politics of the turn of the century were giving way to reform. For example, the Roman Catholic Relief Act of 1829, the Slavery Abolition Act of 1833, the Representation of the People Act of 1832 (more usually called the Reform Act) were all, in their different ways, recognitions of the inappropriateness of the continuation of past practices and ideas in the modern world. There were also numerous attempts to comprehend the emerging 'Condition of England' through commissions of enquiry into such issues as factory conditions and child labour, and later into education, housing, health and sanitation.

Despite these efforts to cast off the past or to illuminate the present, the effect is often a Gothic one, in which the shadows become darker and more mysterious as the light that is shone on the subject grows brighter. Legal change does not make Catholicism or race disappear as locations of anxiety, but the expressions of those anxieties become more convoluted and more strange. Likewise, the constitution of the working classes as a new 'problem' requiring investigation does not produce understanding, but rather renders them separate, alien, mysteriously different in all their habits, practices and beliefs. If the Reform Act was meant in some measure to bring the light of parliamentary democracy to previously unrepresented cities such as Manchester, its shadow, the Poor Law Amendment Act of 1834, is instrumental in producing a new urban darkness. As the Reform Act goes some way to creating a middle class, the Poor Law Amendment Act plays a crucial part in creating an underclass of the poor. The representation of that underclass and its environment becomes one of the principal ways in which Gothic reappears in the Victorian period.

Mrs Lovatt's pie shop. Illustration from *The String of Pearls; or, The Barber of Fleet Street* by James Malcolm Rymer, 1850.
British Library C.140.d.6.

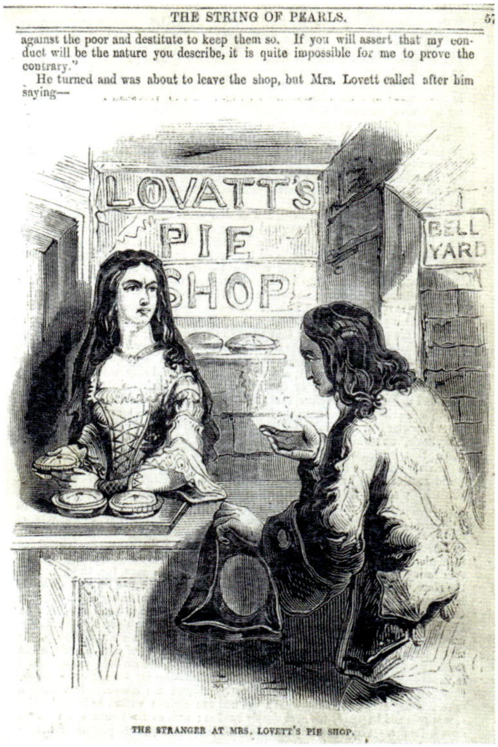
THE STRING OF PEARLS.

against the poor and destitute to keep them so. If you will assert that my conduct will be the nature you describe, it is quite impossible for me to prove the contrary."

He turned and was about to leave the shop, but Mrs. Lovett called after him saying—

THE STRANGER AT MRS. LOVETT'S PIE SHOP.

Poverty and the Gothic City

Throughout the eighteenth century social and technological changes had brought about an expansion in cheap printed material. As well as newspapers and political pamphlets, the age witnessed a mass of popular 'street literature' – dramatic ephemera such as the highly coloured accounts of criminals' careers that were sold at their executions. Such semi-fictional prose forms were among those that contributed to the emergence of the novel, thence to the Gothic novel, and a direct legacy can be traced into the 'penny dreadfuls' of the nineteenth century. Although the monthly instalments of novels by writers such as Charles Dickens were much cheaper than a whole volume (they cost about a shilling, or twelve old pence), the penny dreadfuls, as their nickname suggests, cost even less. Thousands of titles were published in this form, many of them highly successful and with a wider readership than their ostensible working-class audience.

Many of the figures that become part of a familiar Gothic landscape originate in the penny-bloods of the nineteenth century: Sweeney Todd, for example, the murderous barber and supplier of human flesh for pie production, first appears in the series 'The String of Pearls' that ran from 1846 to 1847. The series was the work of James Rymer and Thomas Prest, both prolific hack writers in the period. Rymer was also probably the author of *Varney, the Vampire* (1845–7), a florid elaboration of the vampire figure over some 220 chapters. Tremendously successful, it was also adapted for the stage, and it is important to remember that for the Victorians 'their' vampire was not Bram Stoker's Count Dracula (published in 1897), but the rather different figure of Sir Francis Varney.

Perhaps the most influential of the penny dreadfuls, however, was G W M Reynolds's serial *The Mysteries of London*, published in weekly penny instalments from 1844. It was immediately popular, selling some 40,000 copies a week, and its sequel, *The Mysteries of the Court of London*, started in 1845, continuing on and off with different writers through to 1856. Reynolds's work was heavily influenced by Eugène Sue's *Les Mystères de Paris* (1842–3), but it was only the first of many imitators in the 'city mysteries' genre, with versions appearing that depicted, among others, New York, Boston, Lisbon, St Petersburg, Munich and Naples. City mysteries presented the

BELOW LEFT:
Page from *Varney, the Vampyre; or, the Feast of Blood* by James Malcolm Rymer, 1845–7.
British Library C.193.a.26.

BELOW:
Page from George W M Reynolds, *The Mysteries of London*, 1846–50.
British Library 1456.i.23–25.

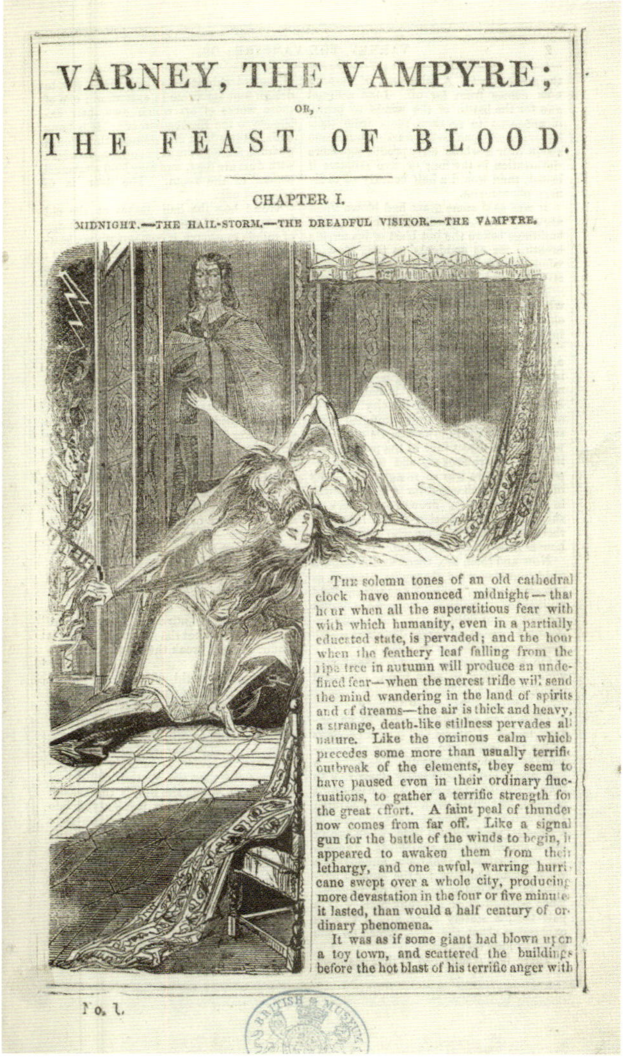

VARNEY, THE VAMPYRE;
OR,
THE FEAST OF BLOOD.

CHAPTER I.
MIDNIGHT.—THE HAIL-STORM.—THE DREADFUL VISITOR.—THE VAMPYRE.

The solemn tones of an old cathedral clock have announced midnight—that hour when all the superstitious fear with with which humanity, even in a partially educated state, is pervaded; and the hour when the feathery leaf falling from the ripe tree in autumn will produce an undefined fear—when the merest trifle will send the mind wandering in the land of spirits and of dreams—the air is thick and heavy, a strange, death-like stillness pervades all nature. Like the ominous calm which precedes some more than usually terrific outbreak of the elements, they seem to have paused even in their ordinary fluctuations, to gather a terrific strength for the great effort. A faint peal of thunder now comes from far off. Like a signal gun for the battle of the winds to begin, it appeared to awaken them from their lethargy, and one awful, warring hurricane swept over a whole city, producing more devastation in the four or five minutes it lasted, than would a half century of ordinary phenomena.

It was as if some giant had blown upon a toy town, and scattered the buildings before the hot blast of his terrific anger with

No. 1.

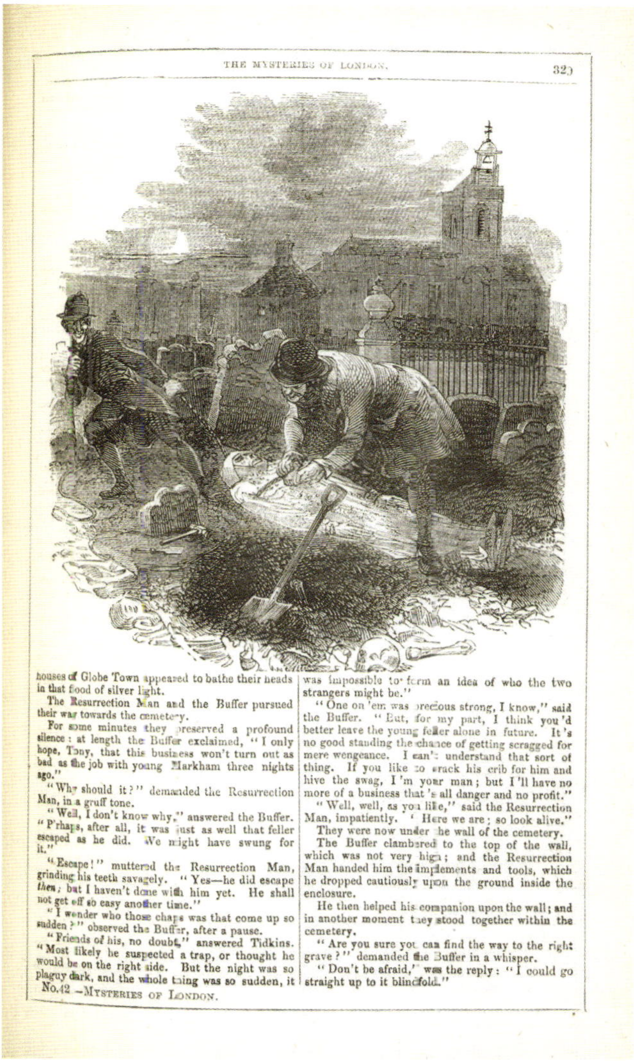

THE MYSTERIES OF LONDON.

houses of Globe Town appeared to bathe their heads in that flood of silver light.

The Resurrection Man and the Buffer pursued their way towards the cemetery.

For some minutes they preserved a profound silence: at length the Buffer exclaimed, "I only hope, Tony, that this business won't turn out as bad as the job with young Markham three nights ago."

"Why should it?" demanded the Resurrection Man, in a gruff tone.

"Well, I don't know why," answered the Buffer. "P'rhaps, after all, it was just as well that feller escaped as he did. We might have swung for it."

"Escape!" muttered the Resurrection Man, grinding his teeth savagely. "Yes—he did escape *then*; but I haven't done with him yet. He shall not get off so easy another time."

"I wonder who those chaps was that come up so sudden?" observed the Buffer, after a pause.

"Friends of his, no doubt," answered Tidkins. "Most likely he suspected a trap, or thought he would be on the right side. But the night was so plaguy dark, and the whole thing was so sudden, it was impossible to form an idea of who the two strangers might be."

"One on 'em was precious strong, I know," said the Buffer. "But, for my part, I think you'd better leave the young feller alone in future. It's no good standing the chance of getting scragged for mere wengeance. I can't understand that sort of thing. If you like to crack his crib for him and hive the swag, I'm your man; but I'll have no more of a business that's all danger and no profit."

"Well, well, as you like," said the Resurrection Man, impatiently. "Here we are; so look alive."

They were now under the wall of the cemetery.

The Buffer clambered to the top of the wall, which was not very high; and the Resurrection Man handed him the implements and tools, which he dropped cautiously upon the ground inside the enclosure.

He then helped his companion upon the wall; and in another moment they stood together within the cemetery.

"Are you sure you can find the way to the right grave?" demanded the Buffer in a whisper.

"Don't be afraid," was the reply: "I could go straight up to it blindfold."

No. 42.—MYSTERIES OF LONDON.

modern urban experience as dark and dangerous, particularly through, as Gertrude Himmelfarb phrases it, 'Gothicizing poverty, making it seem barbarous, grotesque, macabre' (1984: 452). Sue's text opens 'on a cold and rainy night, towards the end of October 1838' with a man darting into 'that labyrinth of obscure, narrow and winding streets which extends from the Palais de Justice to Notre Dame' and which is 'the lurking-place [...] of a vast number of the very dregs of society in Paris'. It is dirty and smelly, filled with 'black slush' and monstrous inhabitants (1845: 1–2). The date and place are crucial: this horror is happening in the present and in a dark urban labyrinth that lies between the twin pillars of church and state.

Reynolds begins in an almost identical manner:

> Our narrative opens at the commencement of July, 1831. The night was dark and stormy [...] Accident conducted the interesting young stranger into that labyrinth of narrow and dirty streets which lies in the immediate vicinity of the north-western angle of Smithfield-market [...] He was evidently shocked at the idea that human beings could dwell in such fetid and unwholesome dens; for he gazed with wonder, disgust, and alarm upon the houses on either side. It seemed as if he had never beheld till now a labyrinth of dwellings whose very aspect appeared to speak of hideous poverty and fearful crime. (2013)

The scene is lit only by some dim lamps and flashes of lightning, and as the man goes in through a door he finds himself:

> ...in a room entirely empty; but in the middle of the floor – only three feet from the spot where he stood – there was a large square of jet blackness [...] He was alone – in an uninhabited house, in the midst of a horrible neighbourhood; and all the fearful tales of midnight murders which he had ever heard or read, rushed to his memory; then, by a strange but natural freak of the fancy, those appalling deeds of blood and crime were suddenly associated with that incomprehensible but ominous black square upon the floor. (2013)

The Gothic is now firmly located in urban squalor. It is no longer set in the isolated feudal castles or lofty abbeys of medieval Europe, but in the present of the populous modern city. The crimes – murders, sexual violence, illegitimate births and robberies – are much the same as they are in the eighteenth-century Gothic, and their structural implications are similar, especially the ways in which the consequences of the crimes tangle the characters together. The illustrations that accompanied the text of the penny dreadfuls were also important in establishing a visual vocabulary of the urban environment. Such figuration of the city and its underclass intensifies throughout the century, gathering further associations in post-Darwinian thinking about issues of degeneration, race and empire. Their very full flowering appears in the fictions of

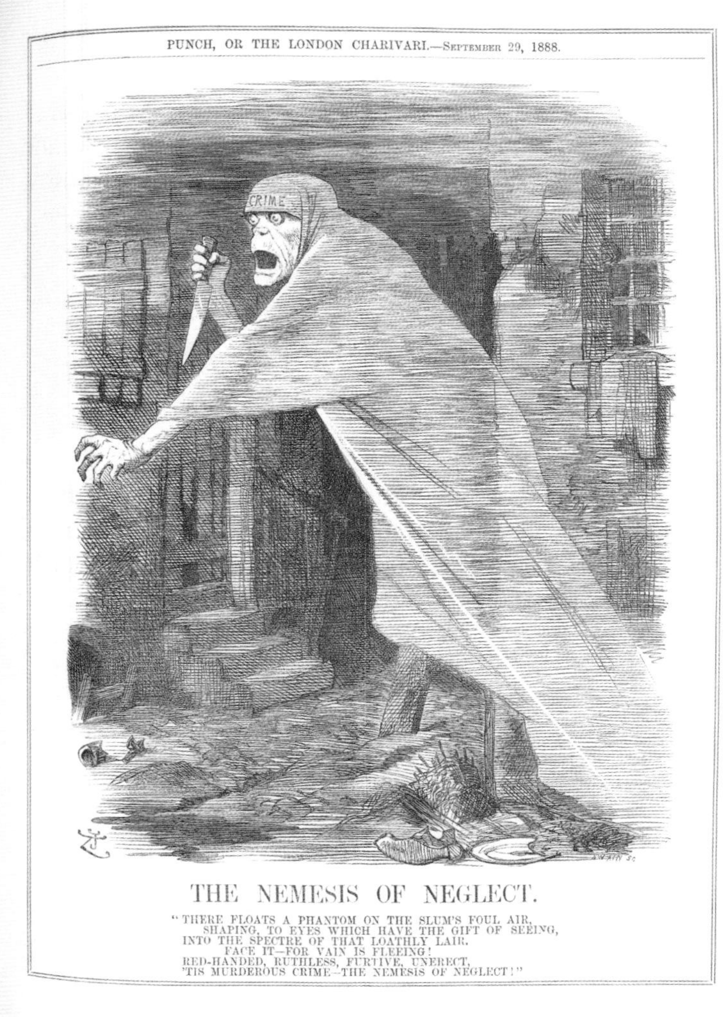

'The Nemesis of Neglect', cartoon from *Punch*, 29 September 1888.

John Tenniel's illustration explicitly linked crime with poverty. The Jack the Ripper murders were at their peak when the cartoon appeared.

the *fin de siècle* and the Gothic responses to real events, such as the Whitechapel murders of 1888.

Paradoxically it is one of the people most publicly opposed to this Gothicising of the real poor who contributes most to the representation of the city, especially London, in enduringly Gothic fashion: Charles Dickens. The plots of his novels thicken with characters and sub-plots, producing a sense of London as a dense web in which all, from the highest in society to the lowest, are connected by hidden acts and secrets. However much the fabric of the city seemed to be designed to separate the classes from one another in the construction of the railways, the omnibus routes, new housing and grand public buildings, the connections between them draw ever tighter, making the webs of Dickensian interconnectedness ever more inescapable. There is a transition in form and content in his work from *The Pickwick Papers* (1836–7), which is essentially picaresque in the eighteenth-century mode, through the progressively darkening visions of *Oliver Twist* (1837–8) to *Bleak House* (1852–3) and *Our Mutual Friend* (1864–5). *Oliver Twist,* written partly in protest at the human consequences of the Poor Law Amendment

Illustration by F W Pailthorpe for an edition of Charles Dickens, *Oliver Twist*, 1885.
British Library Dex. 312.

Oliver Twist contains many moments of horror, none more dramatic than the fatal encounter between Sikes and Nancy.

OPPOSITE:
Poster for a theatrical production of Charles Dickens's *A Christmas Carol*.
British Library Dexter 316 vol.2.

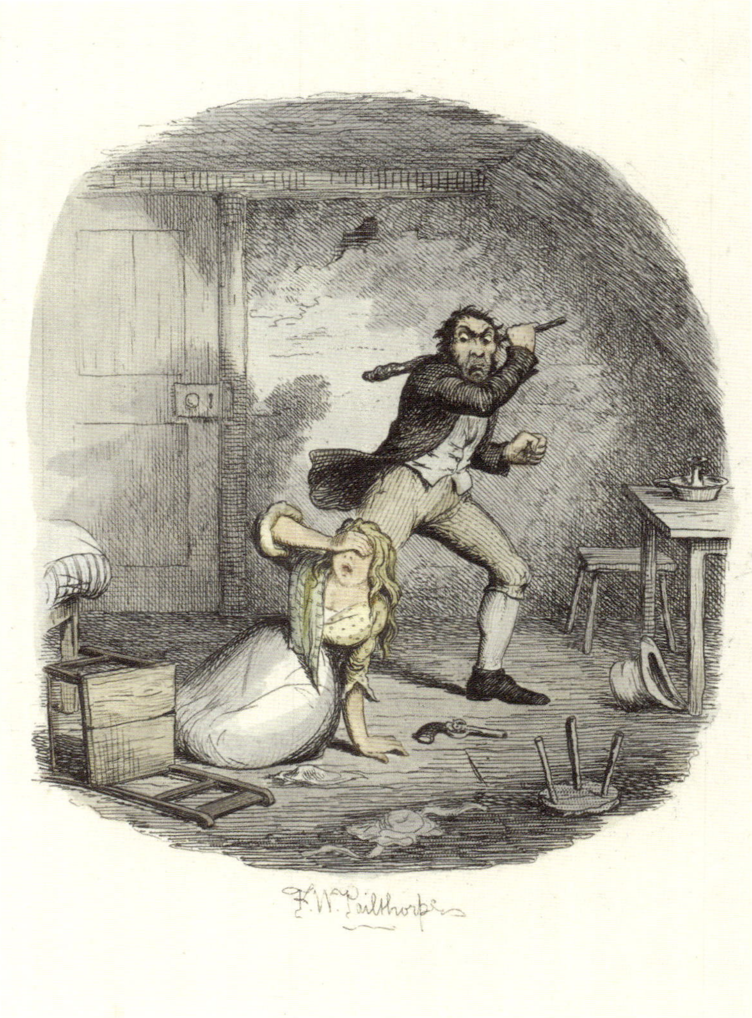

Act, nevertheless consolidates a vision of the city as undermined by crime. London is not the possession of the naïve heroes and heroines; it rather belongs to the criminal and the grotesque, and indeed actively seems to facilitate them. Fagin and his gang move easily and invisibly through the streets that impede Oliver and Mr Brownlow. Nancy, the prostitute, can go where the respectable Rose Maylie cannot.

Bleak House is the most complex of Dickens's urban fictions. It opens with just a single word, 'London', followed by a tumbling of images of history, pre-history, law, geology, thermodynamics and finance in which the city is situated simultaneously in the past, after the biblical Flood, and in the far future, after the death of the sun. The whole is covered in accumulating mud, as though it were one of the ancient cities being excavated by contemporary archaeologists, but the mud is also the metaphor of modern economics, 'accumulating at compound interest' (2003: 13).

This strange double vision of London, bursting with life yet simultaneously dead and buried, is characteristic of Dickens's writing, and there is often a similarly odd distribution of energy

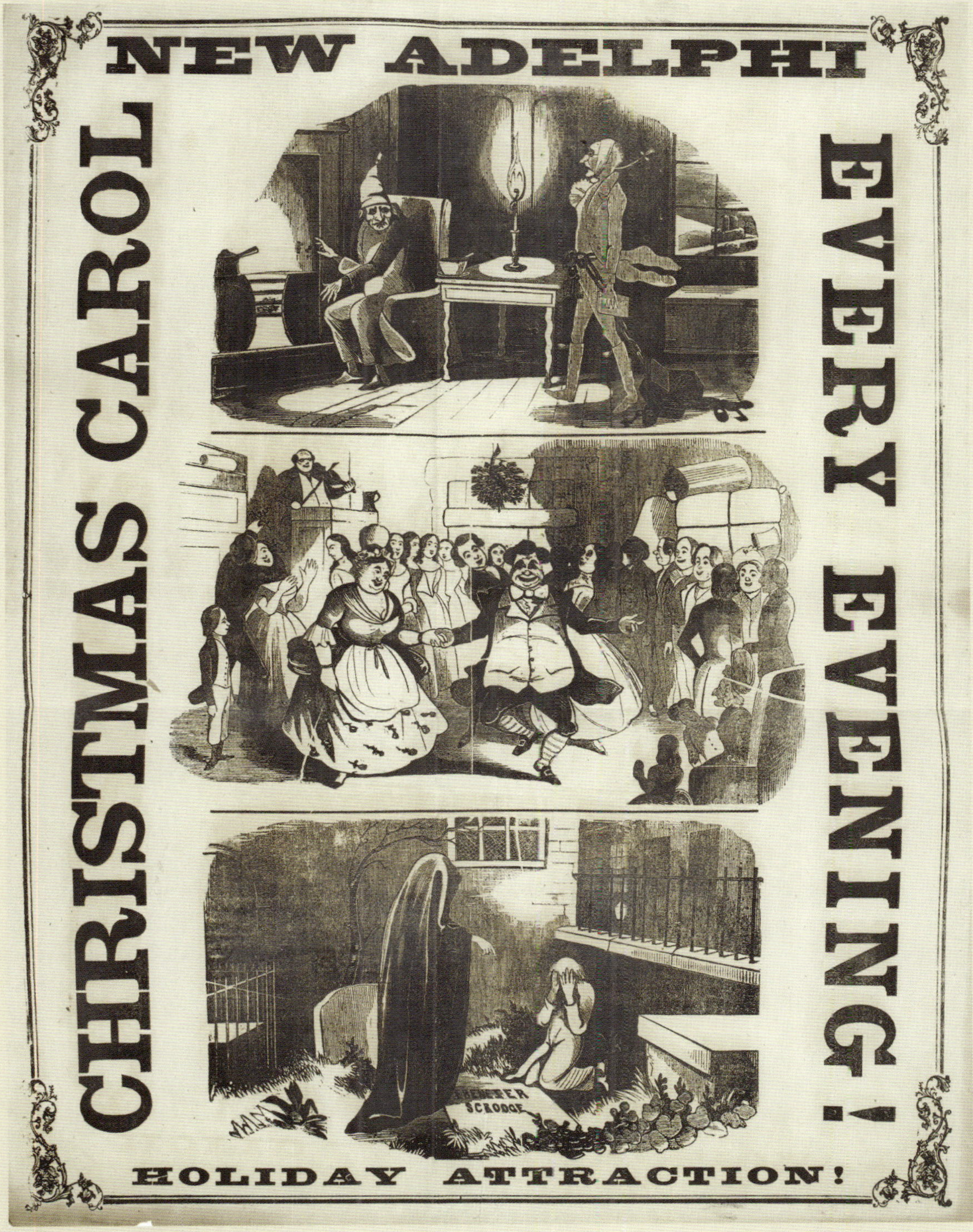
NEW ADELPHI
CHRISTMAS CAROL
EVERY EVENING!
HOLIDAY ATTRACTION!

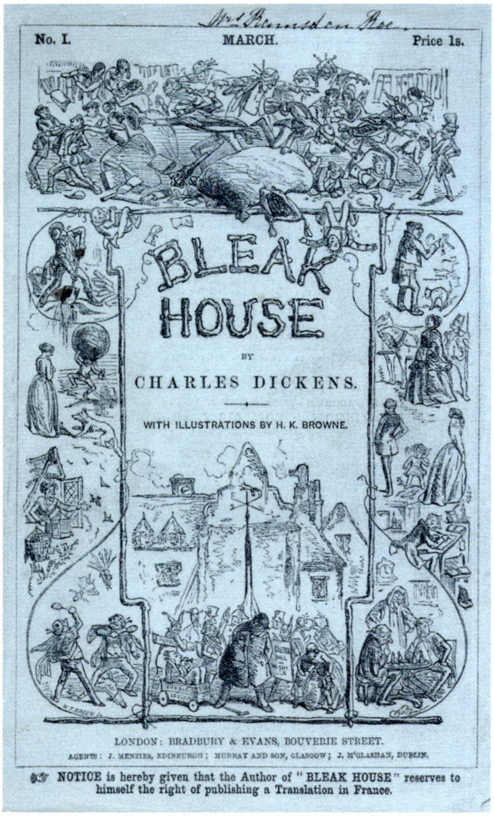

Front cover of the first issue of Charles Dickens, *Bleak House*, March 1852.
British Library Dex 287.

Engraving by Gustave Doré from *London: A Pilgrimage*, 1872.
British Library WF1/1856.
Wentworth Street, Whitechapel, as depicted by Gustave Doré. London's run-down urban landscapes provided popular settings for Victorian Gothic novels.

across the living and the dead, across animate and inanimate objects. Many of Dickens's ghosts are lively and talkative; those in *A Christmas Carol* (1843), for instance, contrast with the shrivelled, life-in-death existence of Scrooge. Similarly, Mr Venus's shop in *Our Mutual Friend* contains articulated bones, stuffed animals and pickled specimens that are as vivacious as their grotesque human visitors. Miss Havisham is only the most obvious of Dickens's living/dead characters; grotesque figures abound in all the novels. The physically and morally deformed Daniel Quilp in *The Old Curiosity Shop* acknowledges himself to be 'a little hunchy villain and a monster' (2000: 46), but he moves as fluidly and quickly about the city as Fagin's gang. The original illustrations of scenes such as Mr Venus's shop (by Marcus Stone), the Ghost's Walk in *Bleak House* (by 'Phiz' or Hablot Browne) or the ghosts in *A Christmas Carol* (by John Leech) were, like those from the penny dreadfuls, significant in the visualising of Gothic; new printing techniques of etching and engraving lent themselves to stark contrasts of black and white, and to the use of cross-hatched shadows. The dense lines of the illustrations seem perfectly matched to the webs of the plots and to the complex conditions of the city itself.

The Living and the Dead

The modern city produces another Gothic problem, this one not confined to the poor, but resting in the recognition that a very high proportion of London's inhabitants were, in fact, dead. The dead are a particularly awkward category in the 1820s and 1830s. As the cities expanded and housing stock became insufficient to the booming population, so graveyards too became horrifically inadequate in accommodating the capital's late citizens. New urban churches had no room for burial grounds, and in the old church graveyards graves were placed on top of one another, with the newest eventually so close to the surface that coffins often re-emerged in bad weather. Vaults under churches were so full that the noxious and flammable gases produced in the decomposition of corpses presented serious hazards to health. The civil engineering works that tore through the city often cut through old burial places, such as plague pits from the sixteenth and seventeenth centuries, although the modern population was much more at risk from the contamination of water supplies by putrefying recent corpses than it was from the ghosts of the plague.

One of the central places in *Bleak House* (which is set in the late 1820s) is the city graveyard where 'Nemo' is buried, described as 'a hemmed-in churchyard, pestiferous and obscene' (2003: 180); it is here that his erstwhile lover, Lady Dedlock, later dies on his grave. One of the novel's secrets, the true parentage of Esther Summerson, is figuratively buried there, and the unfolding of the plot brings about its exhumation. Dickens also takes the 'reeking' graveyard, positioned 'with every villainy of life in action close on death, and every poisonous element of death in action close on life', as the emblem of the shame of social injustice, a manifestation of how 'civilization and barbarism walked this boastful island together'

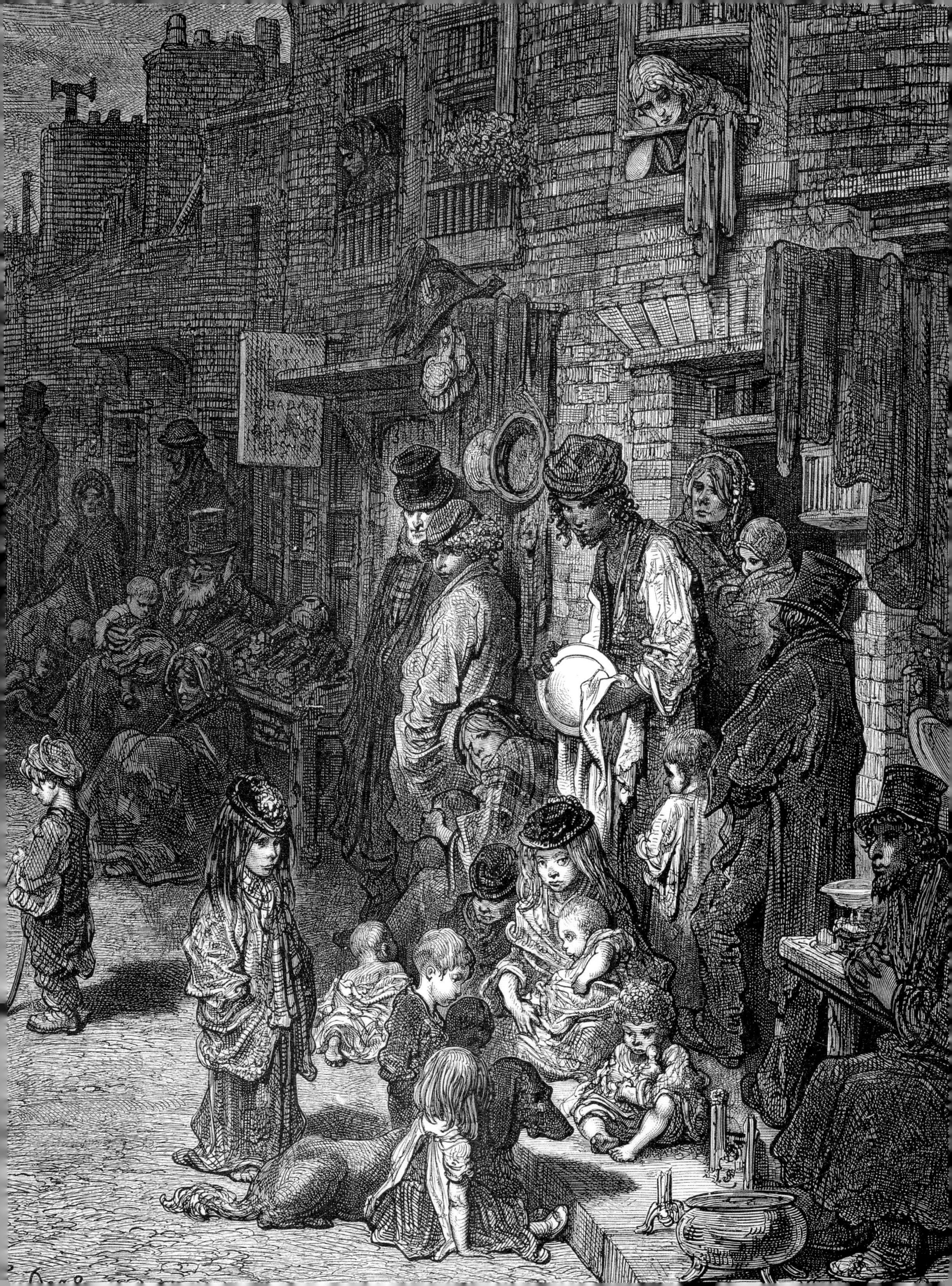

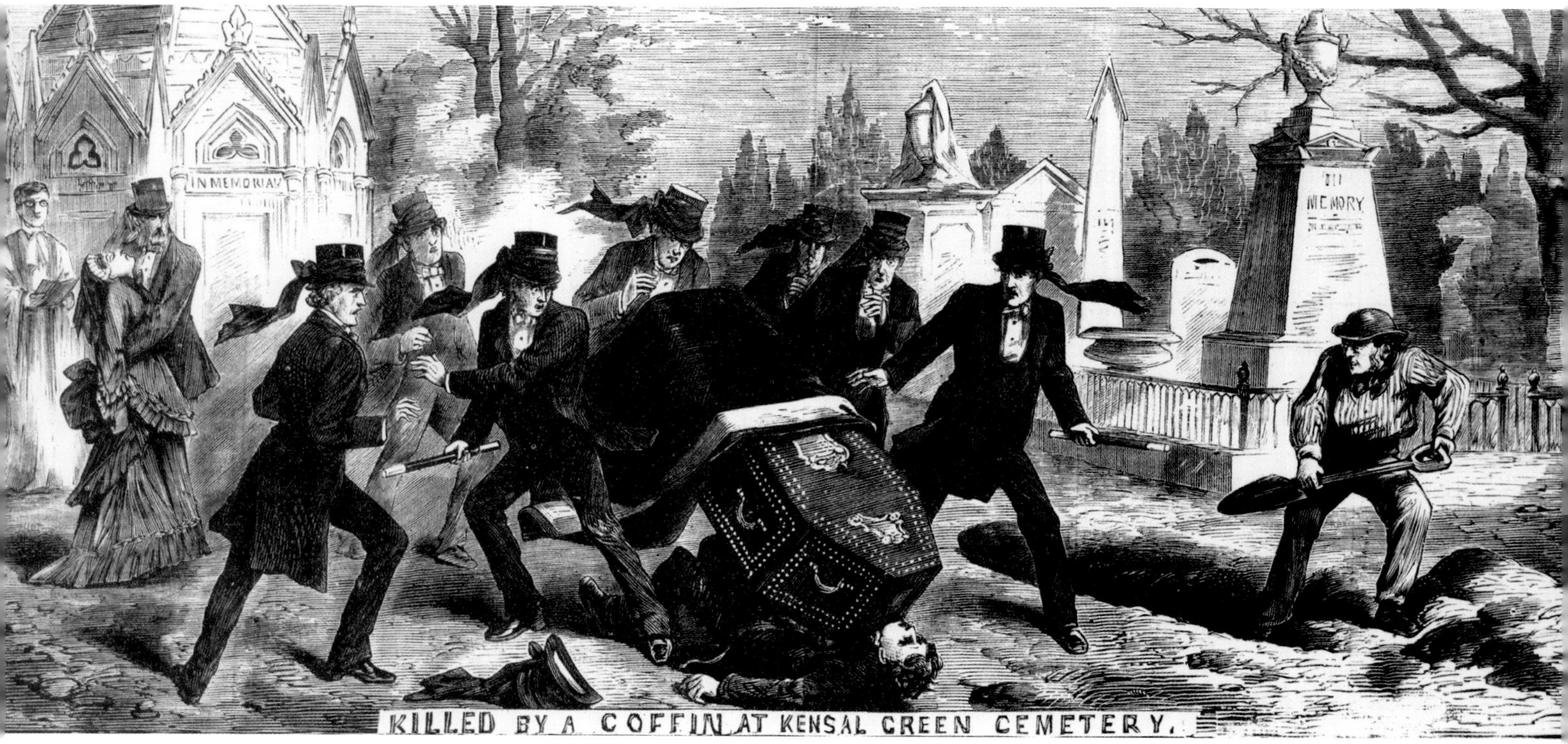

'Killed by a Coffin at Kensal Green Cemetery' from the *Illustrated Police News*, 9 November 1872.
British Library.

(2003: 180). For Dickens, the Gothic is not simply a source of dramatic thrills, but also a means of making plangent commentary on contemporary society.

Corpses such as Nemo's might also experience premature resurrection at the hands of the body snatchers, the work of whom was made easy by the shoddiness of burial practices – though not so easy as to discourage those who, too impatient to wait for dead bodies to appear naturally, hurried them along by the expedient of murder. The dwindling rate of legal executions in the early nineteenth century, coupled with the rise of medical schools, meant that the cadaver had become a valuable commodity. William Burke and William Hare in Edinburgh were only the most notorious body snatchers; there were many others. Burke was executed in 1829, having confessed to sixteen murders, mostly of destitute women, but this did not discourage the trade. John Bishop, after being arrested in 1831 for the murder of a fourteen-year-old street boy in the East End of London, confessed to having sold somewhere between 500 and 1000 bodies to hospitals; most were obtained by exhumation, but some by the murder of marginalised members of society.

The scandal of cases such as these led to the passage of the Anatomy Act in 1832. This changed the law under which the bodies of executed criminals were the property of the dissecting surgeons; their subjects were now the bodies of those who died paupers in the new workhouses created by the Poor Law Amendment Act. As paupers' bodies were more plentiful, it solved the problem for medical students, but transferred the fears of the poor from death at the hands of 'burkers' to the institutions of the workhouses, where they believed that they would be allowed (or assisted) to die for the profit their bodies represented. The poor thus become objects of fear for the rest of society, but they also cast themselves within a modern Gothic narrative, here as the victims of the faceless monstrosity of state systems and institutions.

The difficulty of dealing with the dead was partly solved in civic terms by the construction of the great new cemeteries. By 1841 seven huge necropolises had been built in London, beginning with Kensal Green in 1833; they were constructed by private companies established for the purpose. The cemeteries mimic urban construction, reproducing wealth and class in their layout with large and elaborate tombs on the main broad avenues and the graves of less august persons in the more crowded and narrow 'streets' behind them. Perhaps regrettably, however, the most fantastic of these necropolises, Thomas Willson's 1829 design for a colossal pyramid on Primrose Hill in North London, was never built. It would have been taller than St Paul's Cathedral, ninety-four storeys in height, and, situated on one of the highest points in London, would have loomed ominously over the city. The prospectus for the Pyramid Cemetery Company proposed that it would take 40,000 bodies a year, with funerals managed by means of steam-powered lifts. The eventual occupancy was estimated to be five million dead. Although the pyramid was never built, Willson continued his career on the board of the General Cemetery Company which constructed Kensal Green.

The 'Battle of the Styles'

As well as being a very visible part of what has been called the 'Victorian cult of death' (see Schor 1994), the new cemeteries were the site of an important skirmish in the 'Battle of the Styles'. This very public debate about the presence of Gothic architecture in contemporary Britain was initiated in discussions about the most appropriate style for the rebuilding of the Houses of Parliament in the mid-to-late years of the 1830s. The great champion of the Gothic, Augustus W N Pugin, devoted sections of his polemics *Contrasts* (1836) and *An Apology for the Revival of Christian Architecture in England* (1843) to criticism of cemetery style and the crass commercialism that had displaced Christian dignity. In *Apology* he writes:

> The entrance gateway is usually selected for the grand display of the company's enterprise and taste [. . .] This is generally Egyptian, probably from some association between the word catacombs, which occurs in the prospectus of the company, and the discoveries of Belzoni on the banks of the Nile; and nearly opposite the Green Man and Dog public house, in the centre of a dead wall (which serves as a cheap medium of advertisement for blacking and shaving strop manufacturers).
> (1853: 12)

As Pugin continues, 'The "New Economical Compressed Grave Cemetery Company" has its name displayed on the exterior wall in '*Grecian* capitals interspersed with hawk-headed divinities', and the

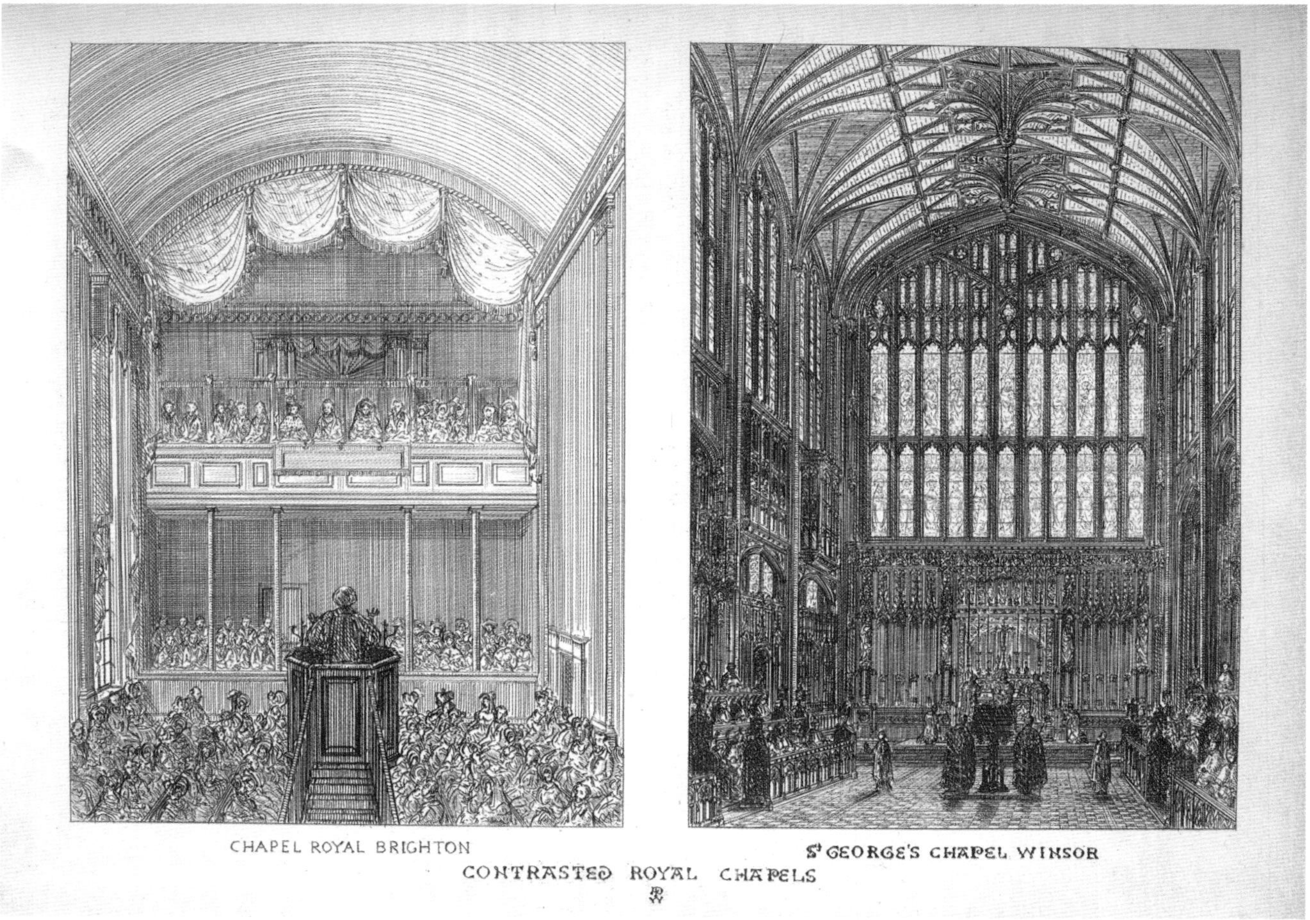

Plate from Augustus W N Pugin, *Contrasts*, second edition, 1841.
British Library 560*.d.33.

whole is topped off with a statue that is 'a huge representation of the winged Osiris bearing a gas lamp' (1853: 12).

The cemeteries were indeed a heterogenous jumble. Kensal Green chapel (1833) is a Greek Doric temple, West Norwood (1837) and West Highgate (1839) are Gothic in their gates and chapels, and Abney Park (1839) has an Egyptian gateway. However, the avenues and monuments within reveal some spectacular examples of fantasies of styles unconnected with any single scheme. Most notable, perhaps, is the Egyptian avenue in Highgate, built as part of the original 'Gothic' design yet consisting of a huge gateway, flanked by tall obelisks and a long tunnel of massive vaults. Pugin's observation of the influence of Belzoni's discoveries is an accurate one. After the defeat of Napoleon's armies in Egypt, English antiquarians and adventurers began bringing Egyptian artefacts back to London in large quantities. Ancient Egypt was a mysterious culture for the Victorians. Its texts were unreadable until the decipherment of hieroglyphics in the 1820s, and because only tombs and temples remained visible rather than buildings of domestic or commercial type, ancient Egyptian culture seemed concerned only with death and strange ritual.

Thomas De Quincey's opium nightmares summarise this Gothic Orientalism well. In his vivid account of his own laudanum addiction, published in 1821, De Quincey's hallucinations culminate in a confrontation with the gods Isis and Osiris that clearly shows the ideas of death and mysterious ritual that Egypt evoked in the nineteenth century. After judgment by the gods he dreams he is buried 'for a thousand years, in stone coffins, with mummies and sphinxes, in narrow chambers at the heart of eternal pyramids. I was kissed, with cancerous kisses, by crocodiles; and laid, confounded with all unutterable slimy things amongst reeds and Nilotic mud' (1971: 109). A visit to Highgate's Egyptian avenue was, for many, a vicarious expedition: 'As we enter the massive portals, and hear the echo of our footsteps intruding on the awful silence of this cold, stony death-palace, we might also fancy ourselves treading through the mysterious corridors of an Egyptian temple'. The guide also notes the 'solemn association' that makes the architectural style appropriate (Justyne 1865: 33).

It was not only the dead cities of Egypt that influenced public taste. In Italy the excavations of Pompeii and Herculaneum, engulfed by the eruption of Vesuvius, were continuing apace, and the unique nature of their destruction meant that many fascinating details of daily life, as well as poignant tableaus of death, had been preserved. Egypt and Pompeii were everywhere in Britain in the early nineteenth century, their popularity enhanced by fictional works such as Edward Bulwer-Lytton's *The Last Days of Pompeii* (1834). Jewellery, clothing, interior and exterior design, even paint production sought to imitate the styles and colours uncovered in various excavations, and archaeology was a source of great public interest. The *Illustrated London News,* for example, carried an 'Archaeology of the Month' column from the 1840s that featured smaller discoveries as well as the large and spectacular finds, such as those of Austen Layard at Nimrud and Nineveh in the 1840s and 1850s and Charles Newton at Halicarnassus in 1857. This excitement increased in intensity as the objects began to arrive at the British Museum (built to a neoclassical design by Robert Smirke in 1847). The past poured into London at an unprecedented rate and became the subject of much of its entertainment: in highbrow form in the educative parade of culture in museums, but far more widely in dioramas and other shows, the pages of the popular press, and in the Greek, Roman, Egyptian, Assyrian and Moorish halls of the relocated Great Exhibition. The distant past was not, however, assimiliated into contemporary culture without difficulty. There was not enough storage or display space in the new museums for the physical objects being sent by archaeologists and many of the non-European objects also challenged the Eurocentric evolutionary narrative of civilisation that was being established. Their spectacular strangeness could also, as in De Quincey's dreams, become threatening rather than entertaining. Even items dug from the English landscape could suggest uncomfortable ideas of 'deep time' and the primitive origins of humanity. It is this 'unruliness' of the archaeological objects, later compounded by the anxieties of imperialism, that lays the foundations for the 'museum Gothic' of the *fin de siècle* with its vengeful mummies, cursed rings and other dangerous imports.

Study for 'Stones of Venice' by John Ruskin. Drawing, 1851–3.
British Museum.

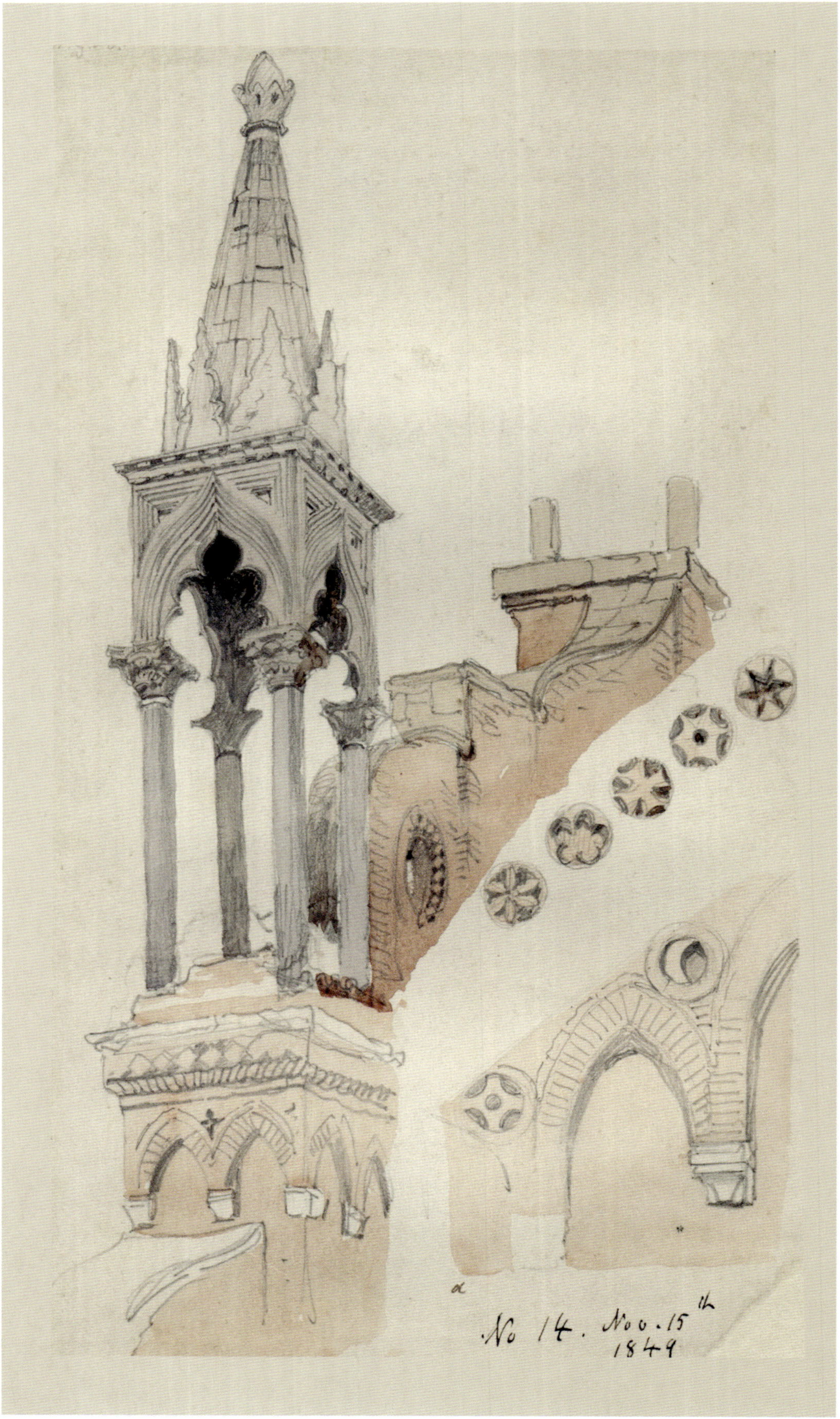

The Victorian 'Battle of the Styles' was more than just a tussle over architectural design or funerary taste, however. The period also saw the attempt to reinforce Gothic, not as mere decoration, but as an expression of real moral and spiritual truths. In *Apology* Pugin describes the 'Babel of Confusion' that is 'the *carnival* of architecture', and complains that buildings are designed 'not on consistent principle, not on authority, not as the expression of our faith, our government, or country, but as one of the disguises of the day' (1853: 2). As well as bemoaning the failure of the cemetery and railway companies to take advantage of new civic construction opportunities, he repeats his manifesto for church architecture and public buildings, first articulated in *Contrasts* in 1836. In this work he argued for a revival of medieval Gothic architecture, and with it a return to the religious practices and social structures of the Middle Ages. He identified 'revived Paganism and Protestantism' as the 'two monsters' of the fifteenth century that had destroyed both the true faith of England and the social and material expression of it (1898: iii).

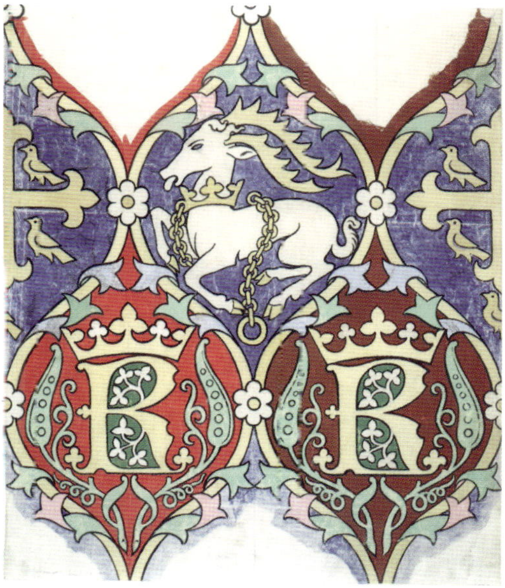

Sketch for wallpaper design for the Houses of Parliament by Augustus W N Pugin.
Victoria & Albert Museum.

For Pugin and his followers, architecture was representative of national character, and the use of any style other than Gothic in England was a betrayal of that character. John Ruskin, in his essay 'The Nature of Gothic' (1853), describes the Northern 'Gothic heart' as having 'strength of will, independence of character, resoluteness of purpose, impatience of undue control, and that general tendency to set the individual reason against authority, and the individual deed against destiny', a set of characteristics quite opposed to the Southern 'languid submission of thought to tradition and purpose to fatality' (1959: 241). England's spirit is free, individualistic and resistant to tyranny, unlike the lazy, superstitious and submissive character of the southern nations; therefore through its art England should lead its people back to their 'Gothic hearts'.

Pugin was only twenty-three when he published *Contrasts*, but he and his ideas were to prove hugely influential. By the time he was thirty he had built twenty-two churches, three cathedrals, three convents, several houses and schools and a Cistercian monastery. The national importance of his work was exemplified in the rebuilding of the Houses of Parliament. The medieval Parliament buildings had been spectacularly destroyed by fire in 1834, and the design competition announced in 1835 stipulated that the new buildings should be either Gothic or Elizabethan in style (Eastlake 1970: 169). The designs of Charles Barry won, and Pugin was asked to design the interiors and the furnishings. Furious objections were raised, and the long, essay-like letters to the Earl of Elgin (acquirer of the Parthenon sculptures) from his secretary, the antiquary William Hamilton, reveal the grounds of the general objections: fervent belief in the superiority of the neoclassical values of the Greek legacy (Pugin's 'revived Paganism') and the lingering suspicion of Catholicism (Hamilton 1836).

Nevertheless, Gothic was firmly established as a national style with the rebuilding of the Houses of Parliament, and hundreds of churches across Britain were built or re-modelled in accordance with Pugin's principles. In architectural history the period between 1855 and 1885 has come to be called 'High Victorian Gothic', since so many other buildings were constructed in the style. They include Keble College Chapel (William Butterfield, 1876) and St Pancras Station and Midland Grand Hotel (George Gilbert Scott, 1876). Not all adhered to the strict 'Decorated' variety of Gothic that Pugin preferred, and he was disappointed in much of what he saw constructed. Ruskin was also frequently enraged by poor use of the style; indeed, he described the new Houses of Parliament as 'the most effeminate and effectless heap of stones ever raised by man' (1880: 254).

Such architectural squabbling would seem to bear limited relation to the Gothic in literature, but it is through Ruskin that the connection can be made. In *The Seven Lamps of Architecture* (1849) Ruskin writes of the significance of shadows in the Parthenon sculptures. He says that shadow is employed as the dark field upon which shapes are made:

> ... but the use of that shadow is entirely to show the confines of the figures, and it is to *their lines*, and not to the shapes of the shadows behind them, that the art and the eye are addressed [...] the sculptors have dispensed with, or even struggled to avoid, all shadows which were not absolutely necessary to the explaining of the form. On the contrary, in Gothic sculpture, the shadow itself becomes the subject of thought. (1959: 206)

This is, in the simplest terms, a definition of the Victorian Gothic: here, the shadow becomes the subject of thought. Again we can see that it is not a crude opposition of black and white, or a reactive turn against the light, but rather that the shadow is an integral part of the whole, requiring a shift of perspective to see that which is more usually left unseen. Thus, unlike the more obvious mode of the eighteenth century, the Gothic of the period 1820–80 is one that requires a deliberate act of 'seeing', a shift of view that can offer an alternative explanation of reality. It is for this reason that so much of Victorian literary Gothic is embedded in realism, where uncanny moments in the texts cause the attention to refocus on the shadows and the occluded alternative reality comes into view.

Gothic Politics

For Ruskin this making of the shadow is not only a question of the aesthetic, the play of light and shade upon surfaces: crucially, it is a social question too. In a famous passage he writes:

> And now, reader, look around this English room of yours, about which you have been proud so often, because the work was so good and strong, and the ornaments of it so finished. Examine again all those accurate mouldings, and perfect polishings, and unerring adjustments of seasoned wood and tempered steel. Many a time you have exulted over them and thought how great England was, because her slightest work was done so thoroughly. Alas! if read rightly, these perfectnesses are signs of a slavery in our England a thousand times more bitter and more degrading than that of the scourged African or helot Greek. (1959: 233–4)

He emphasises that the perfection of the commodity is gained because 'the animation of [England's] multitudes is sent like fuel to feed the factory smoke and the strength of them is given daily to be wasted into the fineness of a web, or racked into the exactness of a line'. The 'old cathedrals' on the other hand exhibit in their 'ugly goblins and formless monsters' the 'signs of the life and liberty of every workman who struck the stone; a freedom of thought and rank in scale of being, such as no laws, no charters, no charities can secure; but which it must be the first aim of all Europe at this day to regain for her children' (1959: 233–4).

To 'see' Gothic in architecture requires a willed act of observation, and what can be seen is the labour of the workman who is free in body, spirit and artistry. The same willed act of looking at the products of industrialised processes also allows the observer to see the labour of the enslaved worker that is concealed in the perfection of a finished surface. Ruskin's theory of the nature of Gothic is striking in its resemblance, particularly in the imagery it deploys, to another nineteenth-century thinker less usually associated with the Gothic: Karl Marx. This is Ruskin writing of architecture on the Greek and Roman model:

> Pagan in its origin, proud and unholy in its revival, paralyzed in its old age, yet making prey in its dotage of all the good and living things there were springing around it in their youth, as the dying and desperate king, who had long fenced himself so strongly with the towers of it, is said to have filled his failing veins with the blood of children. (1959: 255)

Ruskin's vampiric metaphor might fruitfully be compared with that of Marx, who characterises capital as 'dead labour which, vampire-like, lives only by sucking living labour, and lives the more the more it sucks' (1990: 342). He reiterates that 'the vampire will not let go while there remains a single muscle, sinew or drop of blood to be exploited' (1990: 416). These are just two of dozens of examples of the violently Gothic imaginary that Marx uses throughout his work, but especially in *Capital* (1867).

That Marx's theorisation of capital employs so many Gothic figures is testament to how thoroughly the vocabulary and figures of Gothic had permeated the cultural imagination by the middle of the nineteenth century. Marx had been writing *Capital* for two decades by the time the first volume was published in 1867, and it is clear that he had read at least one Gothic fiction: he discusses Sue's *Les Mystères de Paris* at length in his and Engels's *The Holy Family*, written only one year after Sue's series was completed. Marx's use of Gothic also points to a more crucial element in the understanding of nineteenth-century culture, namely his assertion that modern society is animated by the profound, mysterious and invisible force of capitalism. In his famous explanation of the nature of the commodity Marx writes about ordinary wood, and how it is transformed when made into a table:

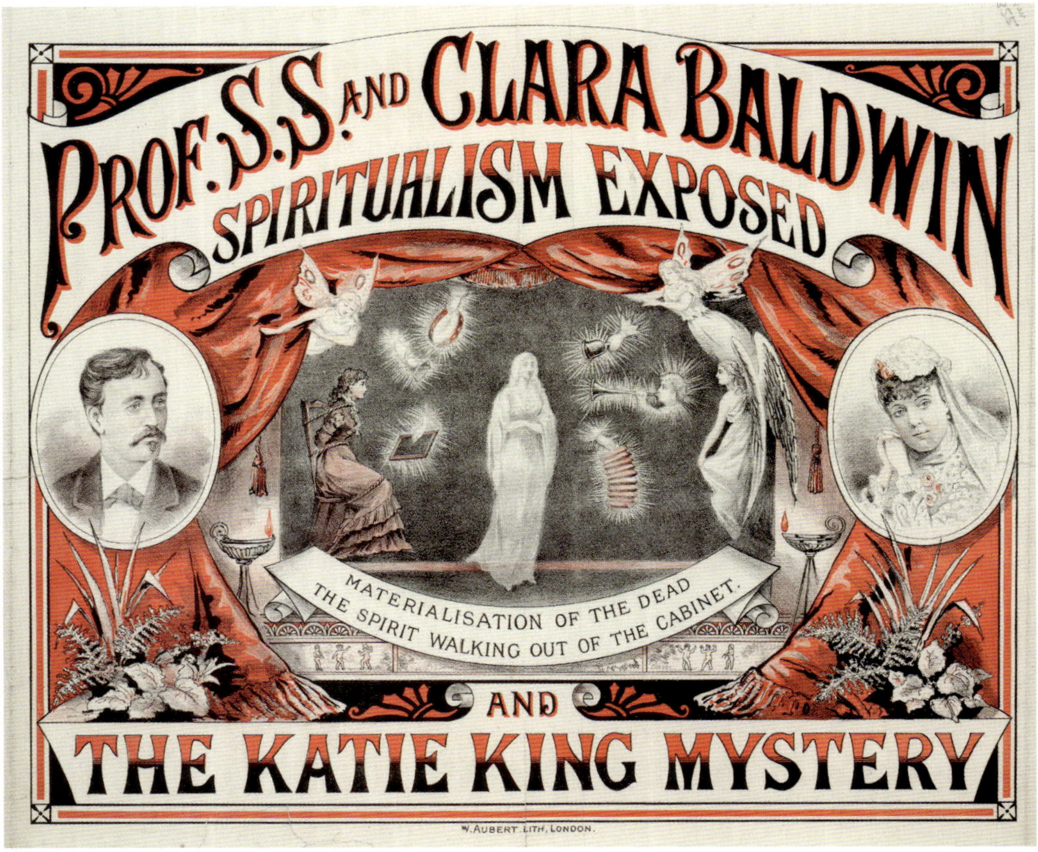

Poster for a stage séance.
British Library, Evanion 355.

Stage magicians took ideas from séances to create dramatic new acts. 'Katie King' refers to a spirit manifested by the medium Florence Cook during the early 1870s.

> But as soon as it emerges as a commodity, it changes into a thing which transcends sensuousness. It not only stands with its feet on the ground, but, in relation to all other commodities, it stands on its head, and evolves out of its wooden brain grotesque ideas, far more wonderful than if it were to begin dancing of its own free will. (1990: 163–4)

The dancing table is a reference to the craze for spiritualist séances that swept across Britain after the importation of the Fox sisters' methods from America in the 1850s. The ordinary table of the domestic interior is far stranger than those used in the séance. For Marx, this is not the primitive survival of pre-modern superstition into the modern age, but a new belief that is the product of modernity itself, a 'fetishistic' belief in the independent life of commodities. Marx's point is that many of the essential features of capitalism, indeed capital itself, are not immediately visible, but require a willed act of 'seeing'. Marx directs the eye to the horrible testimony present in the domestic object and past the enchantment of capitalism, past our necessary 'forgetting' that the object is a human product and our consequent sense that the commodity possesses a life of its own.

Ruskin, though he would certainly have resisted identification with Marx, saw such testimony in the work of the Pre-Raphaelite Brotherhood, the group of artists and critics formed by the painters

Dante Gabriel Rossetti, John Everett Millais and William Holman Hunt in 1848. For the PRB, as they all originally signed their work, Raphael was the equivalent of Pugin's 'revived paganism and Protestantism', representing the moment when art fell away from true principles. The brotherhood and its work were controversial in ways that, today, are hard to grasp. At the time, even their name suggested both secretive revolutionary organisations that were still feared, especially in 1848, the 'year of revolutions' in Europe, and a religious order of some kind, implicitly Catholic.

Alongside the pre-Reformation architectural enthusiasm of Pugin and Ruskin and the theological concerns of churchmen such as John Henry Newman and the Oxford Movement, which sought to reform elements of worship, particularly in matters of ritual and outward display, along Catholic lines, the re-visiting of religious subject matter in Pre-Raphaelite paintings was a source of deep unease. Millais' painting *Christ in the House of His Parents* (1849–50) caused debate because it depicted the family of Jesus in a carpenter's workshop, realistically painted. There were scathing and shocked reactions, most famously in Charles Dickens's review of 1850, which criticises both the depiction of the boy Jesus and his mother Mary as 'she would stand out from the rest of the company as a monster in the vilest cabaret in France or in the lowest gin-shop in England' (1850: 264–5). As Dickens describes it, this holy family is more likely to be seen in the pages of city mysteries.

The Secret Theatre of Home

Ruskin defended Millais and the group generally, though he was not always fully enthusiastic about the works themselves. His defence

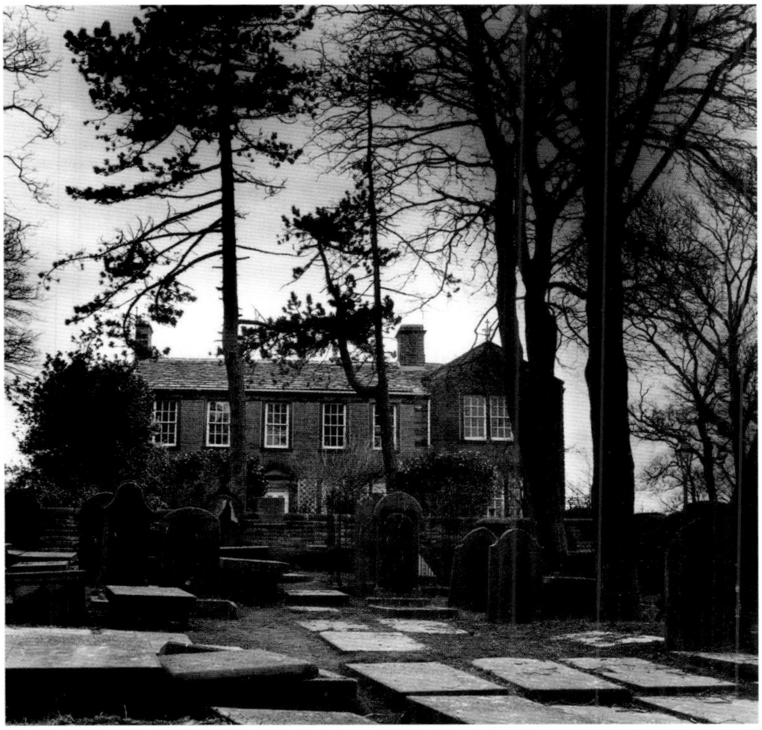

Haworth Parsonage. Photograph by Fay Godwin.
British Library FG2857-3.

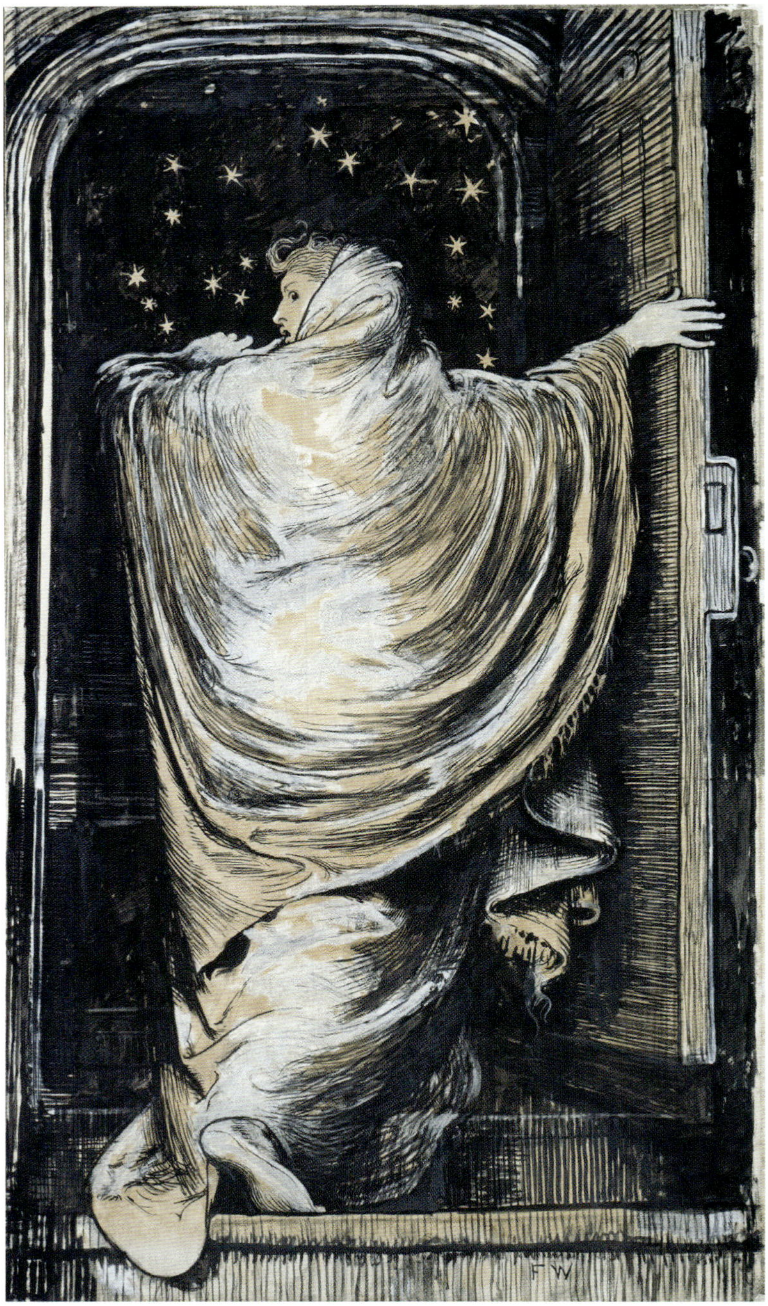

'The Woman in White', poster by Frederick Walker, 1871.
Tate.
Frederick Walker's illustration to promote a stage adaptation of Wilkie Collins's sensation novel *The Woman in White* links mystery and suspense with Pre-Raphaelite style.

was based in his Gothic morality, particularly in relation to the 'modern life' subjects that the PRB produced. In a letter to *The Times* about Holman Hunt's *The Awakening Conscience* (1853), Ruskin writes: 'There is not a single object in all that room, common, modern, vulgar [...] but it became tragical, if rightly read. That furniture [...] is there nothing to be learned from that terrible lustre of it, from its fatal newness; nothing there that has the old thoughts of home upon it, or that is ever to become a part of home' (1854: 7). His letter goes on to mention the possible sad fate of the kept woman, but in spite of their sympathetic depictions of trapped women, both modern and legendary, the gender politics of Ruskin and the Pre-Raphaelites remain troubling. It is in the literary Gothic that challenges to dominant ideologies of gender find their strongest expression.

As the ordinary home replaces the castle as the place of terror, the newer villains are more often lovers and husbands than forbidding fathers. This 'domestic Gothic' is powerfully articulated in the work of the Brontë sisters, where the home is represented as, at best, ambiguous, and, at worst, a place of imprisonment, fear and even death. Such a concept appears most starkly in the incarceration of the first Mrs Rochester in Charlotte Brontë's *Jane Eyre* (1847), but it is also evident in the frequent and repeated images of freedom and enclosure in all their work. Jane Eyre moves between small domestic spaces, such as the window seat where she is first seen and where she finds freedom in reading; in her room at Thornfield she feels trapped and wishes for nothing more than to be outside the 'home' of patriarchy. Similarly, in Emily Brontë's *Wuthering Heights* (1847) we find Cathy (both alive and dead) at a series of windows, either looking in and desperate to be inside, or looking out and wishing for freedom. Peace and resolution for both are only found in a final strange enclosure, Jane with the maimed Rochester in a small, secluded house in the woods and Cathy, more grotesquely, in her coffin beneath the moors, between the corpses of her husband and lover.

The legacy of the Brontës and the Gothicising of domestic space through commodity culture expands in the sensation fiction of the 1860s and 1870s. This genre is exemplified in the novels of Wilkie Collins, in particular *The Woman in White* (1860). Here, in a significant transition, a figure first taken to be a more traditional ghost turns out to be a very material woman who has endured domestic abuse and various incarcerations in the institutions of patriarchy. What Collins himself called 'the secret theatre of home' (1990: 76) provided a rich field for women writers and readers, who used sensation fiction both to elaborate on the metaphor of marriage as Gothic imprisonment, and to imagine the possibilities of 'bad' women who present a challenge to the structures of authority.

Now almost forgotten, Ellen Wood's *East Lynne* (1861) was immensely popular when published and became known to many more people through its equally successful dramatisation. While Wood's adulterous heroine is punished for leaving her husband and children by being disfigured in a train crash, abandoned by her lover and obliged to work as a governess to her own children, some other sensation novels, such as Collins's, or Mary Braddon's *Lady Audley's Secret* (1862), are more ambiguous about their unconventional female characters. Charles Reade's *Hard Cash* (1863) is unusual in taking the familiar sensational theme of wrongful incarceration (here in a lunatic asylum), but making the subjects male: here, a father has his son locked away for financial gain.

The implicit, and sometimes explicit, criticism of the institutions of the family found in sensation fiction is part of the reason why reactions to the mode were so strong. A long article in the *Quarterly Review* spoke of 'diseased appetites' and 'morbid anatomy', questioned the plausibility of the events and the quality of

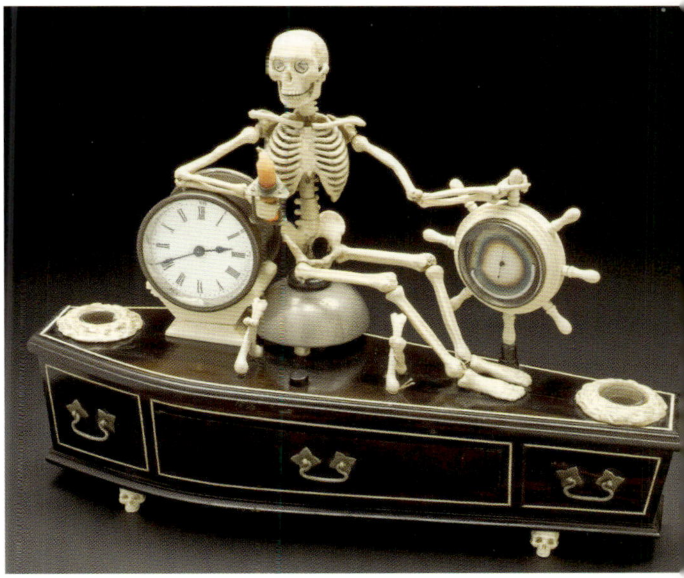

Memento mori alarm clock, nineteenth century.
Science Museum, London.

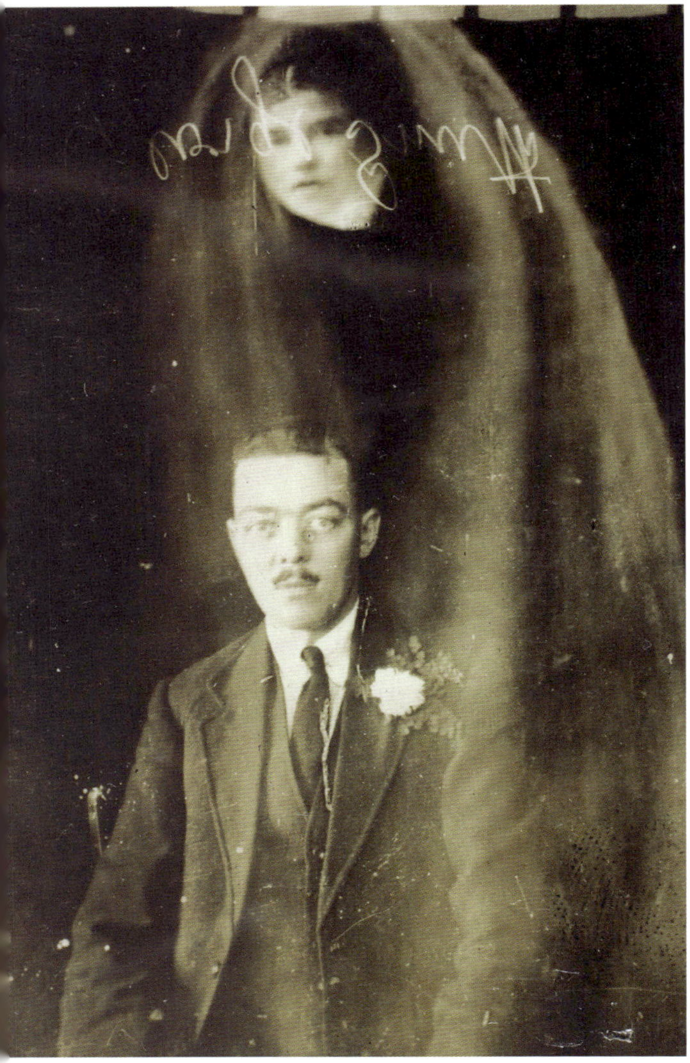

Spirit photograph by Fred Barlow, 1870.
British Library Cup.407.a.1.

Spirit photographs combined two Victorian passions: modern technology and the supernatural.

the writing, sneered at the 'commercial atmosphere [...] redolent of the manufactory and the shop' and attributed blame to 'periodicals, circulating libraries, and railway bookstalls' for the production of such trash. The writer goes on to notice bigamy and the divorce courts as related to the moral decline that sensation fiction represents (Mansel 1863). The class and gender basis of the criticism closely resembles criticism of eighteenth-century Gothic, as does the emphasis on the physicality of reaction to the texts, or what Mansel refers to as their 'preaching to the nerves' (1863: 482). And yet the thrill and the perceived threat of sensation fiction was precisely that it relocated the Gothic to the 'here and now' of contemporary England. Furthermore, as so tellingly happens in *The Woman in White* and *Lady Audley's Secret*, and indeed earlier in Charlotte Brontë's *Villette* (1853), the horrors of the supernatural are revealed actually to be earthly in origin, but all the more horrifying for it.

At the same time as the familiar world is being defamiliarised in this Victorian Gothic realism, a reverse process is taking place in re-imagining the world of the dead. In 1848, after the supposed communications of Katherine and Margaret Fox with the ghost of a murdered peddler in their haunted home, they and their methods became a national sensation. Within a few years thousands of people in the United States were practising table rapping, and by 1852 the spirit séance had arrived in England, where varieties of spiritualism quickly became widespread. Although some séances tried to summon the shades of the famous dead or speak to unknown spirits, people overwhelmingly wanted communication with their own lost loved ones, to reconstitute the broken circle of the bourgeois family in a Ruskinian cluttered drawing-room.

Spiritualism also projects the domestic into the afterlife. Indeed, it reconstructs the afterlife so that the primary existence of the spirit is not the communion of the soul with God, but the participation of the spirits in a society that closely resembles that of the living. In some forms developed by the later years of the century, this includes homes and possessions, even towns, but from the start it remains intensely familial. Although convincing arguments have been made for the liberating potential for women of the medium's role (Oppenheim 1985; Owen 1989) and the alternative communities of authority offered for the working classes (Barrow 1986), the ideal of spiritualism nevertheless remains firmly bourgeois and familial. The awkward dead, as in the civic necropolises, are re-domesticated and folded back into the fabric of the lives of the living.

Perhaps the most conspicuous and emblematic realisation of this is the Queen herself. On the death of Albert in 1861 Victoria, then aged only forty-two, assumed the role of widow, a part she insisted upon performing for the remaining forty-two years of her life and reign. In 1863 work began on a memorial to Albert, to be constructed in Kensington Gardens. Although other designs were submitted (including a massive classical scheme by Charles Barry), George Gilbert Scott's Gothic design was chosen. Scott claimed that medieval reliquaries, the elaborate cases made for the physical relics of saints and martyrs, were the model for his design (Jenkyns 1991: 3).

At the four corners of the memorial are groups of figures representing the four quarters of the globe, 'referring indirectly to the International Exhibition of 1851', as Scott described it (anon.1872: 14), but probably more directly in the public mind to Victoria's rapidly expanding empire. Next to the columns are four more groups, Manufactures, Commerce, Agriculture and Engineering, and the niches and friezes have nearly 200 further historical or allegorical figures that represent the arts and sciences. The late Prince Consort appears as a medieval martyr whose attributes are the emblems of modern industrial economy: the patron saint of progressive science. Albert's other shrine was in his rooms at Osborne House, the royal family's summer home on the Isle of Wight. Victoria kept these rooms just as Albert had left them at his death; his clothes were laid out and hot water brought for shaving every morning, as if he were just about to rise from sleep. These two spaces, the strange giant reliquary of South Kensington and the haunted home of Osborne House, are exemplary of the elaborate public and private performances of Gothic in the built environment. Fittingly, both were commissioned by the widow who gave her name to the century.

It is appropriate, too, that Scott's memorial for Prince Albert was completed in 1872, which saw the beginning of what one contemporary commentator regarded as the 'Victorian equivalent of the Wall Street Crash' and the start of 'a most curious and in many respects unprecedented disturbance and depression of trade, commerce and industry' (Hobsbawm 1997: 17). Albert's memorials are not just testaments to the dead prince, but markers of another end of Gothic. The 'age of anxiety' that began in the late 1870s brings yet another revival of Gothic in the horrific bodies of the *fin de siècle*. This periodic crisis of capitalism picks up the Gothic threads that stretch past to the two abbeys of Northanger and Fonthill and weaves them yet again in ways that ensure that 'Gothic' and 'Victorian' become almost synonymous terms. The shadow that is the nineteenth-century subject of thought is our own modernity.

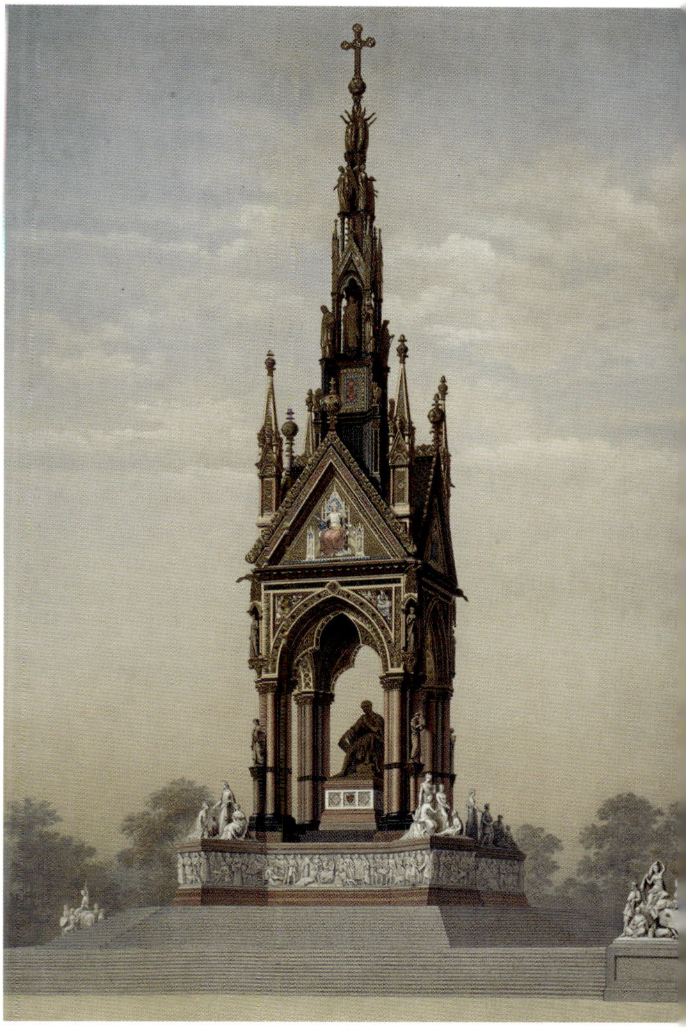

The Albert Memorial. Plate from *The National Memorial to His Royal Highness the Prince Consort*, 1873.
British Library 1731.d.4.

Further Reading

Reynolds, Nicole 2010. *Building Romanticism: Literature and Architecture in Nineteenth-Century Britain* (Ann Arbor: University of Michigan Press). An interdisciplinary study that examines the ways in which the built environment influences literary representations. Taking particular features, such as the casement window and the boudoir, and specific locations such as John Soane's Museum/house, Reynolds illustrates treatment of issues of gender, sexuality and national identity in literature of the period.

Richardson, Ruth 2001. *Death, Dissection and the Destitute*, 2nd edn (London: Penguin). Centred on the passage of the 1832 Anatomy Act, this study discusses beliefs about corpses in pre-Victorian culture, changes in death and burial practices, grave-robbing and the social implications of the link between dissection and poverty created by the act.

Tambling, Jeremy 2009. *Going Astray: Dickens and London* (Harlow: Pearson). Traversing Dickens's journalism and fiction, Tambling reads London not just as the background, but also as the subject of Dickens's work. He also suggests the ways in which it has been instrumental in creating the image of the city itself.

Zimmerman, Virginia 2008. *Excavating Victorians* (Albany, NY: SUNY Press). A study of aspects of Victorian literature and culture through consideration of the disciplines of geology and archaeology. The idea of the 'trace' and of the remains is shown to be important in the understanding of literary texts, including works by Dickens, Hardy and Tennyson.

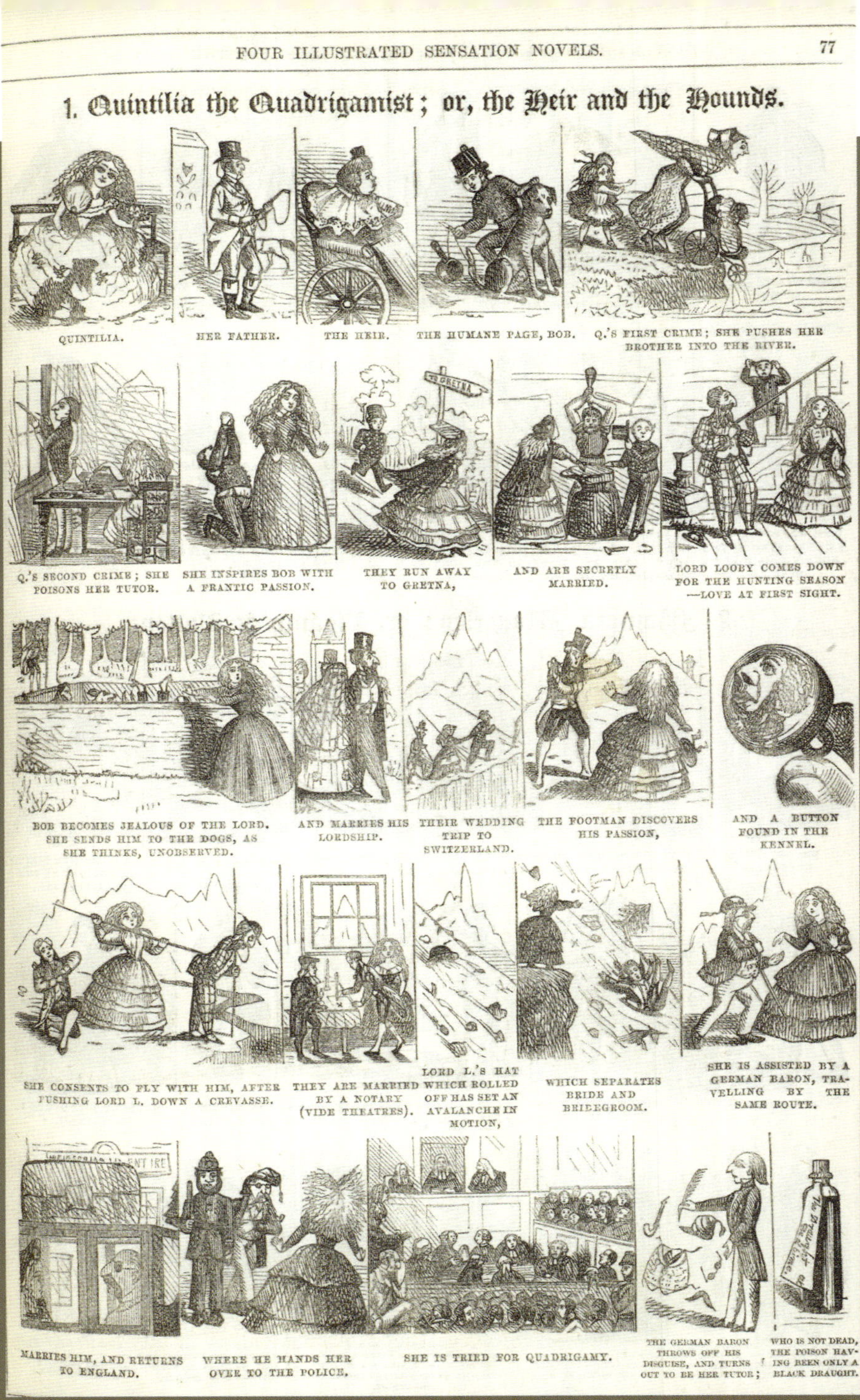

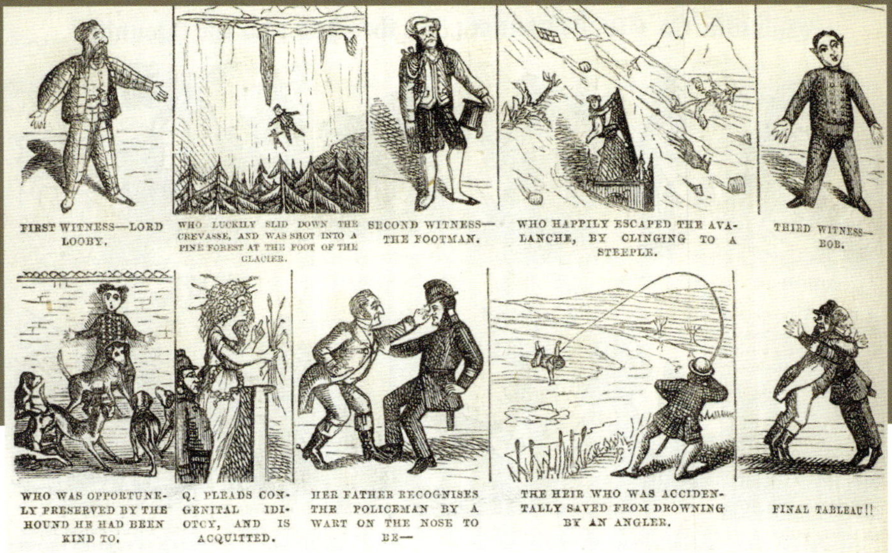

'Quintilia the Quadrigamist; or, the Heir and the Hounds. A satire on the sensation novel from *Beeton's Christmas Annual*, 1865.

British Library P.P.6704.

From the Crypt: *Victorian Sensation Fiction*

'Quintilia the Quadrigamist; or, The Heir and the Hounds'

Sensation fiction, which had its heyday in Britain during the 1860s, presented a quintessentially Victorian variation on the earlier Gothic novels of Ann Radcliffe and Matthew Lewis. Here, the central female characters, formerly so demure, were no longer innocent maidens fleeing the attentions of sex-crazed monks. Rather, they were resourceful and determined, like Marian Halcombe in *The Woman in White* (1860), or else scheming Pre-Raphaelite beauties such as Lucy Graham in Mary Elizabeth Braddon's *Lady Audley's Secret* (1862), and Lydia Gwilt in Wilkie Collins's *Armadale* (1866). The plots of Victorian sensation novels were rife with bigamous marriages, secret identities, forged wills and mysterious dreams. The convents and monasteries in which the heroines of earlier Gothic fictions had been imprisoned were replaced by lunatic asylums and rambling mansions. Doctors, with their numbing supplies of laudanum, took the place of evil abbesses. Sensation fiction brought Gothic themes into the drawing rooms, kitchens and bedrooms of the Victorian upper and middle classes, and made authors such as Wilkie Collins, Mary Elizabeth Braddon and Ellen Wood literary celebrities. Like Gothic literature from the 1790s, however, sensation novels, with their improbable plot twists and relentless emotional intensity, proved a rich source for satire and parody. Just as Jane Austen had affectionately lampooned Radcliffe's *The Mysteries of Udolpho* (1794) and a number of other Gothic fictions in *Northanger Abbey* (1817), so the sensation novel became, in turn, a target for mockery.

In 1865, for instance, *Beeton's Christmas Annual* published a series of four parodic 'Illustrated Sensation Novels', presented in a form similar to today's comic strips. The titles alone give an indication of the content: 'Quintilia the Quadrigamist; or, The Heir and the Hounds'; 'Maurora Maudsley; or, Bigamy and Buttons'; 'Prinvilliers the Poisoner; or, The Live Coal and the Deadly Cup'; and "Arry the 'Eartless; or, A Bad Brother's Aim and End'. Shown here is the first of the tales, featuring the murderous but undeniably appealing Quintilia. With her flowing Pre-Raphaelite locks and endless ability to fascinate, Quintilia owes something to Lucy Graham in *Lady Audley's Secret*. The opening panels introduce the characters: doe-eyed Quintilia, her pompous father and her younger brother, all set to inherit the family fortune, and Bob, the kindly page. From this point onwards, outrageous mayhem ensues as passions become inflamed, murderous desires are acted out and a whole succession of marriages take place. Nothing is merely sensational when it can be downright impossible. Bob is fed to the foxhounds but survives because he has been particularly kind to one of the dogs in the past. The curious German baron who unmasks Quintilia's atrocities is revealed to be the tutor she had attempted to poison at the beginning of the story. Lord Looby survives a fall into an Alpine crevasse by landing on some pine trees, and the infant heir to the family fortune is saved from drowning by an angler with a skilfully wielded fishing rod.

The story of Quintilia's outlandish adventures takes the standard themes of the sensation novel and plays them back in a brilliantly ridiculous fashion. In *Lady Audley's Secret*, Lucy pushes her first husband down a well, considers poisoning her second husband, and sets fire to a hotel in an attempt to do away with the inconvenient Robert Audley, who threatens to reveal her secret. She ends up in an asylum for her troubles. Quintilia does much the same, only to a much greater extent: she does not stop at two husbands, and one of them, Lord Looby, survives a fall into an Alpine crevasse rather than a mere tumble into a well. The plot-twists so deftly employed by Braddon and Collins are all present here, but played for laughs rather than shocks and chills.

GREG BUZWELL

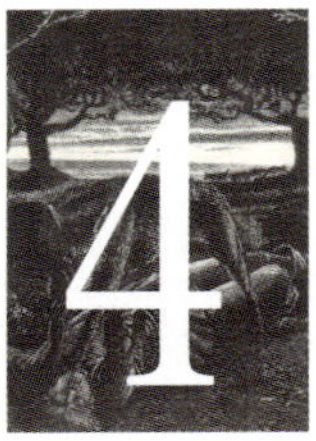

ANDREW SMITH

Gothic and the Victorian *fin de siècle*, 1880–1900

OPPOSITE:
Sabine Baring-Gould, *The Book of Werewolves*, 1865.
British Library 08631.i.24.
One of the titles consulted by Bram Stoker when he was researching his novel *Dracula*.

Degeneration and Decay

Thinking about Gothic writing of the Victorian *fin de siècle* requires us to consider bodies. The period's fascination with ideas of degeneration emphasised the potential corruption lurking within the seemingly civilised body, and within the idea of the body politic. Making sense of how bodies relate to society is a theme that unites Gothic texts as diverse as Robert Louis Stevenson's *Strange Case of Dr Jekyll and Mr Hyde* (1886), Oscar Wilde's *The Picture of Dorian Gray* (1890; 1891), Arthur Machen's *The Great God Pan* (1894), H G Wells's *The Island of Doctor Moreau* (1896) and Bram Stoker's *Dracula* (1897). Such a preoccupation also characterised much of the *fin-de-siècle* social, cultural and political analysis that took place – in part because Britain at the end of the nineteenth century had an odd Gothic look and feel about it.

Max Nordau, a journalist, novelist and playwright, attempted to capture the apocalyptic mood of the time in *Degeneration* (1892). After outlining his highly reactionary account of the newly emerging social and artistic forms – indications for Nordau of the presence of a diseased culture (in which new developments in the novel and theatre, as well as the emancipations being sought by the New Woman, demonstrated signs of cultural pathology) – he concludes that:

> Such is the spectacle presented by the doings of men in the reddened light of the Dusk of Nations. Massed in the sky the clouds are aflame in the weirdly beautiful glow which was

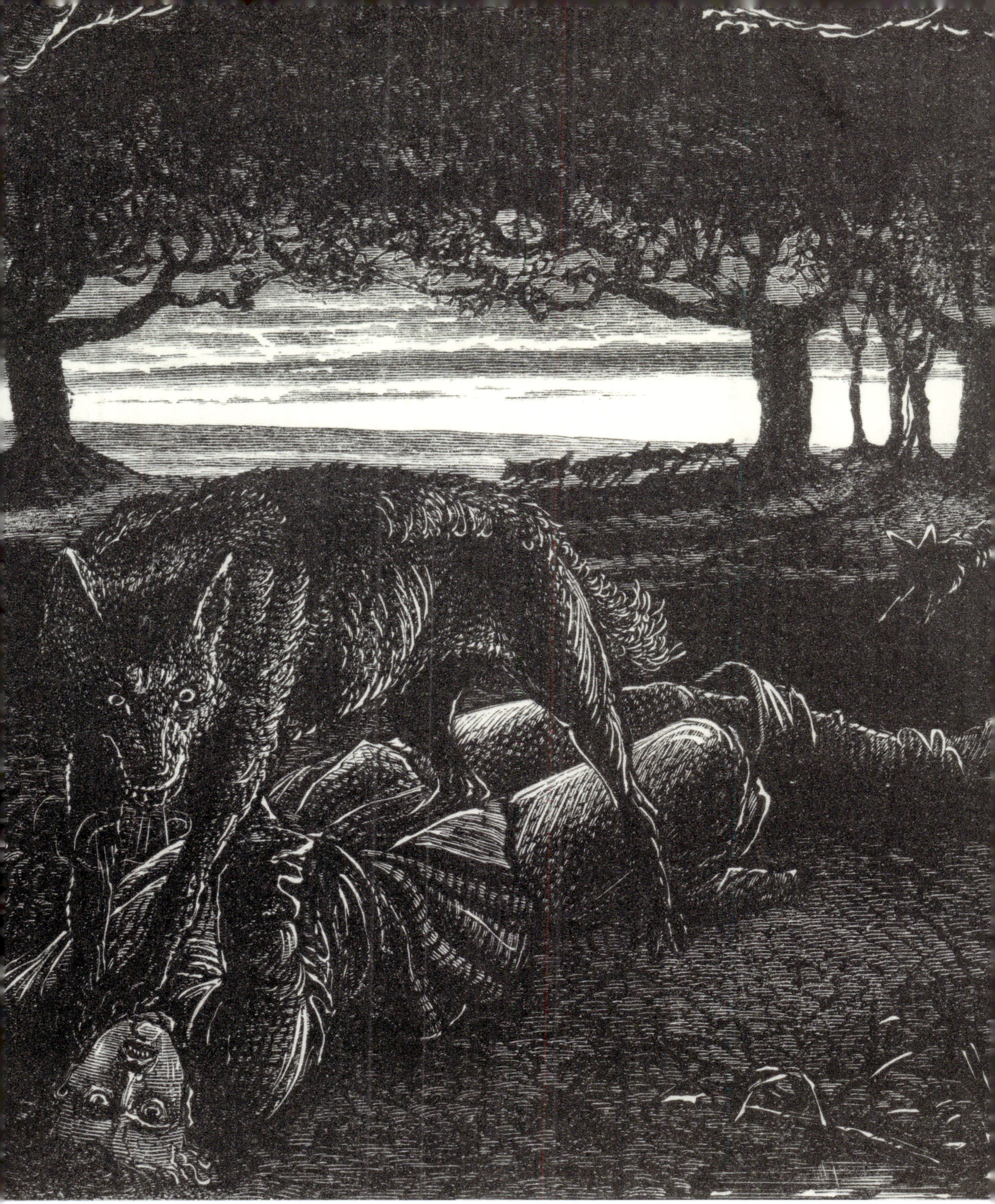

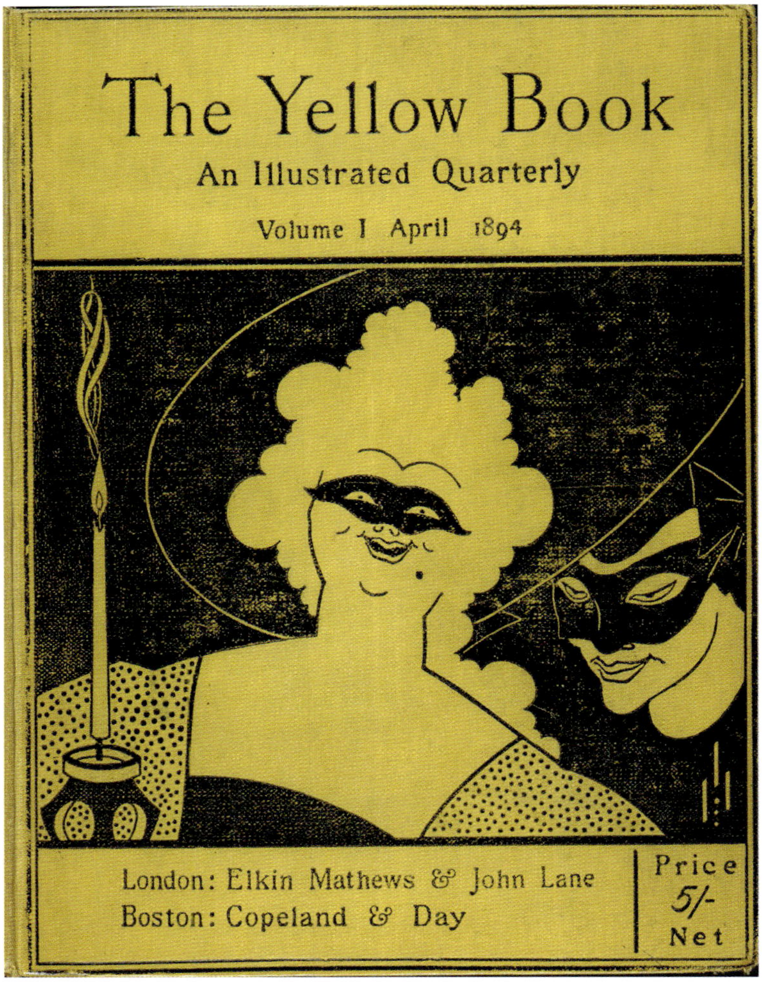

Cover of *The Yellow Book*, volume 1, April 1894.
British Library C.121.b.17/1.
Some saw Aubrey Beardsley's design as brilliant and bold, while others regarded it as a sign of degeneracy.

> observed for the space of years after the eruption of Krakatoa. Over the earth the shadows creep with deepening gloom, wrapping all objects in a mysterious dimness [...] The old anxiously watch its approach, fearing they will not live to see the end. A few amongst the young and strong are conscious of the vigour of life in their veins and nerves, and rejoice in the coming sunrise. (1895: 6)

Krakatoa erupted in August 1883, and the tons of volcanic ash pumped into the atmosphere resulted in blood-red sunsets for the best part of a decade. Nordau's image of the apocalypse is not, however, without its reassurances. The 'young and strong' can see new possibilities emerging from the rubble, and Nordau is clear that the supposed dissipations manifested by *fin-de-siècle* decadence (Wilde is a bogey figure for Nordau) do not touch those of sound mind and body. It would be tempting to dismiss Nordau's argument on at least two grounds: it is highly emotive and politically slanted. Yet it is not accidental that Nordau is mentioned by name in *Dracula*, when Mina Harker notes that Count Dracula is a degenerate *fin-de-siècle* type identified by Nordau. Beyond Stoker's iconic fiction, models of degeneration shape images of the monstrous that repeatedly recur in the Gothic of the time.

Theories of degeneration had their roots in the version of mental pathology developed in France by Bénédict Augustin Morel in the 1850s. Morel attempted to explain various social problems, such as prostitution, gambling and alcoholism, via a theory of hereditary disposition. This was followed by the work of the Italian criminologist Cesare Lombroso (also mentioned in *Dracula*) who, from the 1870s, attempted to account for crime by arguing that unusual cranial formations indicated the presence of specific criminal proclivities. Nordau's *Degeneration* (which is dedicated to Lombroso) transferred the idea of physical symptom to the realm of culture by claiming that diseased books are symptomatic of a diseased society. However, the roots of this can also be found in a popular British science book from the period, *Degeneration: A Chapter in Darwinism* by Edwin Ray Lankester (1880).

Lankester was an eminent evolutionary biologist of the period. His book on degeneration utilises an image of imperial decline as a metaphor for evolutionary regression. For Lankester:

> Any new set of conditions occurring to an animal which render its food and safety very easily attained, seem to lead as a rule to Degeneration; just as an active healthy man sometimes degenerates when he suddenly becomes possessed of a fortune; or as Rome degenerated when possessed of the riches of the ancient world. (1880: 33)

According to this line of reasoning, civilisation degenerates when it becomes too civilised, as it no longer has a natural enemy against which to test its strength. In Lankester's vision we need enemies, but the chief concern, as it would be for Nordau and indeed for other theorists of degeneration, centres on the enemy within. Society breeds its own degenerates, and the claim that we cannot trust civilisation as it may conceal within it the potential for an atavistic decay gave expression to concerns about Britain's imperial decline (as evidenced by *Dracula*), while also linking the civilised to the barbaric. Nowhere is this more evident than in the apparently unusual theme which Stevenson addresses in the opening of *Jekyll and Hyde* (1886): the problem of middle-class boredom.

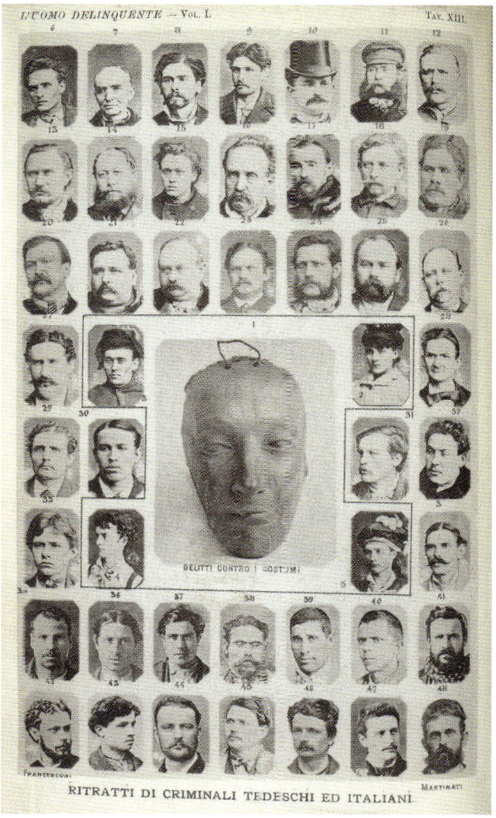

Plate from Cesare Lombroso, *L'uomo delinquente*, 1889. British Library 2228.e.1.

This plate was designed to illustrate Lombroso's theory that criminal types could be recognised by their facial characteristics.

Divided Self, Divided City

The tale begins with a description of the lawyer Mr Utterson, 'a man of a rugged countenance, that was never lighted by a smile' (1984: 29), who ritually undertakes Sunday walks with his 'distant kinsman' Richard Enfield. The joylessness of these walks is emphasised by Stevenson's narrator: 'It was reported by those who encountered them in their Sunday walks, that they said nothing, looked singularly dull, and would hail with obvious relief the appearance of a friend' (1984: 30). However, the narrative continues, 'For all that, the two men put the greatest store by these excursions, counted them the chief jewel of each week, and not only set aside occasions of

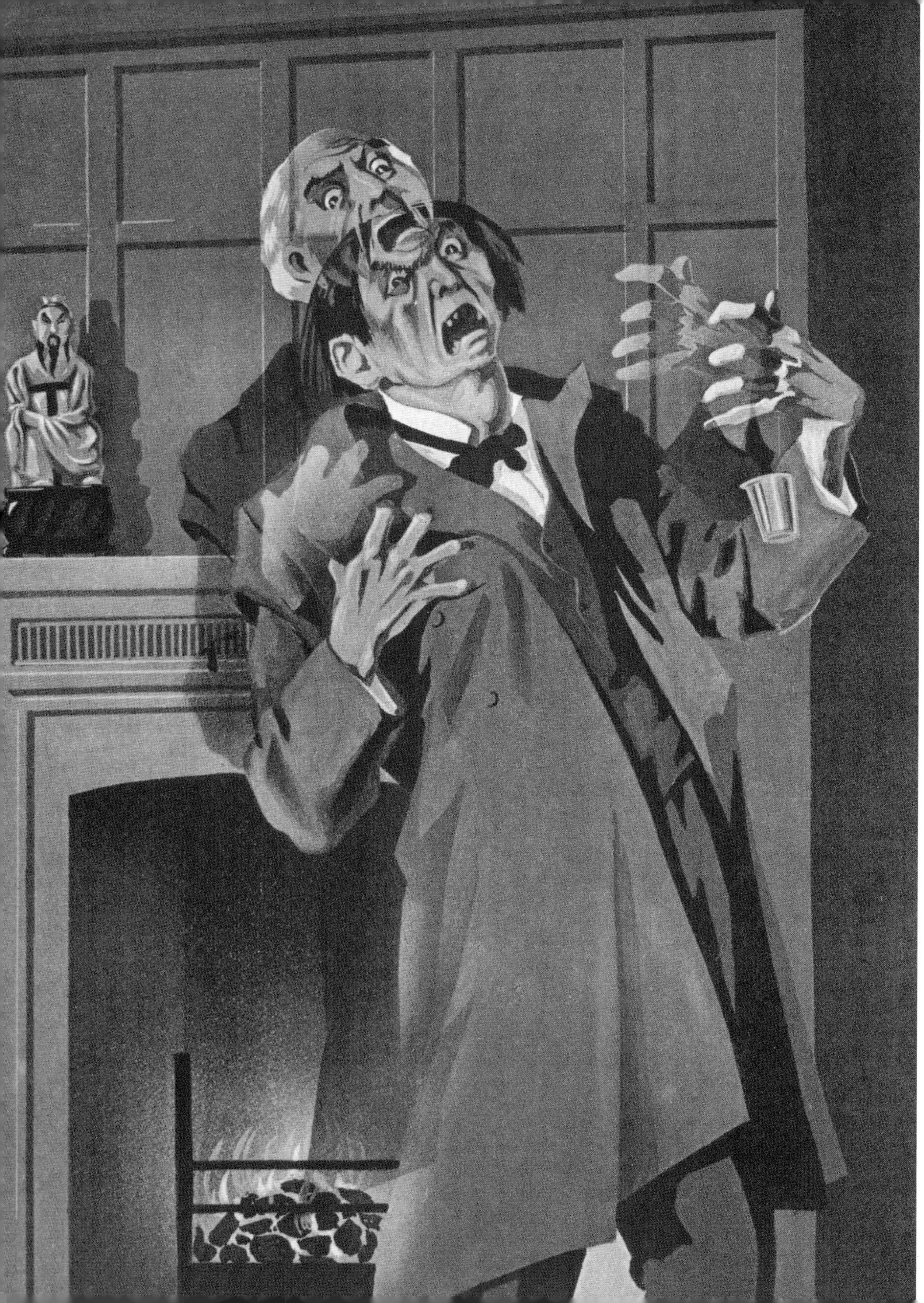

pleasure, but even resisted the calls of business, that they might enjoy them uninterrupted' (1984: 30).

The novella thus begins with a view of middle-class respectability and the tedium that it induces. Stevenson suggests that middle-class ideas of decency, and the empty rituals with which they are associated, are self-destructive. The empty lives of the middle-aged, middle-class professional (*Jekyll and Hyde* focuses on quintessentially Victorian middle-class occupations, medicine and the law) are not the antidote to degeneration; on the contrary, they are its cause. This is not a reactionary critique in the manner of Nordau, nor that touched upon by Lankester, because the bohemian Stevenson seeks to locate degeneration in terms of both class and place. The tale that Enfield relates to Utterson, in order to relieve the tedium, centres on a particular street where he witnessed an uncouth man brutally knock down a child; the man was subsequently apprehended by a crowd that forced him to provide financial compensation for the incident. The description of the street is revealing. One end of the street is governed by trade, light and bustle; its inhabitants are said to be 'all doing well [...] and all emulously hoping to do better still' in this place of 'painted shutters, well-polished brasses, and general cleanliness and gaiety of note' (1984: 30). This contrasts with the scene further down the street, in which 'a certain sinister block of building [...] bore in every feature, the marks of prolonged and sordid negligence' (1984: 30). Here, degeneration is manifest: 'tramps slouched' and 'the schoolboy had tried his knife on the mouldings' (1984: 30).

Hyde is first seen against this backdrop, suggesting that he is a product of it, although in a way in which Enfield finds difficult to explain. Hyde, for Enfield, is 'an extraordinary looking man, and yet I can name nothing out of the way' (1984: 34); and while he might seem to have links with the urban poverty that characterises this part of the street (on which Jekyll's house, too, stands), he also refers to himself as a 'gentleman' (1984: 32) and produces gold and a cheque from Coutts for nearly one hundred pounds to compensate the child's father. It emerges that the signature on the cheque is that of Dr Jekyll, and so begins a series of revelations which link Hyde to Jekyll – not through blackmail, as had been initially assumed by his friends (which include Utterson), but by the disclosure that Hyde is that part of Jekyll which an adherence to civilised values has forced him to repress. As Jekyll puts it, 'I concealed my pleasures' as '[I] began to look around me and take stock of my progress and position in the world' (1984: 81).

Jekyll is thus divided, as is the city of London itself, and Stevenson links these splittings and bifurcations to explore both psychological and social themes. Extremes of wealth and poverty, and their proximity in *Jekyll and Hyde*, reflect emerging concerns during the period about London. Such concerns served to map an idea of degeneracy on to the urban landscape in order to explain the presence of supposedly degenerate urban types. Andrew Mearns, for instance, in *The Bitter Cry of Outcast London: An Inquiry into the Condition of the Abject Poor* (1883), associated slums with what became

OPPOSITE:
Illustration by Edward J. Sullivan from an edition of *Strange Case of Dr Jekyll and Mr Hyde*, 1928.
British Library 012618.ee.38.

a popular image of the urban Jungle, noting 'how can those places be called homes, compared with which the lair of a wild beast would be a comfortable and healthy spot?' (1883: 7). The discussion of the relationship between the rich and the poor of London was explored by the journalist W T Stead in a series of articles entitled 'The Maiden Tribute of Modern Babylon' (1885). In these he famously exposed how a trade in child prostitutes in the East End of London depended upon wealthy clients from the West End.

The relationship between wealth and poverty at this time was mapped, quite literally, by Charles Booth in his *Life and Labour of the People of London* (1889). Booth identified seven social classes in London, ranging from the 'Upper middle class' to the 'The lowest of occasional labourers, loafers and semi-criminals' (1902: 33). Booth's team of researchers colour-coded the social and economic profile of each street, and plotted it on to a map of the city. This revealed that in certain parts of London wealth and poverty, represented on the map in yellow and black respectively, had a particular proximity. The map provided a visual confirmation of what theories of degeneration had conceptually asserted: the apparently civilised was in reality dangerously close to the barbaric. In 1883 Mearns had claimed that 'The churches are making the discovery that seething in the very centre of our great cities, concealed by the thinnest crust of civilization and decency, is a vast mass of moral corruption, of heart-breaking misery and absolute godlessness' (1883: 4).

This thin crust of civilisation is probed in *Jekyll and Hyde*, as Stevenson emphasises the apparently troubling proximity of wealth and poverty in which Hyde lives. Utterson sees that part of Soho as being 'like a district of some city in a nightmare'; he observes 'many ragged children huddled in the doorways, and many women of many different nationalities passing out, key in hand, to have a morning glass' (1984: 48). Such images of the city shape the language used to describe the 'independent denizens' (1984: 82) which inhabit Jekyll. They are again employed, possibly by Hyde, when reference is made to 'Jekyll was now my city of refuge' (1984: 91–2). However, while Stevenson's novella might seem to work through some ideas drawn from theories of degeneration and contemporary accounts of London, he is nevertheless critical of what he perceives to be a specifically middle-class degeneracy.

Jekyll and Hyde, like contemporary theories of degeneration, suggests the presence of the enemy within. Yet, unlike those theories, Stevenson argues that the professional classes destroy themselves because they are inherently empty. Hyde is ultimately little more than the product of middle-class repression. The ending of the novella is revealing in this regard. 'Henry Jekyll's Statement of the Case', which concludes the novella, should explain everything, but raises more questions than it can answer, in the main because by the end of the 'Statement' we cannot be sure who is narrating.

The final narrative begins with a confident voice that is clearly Henry Jekyll's, in which he sketches his family background. However, this 'I' becomes replaced with a third person that claims that in the transformation from Jekyll to Hyde 'It was Hyde [...] and Hyde alone,

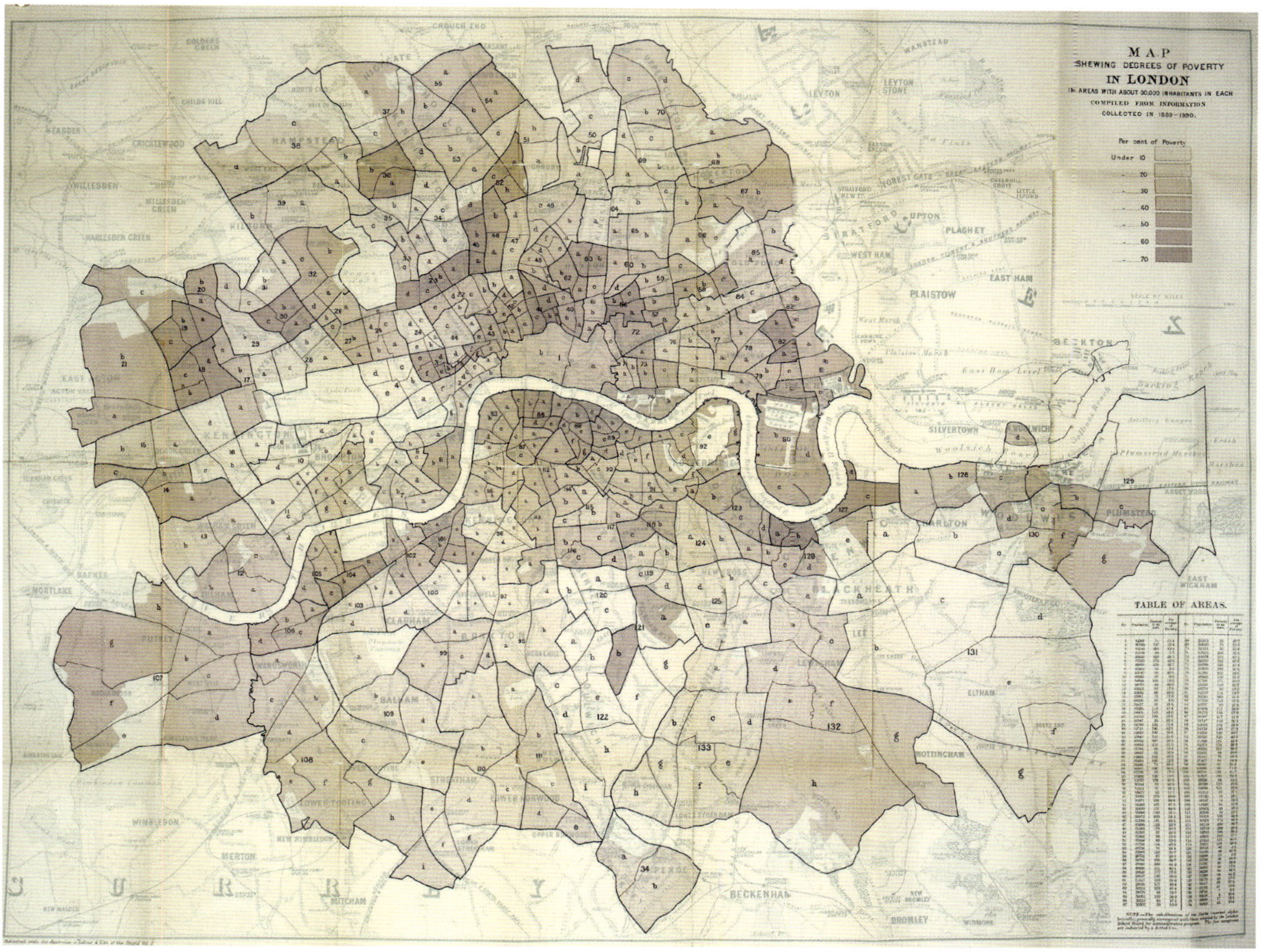

Charles Booth's map of social classes in London, 1891.

British Library Maps.C.21.a.18 map1.

that was guilty. Jekyll was no worse; he woke again to his good qualities seemingly unimpaired' (1984: 87). The subsequent voice that claims that Jekyll was now 'my city of refuge' could arguably be that of Hyde. Nor do the final lines of the novella clarify who this narrator is, as the observation 'I bring the life of that unhappy Henry Jekyll to an end' (1984: 97) could conceivably have been written by either Jekyll or Hyde. Utterson's discovery of the body does not help us either, as he merely notes 'that he was looking on the body of a self-destroyer' (1984: 70). Ultimately, then, we cannot be sure whether Jekyll kills Hyde or whether Hyde kills Jekyll. How we interpret the end determines how we view the theme of middle-class repression that Stevenson has explored throughout.

If we see Jekyll as having killed Hyde, then Stevenson's novella seems to represent the triumph of civilisation over barbarism. If we see Hyde as the victor, however, albeit a self-destructive one, then the self-destructive forces let loose by civilisation prevail. This is the radical conclusion that Stevenson leaves open to us. Such self-destructive tendencies pervade theories of degeneration, too, in rather more reactionary formations. They are also, as we have seen, linked to London, in which urban degenerates occupy locations that are a little too close to comfort for many. William Booth, founder of the Salvation Army, noted in *In Darkest England and the Way Out* (1890):

> As there is a darkest Africa, is there not also a darkest England? Civilisation, which can breed its own barbarians, does it not also breed its own pygmies? May we not find a parallel at our own doors, and discover within a stone's throw of our cathedrals and palaces similar horrors to those which Stanley has found existing in the great Equatorial forest? (1890: 11–12)

The Whitechapel Murders and Their Legacy

The *fin-de-siècle* Gothic is shaped by these social concerns, by anxieties given a quite specific inflection by the Whitechapel murders that took place between 31 August and 9 November 1888. The brutal murder of five women may seem unrelated to the cultural specifics of the Gothic tradition explored here, but, as David Punter has noted, Jack the Ripper became an 'archetype' that captured urban fears, feeding into a Gothic tradition in which the lines between fact and fiction became peculiarly blurred. W T Stead's *Pall Mall Gazette* attempted to develop the class narrative of Stead's earlier account of East End child prostitution in claiming, 'There certainly seems to be a tolerably realistic impersonification of Mr. Hyde at large in Whitechapel' (Curtis, 2001: 77). This view was also endorsed by the *Globe*, which on 1 September 1888 stated that 'One can almost imagine that Whitechapel is haunted by a demon of the type of Hyde, who goes about killing for the mere sake of slaughter' (Curtis, 2001: 77).

Judith R Walkowitz has argued that the press at the time of the murders developed a form of the so-called 'male Gothic' narrative, inviting their putatively male readers to be both appalled and titillated by the suppressed erotic spectacle of the victims' conjectured lives (Walkowitz 1992: 192). In this way, a type of male voyeurism was established in some of the more sensationalist parts of the press, even as a more radical newspaper such as the *Pall Mall Gazette* argued that the killer was a crazed doctor or medical student (London Hospital was in the Whitechapel area). Implicit in this suggestion was the assertion that professional men preyed upon working-class prostitutes.

Jekyll and Hyde, published two years before the Whitechapel murders, provided a particular way of reading them. This suggested that certain types of men were suspect (the 'Mr Hyde' of the *Pall Mall Gazette* quotation above); notably, one minor servant aside, *Jekyll and Hyde* is about middle-class men. Such was the peculiar fragility of the boundaries between Stevenson's novella and real-life events during this crisis that the actor Richard Mansfield, starring as both Jekyll and Hyde in a stage adaptation at the Lyceum Theatre in London's West End, was briefly entertained as a possible suspect because of his apparently realistic on-stage transformations.

The theme of masculinity runs through the *fin-de-siècle* Gothic, a concern that develops some of the links between civilisation and projected barbarism that were prevalent at the time. Images of a fatigued masculinity were later developed by Arthur Machen in

The Great God Pan (1890). His novella begins with an experiment by one Dr Raymond, who describes himself as a follower of 'transcendental medicine' (2006: 9), a phrase borrowed from *Jekyll and Hyde*. Raymond places a young woman called Mary into a surgical trance, intended to give her a glimpse of Pan, and so expose her to the mystical significance of the world; but the brain operation goes wrong, leaving her insane. It transpires that Mary is left pregnant by this encounter, and she gives birth to a child that we first see as an adult, a *femme fatale* named Helen Vaughan. Helen's journey takes her from rural Wales to London, where she works her way into (and up) society through various relationships, only to kill off her paramours by driving them to suicide. Such is the spate of suicides that it seems to indicate that some form of serial killing is taking place. However, 'The police had been forced to confess themselves powerless to arrest or to explain the sordid murders of Whitechapel; but before the horrible suicides of Piccadilly and Mayfair they were dumbfounded'

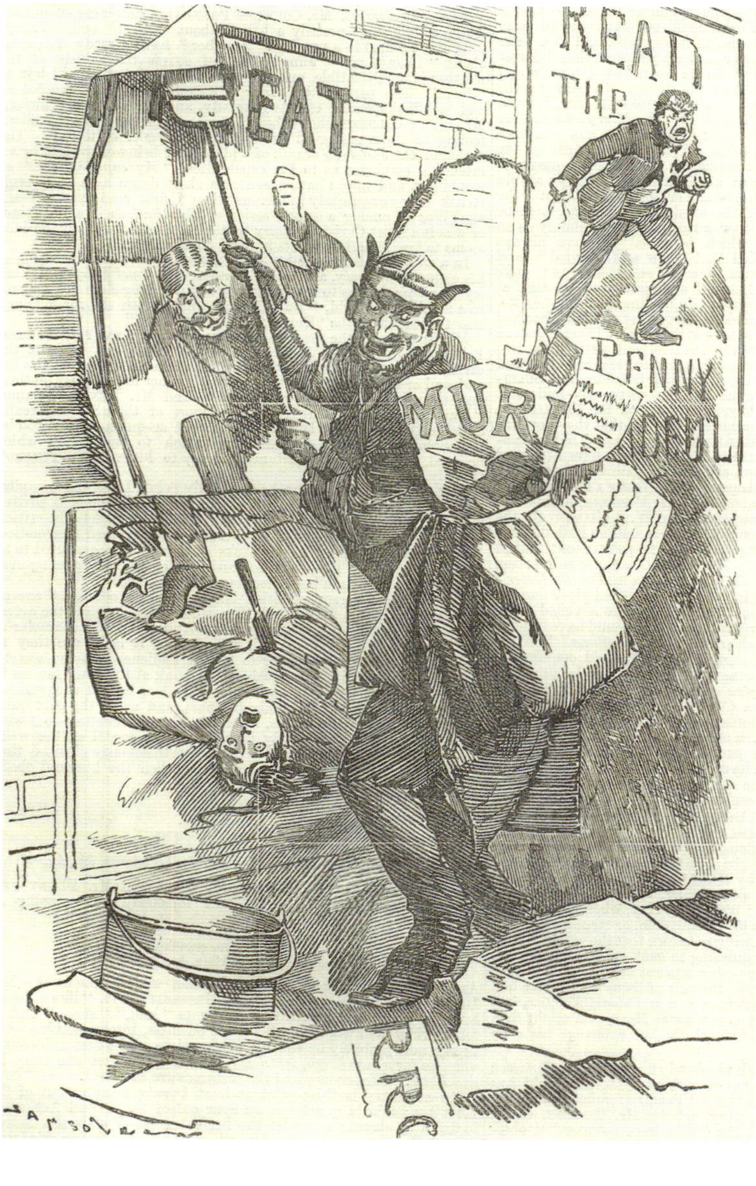

'Horrible London, or the Pandemonium of Posters', cartoon from *Punch* magazine, 1888.
British Library C.194.b.199.

The cartoon, which appeared while the East End was in the grip of the Ripper murders, makes a link between sensational literature and crime.

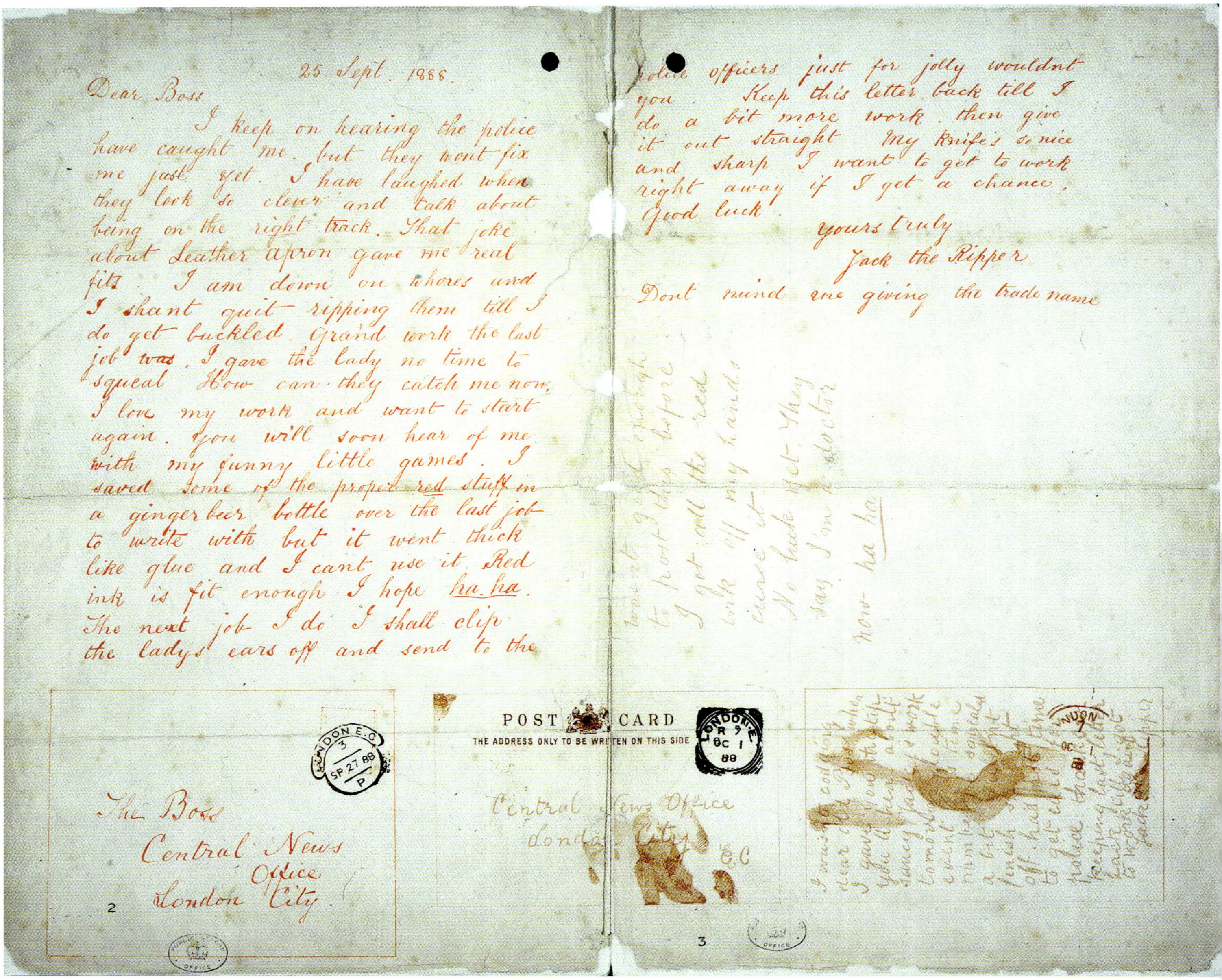

25. Sept. 1888.

Dear Boss

I keep on hearing the police have caught me but they wont fix me just yet. I have laughed when they look so clever and talk about being on the right track. That joke about Leather Apron gave me real fits. I am down on whores and I shant quit ripping them till I do get buckled. Grand work the last job was, I gave the lady no time to squeal. How can they catch me now. I love my work and want to start again. You will soon hear of me with my funny little games. I saved some of the proper red stuff in a ginger beer bottle over the last job to write with but it went thick like glue and I cant use it. Red ink is fit enough I hope ha. ha. The next job I do I shall clip the ladys ears off and send to the police officers just for jolly wouldnt you. Keep this letter back till I do a bit more work, then give it out straight. My knife's so nice and sharp I want to get to work right away if I get a chance. Good luck.

Yours truly

Jack the Ripper

Dont mind me giving the trade name

wasnt good enough to post this before I got all the red ink off my hands curse it. No luck yet. They say I'm a doctor now ha ha

The Boss
Central News
Office
London City

LONDON E.C. 3 SP 27 88 P

2

POST CARD
THE ADDRESS ONLY TO BE WRITTEN ON THIS SIDE

Central News Office
London City
E.C

LONDON E. OC 1 88

3

Letter from 'Jack the Ripper' to the Central News Agency, 25 September 1888.
The National Archives, Kew.

(2006: 46). Helen effectively becomes a female Jack the Ripper. She uses socially well-connected and wealthy men to socially advance, only to dispose of them when they are no longer of any use to her, apparently by revealing her true identity.

Machen parodies the alarm caused by the Jack the Ripper murders in the cry of a street newspaper vendor: 'The West End Horrors; Another Awful Suicide; Full Details!' (2006: 49). Such language echoes the newspaper headlines, shouted aloud by street vendors, that described horrors of the East End murders in 1888. The police are baffled because whereas the East End's violent atmosphere could be used to explain the murders, there is no such accounting for the deaths in the affluent West End, in which 'Each of these men who had resolved to die a tortured, shameful death was rich, prosperous, and to all appearance in love with the world' (2006: 46). Indeed,

Helen functions like a female Hyde. As an eyewitness recalls, 'I saw her entering a house in one of the meanest and most disreputable streets in Soho', an area that is 'hardly [...] a place where you would expect to see a lady who lives in Ashley Street, Piccadilly' (2006: 54). Helen is eventually confronted with her actions and, as in *Jekyll and Hyde*, the novella concludes in an act of self-destruction when Helen hangs herself. However, as in Stevenson's novella, the conclusion is not as clear-cut as it initially appears.

The penultimate document in Machen's text is an account of Helen's death. Written by one Dr Robert Matheson, it is apparently found among his papers after his own death, some seven years after the event it describes. The chapter is tellingly entitled 'The Fragments', and while at one level this relates to Matheson's cryptic notes (which have been written in Latin and are subject to abbreviation) and the fragmentary notes of Dr Raymond and his associate, Clarke, it also relates to the strange physical dissolution of Helen herself. As Matheson records, 'The skin, and the flesh, and the muscles, and the bones, and the firm structure of the human body that I had thought to be unchangeable, and permanent as adamant, began to melt and dissolve' (2006: 62). In her death Helen recapitulates a history of life, as Matheson recalls witnessing:

> ... all the work by which man has been made repeated before my eyes. I saw the form waver from sex to sex, dividing itself from itself, and then again reunited. Then I saw the body descend to the beasts whence it ascended, and that which was on the heights go down to the depths, even to the abyss of being. The principle of life, which makes organism, always remained, while the outward form changed. (2006: 62)

This biological history of living organisms suggests a wider engagement with 'life' on Helen's part than that found in the restricted world of the London aristocrats on whom she preys. The ostensible escape from social constraint that she seemingly offers reflects the potential freedoms enacted by Hyde. Indeed, David Punter has noted a similarity between *The Great God Pan* and *Jekyll and Hyde* when he claims that 'The paradox of *The Great God Pan* is that the visitation which liberates the human being from the repression of false assumptions also destroys the barriers which retain human individuation' (1996: 23) – or, as it is phrased in Stevenson's novella, Jekyll had become 'a composite' (1984: 89). Helen is also a composite, being part-human and part-Pan. The critic Kelly Hurley, following a term coined by the novelist William Hope Hodgson, has usefully examined the presence of the 'abhuman' in the Gothic literature of the period. Hurley notes of this abhuman that it 'retains vestiges of its human identity, but has become, or is in the process of becoming, some half-human other' (Hurley 2002: 190).

Such a category brings together *Jekyll and Hyde* and *The Great God Pan*, and helps to identify the shared context of degeneration as the place where 'uncanny human metamorphoses' (Hurley 2002: 196) demonstrated the concern that 'natural born criminals' represented

Richard Mansfield as Jekyll and Hyde, from the Richard Mansfield calendar for 1900.
British Library LD.31.b.1745.
The actor's transformation between mild Dr Jekyll and brutal Mr Hyde was so convincing that one member of the public accused him of being the Ripper.

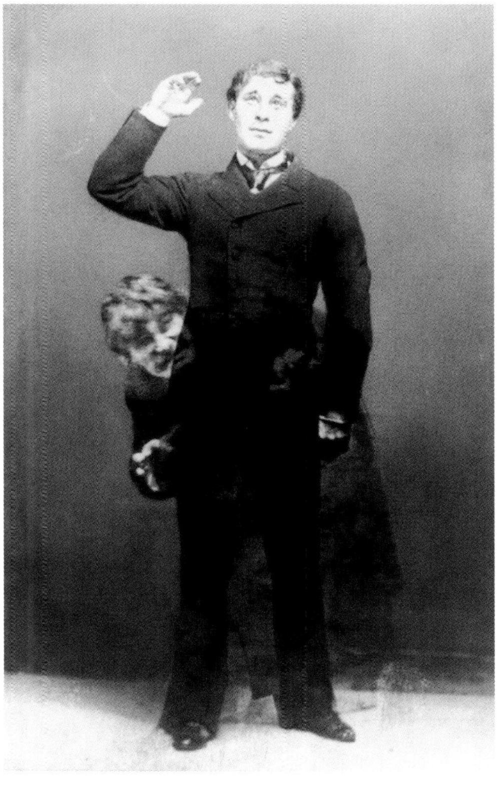

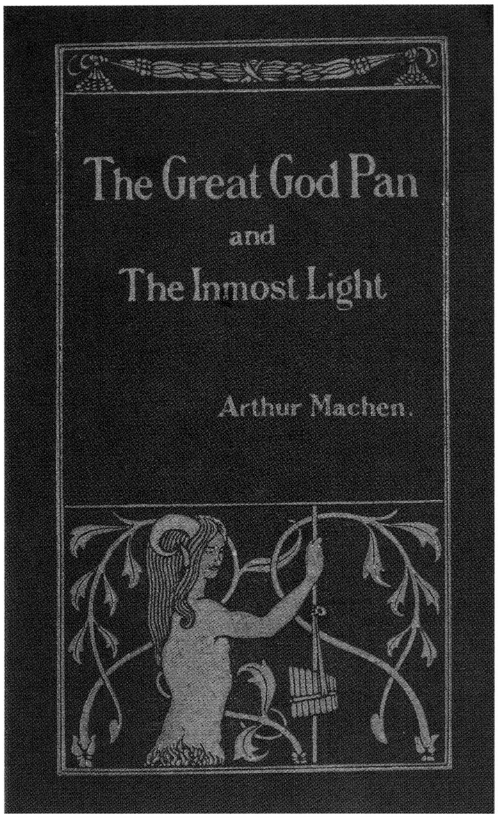

Arthur Machen, *The Great God Pan*, 1894. Cover design and illustration by Aubrey Beardsley.
British Library 012627.g.5.

an atavistic throwback that aligned people with animals. Indeed, as the two novellas explored here indicate, the borderline between human and animal seemed oddly porous, with the presence of science not so much policing this boundary between the human and the animal as producing it. As Hurley argues, 'it is notable that in both *Pan* and *Jekyll* seemingly supernatural phenomena are produced through scientific practice' (2002: 192). The demonisation of science, and especially medicine, is notable in the era; this is due, at least in part, to a longstanding suspicion that medical doctors were amoral butchers whose discoveries were underpinned by vivisection. The strong anti-vivisection movement of the time focused attention on the apparent moral poverty of medical investigations, an issue given stark treatment by H G Wells in *The Island of Doctor Moreau* (1896).

The Beast Within

Wells's novel centres on an eyewitness account given by one Edward Prendick, who is shipwrecked somewhere in the South Pacific and finds himself on an island occupied by Doctor Moreau, a vivisectionist forced out of London because of his scandalous medical experiments. He has used his island retreat to assemble, from animal parts, humanoid figures referred to as the Beast People. These strange creatures are taught the rudiments of language in the form of a series of prohibitions designed to 'civilise' them (including a law that they must not eat any flesh). The experiments fail as the creatures revert to animal type and Prendick records the pathos that is engendered by the sight of them: 'Before they had been beasts, their instincts fitly adapted to their surroundings, and happy as living things may be. Now they stumbled in the shackles of humanity, lived in a fear that never died' (2000: 93). Wells's novel turns the post-evolutionary idea of the animal within on its head, as it shifts the focus to an explicit condemnation of a certain mode of medical experimentation that creates monsters. It also has a continuing effect on Prendick when he returns to England:

> I could not persuade myself that the men and women I met were not also another, still passably human, Beast People, animals half-wrought into the outward image of human souls, and that they would presently begin to revert, to show first this bestial mark and then that. (2000: 128)

The enemy, yet again, is seemingly to be found within, but this picture is complicated by Wells because his novel has clear racial undertones in its distant island setting and in the implicit links between the 'beast' and racial 'otherness' that it sets in place.

The Gothic narratives of Stevenson, Machen and Wells play out their fears at a physical level. In these fictions the beast is manifested from within, or is reassembled by a seemingly deranged scientist. There are points of contact here to the discourse on degeneration, and one significant contribution to that Gothic dialogue is Oscar Wilde's *The Picture of Dorian Gray*. The representation of diseased art in this novel appeared to link a

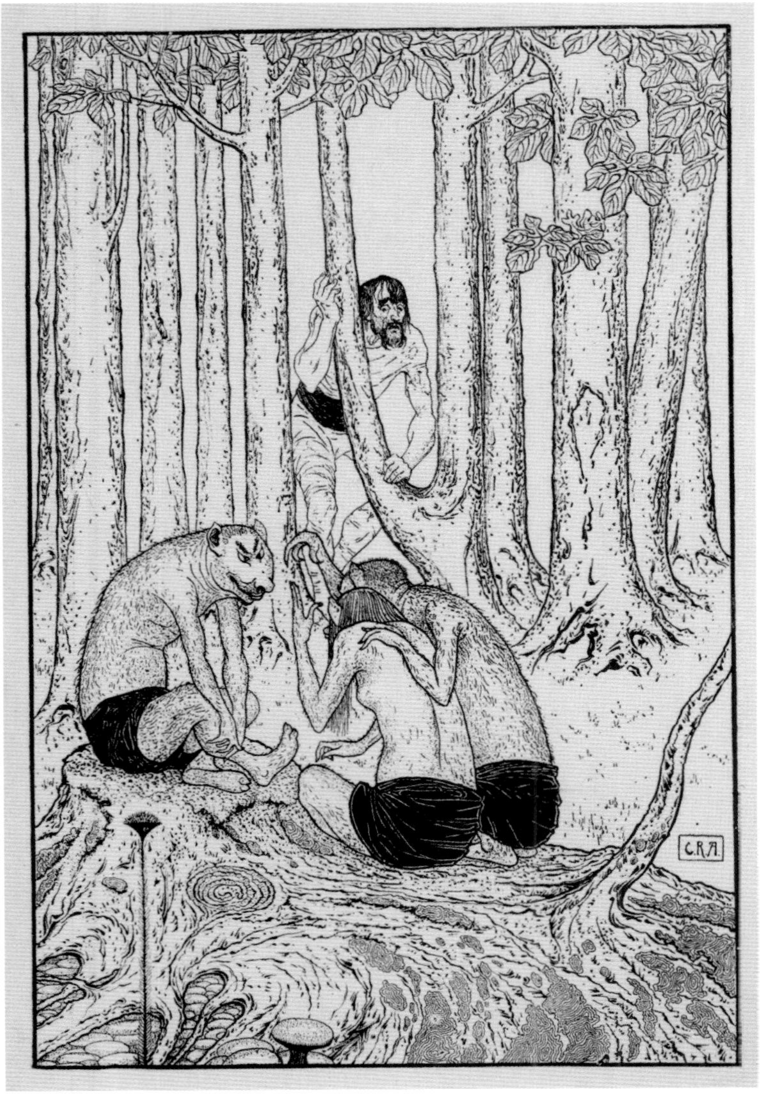

Frontispiece to H G Wells, *The Island of Doctor Moreau*, 1896.
British Library 012627.1.2.

Decadent aesthetic with the type of moral corruption that Nordau claimed to have observed more generally in Wilde's work.

The idea that Wilde's novel might be the source of corruption took a literal turn in 1895, when Edward Carson QC (the Marquess of Queensberry's barrister in the libel trial initiated by Wilde) referred to the novel in court in an attempt to incriminate Wilde. The author deftly sidestepped such an interrogation by asserting that the novel was about art and matters of artistic influence. The passages identified by Carson are nevertheless revealing, as they centre on the artist Basil Hallward's feeling for Dorian Gray. Basil's adoration of Dorian could be construed, as Wilde would assert in court, as a love of beauty. However, the artist's concern that the painting should not be seen publicly raises another issue. Hallward tells Lord Henry Wotton that the painting reveals nothing about Dorian, but everything about Hallward's feelings for the subject, so that 'I am afraid that I have shown in it the secret of my own soul' (1985: 9). Degenerating bodies become replaced by art that goes 'bad' as

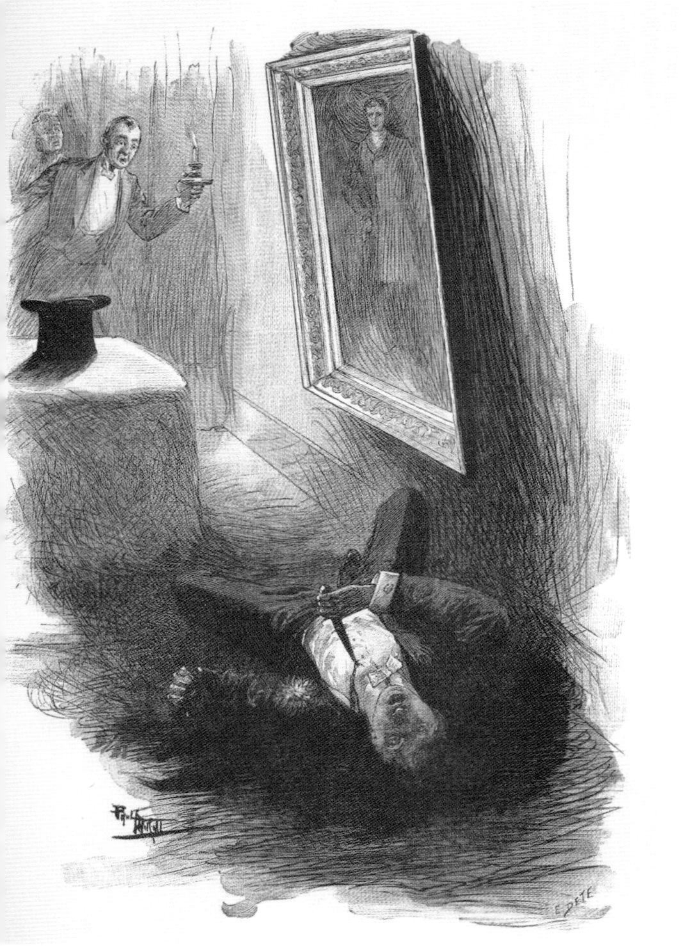

Illustration by Eugène Dété from an edition of *The Picture of Dorian Gray*, 1910.
British Library Cup.501.c.13.

Dorian, so the narrative subsequently relates, fails to lead a beautiful life, but rather one that includes blackmail, drug-taking and murder, the effects of which all become registered on the corrupted painting.

One of the questions raised by the novel relates to the consequences of what a Decadent 'Art for Art's sake' attitude produces and generates. While Carson sought to incriminate Wilde over the specific nature of Hallward's guilty 'secret', Nordau had more broadly condemned Wilde for his amoral Decadent sympathies. The novel is, however, more complex than this. Dorian's attempt to transform a Decadent aesthetic into a metaphysic has disastrous consequences for him, for others and for art itself. Paradoxically, however, the novel seems to be a critique of Decadence rather than a celebration of it. At its end Dorian plunges the knife he has used to kill Basil into the painting, and is transformed into a corpse that was 'withered, wrinkled, and loathsome of visage' (1985: 246). In effect, Dorian has become 'bad' Art. While at one level the novel seems like an exercise in *fin-de-siècle* ennui, it also stands as a trenchant criticism of the self-destructive amoral life that critics such as Nordau had attributed to writers such as Wilde.

Empire Gothic

Empire, and anxieties about its associated 'great game', represent another key theme of *fin-de-siècle* Gothic. Rudyard Kipling addressed ideas about empire and British colonial expansion in a series of tales including 'The Mark of the Beast' (1890), 'The Strange Ride of Morrowbie Jukes' (1885), 'The Phantom 'Rickshaw' (1888) and 'My Own True Ghost Story' (1888). 'The Mark of the Beast' centres on how, on New Year's Eve, a drunken Englishman named Fleete desecrates a temple statue of the Indian monkey god, Hanuman. Fleete is subsequently touched by a leper and transformed over the next day into a wolfish animal. Only when his friends, Strickland and the narrator, capture the leper and torture him into lifting the curse is Fleete restored to his human self. The post-Darwinian idea of the animal within may seem to have been disciplined and corrected in this tale, but the narrative reveals consequences for both Strickland and the narrator. It records how, after Fleete has been restored to himself, Strickland 'went into an amazing fit of hysterics' while the narrator 'laughed and gasped and gurgled just as shamefully'; both know they have 'disgraced ourselves as Englishman for ever' (1891: 258) by torturing the leper with a red-hot gun barrel. As Hurley notes of this story, what is intended to be horrific is the rapid decline from the civilised to the barbaric (2002: 195), a process in which Strickland and the narrator are also marked by the beast in their treatment of the leper.

In 'The Strange Ride of Morrowbie Jukes', the eponymous Jukes, a colonial administrator in India, loses consciousness; he comes to in a strange world, inhabited by Indian subjects who openly mock his attempts to assert authority. Jukes is in a limbo-world populated by people who have been falsely identified as dead and their social authorities suspended, including his own. In this strange world an informal hierarchy is presided over by the malevolent Gunga Dass, a high-ranking Brahmin, once the manager of a branch telegraph office, who thwarts Jukes's attempts to escape. Jukes's social invisibility makes him almost ghost-like; at one point he is trampled by some natives who apparently cannot see him. Colonial authority is rendered spectral, and it is with some difficulty that Jukes is finally able to escape.

Colonial history is addressed in 'My Own True Ghost Story' through a similar language of spectrality, although the narrator reassuringly notes that 'No native ghost has yet been authentically reported to have frightened an Englishman' (2007a: 36). He occupies a dâk-bungalow, a typical residence for colonial officials such as himself, and the type of building reputedly haunted by the troubled ghosts of colonial administrators. As the narrator notes, 'A ghost that would voluntarily hang about a dâk-bungalow would be mad, of course; but so many men have died in dâk-bungalows that there must be a fair percentage of lunatic ghosts' (2007a: 37). The narrator, while in bed, hears what sounds like a game of billiards being played in the next room; he subsequently discovers that the room had been a billiard room some ten or twenty years earlier. The presence of a certain type of Britishness, represented by the billiards, is ultimately undermined when a narrative turn reveals that the noises have been caused by the wind rattling the window bolts, possibly combined with the sound of a gnawing rat. These 'ghosts' are self-generated, a potent image of British colonial power haunted by recollections of itself, even as it seeks unnaturally to replicate its power.

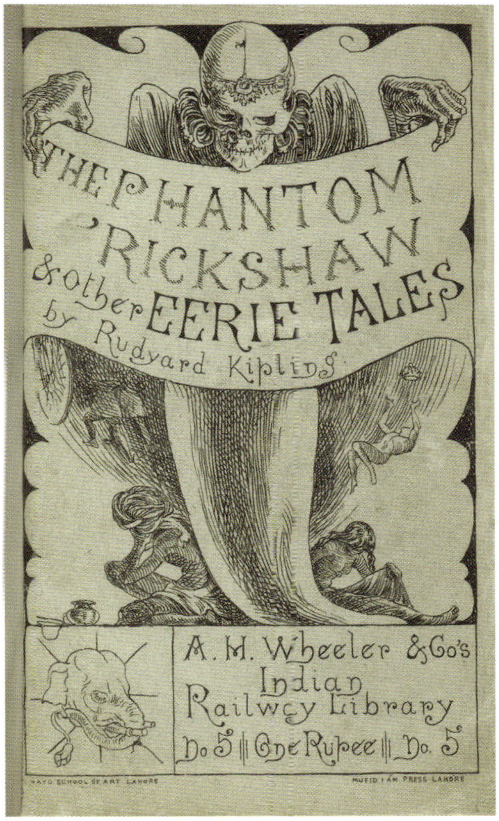

Front cover of an edition of Rudyard Kipling's *Phantom Rickshaw*, 1888.
British Library File 460.

'The Phantom 'Rickshaw' focuses on the narrow world of the Anglo-Indian. The tale centres on Theobald Pansay's affair with, and subsequent rejection of, one Mrs Wessington, who dies when Pansay becomes engaged to Kitty Mannering. The ghost of Mrs Wessington complete with her rickshaw and its four-strong crew, comes to haunt him, although only he can see her. The emphasis here is on the social world of the Anglo-Indian class, its limitations and ultimately self-destructive behaviours. As Bart Moore-Gilbert has noted of this time, 'A great preoccupation of Anglo-Indian culture [was] the problem of demoralisation in the subcontinent' (1986: 139). Pansay dies, trapped between two worlds in which 'By day I wandered with Mrs Wessington almost content. By night I implored Heaven to return me to the world as I used to know it' (2007b: 33). In effect he is trapped somewhere between the Gothic and a stifling colonial culture from which he cannot escape.

Images of empire, and the anxieties surrounding Britain's late-Victorian colonial practices, can also be found in *Dracula* (1897). Stoker's novel moves from Transylvania to London and back again, as the Count is ousted from the city as an invading presence who has migrated to London to feast on its 'teeming millions' (1996: 179) and so vampirically colonise the city. His eventual defeat represents the triumph of the West over the East.

Jonathan Harker's opening journal is the key to understanding the novel's themes. A newly qualified solicitor, Harker is on his first overseas journey, to complete the legal documentation relating to the purchase of Carfax, the house that Count Dracula is buying in

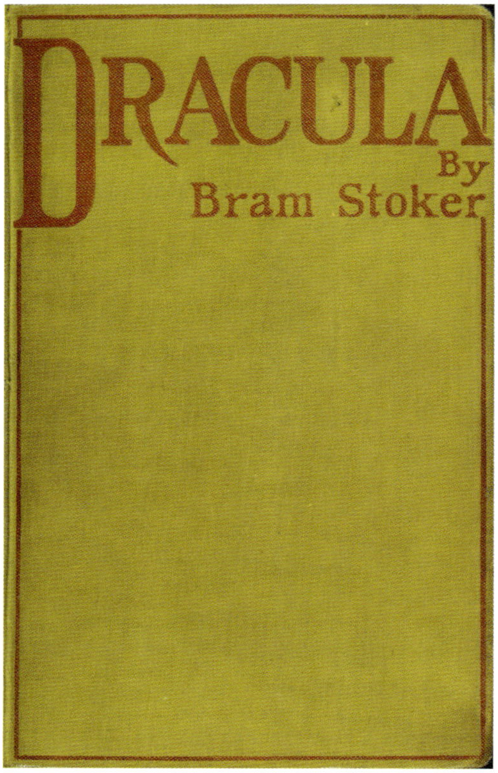

ABOVE:
Front cover of the first edition of Bram Stoker's *Dracula*, 1897.
British Library Cup.410.f.718.

BELOW:
Woodcut illustration of Vlad the Impaler, 1491.
British Library IA 2673.

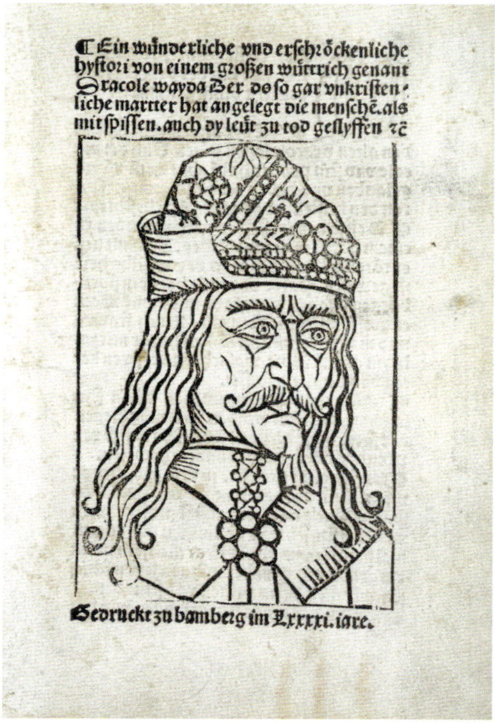

Purfleet, near the Thames. Harker, engaged to the resourceful Mina Murray, is at a turning-point in his professional and personal life, owing to his recent promotion and pending marriage.

This middle-class narrative of upward social and economic mobility contrasts with the feudal world of the Count, a world which is retrospective but somehow still relevant; as Harker notes, 'unless my senses deceive me, the old centuries had, and have powers of their own which mere "modernity" cannot kill' (1996: 36). It is a view that the Count emphasises when plotting his blood-line back to Attila. He condemns the sterile 'modernity' associated with Harker (with his newly made Kodak camera and knowledge of shorthand): 'Blood is too precious a thing in these days of dishonourable peace; and the glories of the great races are as a tale that is told' (1996: 30). Such an indictment could have been made by Nordau, despite the novel's assertion that the Count himself is a degenerate figure. However, therein lies the irony: it is Harker, prone to fainting fits, who needs to become transformed into a man of action so that, at the end of the novel, he can participate in the killing of the Count. Harker, in effect, needs to become more like the heroic, war-like Count in order to regain a masculine identity subsumed by notions of middle-class duty. Stoker's use of paradox is less sophisticated than Wilde's. However, the assumption in *Dracula* that in order to defeat a degenerate such as the Count one needs to become more like him is an incoherence generated by the text, but never resolved. It is in the area of sexuality, though, that the novel also engages with ideas of degeneration.

At Castle Dracula, Harker encounters three female vampires who are on the verge of seducing him. He recalls that 'I felt in my heart a wicked, burning desire that they would kiss me with those red lips' (1996: 37), with Harker rendered passive by the encounter. The Count disrupts their assault by throwing them a baby to feast upon. His action introduces a theme about women and mothering that Stoker explores throughout the novel. In his encounter with the three female vampires, Harker notes that he seemed to recognise the face of one of them 'and to know it in connection with some dreamy fear' (1996: 37). The reason for this strange recognition is that she resembles Mina's friend Lucy Westenra, around whom issues of sexuality are further developed.

Lucy's early letter to Mina recounts her three marriage proposals from different suitors. It occurs just after Harker's opening journal concludes, so that the three proposals echo the three female vampires who seek to seduce Harker at the outset of the narrative. Lucy dwells on her rejection of the American frontiersman Quincey P Morris and the asylum administrator Dr John Seward, noting provocatively, 'Why can't they let a girl marry three men, or as many as want her, and save all this trouble? But this is heresy, and I must not say it' (1996: 59). This implicit desire for sexual promiscuity is reinforced by her relegation of the proposal that she accepts, from Arthur Holmwood, to the postscript, a move that effectively means that her letter dwells for the most part on missed conjugal opportunities.

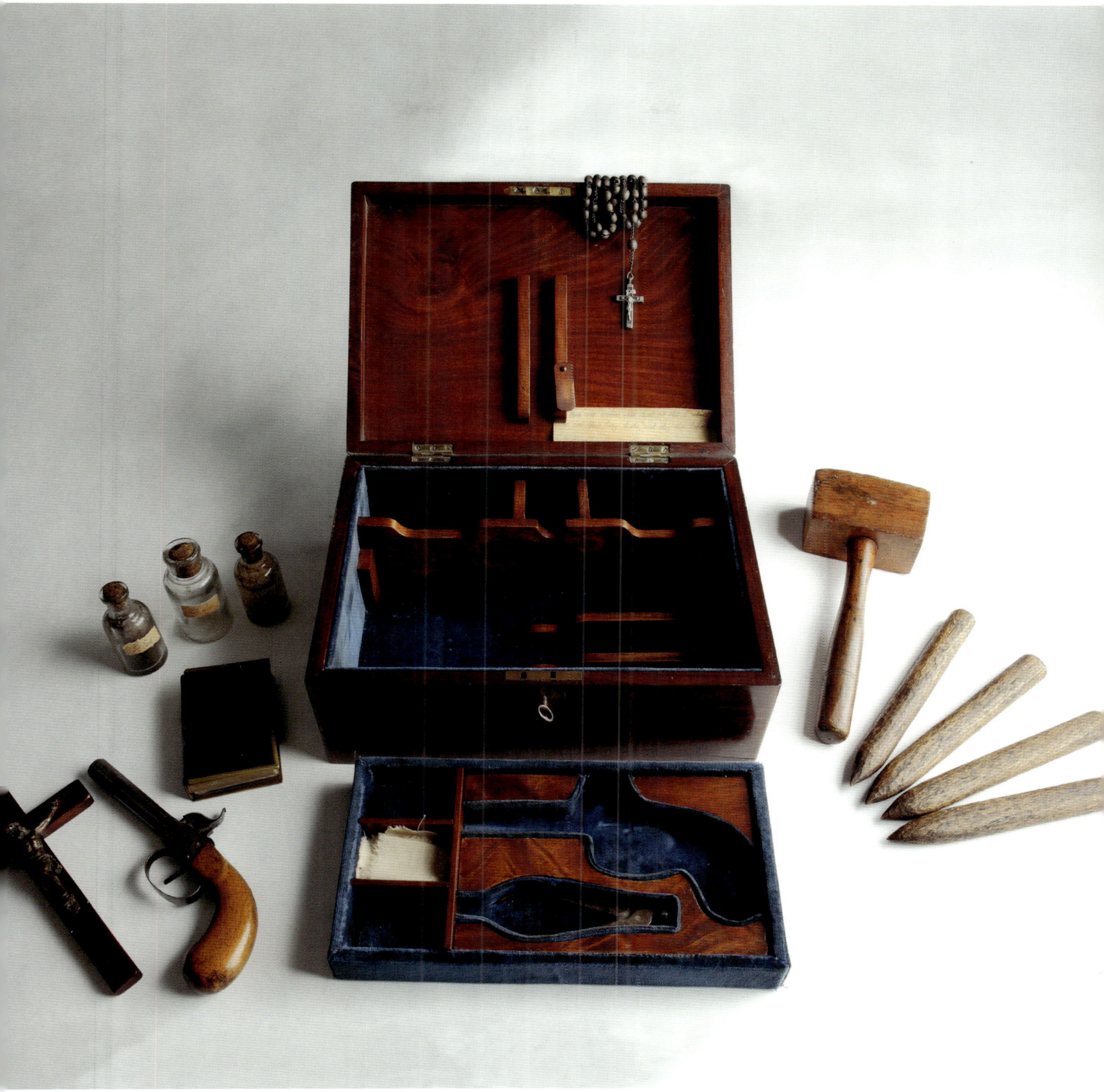

Vampire slaying kit.
Royal Armouries, Leeds.

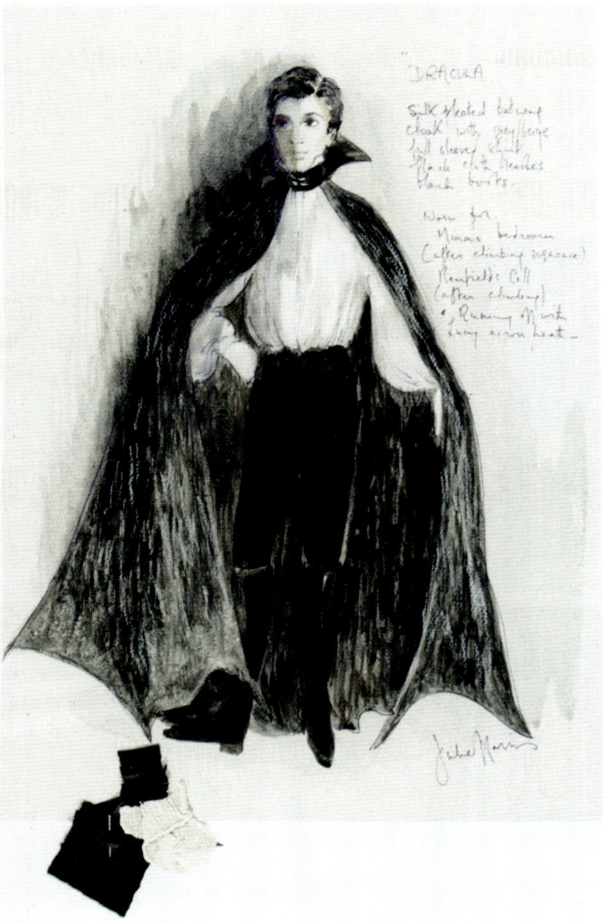

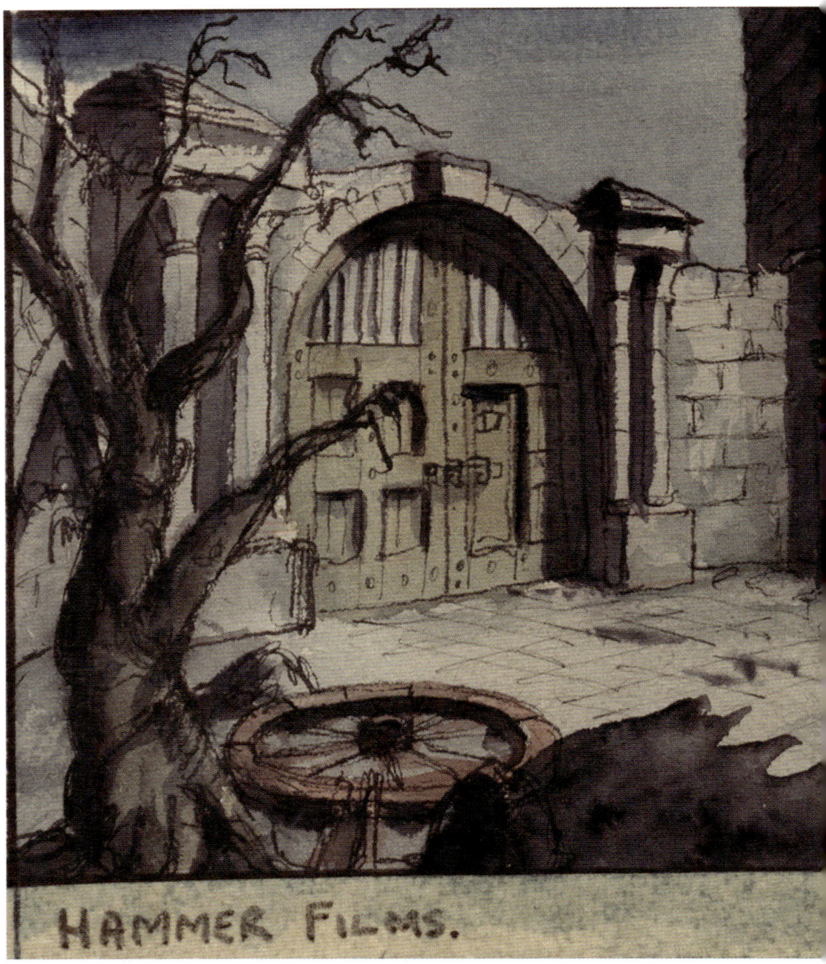

Costume design by Julie Harris for *Dracula*, film version, 1979.
British Film Institute.

Lucy is subsequently infected by the Count, and as a vampire is transformed into the 'Bloofer Lady', a name coined by the cockney children, upon whom she preys, in their attempts at describing her as the 'beautiful lady'. As a vampire, she attacks rather than nurtures young children, a shocking inversion of the maternal instinct: rather than allowing the young to suckle, Lucy is a mother who sucks. She transgresses all rules for being a proper mother, rules upheld in the novel through the conclusion's image of the naturally maternal Mina. Set some seven years after the Count's death, it describes a scene in which Mina's child sits on Van Helsing's knee. Lucy is an 'improper' woman in *Dracula* because her demands for freedom align her with the late Victorian figure of the New Woman, whose demands were mocked by Nordau in *Degeneration* as 'the cravings of travailing women' (1895: 7). The more motherly Mina caustically notes of the 'New Woman' that one day 'she will do the proposing herself. And a nice job she will make of it, too!' (1996: 89). Women such as Lucy, so Stoker suggests, require disciplining or even complete social eradication.

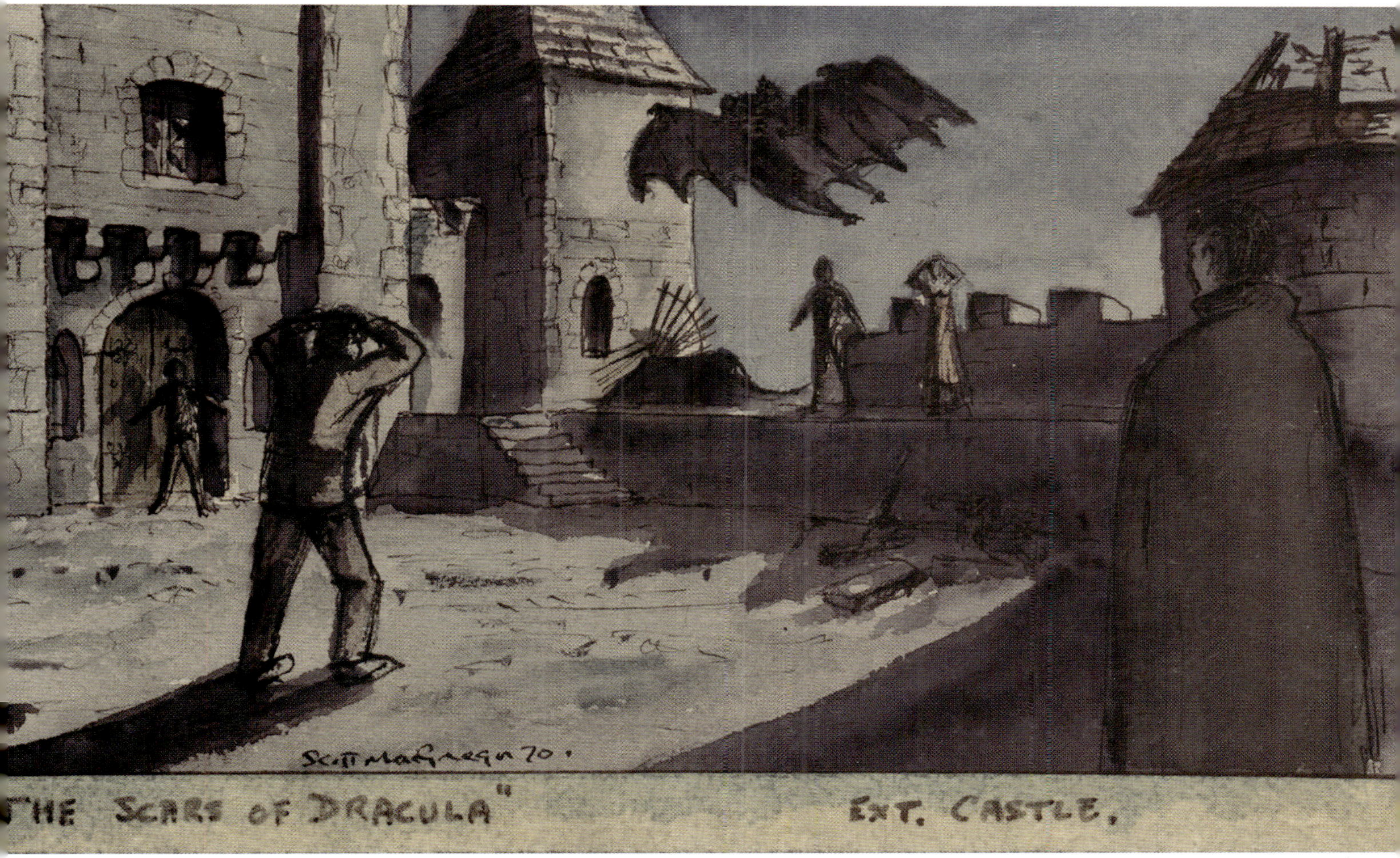

Set design for *Scars of Dracula*, Hammer Film Productions, 1970.
British Film Institute.

Ancestral Blood

This demonisation of women was given a racial inflection by Florence Marryat in *The Blood of the Vampire* (1897). Marryat was a prolific writer of sensation novels from the 1860s onwards, as well as a spiritualist and an occasional actress, and *The Blood of the Vampire* was seen by an anonymous reviewer in the *Speaker* as part of a trend of vampire novels stimulated by *Dracula*. The reviewer somewhat churlishly claimed that 'Mr. Bram Stoker has much to answer for', adding, 'The book is a mistake' (Marryat 2010: 213–14) because its vampire is not frightening enough.

This vampire, Harriet Brandt, is an independently wealthy, eighteen-year-old Creole who, on completion of her education, finds herself a part of British fashionable society. The tale ranges from a Belgian resort, her residence in London and her subsequent marriage to a writer, Anthony Pennell, who dies weeks after they marry while on an extended honeymoon in Florence. Harriet is described as emotionally depleting all who come into contact with her as she feasts on their vitality; Anthony is her final victim, while others whom she encounters, including a baby, also die in this way. A certain Dr Phillips, who knew Harriet's parents in the West Indies, states the case against Harriet when trying to warn Pennell about

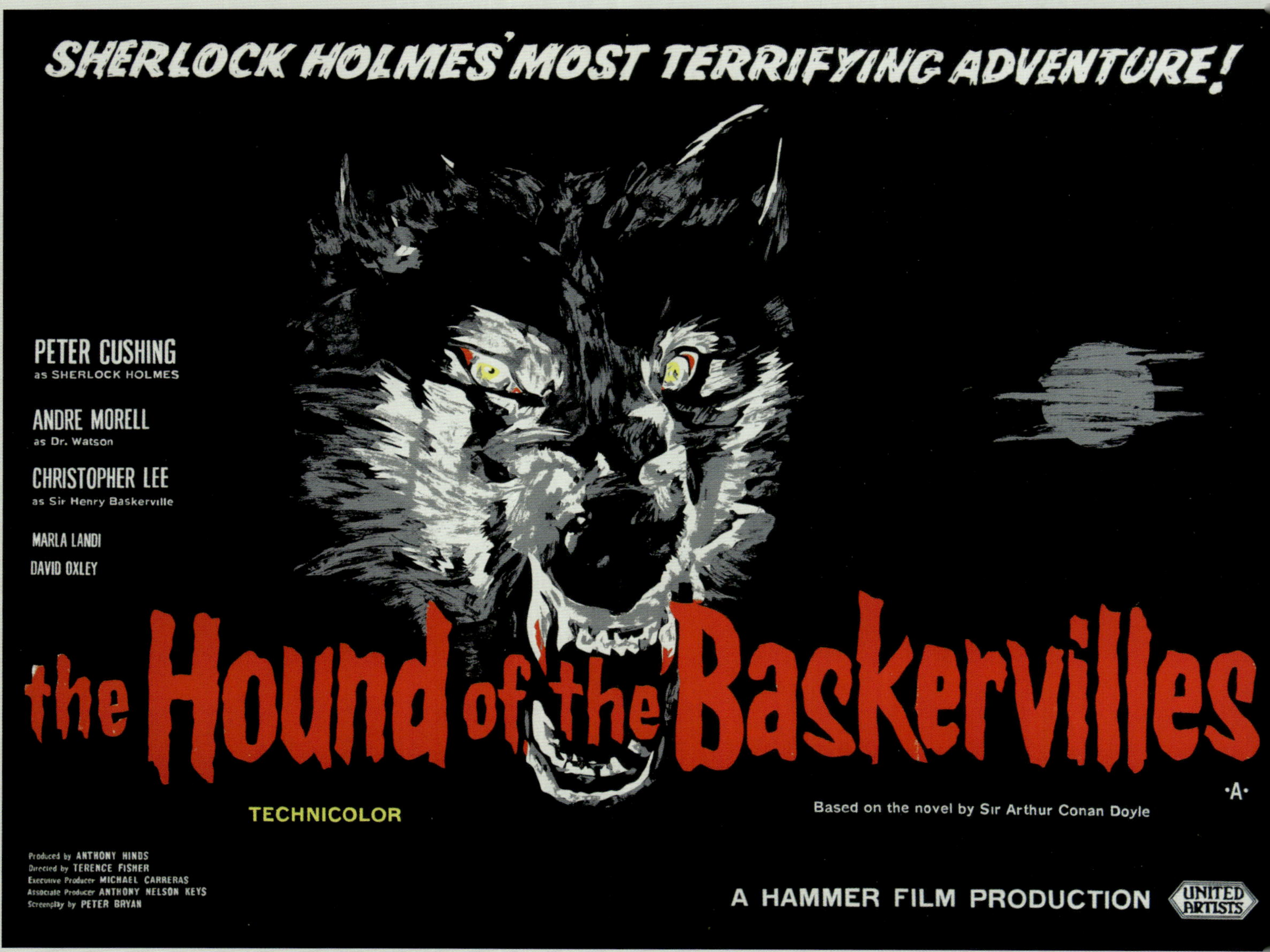

Poster for *The Hound of the Baskervilles*, Hammer Film Productions, 1959.
British Film Institute.

her: 'I knew her parents in the West Indies and could never believe in anything good coming from such stock. Whatever the girl may be, she inherits terrible proclivities, added to black blood. She is in point of fact a quadroon and not fit to marry into any decent English family!' (2010: 118).

Harriet's mother is described as half-black, obese, mentally compromised and addicted to food and sights of violence. Her husband is a white scientist who, like Wells's Doctor Moreau, is an enthusiastic vivisector. He extends his experiments to the sick and elderly slaves that populate his plantation, slaves who are routinely whipped to satiate his and his wife's love of violence. The slaves, aware of the experiments on the old and ill among them, murder Harriet's parents while she is a child. She is saved and sent to a convent, from which, at the opening of the novel, she has just emerged.

The novel reworks ideas about hereditary disposition that underpin theories of degeneration. Harriet has inherited dangerous propensities from her parents, and it is Dr Phillips's role repeatedly to outline what these are. As he tells Mrs Pullen, 'We medical men know the consequences of heredity better than outsiders can do. A woman born in such circumstances – bred of sensuality, cruelty, and heartlessness – cannot, in the order of things be modest, kind or sympathetic' (2010: 70). The irony here is that Harriet is kind and sympathetic, but she has also inherited a capacity to destroy others – a dangerous and involuntary power over which she seems to have no control. Her vampirism might be in her blood, but she thirsts consciously for love and affection; in doing so, however, she drains those that form emotional attachments to her. Harriet becomes aware of this, realising that she is responsible for a number of deaths, including Pennell's; she concludes that she can never be happy because she will always unwittingly kill those whom she loves. Harriet commits suicide after sending Mrs Pullen (whose baby died as a consequence of Harriet's affections) a note in which she poignantly requests, 'Do not think more unkindly of me than you can help. My parents have made me unfit to live' (2010: 187).

The Blood of the Vampire entertains racist imagery which links the animal within – Harriet is repeatedly likened to a tiger – to the idea of having black blood. In the end she can never be assimilated into polite, middle-class, white society, as the novel appears to uphold a view on biological inheritance that we have seen elsewhere in accounts of London and models of degeneracy.

This idea of heredity is given an interesting Gothic twist by Sir Arthur Conan Doyle in *The Hound of the Baskervilles* (1902), a novel which invalidates one Gothic narrative by embracing another. The family curse of the Baskerville family centres on an aristocratic abuse of power in the seventeenth century for which the family were punished by the killing of the dissolute Hugo Baskerville by a mysterious and terrifying hound. The apparent return of this ancestral curse, evidenced by the clues left at the recent death of Sir Charles Baskerville, prompt Holmes's investigation. However, Holmes, ever the pragmatist, realises that the solution is to discover the individual who is attempting to exploit this family Gothic narrative. At one level the tale is about ancestral inheritance built around a family curse; but the real family inheritance turns out to be a recessive faulty trait, able to skip generations and specific individuals, that the family cannot quite cast off. At Baskerville Hall, Holmes observes a portrait of the dissolute – and, indeed, degenerate – Hugo Baskerville; he is struck by the physical likeness to the naturalist Stapleton, who he now tells Watson 'is an interesting instance of a throwback' (1981: 750). This serves to identify Stapleton as the killer: he had aspired to inherit the baronetcy and Baskerville Hall by arranging the death of those who stood between him and his succession.

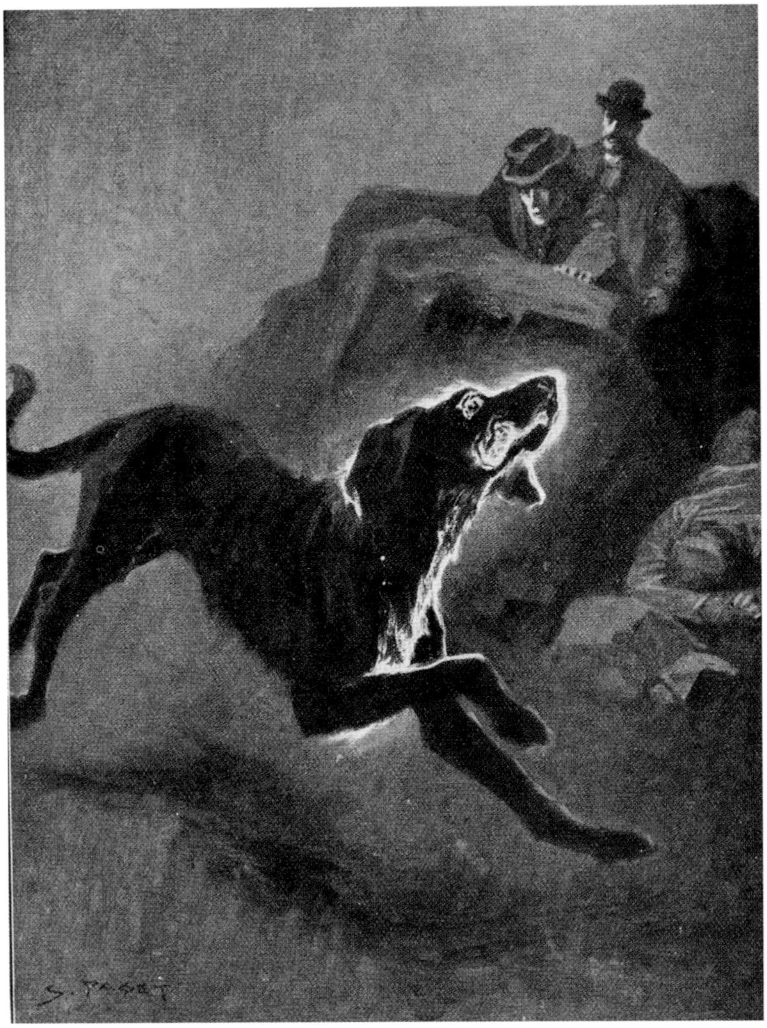

Illustration by Sidney Paget for *The Hound of the Baskervilles*, first published in the *Strand* magazine.
British Library PP.6004.glk.

As theories of degeneration do, the novel suggests that real dispositions will out, and it is noticeable that all of the main characters in Conan Doyle's narrative are in disguise. Holmes has hidden in disguise on the moor to keep watch over the principal characters, Stapleton is a Baskerville in disguise and his supposed sister is actually his wife. Even the dog has been painted with phosphorous in order to make him look more diabolic; only later does the animal reveal its true genetic identity when Watson, observing its dead body, notes that 'it was a terrible creature which was lying stretched before us. It was not a pure bloodhound and it was not a pure mastiff; but it appeared to be a combination of the two' (1981: 757). Breeding, here, is given a specific biological significance that displaces the idea of aristocratic 'breeding' or ancestral blue blood.

Nor is Holmes himself entirely immune. Across the Holmes corpus it is clear that his feelings of ennui and a predilection for drug-taking mark him out as being on the spectrum of nineteenth-century degenerates, a finely graded scale that at one end places the criminal, and at the other the genius, since both represent an aberration from the 'norm'. This fact is brought home to us at the beginning of *The Hound of the Baskervilles* when Holmes receives a visit from Dr Mortimer (a friend of the Baskerville family), who is the author of essays entitled 'Is Disease a Reversion?', 'Some Freaks of Atavism' and 'Do We Progress?' Mortimer is also a collector of the primitive skulls that he finds in the Neolithic sites on the Grimpen Mire, the moor where much of the action takes place, and on first meeting Holmes he indicates that he would like to add his skull to the collection because of its unusual formation. The genius and the primitive thus represent different ends of an evolutionary scale.

As this essay has argued, the Gothic of the *fin de siècle* has many issues that are specific to it. We have seen that theories of degeneration are engaged with in a variety of ways as a means of making sense of the anxieties of change at the end of the nineteenth century. Nordau wanted to turn the clock back, and to renounce the modern world as one vulnerable to collapse under its self-generated fragility. The modern world seemed, in many of these Gothic narratives, to be haunted by the pull of the past in the guise of hereditary taints. In some ways, this represented a desperate attempt to assert a new purity; yet it would shortly lead to a dangerous enthusiasm for eugenics. This pervasive European discourse was to have disastrous consequences for views about race, crime and sexuality for much of the twentieth century.

Further Reading

Killeen, Jarlath 2010. *Gothic Literature: 1825–1914* (Cardiff: University of Wales Press). An introductory guide to the developments in Gothic literature during the period. It provides some very useful material on the genesis of particular forms, such as the ghost story, and explores a number of relevant themes, such as an interest in the occult, which help to contextualise the *fin-de-siècle* Gothic.

Margee, Victoria and Bryony Randall 2012. 'Fin-de-Siècle Gothic', Andrew Smith and William Hughes (eds), *The Victorian Gothic: An Edinburgh Companion* (Edinburgh: Edinburgh University Press), pp. 217–33. The chapter offers a very helpful analysis of a range of themes and authors from the period. In particular, its focus on figures such as the vampire, the scientist and the ghost helps to develop an interesting, gender-aware reading of texts from the period.

Navarrette, Susan J 1998. *The Shape of Fear: Horror and Fin de Siècle Degeneration* (Lexington: University Press of Kentucky). This study of the Gothic provides an innovative focus on how the prose style of certain Gothic narratives can be read as a degenerated form of expression that reflect the wider themes of degeneration in the period.

Smith, Andrew 2004. *Victorian Demons: Medicine, Masculinity and the Gothic at the fin de siècle* (Manchester: Manchester University Press). The book explores a series of narratives about masculinity that link Joseph Merrick (the 'Elephant Man'), the Whitechapel murders, the trials of Oscar Wilde and medical textbooks on syphilis to the Gothic culture of the period.

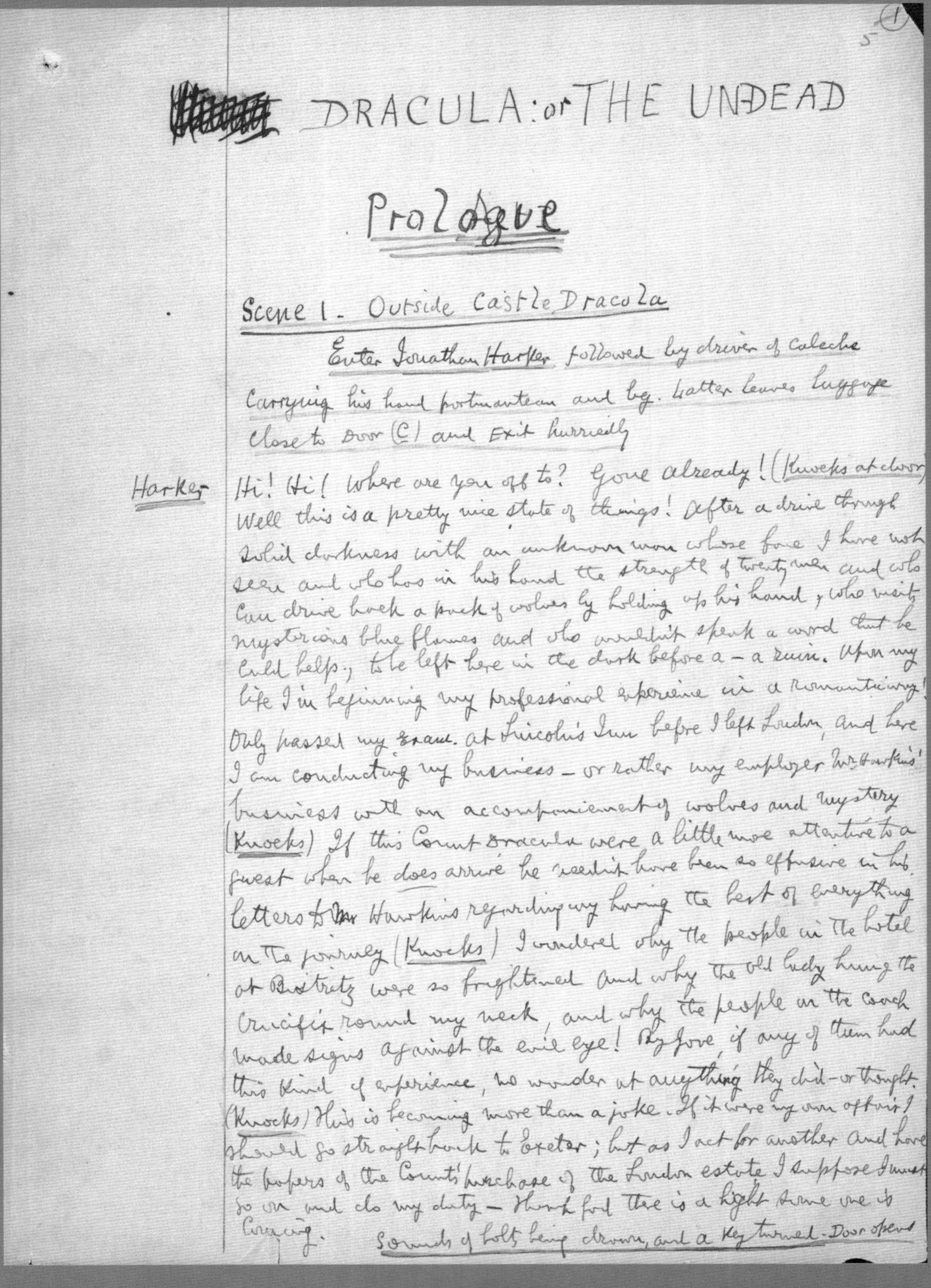
DRACULA: or THE UNDEAD

Prologue

Scene I. Outside Castle Dracula

Enter Jonathan Harker followed by driver of Caleche carrying his hand portmanteau and bag. Latter leaves luggage close to Door (C) and Exit hurriedly

Harker Hi! Hi! Where are you off to? Gone already! (Knocks at door) Well this is a pretty nice state of things! After a drive through solid darkness with an unknown man whose face I have not seen and who has in his hand the strength of twenty men and who can drive back a pack of wolves by holding up his hand, who visits mysterious blue flames and who wouldn't speak a word that he could help, to be left here in the dark before a – a ruin. Upon my life I'm beginning my professional experience in a romantic way! Only passed my exam. at Lincoln's Inn before I left London, and here I am conducting my business – or rather my employer Mr Hawkins' business with an accompaniment of wolves and mystery (Knocks) If this Count Dracula were a little more attentive to a guest when he does arrive he needn't have been so effusive in his letters to Mr Hawkins regarding my having the best of everything on the journey (Knocks) I wondered why the people in the hotel at Bistritz were so frightened and why the old lady hung the crucifix round my neck, and why the people on the coach made signs against the evil eye! By Jove, if any of them had this kind of experience, no wonder at anything they did – or thought. (Knocks) This is becoming more than a joke. If it were my own affairs I should go straight back to Exeter; but as I act for another and have the papers of the Count's purchase of the London estate I suppose I must go on and do my duty – Thank God there is a light some one is coming. Sounds of bolt being drawn, and a key turned – Door opens

Manuscript of Bram Stoker, *Dracula*.
British Library Add MS 53630F f.5.

From the Crypt: *Dracula*

'DRACULA, OR, THE UNDEAD'

The year 1897 was a good one for vampires. Philip Burne-Jones's painting *The Vampire*, depicting a woman straddling a prone man lying across a bed, caused a sensation with its overt portrayal of female sexuality; inspired by Burne-Jones's painting, Rudyard Kipling penned his chilling poem 'The Vampire'. In the same year, Florence Marryat, the author and spiritualist, published a novel about psychic vampirism entitled *The Blood of the Vampire* and, most enduringly of all, Bram Stoker published *Dracula*, a tale of an ancient, European count with a taste for blood. The manuscript of *Dracula* is not thought to exist, although there are extensive author's notes for the book currently held in the Rosenbach Museum and Library, Philadelphia. What does remain, however, is a manuscript for a theatrical adaptation of the novel produced by Stoker himself, a dramatic script which offers fascinating insights into this iconic late-Victorian Gothic tale.

The script for the theatre version of *Dracula* is a mixture of Stoker's own handwriting and printed extracts cut and pasted from the novel. Originally titled 'Count Dracula: or The Un-Dead', the play was written by Stoker in order to protect the dramatic rights to the book. A copyright reading took place at the Lyceum Theatre in London, of which Stoker was the business manager, on the morning of 18 May 1897. The role of Mina Murray was taken by Edith Craig, daughter of the actress Ellen Terry and a pioneer of the women's suffrage movement in England. Copies of the novel itself, with its iconic yellow cover and red lettering, appeared for sale later the same month.

The play follows the plot of the novel closely, but, in order to propel the action forwards at a pace suitable for a theatre audience, many of the purely atmospheric elements included in the book have been cut. As a result, much of the dialogue reads like plot exposition rather than natural speech. For example, in the opening scene, the character of Jonathan Harker finds himself at the door of Dracula's castle, but somewhat artificially has to relate his preceding nightmarish journey with the mysterious coachman to the audience in order for subsequent events in the play to make sense:

> After a drive through solid darkness with an unknown man whose face I have not seen and who has in his hand the strength of twenty men and who can drive back a pack of wolves by holding up his hand, who visits mysterious blue flames and who wouldn't speak a word that he could help, to be left here in the dark before a – a ruin.

In Stoker's novel, Harker's journey to the castle is related via diary entries and, as a result, is conveyed to the reader in a measured, atmospheric fashion. Even allowing for what appears to have been the rather hasty composition of the script, there is a suggestion that the reason why the book works so well, and why the theatrical version is somewhat stilted, is because Stoker was always more comfortable with evocative descriptions and the portrayal of setting and atmosphere than he was with dramatic dialogue. As a formally innovative novel, *Dracula* works so well because it is largely told in the form of diary entries, newspaper articles and letters that take the place of conventional dialogue between the characters. As the script progresses, the number of printed extracts cut directly from the book and pasted to the pages increases significantly, suggesting once again the haste with which the theatre script was put together. Even so, the play provides a unique glimpse into the working methods of an author who, in *Dracula*, produced one of the most, enduring, inventive and eerily compelling novels of the nineteenth century.

GREG BUZWELL

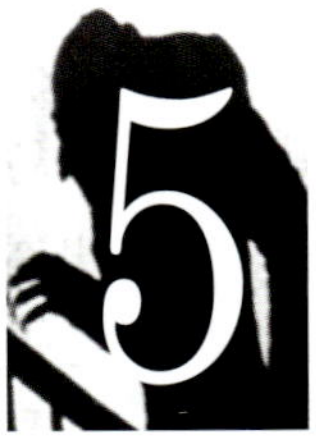

LUCIE ARMITT

Twentieth-Century Gothic

OPPOSITE:
Still from the film *Nosferatu*, 1922.
This influential German Expressionist horror film, directed by F W Murnau, brought a modernist feel to the vampire myth. Depicted here is Max Schreck as Count Orlok.

A Changing Perspective

The greatest challenge facing the Gothic in the twentieth century is that voiced by Sigmund Freud at the end of its second decade: 'All supposedly educated people have ceased to believe officially that the dead can become visible as spirits' (1990: 361). Nevertheless, the Gothic remains a highly popular and compelling form of literary and cinematic storytelling. The answer to this conundrum, it seems, is that, in the active pursuit of what most frightens us, we continually reshape our Gothic monsters to fit society's changing fears. Thus the Gothic, for all its apparent connection with antiquarianism, tradition, the long dead and the undead, actually says as much about the period of modernity in which it is written or read as does the most avant-garde form of modernist writing.

At the start of the twentieth century, Gothic literature remains largely informed by the Victorian ghost story. As the century progresses, however, those stories become increasingly informed by psychological possibilities and, later still, the unsettling content in them is increasingly re-read as a metaphor for aspects of our sexuality or bodily secrets deemed 'unspeakable' or deviant at the time of writing. As we become increasingly fascinated by the body, and yet more tolerant of difference, what assumes ever more uncanny status are those unseen metamorphoses that might be taking place undetected within our own cells. By the end of the twentieth century, illness and disease play a central role in our understanding of Gothic terror.

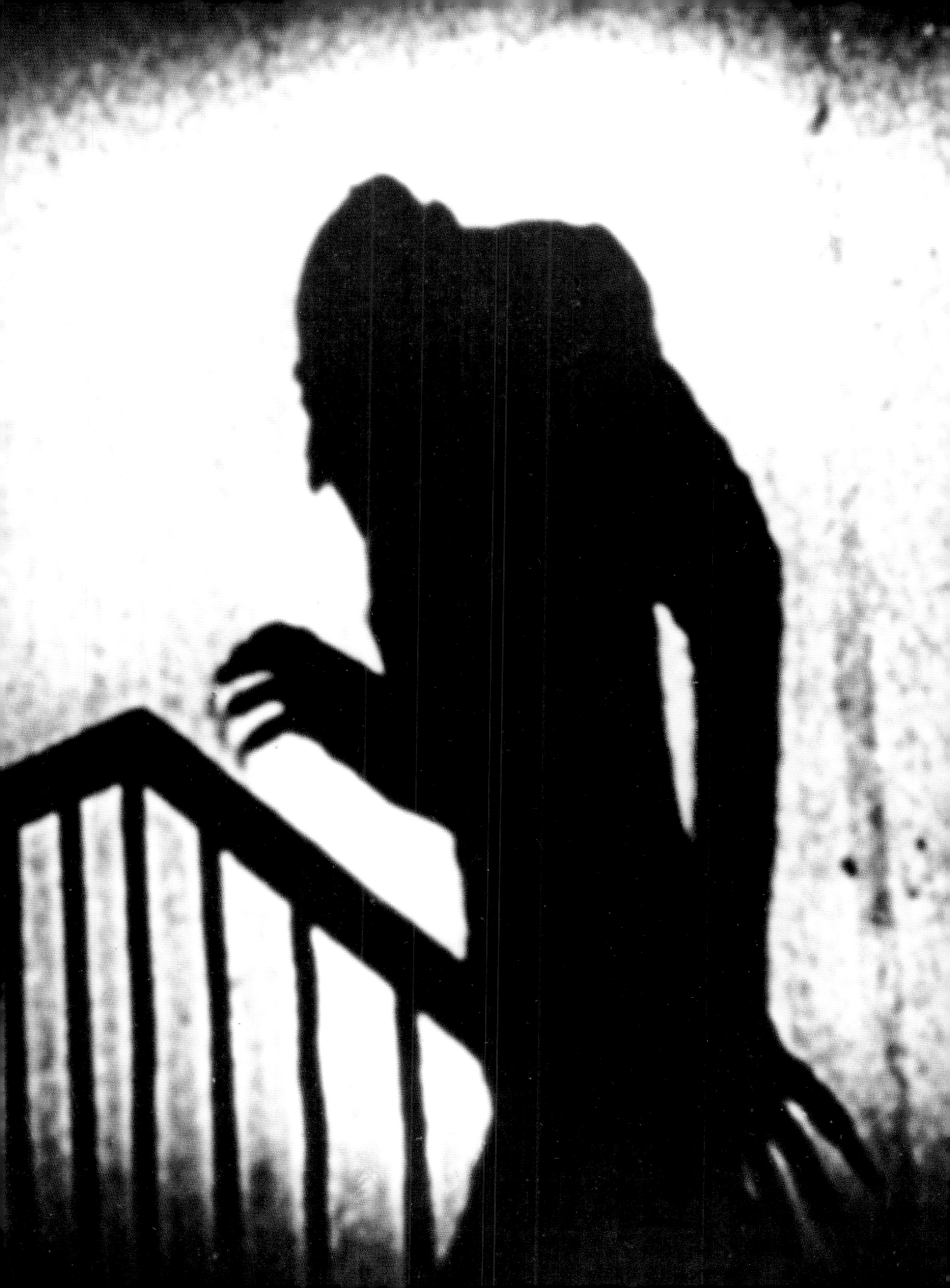

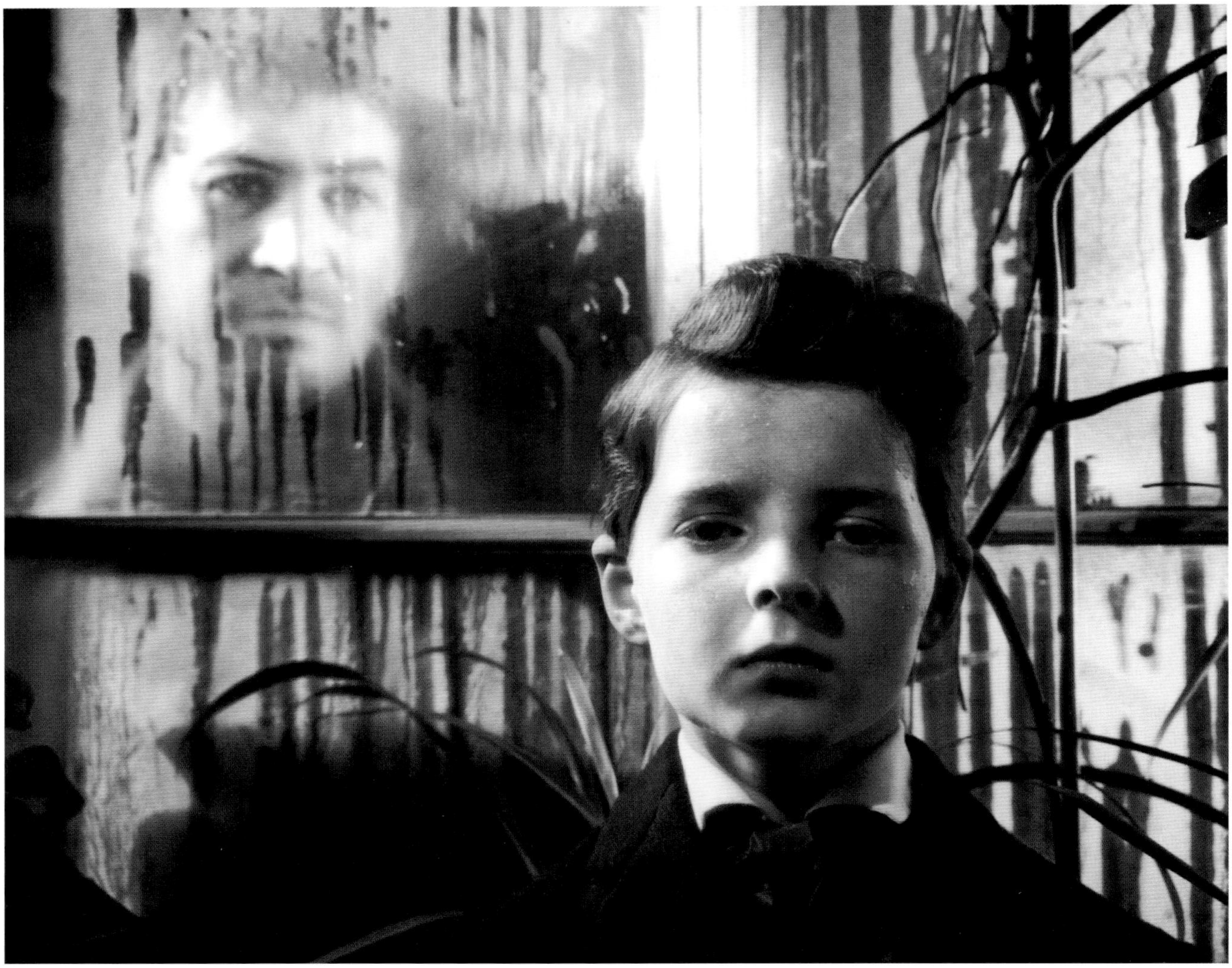

The Innocents is a film adaptation of Henry James's novella *The Turn of the Screw.* Shown here are Peter Wyngarde as the ghost of the servant Peter Quint and Martin Stephens as Miles.

As technology advances, some aspects of the Gothic that rely on things 'unknown and unknowable' start to disappear, but with that shift others appear. Undoubtedly it is the silent but powerful associations of the spirit world that gave Rolls Royce the idea for its Silver Shadow, Silver Wraith, Phantom and Ghost models of luxury car. However, while those supreme icons of mechanisation borrow from the world of the supernatural the ease with which its emanations glide through space, the later innovations of microchip and digital computer technology have endowed technology with the appearance of sentience. Thus is reintroduced into the machine age that type of fear Freud associated with uncertainty over 'whether a lifeless object might not be in fact animate' (1990: 347). Increasingly, too, as the century develops emphasis falls upon understanding the role played by readers or audiences in the construction of uncanny content, often prompted by environmental factors. Evidently listening to a ghost story by candlelight, as are the women depicted in James Gillray's 'Tales of Wonder!' from 1802, must enable a more 'experiential' understanding of the Gothic than listening to it in audio-book format on the car CD-player. Similarly, Helen Wheatley, writing about Gothic television, observes that 'it is the feeling that television is too literal a medium, too obvious, too blatantly visual, which has challenged programme makers and troubled reviewers' (2006: 26). Nevertheless, Gothic continues to resonate with us in new and old ways. The best of Gothic narratives have an enduring influence in shaping more recent Gothic literature, as well as in ever-renewed and repeated film and TV adaptations.

After all, Gothic is a mode of storytelling rooted in our ability to return to our forebears. Henry James's *The Turn of the Screw* (published in episodes in 1898), though emerging on the cusp of the twentieth century, actually sets in place many of the preoccupations that will come to characterise that century's Gothic literature. As is conventional, it is a Christmas Eve tale told to an assembled audience by the fireplace, by a narrator who was one of the original listeners and who now recounts it to us, his readers, at several stages of temporal and spatial remove. The self-conscious literariness of much Gothic writing and its preoccupation with written documents which are 'out of place' (either through the death of their original keepers or through a chain of events beyond the living recipients' control) remains a key feature. *The Turn of the Screw* concerns two upper-class children, Miles and Flora, and the eventual death of Miles in mysterious circumstances involving two mysterious strangers and his own governess. James's novella retains its fascination today because of the many issues it raises: the division between upper and servant classes, and what can and cannot be spoken between them; questions of innocence and guilt in relation to child characters; a perceived crisis in masculinity at the *fin de siècle*; the death of empire. That what is 'horrible' in the narrative emerges from the underside of 'respectable' upper-class society is clear; so is the fact that this is a tale involving class-related guilt. What gives added *frisson* to *The Turn of the Screw* for modern readers, however, is its concern with the death of a child – apparently at the hands of a trusted adult. Ghost stories enjoyed a resurrection in popularity in the final decades of the twentieth century, and a disproportionate number share a central fascination with child deaths. Contemporary monsters have ceased to look unfamiliar and now look 'like us', extending their reach to the terrorist and the psychopath, around whom fears that he will 'go underground' and similar crypt-like metaphors accumulate.

By contrast, the traditional monsters of folklore, such as the vampire or the werewolf, undergo a series of 'taming' transformations during the course of the twentieth century, a development that has been accelerated by Goth fashion and popular television. According to Alison Lurie in *The Language of Clothes* (1992), the 'heavy-eyed, fleshly sensuous vamp of the 1920s' retained her enduring appeal throughout the century and Theda Bara, 'the original vamp' from that period, 'was said to drive men to madness' of an erotically charged nature (1992: 252). It is not only the vamp, however, around whom such erotic appeal accumulates. For Lurie, before Bram Stoker's *Dracula* it is the 'thin white muslin dresses' of the early nineteenth century that associates sensuality with a type of performed invalidity. In later periods it is adapted, 'usually in the

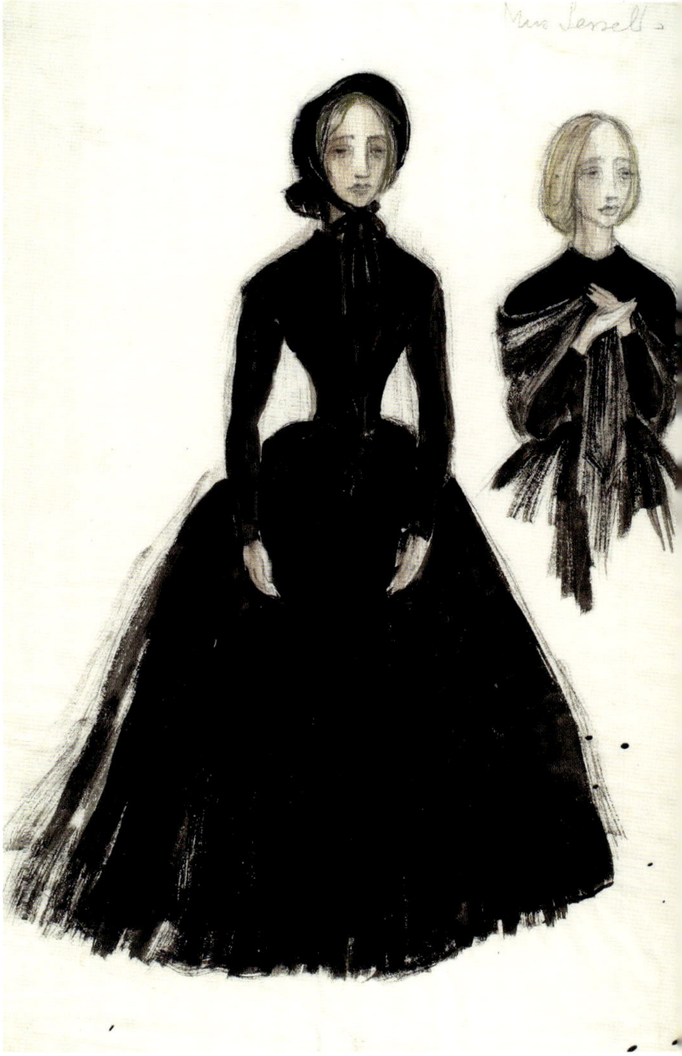

Costume design by Sophie Harris for *The Innocents*, 1961.
British Film Institute.

The mourning dress enhanced the severe, morbid look of the ghostly governess Miss Jessel.

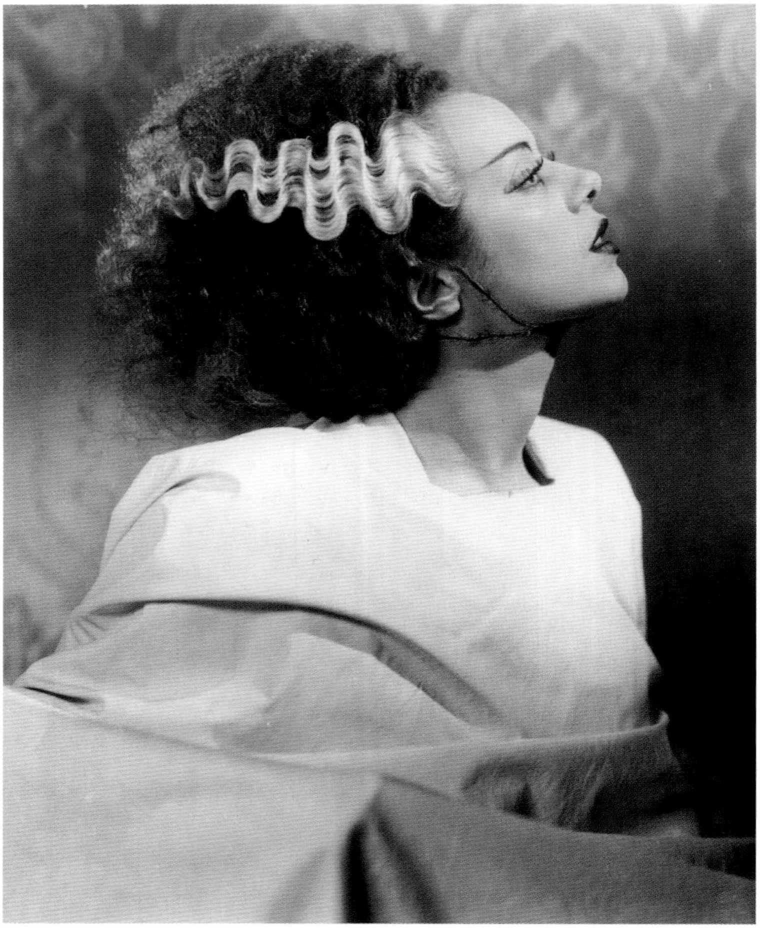

Elsa Lanchester in *The Bride of Frankenstein*, 1935.

Lanchester epitomises Gothic glamour in the 1930s.

form of a nightdress', to become the Gothic heroine's costume of choice (1992: 256). By the final decades of the twentieth century, Lurie reminds us, the influence of the women's liberation movement has produced 'Vampirella, a comic-book heroine whose costume is a kind of space-age female Dracula outfit, scanty and revealing' (1992: 257). This shift from a state of genuine illness to one of performed invalidity, from sensual allure to sexualised parody, is a not unusual development in popular Goth and Gothic culture. At the same time, a new audience of children and teenagers has embraced the vampire and its various fashion styles as it reduces in menace – hence the popularity of television series such as *Buffy the Vampire Slayer* (1997–2003).

Considering Goth sub-culture more generally, it is for this youth audience that the vampire has greatest appeal. According to Sara Martin, the label 'Gothic' may have started to become applied to this group only in the 1980s, largely as a reaction against Thatcherite and Reaganite consumerism in Britain and the US respectively, but it informed the heavy-metal music scene from as early as the 1960s. Citing the work of Elizabeth Jane Wall Hinds, Martin continues:

> [Wall Hinds's] thesis is that heavy metal, inaugurated by the album Led Zeppelin I (1968), transformed rock music in the

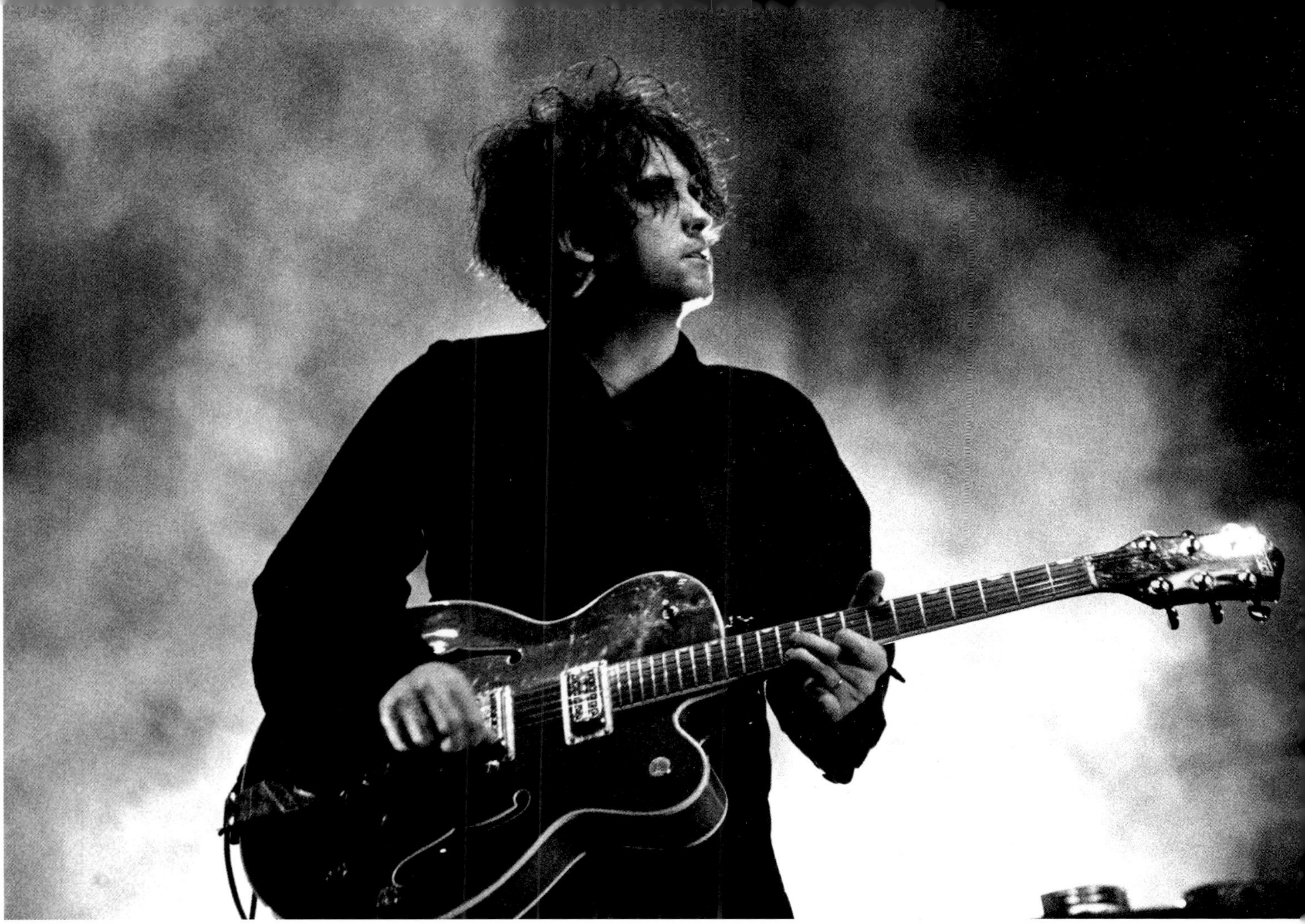

Robert Smith, lead singer of The Cure.

Smith's style – deathly white face, red lips and tangled mop of black hair – was both distinctive and influential.

> same way that Horace Walpole's *The Castle of Otranto* (1764) transformed the novel [...] shock[ing] complacent rock and pop 1960s audiences by introducing openly sexual elements in their lyrics. (Wall Hinds 1992: 159; cited in Martin 2002: 33)

Thus a paradox emerges, between those aspects of Goth culture that resist consumerism and the appetite for merchandise which accompanies certain other forms (such as modern music). These more market-driven areas re-invoke what Franco Moretti might argue to be at the roots of the appeal of vampire literature. In his often-cited book *Signs Taken for Wonders* (1983), Moretti argues that Dracula's ability simultaneously to horrify and compel derives directly from his conspicuous wealth, coupled with his consumerist appetites: 'His ultimate aim is not to destroy the lives of others according to whim [...] but to use them' (1983: 91). For the Western reader, Dracula's appetite may also be reflected in society's ambition: 'Like capital, Dracula is impelled towards a continuous growth, an unlimited expansion of his domain: accumulation is inherent in his nature' (1983: 91)

However, the vampire's appetite is not simply attractive, but also contagious. As we shall see, what is readily interpreted in the nineteenth century as the corrupted bloodline of an aristocratic inheritance 'gone bad' becomes, in the late twentieth century, a cautionary warning of the dangers of appetite, especially when spread through 'bad blood'. In the final decades of the twentieth century, the vampire re-emerges to embody the threat of HIV/AIDS.

The Gothic and Sigmund Freud

A year after the end of the First World War, Sigmund Freud stamped his authority over the Gothic through his highly influential essay 'The "Uncanny"' (1919). Now that shared belief in the supernatural, ghosts and the occult had dwindled, Freud claimed, our enduring fascination for that which frightens us derived from our innermost repressions. Crucially, for Freud the uncanny is a *process* rather than a presence, one requiring an initial sensation of familiarity (the *heimlich*) before the *unheimlich* (unhomely) shift can take place. The more minimal the shift from familiar to unfamiliar the better: just enough to raise the hairs on the back of our necks or to send a chill down our spine. Too little and we will simply be puzzled; too much and we will be repulsed. The Gothic must tease and play with us sufficiently to keep us coming back for more.

Such is the nature of the relationship between the *heimlich* and the *unheimlich* in Susan Hill's novel *The Woman in Black* (1983), when her central protagonist, Arthur Kipps, first hears something go 'bump' in the night. Approaching the locked door from behind which the sound emanates, Kipps reflects that it is 'a sound that, in any other place, would [...] have been enormously comforting, friendly' (1998: 133). According to Mark S Madoff, 'The locked-room mystery [...] nearly is the Gothic' (1989: 49). In Hill's narrative the locked room is a child's nursery and the mysterious bumping is the rocking of a nursemaid's rocking chair, simultaneously prompting happy memories of Kipps's own childhood and fears for the haunting present. For Freud, indeed, toys (especially of a mechanical or clockwork nature) are frequently experienced as uncanny, particularly when half glimpsed in shadows, so that they seem to be about to come to life, or when their faces are so like ours that they might be miniature doppelgängers. Other frequent examples comprise doubles or twins, to which we might add one who appears to be tracing our progress, an occurrence repeating sufficiently to provoke a sense of unease and something Freud describes as the 'omnipotence of thoughts' – namely an event that occurs after we have imagined it in our mind's eye (1990: 362).

So established is Freud's influence upon a modern reading of the Gothic that we tend to lift his essay from its original historical context and use it as a kind of ahistorical template to be placed over any Gothic text, appropriating it to identify the means through which the uncanny works in isolation. However, we need to pause and consider that Freud wrote the essay immediately after the end of the First World War. This devastating conflict split Europe into factions that rested so uneasily they festered like open sores until the 1930s, when the Second World War became perhaps inevitable.

So many people died in the First World War that no clear statistical records of the precise number of dead exist. Death,

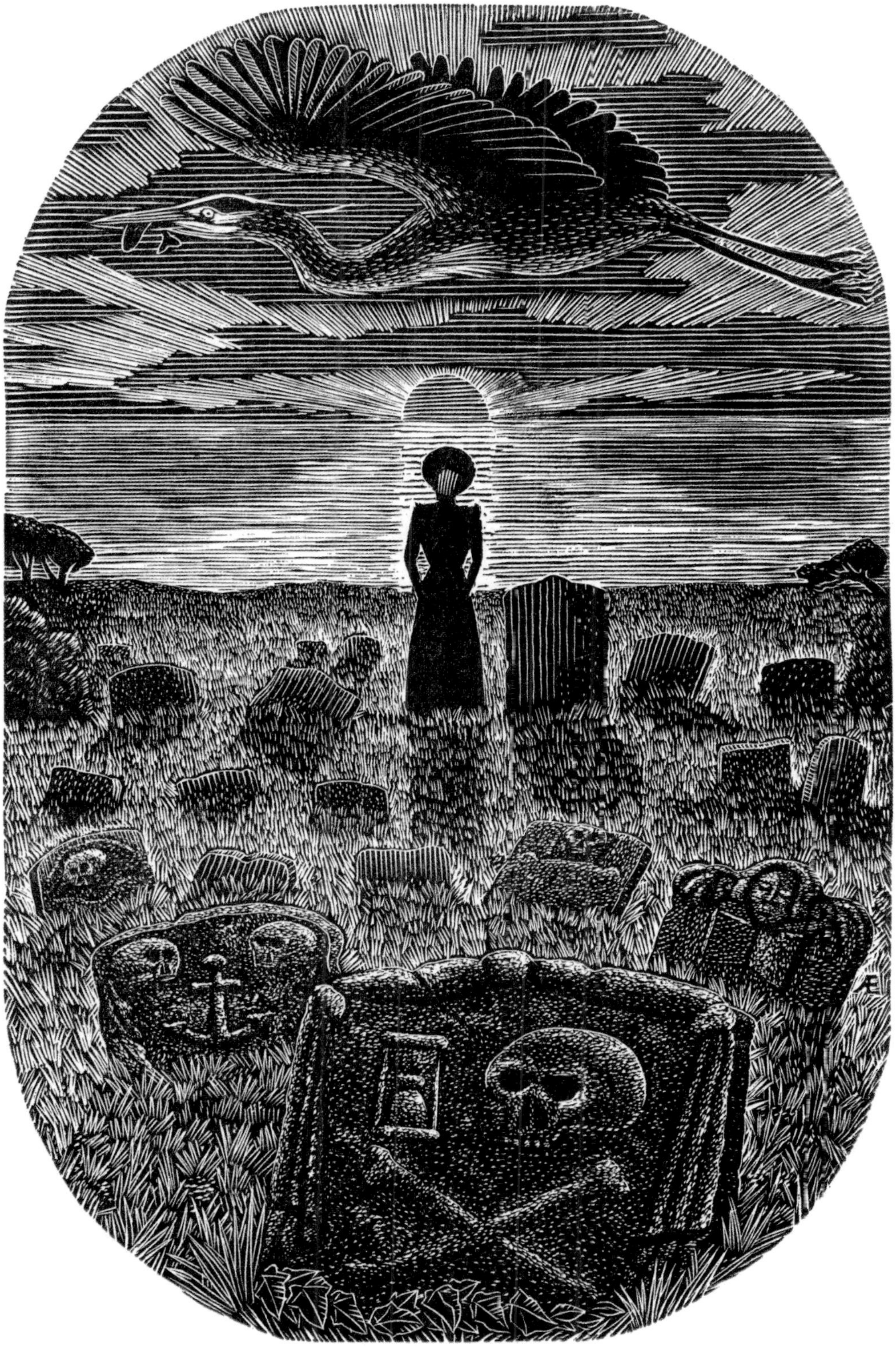

'At the Burial Ground', woodcut illustration by Andy English for *The Woman in Black*, 2011.

then, swept across Europe like a contagion and invaded, one might say 'haunted', the houses of almost every family, bringing to pass a terrible sense of a living death in those left behind. What is more, it was often a death without a body or corpse to mourn: an abrupt absence, the very obverse of an apparition. This desperate sense of longing for the invisible, absent loved one fed the appetites of unscrupulous spirit photographers, social parasites who exploited the mass grief of bereaved families by claiming that the camera lens could capture a spectrum of light beyond that of the human eye, and thus return a photographic image of their child to grieving relatives. This unethical trickery had at least one positive spin-off for the Gothic. It helped to establish the uncanny possibilities afforded by the film camera and its ability to use special effects to complicate questions of perception and invisibility.

During the First World War two young girls, Elsie and Frances, took a series of photographs which they claimed showed fairies playing in the beck near their house. The images, which have come to be known as the Cottingley photographs, though widely believed to be fakes, sparked intense interest in theosophists such as Sir Arthur Conan Doyle. Theosophy offered a scientific rationale for the belief in the supernatural or after-life, and Conan Doyle's interest in it is often attributed to the loss of his own son in the war. He immediately accepted the girls' images as genuine and offered his scientific theory on the existence of things unseen. For Conan Doyle, fairies belonged to 'a race of beings which were constructed in material which threw out shorter or longer vibrations [...] [and] would be invisible' to most people. However, he equally believed there were people whose capability of tuning in to these vibrations enabled them to see 'that which is invisible to others' (1922: 9–10). To Elsie and Frances the fairies were biddable playthings, fantasy forms not dissimilar to those sanitised versions handed down to us from the Victorian nursery. Yet as Conan Doyle's perspective reveals, fairies to a theosophist come from the spirit world. As late as the 1990s one novel and two films were written about the Cottingley images, all of which share a central preoccupation with death: Steve Szilagyi's novel *Photographing Fairies* (1995), Nick Willing's film of the same name (1997) and Walt Disney's *Fairy Tale: A True Story* (1997).

In fact, death and destruction have long been the realm of traditional fairy lore. These beings inhabit a shadow world, gather at twilight and are endowed with second sight; they are dangerous to humans and inflict great harm, including blinding any human who claims to have seen them. Rural communities through the ages made offerings to fairies to prevent them from stealing human children and replacing them with 'changelings', doppelgängers whose resemblance to the original was only a trick. Especially connected with Celtic and English rural superstition, fairies remain at the centre of our doubts about the nature of the real and the unreal, the seen and the unseen. One of the most recent writers of Scottish and Welsh Gothic is Alice Thomas Ellis, whose fiction about the Scottish Selkies and the Welsh Tylwyth Teg (fair folk) can be found in *The Inn at the Edge of the World* (1990) and *Fairy Tale* (1996) respectively.

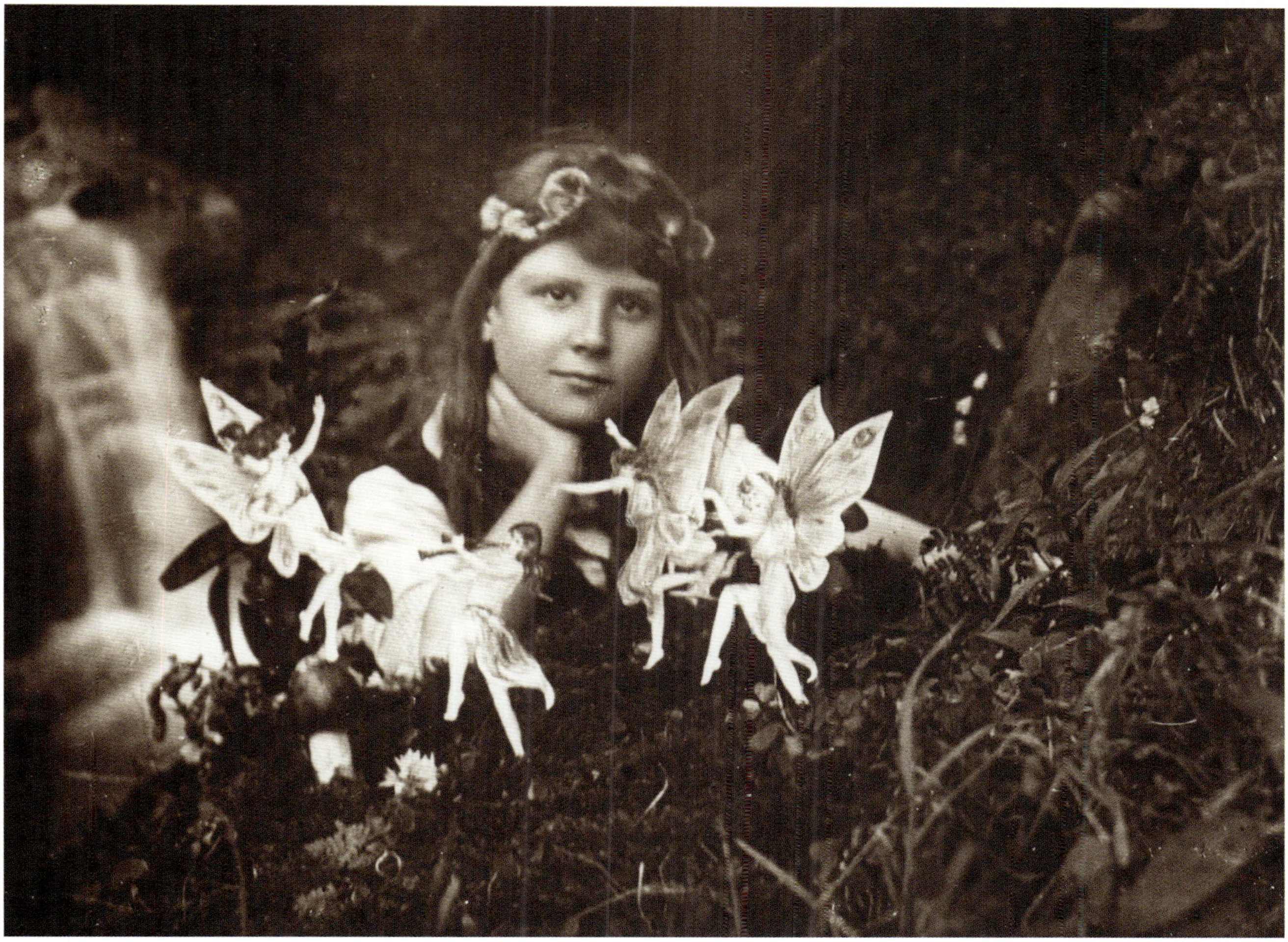

The Cottingley fairies. Photo by Elsie Wright, 1917, published in the *Strand* magazine, 1920.

In other cultures, too, fairy lore takes on an especially Gothic timbre, but always in relation to minority cultures or marginal areas. Thus in a North American context it is the wilderness of the great forests and lakes, often transformed into a haunted landscape, where legendary creatures such as the Wendigo (half-human, half-beast) lurk and hunt human flesh. In Algernon Blackwood's short story 'The Wendigo' (1910), many of the features that a British readership would associate with traditional fairy lore are present. The story tells of an encounter between a group of men and a supernatural presence, whose claim on that natural wilderness is much greater than theirs. One of their number, Joseph Défago, is called or dragged from his bed in the middle of the night by a strange, half-human voice uttering 'a most uncommon sound [...] It rang out, too, in three separate and distinct notes and cries that bore in some odd fashion a resemblance, far-fetched yet recognisable, to the name of the guide' (1910: 46). The elemental nature of the abduction is revealed in Défago's reiterated cry: 'Oh! Oh! My feet of fire! Oh! Oh! This height and fiery speed!' (1910: 47). In the receding imprint of his stumbling footprints his companions track 'a mysterious, reddish tinge that was more like the effect of light than of anything that dyed the substance of the snow' (1910: 53). Though the group manages temporarily to retrace Défago, like the changeling victim of a fairy abduction, they man is returned to them much aged: 'For the Défago who sat huddled by the big fire [...] was no more like the guide they had last seen alive than the picture of a man of sixty is like a daguerreotype of his early youth [...] the features drawn about into wrong proportions, the skin loose and hanging' (1910: 70).

Early Horror Film

As films such as *The Wicker Man* (dir. Robert Hardy, 1973) demonstrate, Celtic and pagan superstition retain their cinematic as well as their literary appeal throughout the twentieth century. One of cinema's key advantages is its ability to realise spectres and apparitions that, like the Wendigo, might otherwise exist only in our imaginations. Very early on, cinema capitalised on this advantage, and 1931 was a vintage year for early horror cinema. Carl Laemmie Jr's *Frankenstein*, starring Boris Karloff, Carl Laemmle Jr and Tod Browning's *Dracula*, starring Bela Lugosi, and Rouben Mamoulian's *Dr Jekyll and Mr Hyde* were all released in that year.

The stage was actually set for these stylised and excessive monsters a decade earlier, however, in F W Murnau's 1922 silent horror classic *Nosferatu*. Murnau's portrayal of Dracula (renamed Count Orlok in this film) is a perfect illustration of appetite. With his piercing fangs and hook-like, clawed nails, the shadowy monster at the heart of this film is a creature of shadows, and much is made of shadow play throughout the screening. If, as Alexandra Warwick's essay in this collection has argued, the shadow becomes an important aspect of Victorian Gothic, its point of destination seems to be the horror cinema of the early twentieth century.

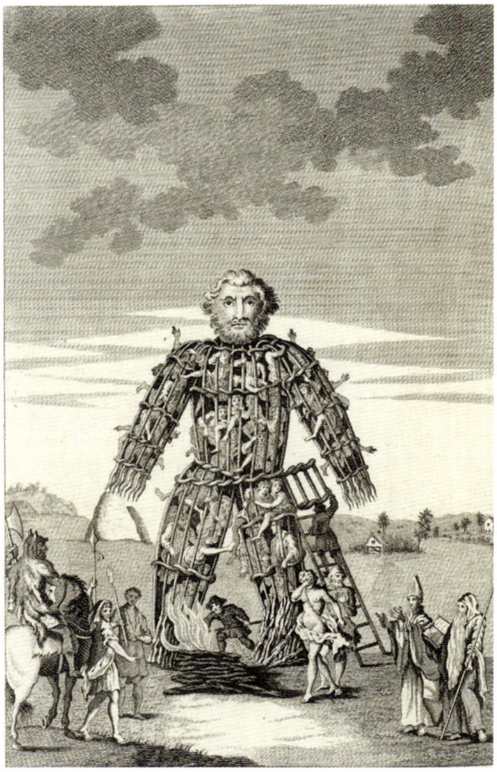

The wicker man. Illustration from Nathaniel Spencer, *The Complete English Traveller*, 1771.
British Library 1854.a.23.

The only contemporary record of Druids burning sacrificial victims in a wicker man comes from Caesar's dubious account in his *Commentaries on the Gallic War*. This image illustrated an eighteenth-century guidebook to England.

However, *Nosferatu* is also a film about storytelling. In typical silent-movie tradition, billboards reading 'Men do not always recognise the dangers that beasts can sense' or 'And when he had crossed the bridge the phantoms came to meet him' are presented to the viewing public. Characters are also depicted reading: first Harker and then Nina open *The Book of Vampires*, and the ship's log later tells the story of Orlok's passage on board the *Demeter* and the deathly excesses he wreaks upon the crew – a necessary narrative device in the absence of any remaining living witnesses. As Harker reads *The Book of Vampires* by candlelight, a flickering screen, just like the one the audience is watching, is played out on the walls of his chamber. The ability of such shadow-play not just to project but also to realise monsters is shown later on in the movie, as Orlok mounts the stairs to feast on the blood of Nina. Only the vampire's shadow is seen as he climbs, grotesquely magnifying his already excessive form.

The use to which shadows are put in the film also enables a more risqué depiction of sexual depravity than would otherwise be possible in the period. As Orlok enters Nina's chamber, the camera angle creates long shadows running from his hands, allowing those to caress torso, belly and breasts without making actual physical contact. At a time when an actor portraying love-making was required at all times to keep one foot on the floor, the shadow play of *Nosferatu* enables otherwise taboo material to be presented on screen.

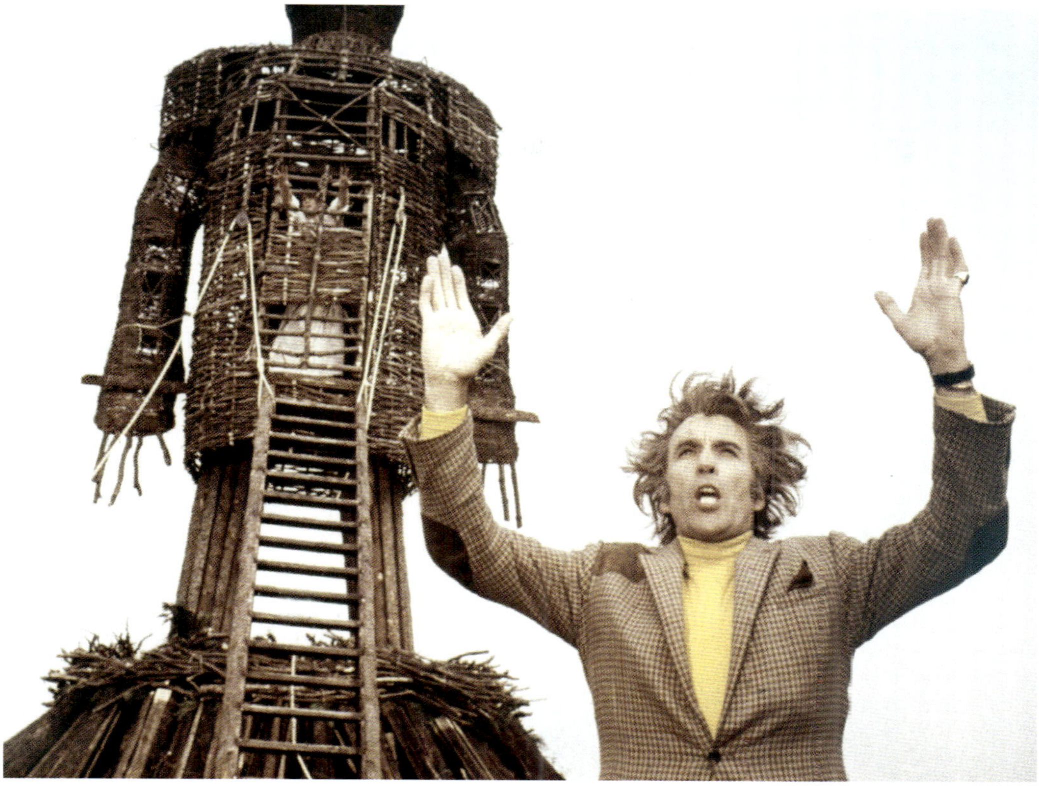

Christopher Lee as Lord Summerisle in *The Wicker Man*, 1973.

The film reflects the late 1960s/early 1970s concern over hippyism and the newly relaxed attitudes towards drug use, religious belief and sexual permissiveness.

Still ffrom the film *Frankenstein*, 1931.

In this iconic scene from James Whale's first Frankenstein film, Boris Karloff as the monster meets a little girl who is not instinctively afraid of him.

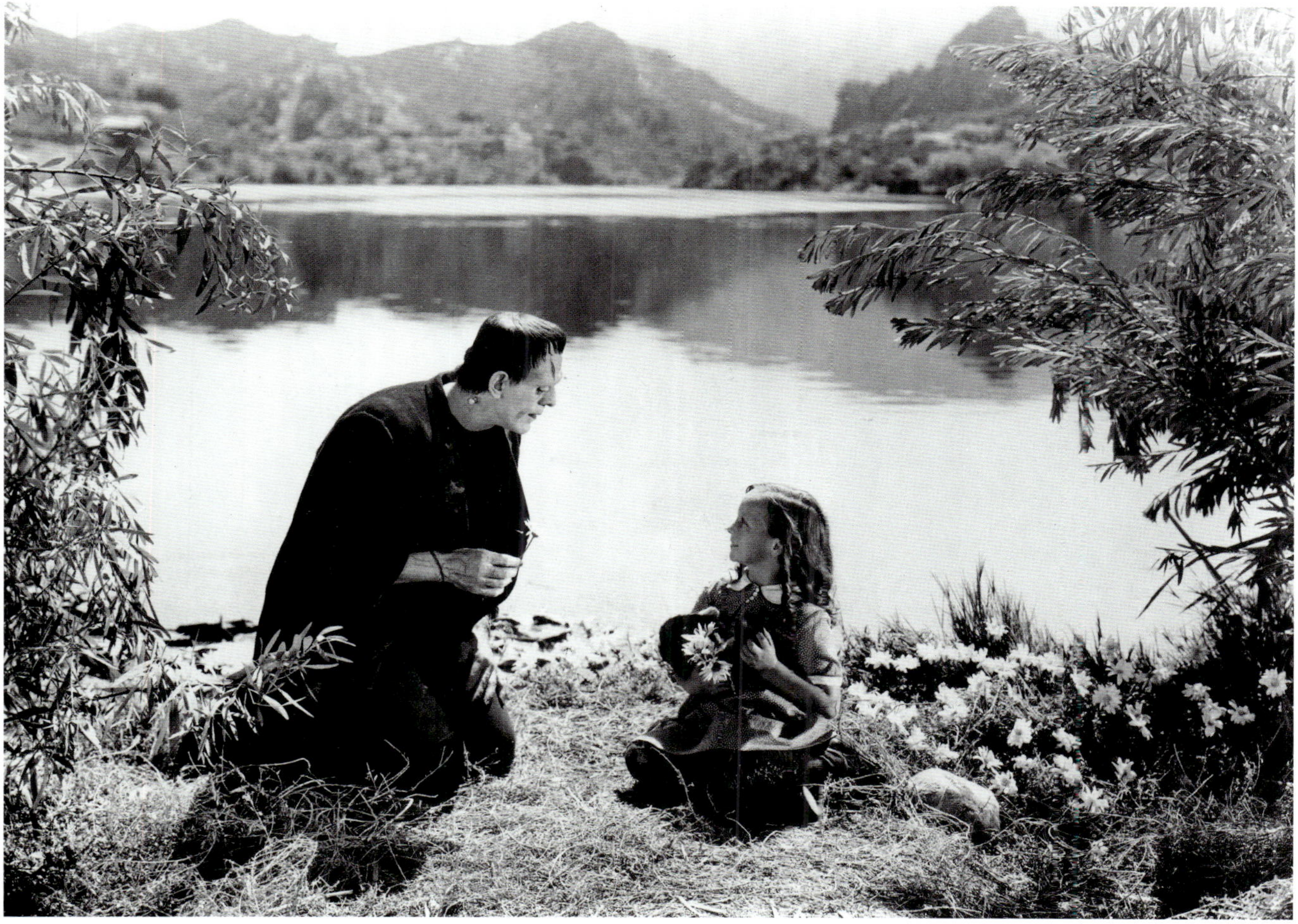

It thus brings to fruition Nina Auerbach's claim that 'Edwardian vampires were, as a rule, more perverse than their later counterparts' (1995: 102) and creates a newly sexualised relationship between audience and film.

As Denis Giles observes, in the twentieth century our interest in film started to move away from a consideration of individual movies *per se*, focusing more upon a film's relationship with 'a viewing subject who has adapted to the text and who, in part, has been produced by the institution of cinema itself' (1984: 38). One can see how Gothic cinema in general, and horror cinema in particular, is especially well placed to flourish within these new, audience-related approaches. There is something peculiarly physical in our response to these kinds of film (chills in our stomachs, hairs rising) and cinema is a profoundly collective form of aesthetic response. By offering audiences safely defined parameters for viewing pleasure, it allows them to enjoy material from which they might otherwise recoil in fear or shame.

The Edwardian Ghost Story

This concept of the seen and the unseen is also a key aspect of the ghost story – a form that is, after all, a tale of 'apparitions' – from the Edwardian period onwards. The importance of the verb 'to appear', unlike those such as 'shout', 'sniff', or 'blink', is that it contains a time delay in its execution within which the gradual shift in states between being invisible and being present takes place. Moreover, unlike the definite state of being 'seen', that which appears carries with it the fragile possibility of error: it may be 'really' there, or it may not; or it may be partially perceived and then vanish. In other words, the ghost story is always a narrative of uncertainty. Such tensions are revealed by the ghost-story writer Edith Wharton, who observed that when she was asked if she believed in ghosts, her characteristic reply was 'No [...] but I'm afraid of them' (1973: 1).

Wharton's response is not dissimilar to Mark Gatiss's observations about M R James. According to Gatiss, James was evasive about his own supernatural experiences, but what matters far more to his storytelling is that James understood the nature of fear. There is a popular maxim that seeing is believing; but what is most compelling about the ghost story is that it deals in things which are half-seen, encounters from which we flinch or flee, terrors which take on imprecise definition and, in doing so, become so malleable that they take on the shape of our own particular fears. This question of the immediate connection between visibility and invisibility, seeing and not seeing, perception and imperception strikes at the heart of the Gothic, especially as it deals with ghostly encounters.

M R James's story '"Oh, Whistle, and I'll Come to You, My Lad"' (1904) is set on the east coast of England in a fictional town called Burnstow, believed to be Felixstowe. The marginal territory where land meets sea provides an especially popular landscape for the twentieth-century Gothic narrative, and its suggestible nature for such tales is amplified in part by tidal patterns that unsettle any clear distinction between water and earth. Thus are we reminded of the

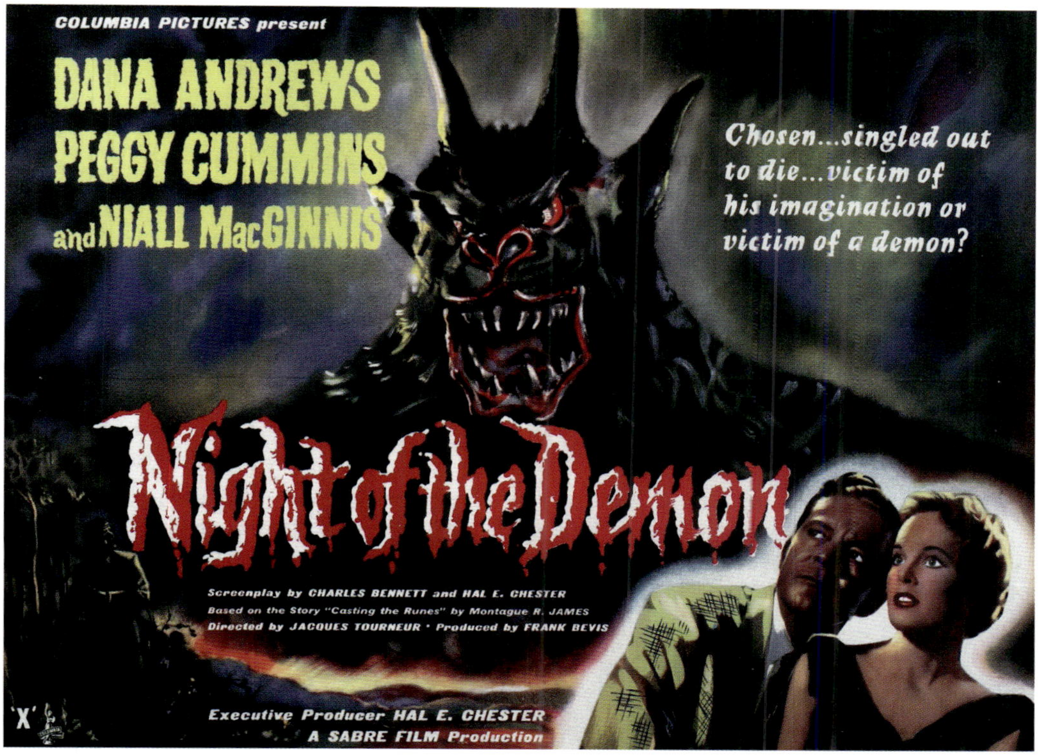

Poster for *Night of the Demon*, 1957.
British Film Institute.
This British horror film was based on the short story 'Casting the Runes' by M R James. The film jettisoned James's minimalistic descriptions of supernatural horrors in favour of a huge monster.

power of the elements and their ability to dominate or destroy. In '"Oh, Whistle, and I'll Come to You, My Lad"', the central protagonist is a Cambridge professor of ontography – the science, according to Richard F Kitchener, of describing 'the theory of the nature of existence' (1988: 76). James's professor, then, is interested in the physical properties of the shoreline, and he makes clear that the trip, though in part a holiday, will offer him an opportunity to work. Like many a Gothic tale since Mary Shelley's *Frankenstein* (1818), the presence of a scientist who unwittingly stumbles upon the occult strengthens the storytelling claims for the meeting point between material science and superstition.

At the request of an archaeologist colleague, Prof. Parkins is asked to take a brief look at an area of the shoreline to ascertain if it appears worthy of excavation. It is when thus diverted that he finds and retrieves 'a metal tube about four inches long, and evidently of some considerable age' (1987: 62). Removing it from the scene, he returns to his lodgings as dusk gathers and falls. As we have already observed in relation to the fair folk, twilight is often an invitation for supernatural happenings – a time when humans may be still in view, but they are far off and receding. Parkins noticeably starts to hasten his steps: 'He quickly rattled and clashed through the shingle and gained the sand, upon which but for the groynes which had to be got over every few yards, the going was both good and quiet' (1987: 62). It is as he glances back to measure his progress that he spies 'the shape of a rather indistinct personage, who seemed to be making great efforts to catch up with him, but made little, if any, progress' (1987: 63).

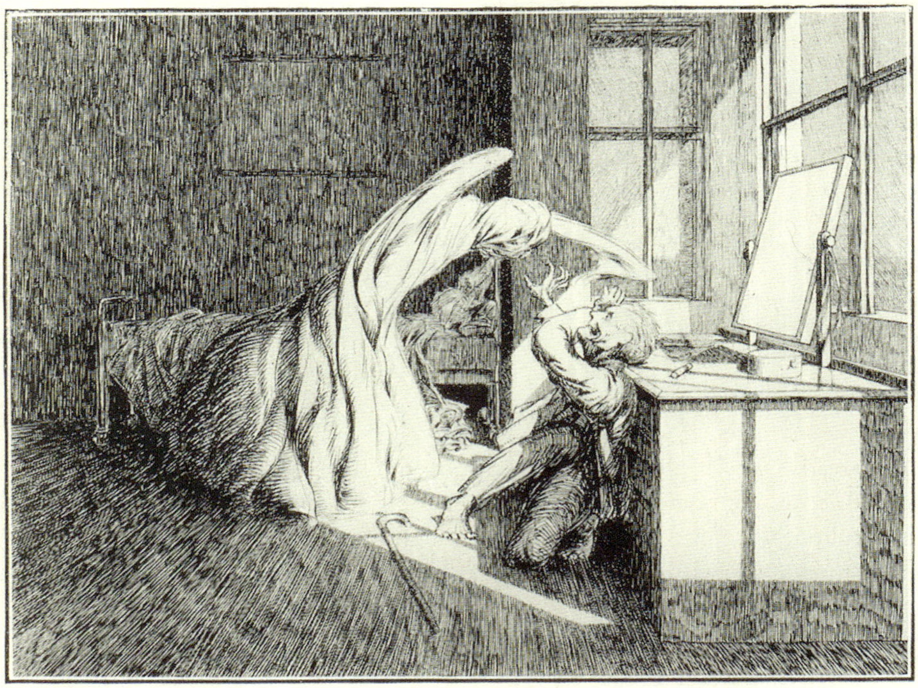

Illustration by James McBryde from M R James, '"Oh, Whistle, and I'll Come to You, My Lad"', from *Ghost-Stories of an Antiquary*, first edition.
British Library 012630.b.1

As the distance between the two persons never changes, two possibilities present themselves: either this is an imagined double left behind on the shore, or Parkins is being pursued. The primary response in the reader is fear: we want him to widen the space between self and other. At the same time a competing response presents itself, deriving from our identification with the shadow self. The apparently futile effort being made by the other party reminds the reader of a common childhood dream, one in which a cherished other (such as a parent or older sibling) refuses to wait as we struggle to catch up but find ourselves rooted to the spot.

In fact the relationship between protagonist and pursuer is more complicated than it would at first appear. Despite Parkins's lack of certainty about the identity of his tracker, he affirms that company might be welcome and, without any apparent show of doubt, identifies this other as 'a gentleman' (1987: 63). The object Parkins retrieves proves to be a whistle, and back at his room he cannot resist blowing it more than once, finding himself 'startled and yet pleased' by the results (1987: 65). Pleasure and danger seem to attach themselves to this strange encounter in equal measure, so much so that Parkins's apparent lack of awareness that there is any connection between the whistle and the stranger starts to become unconvincing to a modern reader. On the second whistle a storm blows up outside, sufficient to force open the casement and 'While you might count twenty' Parkins struggles with it before it re-closes (1987: 65). Having thus gained entry (for so it proves), the stranger seems to do Parkins no harm. He shares his bedchamber for two nights, apparently undetected by any but the maid, who wonders why both beds have been slept in. According to Parkins, only when he wakes to find the stranger in his room does violence ensue, which he passes off as a horrifying encounter with the occult.

However, a more prosaic possibility presents itself if we consider that this story is written less than a decade after the trial of Oscar Wilde. At this time in particular, a man might very well choose to explain away a chance encounter with a stranger on the beach by means of a decoy narrative of the supernatural. Certainly speculation about James's possible homosexuality exists. In a 2013 television documentary accompanying an adaptation of James's 'The Tractate Middoth' (1911), Gatiss associated with such speculation James's fascination with the relationship between horror and tactility in his stories: open mouths, clutching hands, the very 'feel' of an unwanted touch.

If we read '"Oh, Whistle, and I'll Come to You, My Lad"' as an encoded account of homosexual desire, we must surmise that Parkins is fully aware of the stranger's presence in his room, finding him monstrous only when he has tired of him. Certainly Parkins shows himself capable of voicing sexual disgust: 'he could not have borne – he didn't know why – to touch it; and as for it touching him, he would sooner dash himself through the window' (1987: 75). As the resulting confrontation becomes violent enough to attract attention, Parkins forces 'it' (no longer a gentleman, it seems) back through the window, leaving only his crumpled bedsheets behind. Parkins now uses the Gothic as an alibi, under the terms of which he has suffered an attack from a mummified ghoul, one having 'a horrible [...] face of crumpled linen' (1987: 76). Afterwards, the frame narrator tells us, Parkins 'very much dislike[d] being questioned about it' (75) and certainly curiosity is heavily punished in James's stories, as 'A Warning to the Curious' (1925) makes clear. One might say that, in James's writing, any form of prying or 'poking one's nose' (or hand) into somewhere it does not belong is likely to be a cause for regret.

However, despite the many powerful rural locations in which twentieth-century Gothic narratives are set, the countryside does not have a monopoly on the form. Examples of urban Gothic continue to pay homage to the overcrowded streets, poverty-related street crime and inadequate street-lighting of the late nineteenth century. The by-product of Victorian industrialisation, a rich amalgam of factory chimneys, fossil fuels and gas lamps, can be found in some of Conan Doyle's Sherlock Holmes novels, constituting what Susan Hill later describes, in *The Woman in Black*, as 'A London Particular' – a 'yellow fog, a filthy, evil-smelling fog, a fog that choked and blinded, smeared and stained' (1998: 22). Yet as the twentieth century develops a different vision of the urban Gothic pertains. During the Second World War, the most Gothic features of the urban landscape were created by the blackouts: a once familiar cityscape assuming new and sinister shapes in a bombed-out and blinding darkness. This is the backdrop to mid-twentieth-century narratives such as Elizabeth Bowen's 'The Demon Lover' (1945).

Second World War and Post-War Gothic

In Bowen's story, Kathleen Drover is a married mother of two who returns to the family home in London to check on its security while she and the children are staying in the countryside, following evacuation. London is in a state of architectural decrepitude and 'The unoccupied houses opposite [...] meet her look with their damaged stare' (1999: 666). Though the structure of her home appears intact, on arriving she finds a ghostly letter awaiting her, written by a long-dead lover, killed during the First World War. Suddenly it is as if the house has become haunted, and Kathleen starts to feel uncomfortable 'kneeling with her back exposed to the empty room' (1999: 664). The disquieting arrival of the letter forms a perfect illustration of the tiny shift, discussed earlier, that transforms the familiarity of the homely into the uncanny.

As she flees the house, Kathleen's descent down the stairs is met with an increasing sense of unease, and she feels a draught that seems to come from the cellar: 'down there a door or window was being opened by someone who chose this moment to leave the house' (1999: 666). Equally uncannily a taxi awaits, its engine firing as she approaches and its driver requiring no direction. But it is as she sees the identity of the driver's face that her 'mouth hung open for some seconds before [...] she continued to scream freely and to beat with her gloved hands on the glass all round as the taxi, accelerating without mercy, made off with her into the hinterland of deserted streets' (1999: 666). This horror, we assume, emanates from the face of a corpse, a ghost representing the mass dead of one war now come to shadow the dead of another – and simultaneously to haunt those whose lives have continued regardless.

Even in those mid-twentieth-century texts that appear to shape themselves as human versus nature narratives, we can witness the haunting impact of the Second World War. Such is the case in Daphne Du Maurier's 'The Birds' (1952), which has entered into popular knowledge primarily through Alfred Hitchcock's feature film of 1963. In fact the original story and the film are very different, not least because of Hitchcock's decision to set his version in coastal California, rather than Du Maurier's Cornwall. According to his screenwriter, Evan Hunter, Hitchcock claimed 'We're throwing away everything but the title and the notion of birds attacking human beings' (Bouzereau 2000).

One of the elements that Hitchcock's version loses is its post-war focus. Du Maurier's protagonist, Nat Hocken, is a part-time farm labourer, married with two children, existing on a war pension after being wounded in action. At first these details seem to be pure 'background' as the emphasis falls upon the beast narrative part of the story; Du Maurier alternately uses distance and proximity to bring the birds and the humans into closer contact with one another. As with any example of Gothic horror, bloodshed is repeatedly transacted between humans and 'the beasts'. On the first night Nat opens and shuts the window to frighten away a bird at the glass, but sucks at his hand: the bird has drawn blood. Later, when Nat returns inside after another attack, he has to re-bandage his hands, now

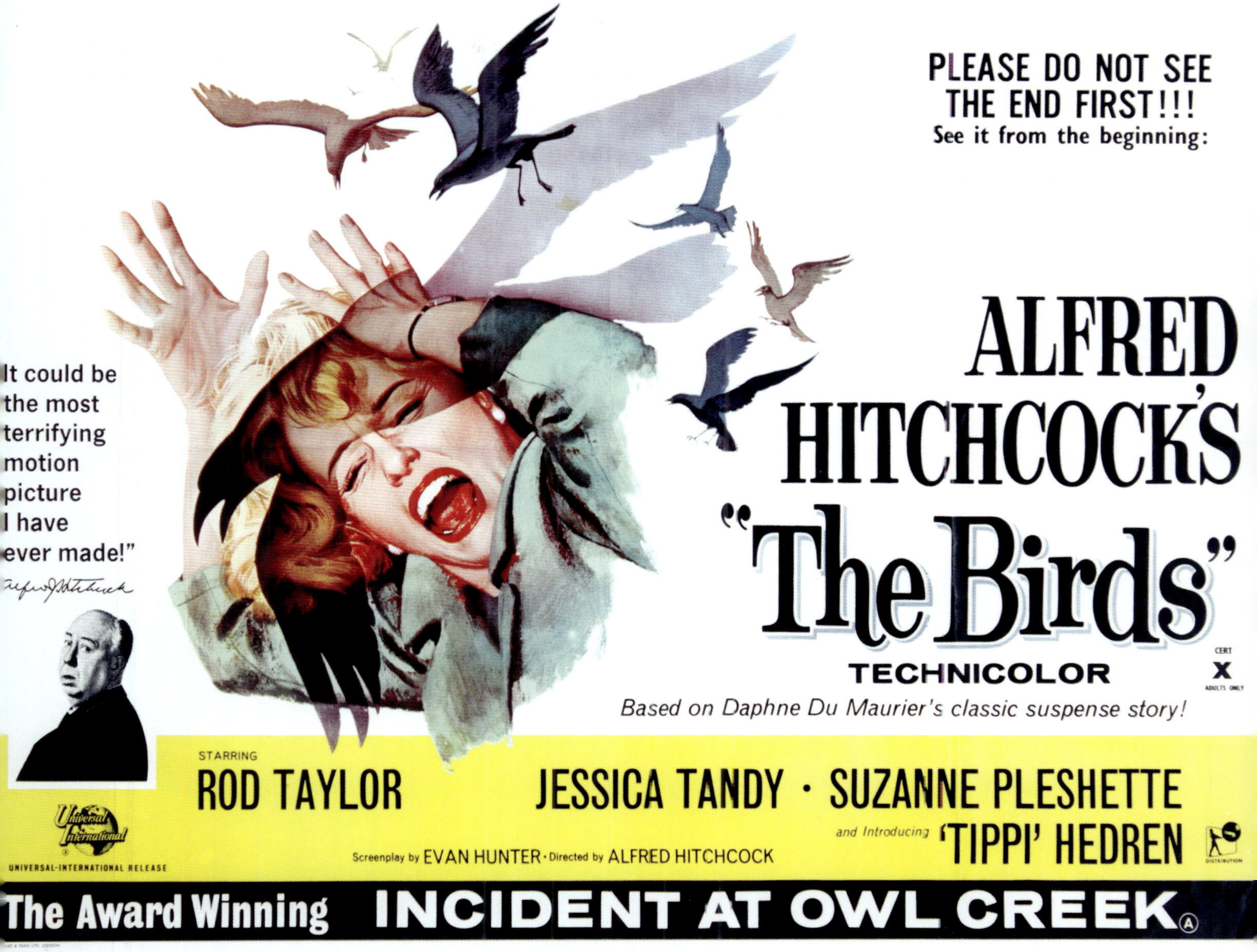

Poster for Alfred Hitchcock's *The Birds*, 1963.
British Film Institute.

'sticky with the birds' blood, not with his own cuts' (2004: 27). Here Nat's sucking, coupled with the placing of the bird at the threshold of the house, invites a reading of this passage as potentially vampiric, and thus invites the return and ultimate breach of more boundaries by the birds.

According to Carol J Clover, a metropolitan viewpoint is assumed by the majority of horror narratives: 'People from the city are people like us. People from the country [...] are people not like us' (1992: 124). This view is implied in both Hitchcock's film and Du Maurier's story, the film also emphasising the comparative isolation of Bodega Bay, to which his leading man, Mitch, retreats at weekends and to which the heroine, Melanie, follows him. Described as being 'about sixty miles north of [San Francisco] [...] About an hour and a half on the freeway. Or two hours if you take the coast highway' (2000), the reference to 'the freeway' introduces one of the key locations for the uncanny in both versions – namely the battleground between machinery and nature.

Here the wartime symbolism of the written story becomes most apparent. For Hitchcock, machinery is land- or water-based and civilian, focusing on the motor car or outboard engine of a boat. In Du Maurier's story, however, it takes to the sky and is centred upon aircraft flight as one means by which humanity has brought itself into conflict with the elements: '"What was that?" asked [Nat's] wife. "Were they dropping bombs on the birds?" [...] He did not want to tell her that the sound they had heard was the crashing of aircraft [...] What could aircraft do against birds that flung themselves to death against propeller and fuselage?' (2004: 25). These air attacks resonate with echoes of the air raids. More than once the birds are implied to have studied the devastating *Blitzkrieg* as a prototype for their tactics, with Du Maurier evoking statements from the Home Office as the birds' attacks widen in scope.

Though Hitchcock removes the connections between human and bird flight, he uses the 'bird's eye view' of the camera to establish a sense of the birds studying and thereby outwitting humans. This is particularly effective in the scene in which the birds attack a gasoline station. A gull swoops on a driver filling up at the pump, leaving him prone on the ground as the pump continues to siphon gasoline across the forecourt. Another customer, startled by what is going on, drops a lighted match in the fuel, and is instantly engulfed in flames. Human excess is implied to be a contributory factor in this scene. The first driver is intoxicated and the 'worse for wear', a state ironically mirrored by the overflow of gasoline pumping across the forecourt. The social critique here, perhaps, is of the excesses of America's post-war 'gas-guzzling' economy.

Manderley and Other Mansions

The Gothic narrative with which Du Maurier is most commonly associated, of course, is her 1938 novel *Rebecca*, also made into a classic film by Hitchcock, in 1940. In part what makes the novel so important to our understanding of the twentieth-century Gothic is its overtly psychological opening:

> Last night I dreamt I went to Manderley again. It seemed to me I stood by the iron gate leading to the drive, and for a while I could not enter, for the way was barred to me [...] Then, like all dreamers, I was possessed of a sudden with supernatural powers and passed like a spirit through the barrier before me. (1992: 5)

In Hitchcock's version, the railings of the gateway part like a semi-transparent gauze as the camera approaches, as if transformed into a soft curtain or veil that entices us to enter. Later in the film this scene is mirrored as Mrs Danvers, the housekeeper, holds up the lace negligee of her former mistress to taunt Maxim's new second wife with its allure: 'Look, you can almost see your hand through it.' The relationship between the women in the film is crucial, for *Rebecca* spawns an important twentieth-century sub-set of the form called 'the female Gothic'. In 1976 Ellen Moers attributed this type of Gothic narrative to a much earlier moment in its history, namely the turn of the eighteenth and nineteenth centuries, when writers such as Ann Radcliffe and Emily Brontë forged a new Gothic vision of 'travelling heroinism' (1976: 126). Nevertheless, Moers also represents one of several Second Wave literary feminists who, in the 1970s and 1980s, started to re-read a variety of 'popular classics' by female writers and re-think their significance in gendered terms. Among these, it is *Rebecca* that provides the clearest formula for Moers's notion of the female Gothic, for this approach enabled a re-reading of the narrative less in terms of the unequal romantic relationship between the wealthy Maxim de Winter and his second, unnamed bride, and more in terms of the power dynamics at work between this second wife and her dead rival, and between both women and Mrs Danvers.

Still from Alfred Hitchcock's film *Rebecca*, 1940.

Shown here are Joan Fontaine as the nameless second Mrs de Winter, and Judith Anderson as Mrs Danvers. The film reuses motifs from ghost stories to heighten the psychological tension.

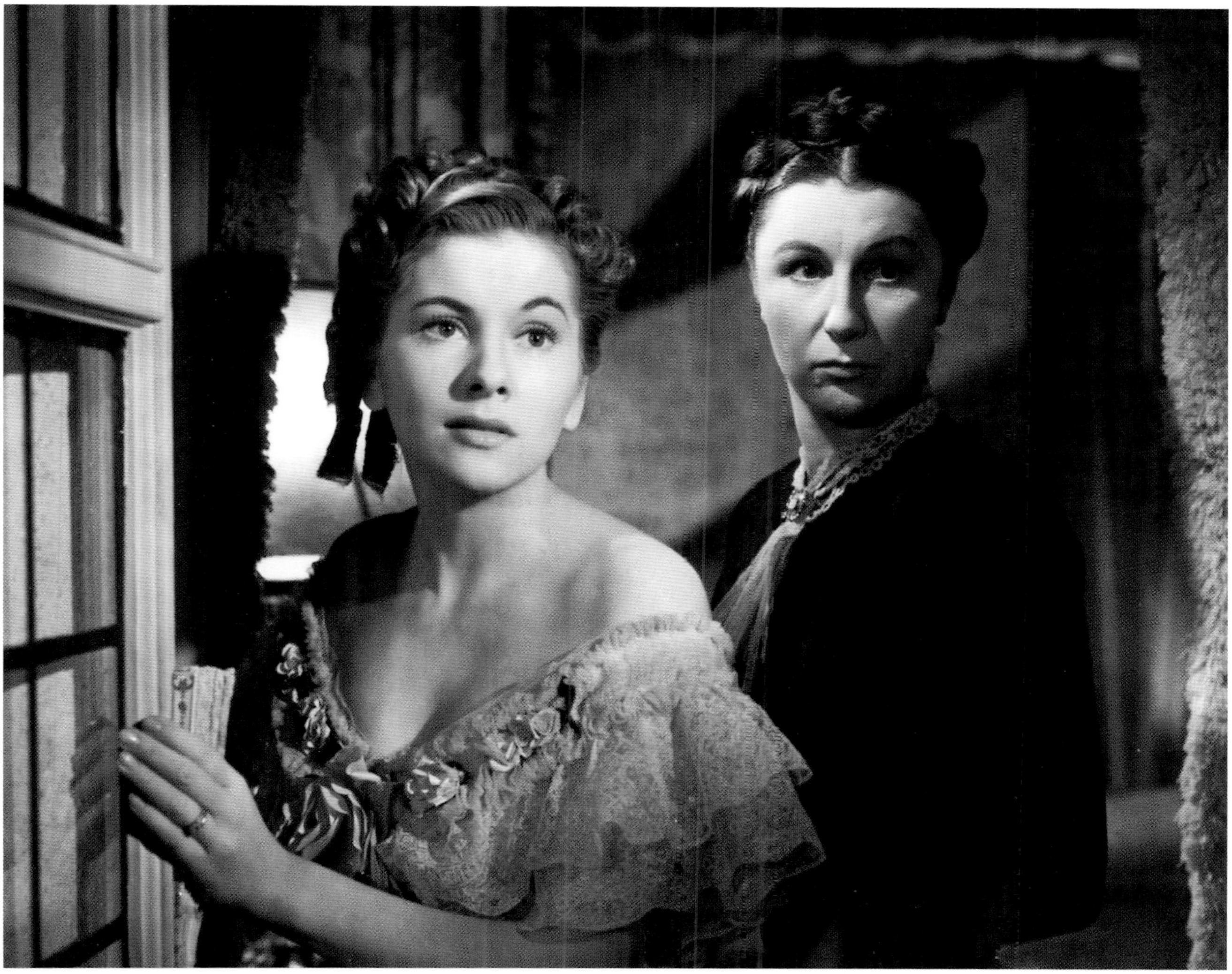

Once we remove our attention from Maxim, we also become able to contemplate what it is that makes Rebecca so feared. Far more threatening than her allure, far more omnipresent than her flamboyant signature that Hitchcock scrolls across several scenes of his film and far more shocking than her adulterous liaisons with other men, what makes Rebecca the embodiment of late twentieth-century dread and horror is the discovery that she was suffering from terminal cancer. By the late twentieth century the medical Gothic really starts to take hold as a powerful source of the uncanny, for if we are afraid neither of ghosts, vampires nor werewolves, we dread the lurking shadow of a malignant tumour, an 'other' that feeds upon us, a shadow self that must be exorcised.

The entrapment of female characters by monsters, ghosts, demons and predators has always been a key preoccupation of the Gothic. Later in the century, however, the influence of Second Wave Feminism starts to inspire a new type of Gothic narrative, allowing for a different portrayal of women and girls. At the forefront of this new trend we find Angela Carter, a writer who revised the conventional fairy tale to bring out its dark origins and utilise the Gothic aspects of those tales to explore more adult themes of desire and sexuality. Most influential of all in this regard is her Gothic collection of short stories *The Bloody Chamber* (1979), one story from which, 'The Company of Wolves', was made into a film by Neil Jordan in 1984.

Jordan's film *The Company of Wolves* counters a growing trend, for while the vampire retains its currency in literature and

Still from Neil Jordan's film *The Company of Wolves*, 1984.

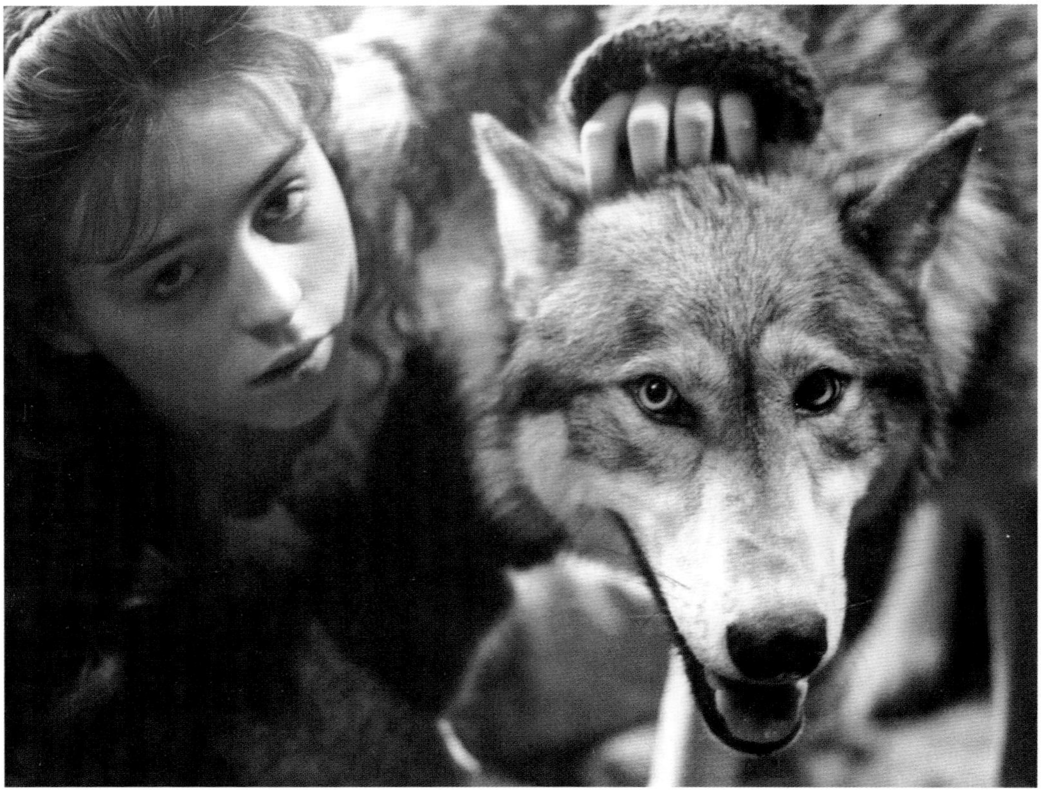

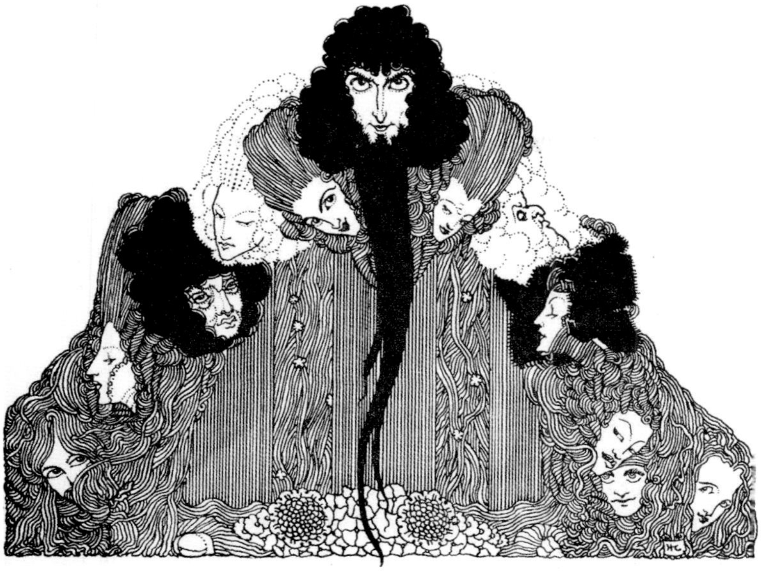

Bluebeard, illustration by Harry Clarke from *The Fairy Tales of Charles Perrault*, edition of 1922.
British Library 12450.v.1.
Angela Carter used the Perrault story as source material for the title story in her collection *The Bloody Chamber* (1979).

film throughout the century, its partner in horror, the werewolf, tends to fall into abeyance. There are exceptions to this rule, especially in cinema, including *Werewolf of London* (dir. Stuart Walker, [1935]), *The Werewolf* (dir. Fred F Sears, [1956]) and *An American Werewolf in London* (dir. John Landis, [1981]), but one of the reasons for its limited success as a Gothic monster is, according to James B Twitchell, because 'the wolf is so irredeemably a beast' (1985: 216). As a result, the uncanniness of the creature becomes lost, with all interest relying on the use of special effects during the transformation scene: 'He is just there to say "boo!" and be gone' (1985: 218). Carter's story succeeds where others fail because she achieves what Twitchell also argued Michael Jackson achieved in his *Thriller* video, namely the attachment of 'the wolf transformation to a clearly sexual scenario' (1985: 219).

Carter's title story 'The Bloody Chamber' is similarly a combination of carnal and carnivorous appetites, based around a rewriting of the Bluebeard folk narrative. In true Gothic tradition, Carter also makes optimum use of Madoff's locked room mystery, the young bride's transgressive determination to access that room, and the horrifyingly hard-core sado-masochistic secrets she discovers therein. The setting is also a major contributor to the story. The male protagonist's castle is built on a remote tidal causeway, this being the eventual destination following a lengthy journey by steam locomotive. Rather like Du Maurier's second Mrs de Winter, this young bride is both excited and daunted by her new bestial bridegroom:

> I could see the dark, leonine shape of his head and my nostrils caught a whiff of the opulent male scent of leather and spices that always accompanied him [...] though he was a big man, he moved as softly as if all his shoes had soles of velvet, as if his footfall turned the carpet into snow. (1979a: 8)

Carter's real accomplishment in these stories is her construction of characters that appear to inhabit a liminal realm, somewhere between the animal and the human. Like the vampire or the werewolf, both of whose excesses are 'red in tooth and claw', this bridegroom is a creature of appetite; but, unlike Moretti's Dracula, this monster's wealth is only a taster of his real pleasure, which comprises sado-masochistic pornography. One of Carter's interests in the Gothic is precisely that it enables her female characters to come into contact with a new type of danger, that of the libertine.

In her non-fictional study *The Sadeian Woman* (1979), Carter argues that 'the chaste kiss of the sentimental lover differs only in degree from the vampirish love-bite that draws blood [...] a disinterested carcass is only quantitively different from a disinterested flogging' (1979b: 24–5). Embracing the libertine excesses of the Marquis de Sade as a pornographer who refused to equate female sexuality with that of the passive victim, Carter's Gothic tales bring her female characters into contact with a sexual excessiveness that requires an active sexual response from them. In this respect Carter's view of the relationship between the Gothic and its female characters is not so very different from Moers's reading of the transgressive potential of Ann Radcliffe or Emily Brontë 150 to 200 years previously. In *Wuthering Heights* (1847), Moers observes, the critics of the time identified the presence of a 'Gothic vice of sadism' (1976: 100). Although this contributed to the distaste with which some critics of the time greeted the novel, it undoubtedly enabled its female characters to be endowed with a 'palpitating vitality' typically denied to literary heroines in the nineteenth century (1976: 107).

Susan Hill's *The Woman in Black* (1983), published four years after Carter's *The Bloody Chamber* collection, perhaps owes something of its dark vision to Carter's tales, not least because of its causeway setting. However, Hill reverses the gender dynamics and returns us to a much more conservative tale of haunting. In *The Woman in Black* it is a young lawyer, Arthur Kipps, who finds himself stranded in the far-flung Gothic mansion and, because her antagonist is female, Hill employs a different type of tyranny with which to terrify him. So far, we have only considered those ghost narratives in which apparitions are half-seen or unclear in outline. In Hill's novel Arthur's early sightings focus upon how utterly clear and life-like the ghost appears – one of the unusual aspects of her portrayal. At first he believes her to be alive, the only sign of decrepitude being illness: her skin appears to be inflicted with a wasting disease. (The Gothic possibilities afforded by narratives of contagious or carcinogenic illness are again in evidence.) This ghost, Jennet Humfrye, is a grieving mother, and her illness, missing from the film version directed by James Watkins in 2012, is an outward manifestation of a twelve-year period of melancholia following her son's death. The loss of her child renders Hill's ghost especially vindictive, determined to exact vengeance even upon this innocent interloper. Arthur's only transgression, acting on his employer's instructions, is to enter Eel Marsh House, home of the recently deceased Mrs Drablow, Jennet's sister, and act as executor to her estate.

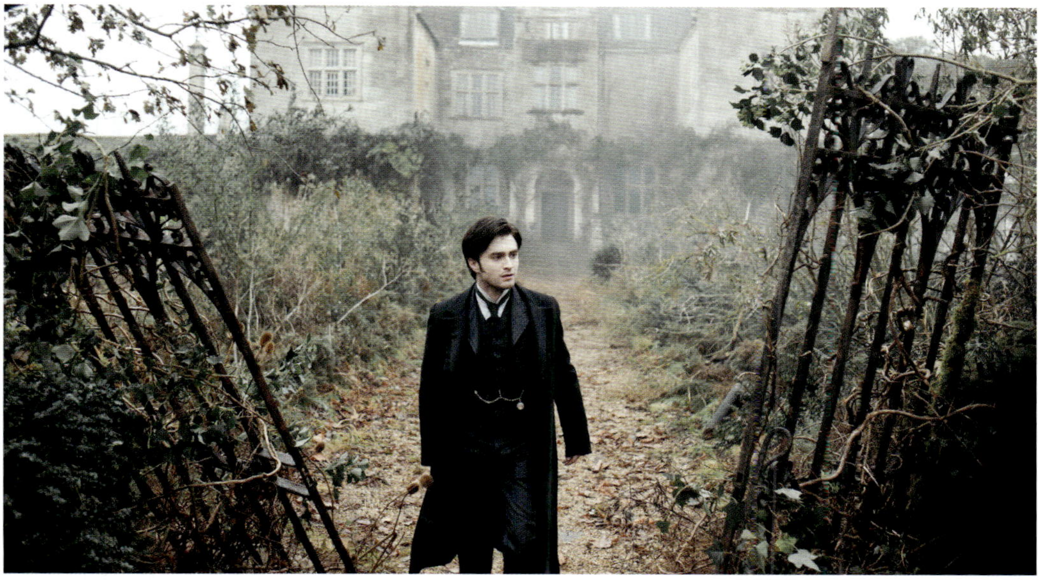

Still from James Watkins's film *The Woman in Black*, 2012.

Daniel Radcliffe as Arthur Kipps in the third release from the new incarnation of Hammer Films.

To understand fully the viciousness of this ghost's attack upon Arthur, we have to consider the relationship between sight and responsibility. Jennet's son dies in full view as she sits in the rocking chair looking out of the nursery window, anxiously anticipating his return along the causeway in the pony and trap (the only vehicular means of access in the nineteenth-century setting of the novel). His death is partly at the hands of the elements, haste being prompted by the returning tide and a sudden 'sea-fret' or fog, but it is just as he comes into sight and apparent safety that the pony loses its way and plunges helplessly into the marsh. This is not only a fully visible but a noisy ghost, and what terrifies Arthur most are the ghostly screams of the boy, as he, his nursemaid and the pony are sucked into the greedy mud.

As is the case with the other film adaptations we have considered, important differences are written into the cinematic version of *The Woman in Black* and they prompt a different ending. In Hill's novel, one of the reasons Jennet punishes Arthur is because he is so badly affected by his ghostly experiences that he becomes ill and is persuaded to abandon his task, fleeing into marriage with his beloved Stella and fatherhood with a baby boy. In the film version, Kipps insists on seeing his task through to the bitter end, irrespective of the physical cost to himself. He recognises that both boy and woman are 'lost' and determines to reconcile them in death. Whereas in the novel the boy's body has already been recovered and buried long ago, in the film it has not been retrieved. Kipps duly sets out, with the help of a local businessman, Mr Daily, and his motor car, to pull the wreckage and boy from the mud. Dressing the boy's body for burial, Kipps summons the ghost to the nursery to allow her the final deathbed farewell denied her in life. He then exhumes her skeletal remains from the tomb and buries her dead son in her arms.

On the face of it, the film is a far more horrifying narrative than Hill's novel. The novel proceeds in a slow and steady manner, a sense of the uncanniness building through the responses of other characters long before Kipps's first arrival at Mrs Drablow's house, as late as the fourth chapter. Film audiences are perhaps less patient, and the need for gratuitous horror to be present in visible and immediate form is much clearer in the film, which is as much a horror movie as a ghost story. In part it is the treatment of dead children that emphasises this shift, for the film magnifies and multiplies the number of child victims. In an entirely invented scene in the film, Kipps opens the front door of Eel Marsh House in response to the rattling of the door handle, only to see the house surrounded by dead children, their bloodied faces and blackened eyes a typical horror trait.

At the same time, one of the questions that all Gothic narratives have to address is of what, exactly, are we frightened? What this may boil down to is the issue of whether or not the ghost, monster or apparition intends physical harm to the innocent interloper, our representative in the text. In the novel Arthur sleeps at the house in the small bedroom, at the opposite end of the landing to the nursery. Though his experiences leave him immobilised with fear at times, at no point does the ghost actually approach him. He feels her pass him as he approaches the staircase, as if she has turned ahead of him towards the nursery; he sees her malevolent look on more than one occasion, as when he returns from the near-death experience of rescuing Mr Daily's dog from the marshes (in a chapter tellingly entitled 'Whistle and I'll Come to You'); as the plot proves, she has obvious malevolent intent for all those he loves. However, violence against Arthur is not part of that intent.

To return for one moment to M R James's '"Oh, Whistle, and I'll Come to You, My Lad"', that story ends on a remarkably anti-climactic note when the narrator considers that 'it is not so evident what more the creature that came in answer to the whistle could have done than frighten' (1987: 76–7). However, this is a key issue for twentieth-century Gothic narratives in general, and for *The Woman in Black* in particular. For the dread that the cinema viewer feels in watching this film is only partly prompted by its horror content. It is also provoked by the kind of fear we respond to in a thriller, namely that a 'real' stranger might be lurking in our house unseen, waiting until darkness falls to come out and attack us.

One reason for the effectiveness of the haunted house narrative is that we can all relate to it as our primary real-life illustration of Freud's uncanny. To recall Wharton's words, we may not believe in ghosts, but we remain frightened by them. Precisely because we all live in houses that become dark at night and begin to creak, that have shadowy corners, cupboards and rooms with closed doors, one of the great successes of the uncanny is the fact that we may well fear, especially when alone, that an antagonist (living if not dead) could be waiting for us. In the film version of *The Woman in Black,* and in absolute opposition to the novel, great use is made of the glimpsed, the half-seen, *something* that gradually comes into view. The camera angle is crucial to this effect. As Giles observes, one of the greatest pleasures in horror cinema is, paradoxically, in choosing not to look,

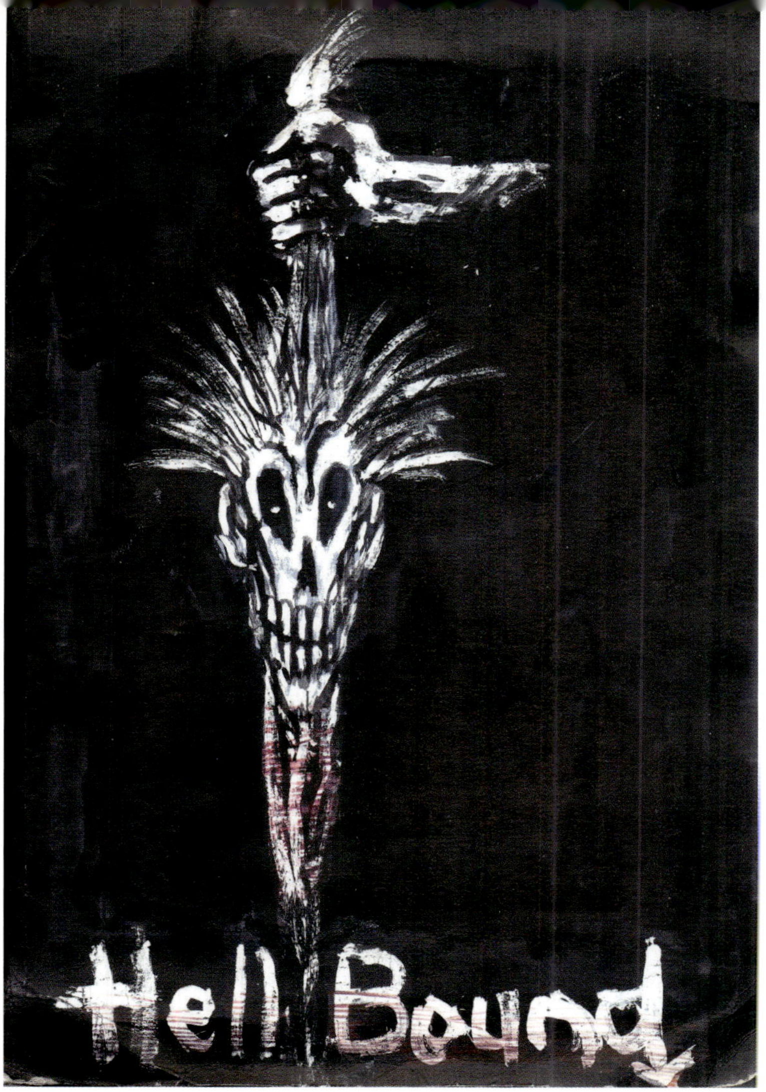

LEFT AND BELOW:
Clive Barker, illustrations for *The Hellbound Heart*, 1986.

Clive Barker's sketch of a cenobite from his draft of *The Hellbound Heart*.

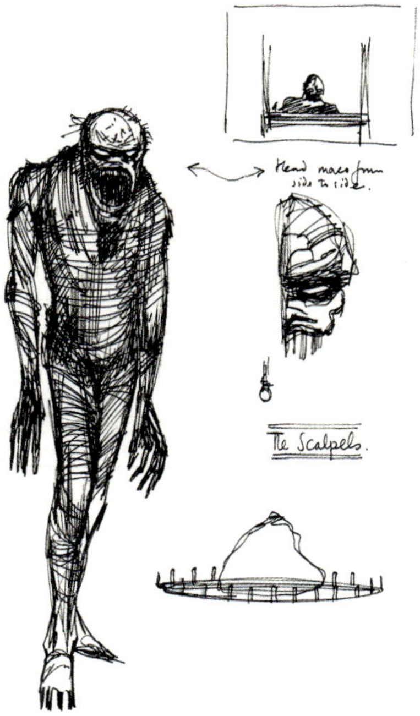

or to look away at the key moment. This leads him to differentiate between two forms of horror cinema, one in which 'the object of fright may be extended indefinitely', such as *The Texas Chainsaw Massacre*, or another, in truth a more affecting one, in which 'the image is only a brief pay-off which proves that the thing is truly terrifying [...] [then] full vision fades [. . .] into a sequence of imagery which anticipates the return of the terrible object but evades it – refuses to face it openly' (1984: 42). This second type is precisely the viewer's experience in the film version of *The Woman in Black*.

The Horrors of the Flesh

By the end of the twentieth century it seems that it is the body itself and its secrets that most haunt our waking nights, a cultural move that, although differently inflected, marks a return to the corporeal nightmares of the late Victorian Gothic. Such preoccupations are to be found in the physical horror of Clive Barker's writing, for example in his 1986 novel *The Hellbound Heart*, adapted for cinema in 1987 under the title *Hellraiser*. In this novel a young married couple, Julia and Rory, move into a suburban house which Rory has inherited from his parents, only to be intruded upon by the husband's renegade brother, Frank, who has equal claims on the property. Driven by licentious desire, Frank obtains and opens a contraption known as Lamarchand's Box. Inside resides a form of psychological torment inflicted upon its curious victims, controlled by a mysterious race called the Cenobites.

As the influence of the box drives Frank further and further into the realm of the taboo, he falls increasingly under the spell of his own extreme practices and his body begins to fester and decay. As the Cenobites suck greater and greater amounts of humanity from him, he is gradually reduced to a husk or festering remnant of human flesh, trapped behind the wall of the house: '[T]he body had been ripped apart and sewn together again with most of its pieces either missing or twisted and blackened as if in a furnace. There was an eye, gleaming [...] and the ladder of a spine, the vertebrae stripped of muscle, a few unrecognizable fragments of anatomy [...] That such a thing might live beggared reason – what little flesh it owned was hopelessly corrupted' (1986: 49). That Frank's transgressive behaviour has a direct anatomical consequence renders Barker's novel a kind of modern-day horror version of Wilde's *The Picture of Dorian Gray* (1890).

At the same time, *The Hellbound Heart* has much in common with what becomes a recurring preoccupation in the final decades of the twentieth century: the Gothicism of the diseased body, most predominantly centring upon two diseases, cancer and HIV/AIDS. Patrick McGrath, in particular, uses much of his late twentieth-century fiction to explore the growing connection between disease and a new medicalised understanding of haunting. In his first novel, *The Grotesque* (1989), the central narrator is Sir Hugo Coal, a paralysed man whose injuries are inflicted as the result of a brain haemorrhage brought on by a sexualised struggle with his butler, Fledge, who later goes on to become involved with Sir Hugo's wife. Believed to inhabit a persistent vegetative state, Sir Hugo is also our first-person narrator, and so fully conscious, but only to us. The novel thus offers readers a deeply disturbing example of a 'live burial' narrative, one of the Gothic conventions most favoured by writers at the end of the eighteenth century.

In *Dr Haggard's Disease* (1993), the first-person narrator, the eponymous Dr Haggard, is again physically diminished. He walks with a stick, having been thrown down the stairs by his mistress's husband, the senior pathologist at the hospital where Haggard works as a surgeon. After his mistress, Fanny Vaughan, dies, Haggard becomes increasingly attached and attracted to her son James, an airman. James also suffers from a regressive anatomical condition, in which his body gradually returns to a 'feminised' pre-pubescent state; as a result, Haggard gradually starts to believe that the cause of this condition is Fanny's possession of her son's body. Looking to re-attain physical intimacy with Fanny at all costs, Haggard, following an air crash, holds the dying James in his arms. Suddenly Haggard is overcome with longing and, in a horrifyingly vampiric kiss, forces his tongue into the dying James's mouth.

Such horror is characteristic of McGrath's narrative vision. In one of his early and best-known stories, 'The Angel' (1988),

McGrath openly explores the fearful contagion of HIV/AIDS and its connection with social paranoia, through a narrative concerning a wealthy elderly man, Harry Talboys, who lives in an apartment by the Chrysler Building in New York. Much is made, in the story, of the phallic connotations of the building's spire, while Talboys himself exists as a type of living corpse. McGrath describes his protagonist's torso in a manner that recalls Barker's Frank in *The Hellbound Heart*: a rotted mass to which 'the clotted skin' clung 'in a state of gelatinous putrescence' (1988: 15). Constructed using the imagery of horror, McGrath's representation of this homosexual male character during the HIV panic both challenges regressive social attitudes and reinforces the increasingly Gothic features that we attach to disease.

However, it is in returning to questions of medical interventions into the diseased body that twentieth-century writing draws us back to territory reminiscent of early Gothic narratives, such as *Frankenstein*. Perhaps this also explains why, in the final decade of the century, two Gothic films, *Bram Stoker's Dracula* (dir. Francis Ford Coppola, [1992]) and *Mary Shelley's Frankenstein* (dir. Kenneth Branagh, [1994]) re-attach the literary origins to what had become quite detached cinema metamorphoses of these tales. Freud's curiosity about what continues to motivate our interest in the uncanny long after we have ceased to believe in the supernatural is perhaps also best answered in this way: nothing is more horrifying to us than those unseen mysteries, terrors and wonders that lurk in the anatomical 'locked room' to which only the medical profession holds the key.

Further Reading

Armitt, Lucie 2011. *Twentieth-Century Gothic* (Cardiff: University of Wales Press). This monograph examines issues of haunted childhood, the architectural uncanny, Gothic inhumanity and the queer in its exploration of the long twentieth-century Gothic, from Henry James's *The Turn of the Screw* to Sarah Waters's *The Little Stranger*.

Botting, Fred 2008. *Limits of Horror: Technology, Bodies, Gothic* (Manchester: Manchester University Press). A wide-ranging study of twentieth- and twenty-first-century Gothic. In his discussion of the role played by technology in the construction of the modern Gothic, Botting's argument ranges from early cinema to the computer game, and includes the role of technological shock within cultural modernity.

Clover, Carol J 1992. *Men, Women and Chainsaws: Gender in the Modern Horror Film* (London: British Film Institute Publishing). An important book that opens with a discussion of the iconic 1976 film *Carrie* (dir. Brian de Palma) and ends with a discussion of the equally iconic 1991 film *Thelma and Louise* (dir. Ridley Scott). For Clover the horror film, in all its corporeal extremes, plays a crucial role in the gender-orientated negotiations that take place within its primarily adolescent audience members.

Grixti, Joseph 1989. *Terrors of Uncertainty: The Cultural Contexts of Horror Fiction* (London: Routledge). Grixti's study begins with a discussion of *The Twilight Zone* (1983; dir. Steven Spielberg and John Landis), a film which Grixti uses to argue that horror is a mode of cinema that questions the perceived binary divide between fantasy and reality. Like many critics of the Gothic, Grixti perceives the stuff of horror narratives to be socially constructed, irrespective of whether the outward manifestation of that social horror takes the form of the vampire, the beast or the psychopath.

Hock-soon Ng, Andrew 2004. *Dimensions of Monstrosity in Contemporary Narratives: Theory, Psychoanalysis, Postmodernism* (London: Palgrave Macmillan). A conceptually sophisticated study that defines monstrosity primarily in relation to the psychoanalytic theories of Jacques Lacan, Slavoj Žižek and Julia Kristeva. In contrast to our more conventional understanding of monstrosity as an 'other' or 'scapegoat' that must be defeated, Hock-soon Ng identifies monstrosity in late twentieth-century narratives as a mode of self-reflection upon the human condition.

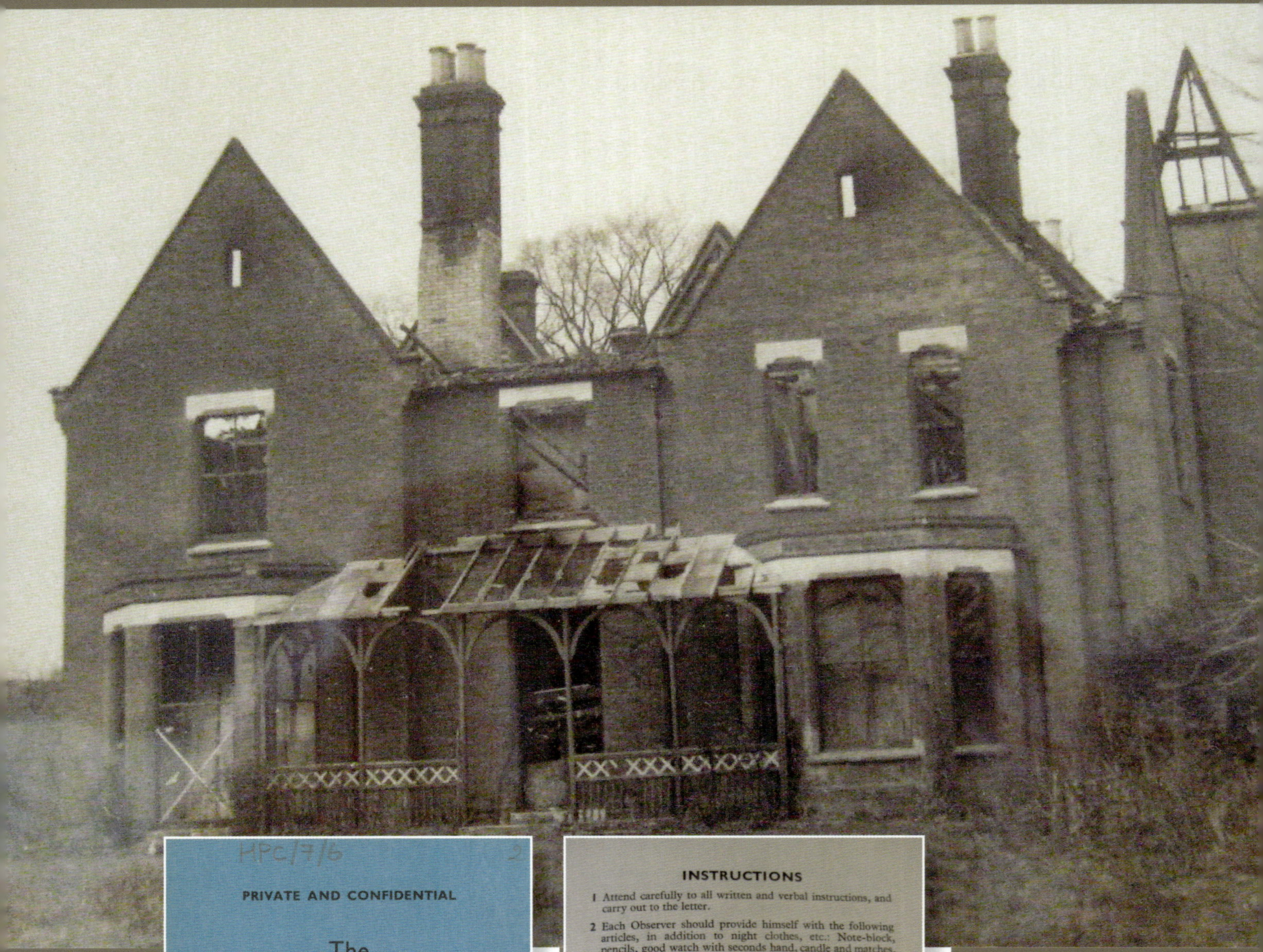

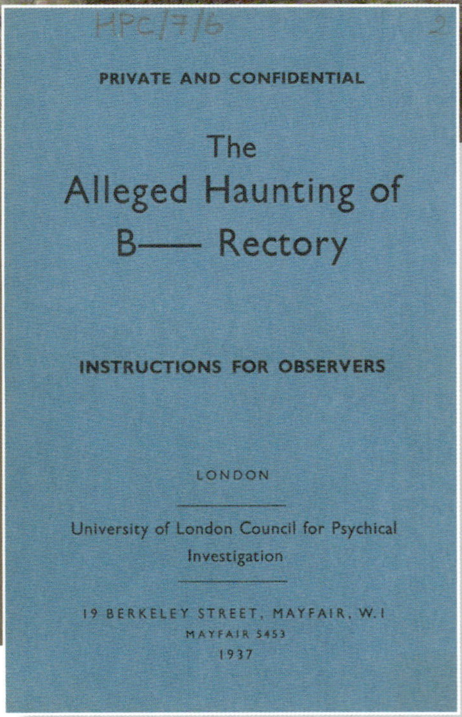

HPC/7/6 2

PRIVATE AND CONFIDENTIAL

The
Alleged Haunting of
B—— Rectory

INSTRUCTIONS FOR OBSERVERS

LONDON

University of London Council for Psychical Investigation

19 BERKELEY STREET, MAYFAIR, W.1
MAYFAIR 5453
1937

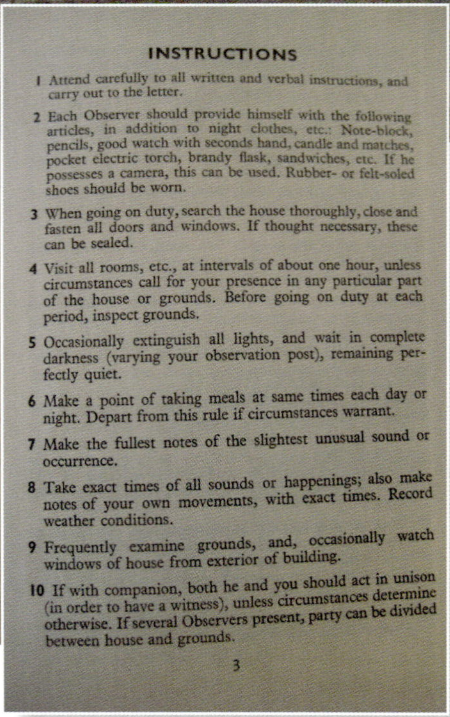

INSTRUCTIONS

1 Attend carefully to all written and verbal instructions, and carry out to the letter.

2 Each Observer should provide himself with the following articles, in addition to night clothes, etc.: Note-block, pencils, good watch with seconds hand, candle and matches, pocket electric torch, brandy flask, sandwiches, etc. If he possesses a camera, this can be used. Rubber- or felt-soled shoes should be worn.

3 When going on duty, search the house thoroughly, close and fasten all doors and windows. If thought necessary, these can be sealed.

4 Visit all rooms, etc., at intervals of about one hour, unless circumstances call for your presence in any particular part of the house or grounds. Before going on duty at each period, inspect grounds.

5 Occasionally extinguish all lights, and wait in complete darkness (varying your observation post), remaining perfectly quiet.

6 Make a point of taking meals at same times each day or night. Depart from this rule if circumstances warrant.

7 Make the fullest notes of the slightest unusual sound or occurrence.

8 Take exact times of all sounds or happenings; also make notes of your own movements, with exact times. Record weather conditions.

9 Frequently examine grounds, and, occasionally watch windows of house from exterior of building.

10 If with companion, both he and you should act in unison (in order to have a witness), unless circumstances determine otherwise. If several Observers present, party can be divided between house and grounds.

3

ABOVE:
Photograph of Borley Rectory taken after it was badly damaged by fire in 1939.
Harry Price Archive, Senate House Library.

LEFT:
The 'Blue Books' of instructions were given by Harry Price to each of his fellow psychical investigators during his 1937 tenancy at Borley, to guide their investigations when Price was not present.
Harry Price Archive, Senate House Library.

From the Crypt: The Haunting of Borley Rectory

Borley Rectory in rural Essex, once known as 'the most haunted house in England', was made notorious by the investigation of psychical detective Harry Price and his related works, *The Most Haunted House in England* (1940) and *The End of Borley Rectory* (1946). Built in 1863 by the Reverend Henry Bull as a home for his large family, Borley Rectory was said to have been haunted almost immediately after its construction, with the ghosts of a nun and a headless coachman plaguing its first inhabitants. The next tenants of the rectory, the Reverend and Mrs G. Eric Smith, were so disturbed by these ghostly accounts that they decided to hire a psychic investigator to determine their veracity, and wrote to the *Daily Mirror* for advice on locating a suitable person for the job. The *Mirror* responded by dispatching Harry Price and a journalist to the scene.

These items relate to the investigations that Harry Price carried out at Borley Rectory between 1929 and 1946. The most intense period of psychical incidents occurred during the tenancy of the Reverend Lionel and Mrs Marianne Foyster. During this time various pieces of automatic writing appeared on the rectory walls. Some of it appeared to be appealing to Mrs Foyster by name, and was later deciphered as reading 'get help well tank bottom me' – a statement that seemed less cryptic following the excavation of an old well and a female human jawbone in the rectory's basement. Mrs Foyster wrote back to the 'spirit' and appeared to receive further illegible replies. The Foysters reported several paranormal incidents during the 15 months they resided at Borley, including the vanishing and mysterious reappearance of objects; the spontaneous combustion of a skirting board; pervasive smells; incessant bell ringing; and the violent hurling of pebbles, books and even furniture across rooms. There is strong evidence to suggest that almost all of these occurrences were perpetrated by Mrs Foyster herself, possibly in an attempt to persuade her much older and infirm husband of the necessity of leaving the isolated rectory (which had no electricity, central heating or running water) for somewhere more civilised. For example, the automatic writing of her name 'Marianne', supposedly by the poltergeist, bore some similarity to her own signature.

The blue booklets seen here were a key part of the building of the Borley legend. After the Foysters left the rectory, Harry Price himself took on the tenancy of Borley for the purpose of carrying out further investigation. Rather than embarking upon this alone, he recruited a small army of amateur ghost-hunters to assist him, arming them with such sets of instructions and setting them to work. The wording of the instructions strongly led these susceptible investigators to interpret ordinary noises caused by mice or the wind as the tappings and knockings of the spirit-world. In 1939 the rectory burned down, but some limited investigation continued. In 1944, shortly after this photograph was taken, the last remains of the building were demolished. Although most of the evidence has since been shown to be unreliable at best, or fraudulent, at worst, the legend of Borley Rectory has provided inspiration for a number of classic ghost fictions, including, most notably, Shirley Jackson's *The Haunting of Hill House* (1959) and its film adaptations, *The Haunting* (1963; 1999), as well as Sarah Waters's *The Little Stranger* (2009). TANYA KIRK

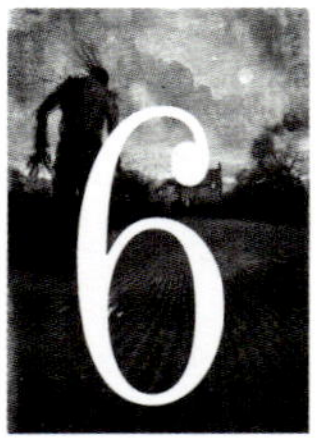

CATHERINE SPOONER

Twenty-First-Century Gothic

OPPOSITE:
Jim Kay, illustration for *A Monster Calls* by Patrick Ness, 2011.

Twenty-first-century literature for children and young adults increasingly uses the Gothic as a way of exploring the pain of growing up.

Bloodsuckers, Beasts and Zombies

It may seem premature to identify a specifically twenty-first-century Gothic. In many ways twenty-first-century Gothic resembles that of the twentieth century; its distinctive trends and themes generally cultivate ideas seeded earlier in the preceding century rather than plant entirely new ones. The sympathetic vampires of Stephenie Meyer's *Twilight* saga (2005–08) and the 'paranormal romance' genre are anticipated by Anne Rice's *Vampire Chronicles* (1976–2003), if not by still earlier Gothic romances with dangerous yet attractive heroes. The apocalyptic scenarios of books such as Max Brooks's *World War Z* (2006) and Justin Cronin's *The Passage* (2010) recall Richard Matheson's *I Am Legend* (1954), and can be traced still further back to Mary Shelley's *The Last Man* (1826). Even the trend towards extreme horror in films such as James Wan's *Saw* (2004) or Tom Six's *The Human Centipede* (2009) can be regarded as a continuation of the experimentation with violence found in earlier titles, such as Michael Powell's *Peeping Tom* (1960), Tobe Hooper's *The Texas Chainsaw Massacre* (1974) and Abel Ferrara's *The Driller Killer* (1979).

One distinctive feature of twenty-first-century Gothic texts is the way in which vampires have been joined by other mythical beings, including demons, fairies, werewolves and, most prominently, zombies, in a revitalised bestiary of Gothic creatures. Many of these derive from folkloric traditions newly appropriated into the Gothic through the processes of globalisation. The Caribbean soucouyant, or bloodsucking female spirit, in Helen Oyeyemi's *White Is for Witching* (2009), for example, haunts a boarding house in Dover,

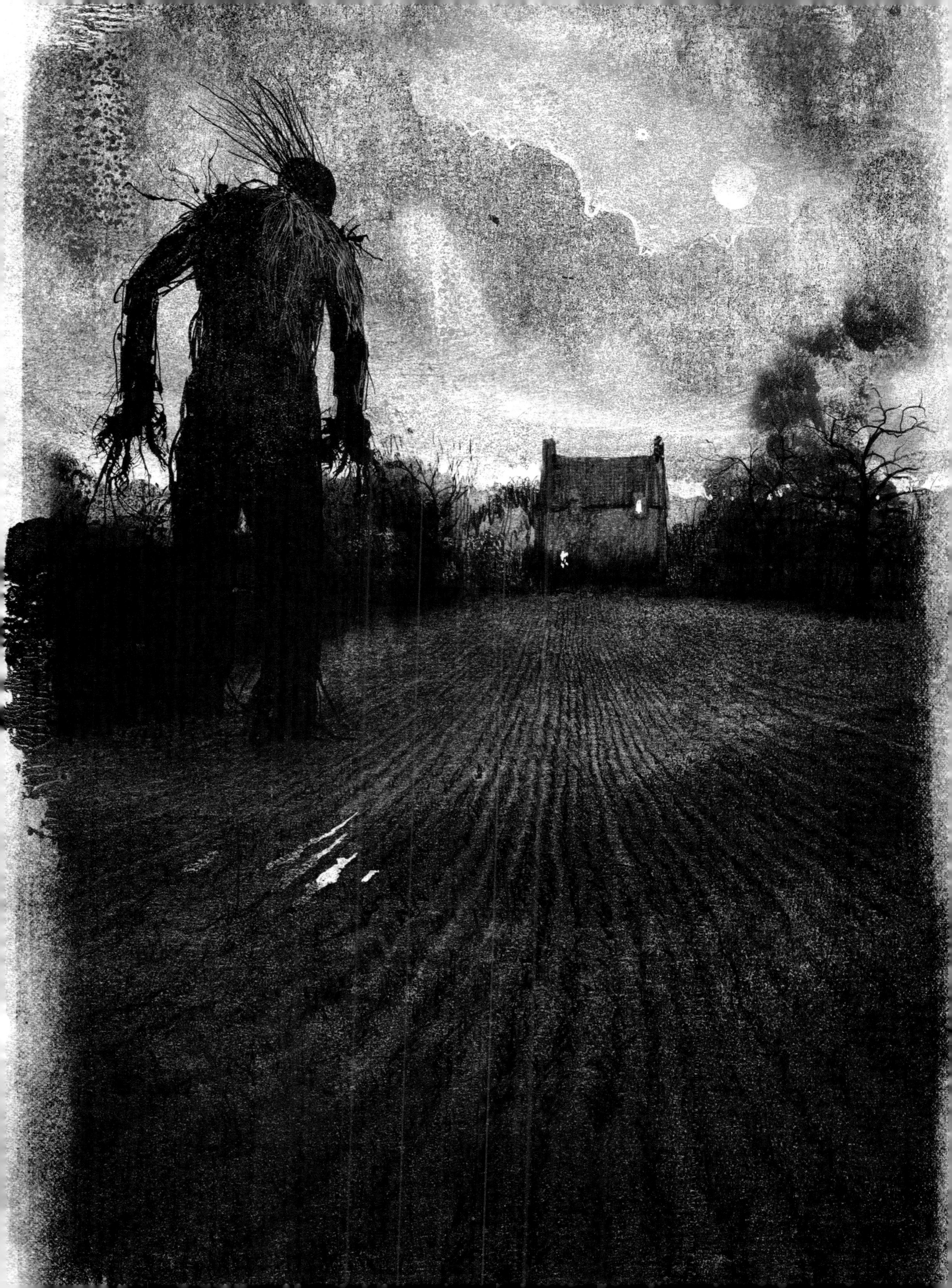

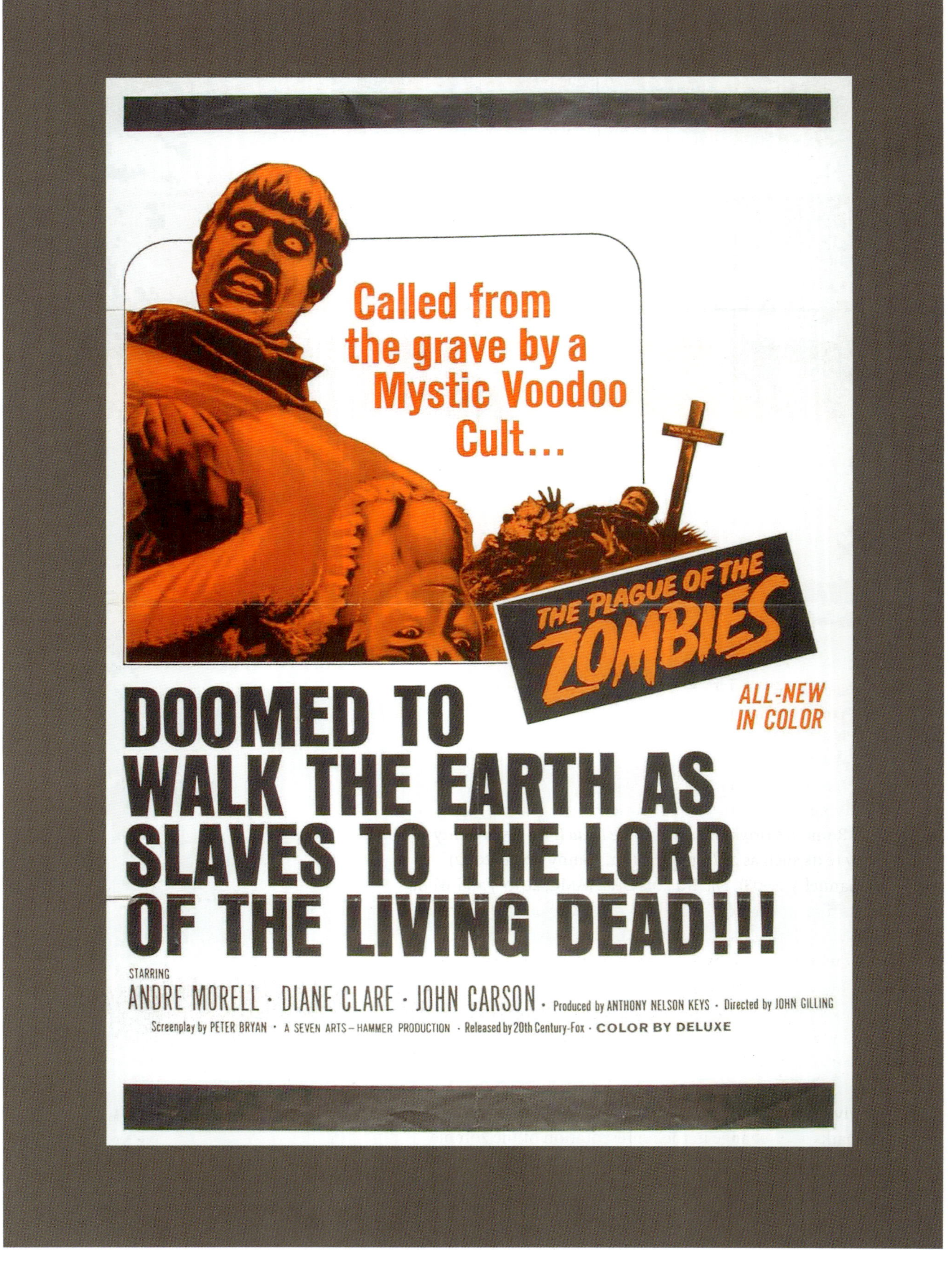
Called from the grave by a Mystic Voodoo Cult...
THE PLAGUE OF THE ZOMBIES
ALL-NEW IN COLOR
DOOMED TO WALK THE EARTH AS SLAVES TO THE LORD OF THE LIVING DEAD!!!
STARRING
ANDRE MORELL · DIANE CLARE · JOHN CARSON · Produced by ANTHONY NELSON KEYS · Directed by JOHN GILLING
Screenplay by PETER BRYAN · A SEVEN ARTS–HAMMER PRODUCTION · Released by 20th Century-Fox · COLOR BY DELUXE

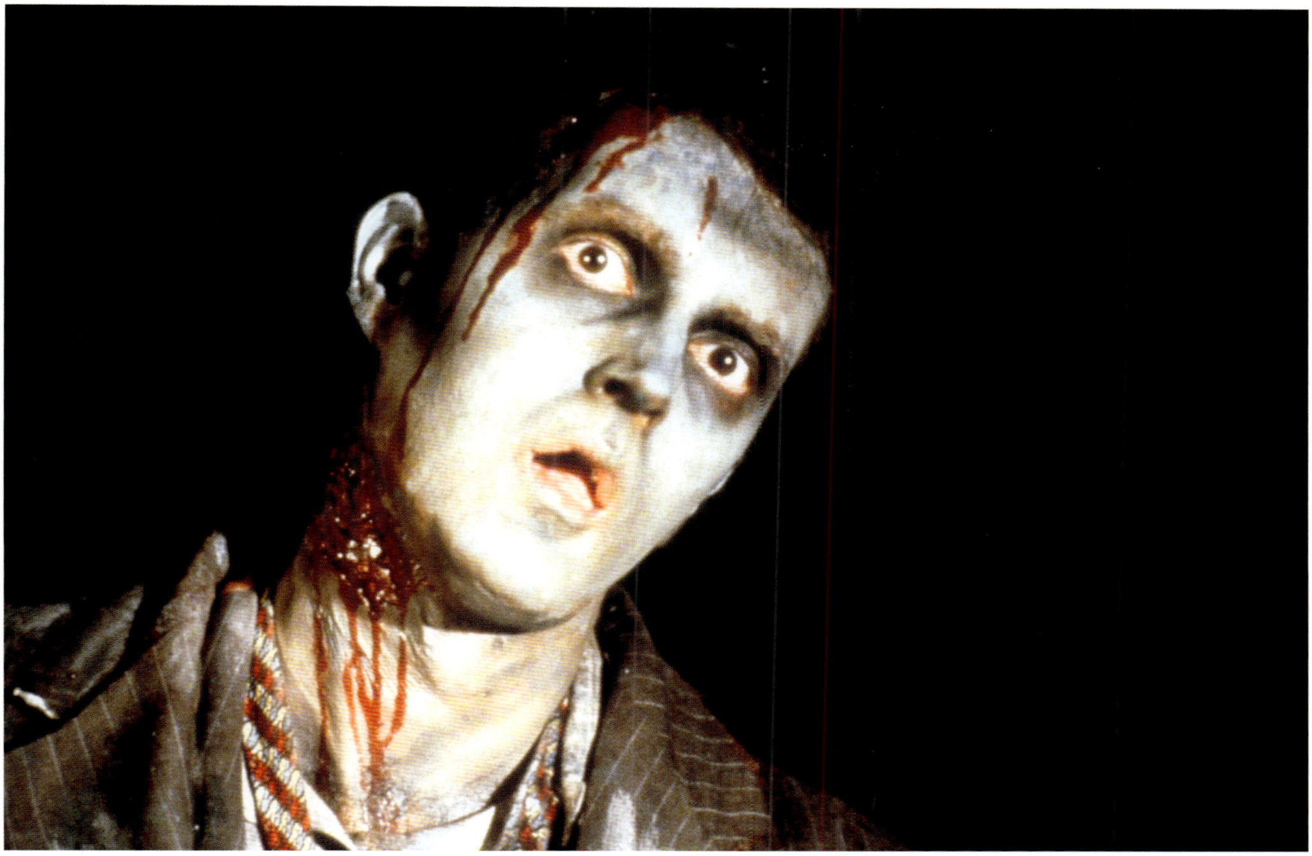

Still from the film *Day of the Dead*, 1985.

This was the third of George A Romero's six 'Dead' zombie films.

the symbolic gateway for British immigration. Zombies derive from Haitian folklore and were fictionalised in that guise in twentieth-century films such as Victor and Edward Halperin's *White Zombie* (1932) and Jacques Tourneur's *I Walked with a Zombie* (1943).

These quasi-folkloric zombies, however, bear little resemblance to their manifestation in the late-twentieth and early twenty-first centuries. Taking inspiration from twentieth-century films such as George A Romero's original *Trilogy of the Dead* (1968–85), twenty-first-century texts such as *28 Days Later* (dir. Danny Boyle, 2002), *Dead Set* (Channel 4, 2008), *The Walking Dead* (AMC, 2010–) and *World War Z* and its film remake (dir. Marc Forester, 2013) use zombies to explore a variety of globalised threats: consumer capitalism, viral pandemics, environmental disaster, military irresponsibility and celebrity culture. Just as vampires and werewolves are increasingly portrayed as assimilating into contemporary society, so zombies are rehabilitated in many recent texts. Nick Frost's zombie Ed ends the 'zom rom com' *Shaun of the Dead* (dir. Edgar Wright, 2004) playing videogames in the garden shed, his friendship with Simon Pegg's human survivor Shaun still conducted on largely the same terms.

This marks a sea change in the representation of the zombie, a figure that in recent years has frequently appeared not as the most abject and inhuman of Gothic monsters, but rather as a metaphor for alienated otherness, particularly that of young white masculinity. In novels including Daniel Waters's *Generation Dead* (2008), S G Browne's

OPPOSITE:
Poster for *The Plague of the Zombies*, Hammer Film Productions, 1966.
British Film Institute.

This was Hammer's only zombie film. Highly effective, it influenced later, better-known films such as George A.Romero's *Night of the Living Dead*.

Breathers (2009), Isaac Marion's *Warm Bodies* (2010, filmed by Jonathan Levine in 2013) and the BBC TV series *In the Flesh* (2013–), scripted by Dominic Mitchell, zombies learn to live in 'regular' society, conducting romances and campaigning for their human rights. In these iterations of twenty-first-century Gothic, zombies have become the ultimate means of investigating and exploring a number of pressing contemporary questions, not least of which is what it means to be human.

History's Returns

Paradoxically, however, what is most current about contemporary Gothic is the way in which it engages with the past. Gothic literature is a product of modernity: it is often characterised as the counter-narrative of Enlightenment, and its emergence in the later eighteenth century is roughly contemporary with the earliest stirrings of the Industrial Revolution. As Fred Botting states, 'Gothic figures [...] mark the turning points in cultural historical progress, points at which feudalism is apprehended and dismissed as a ruined past in a movement towards a more enlightened future' (2002: 278–9). From the outset individual Gothic writers could be progressive or conservative in their politics, but all were responding to a sense of the world as new and firmly differentiated from 'the past'. In Gothic fiction the past possesses a sense of otherness that may be feared or desired, but it always returns nonetheless.

The notion of the weight of history and the terror of the past dominates critical definitions of Gothic, from Horace Walpole's evocation of the biblical 'sins of the fathers' motif in *The Castle of Otranto* (1764) to the Freudian notion of the 'return of the repressed'. Undead revenants, ancient curses, outmoded belief systems, hauntings, trauma – all are central to Gothic narrative. But precisely *what* comes back – what returns – is determined by the concerns of the present. Robert Mighall explains that nothing is essentially Gothic, but rather that different things become Gothicised at different times and places: 'Epochs, institutions, places, and people are Gothicized, have the Gothic thrust upon them. That which is Gothicized depends on history and the stories it needs to tell itself' (1999: xxv). In twenty-first-century Gothic fiction, the stories that history needs to tell are about books themselves.

Gothic Aesthetics

Since the early 1990s two features of Gothic are increasingly in evidence. One is the increasingly visual aspect of Gothic: the codification of a distinctly Gothic 'look', duly deployed in design and marketing to target consumers with a taste for Gothic. While demonstrating multiple variations, twenty-first-century Gothic style in fashion, film production, design and illustration can be recognised by a combination of features, including intensive chiaroscuro, crowded space, intricate detailing, distorted proportions, a saturated colour palette, ornate fonts and deliberately retro or aged styling.

This is distinct from a parallel movement towards the Gothic in contemporary fine art, governed by the adoption of narrative themes and tropes of the Gothic rather than a consistent 'look'. Douglas Gordon, for example, explicitly draws on fellow Scots Robert Louis Stevenson's *Strange Case of Dr Jekyll and Mr Hyde* (1886) and James Hogg's *Private Memoirs and Confessions of a Justified Sinner* (1824) to create new images of uncanny doubling in *Monster Reborn, Fog* and *Black Star* (all 2002). Elsewhere artists such as Louise Bourgeois, Jane and Louise Wilson, Cathy de Monchaux and Jake and Dinos Chapman project more general concerns with traditional Gothic themes, including haunted or constricting spaces, monstrosity and abjection. In *Insult to Injury* (2003) the Chapmans added comical and grotesque doodles to a set of original prints of *Disasters of War* (1810–20), playing the Gothic barbarians to Goya's supposed pillar of the Enlightenment. This served to provide a metacritical commentary on the properties of horror and taboo found in Goya's work and the value that contemporary culture places on the original artefact. Yet even as fine art turns for inspiration to the literary Gothic, style increasingly supersedes narrative content in the production and marketing of Gothic fiction. While Gregory Crewdson's photographs, therefore, communicate an entire Gothic story through a single image, Erin Morgenstern's novel *The Night Circus* (2011) offers a plot that is little more than a succession of highly visual tableaux,

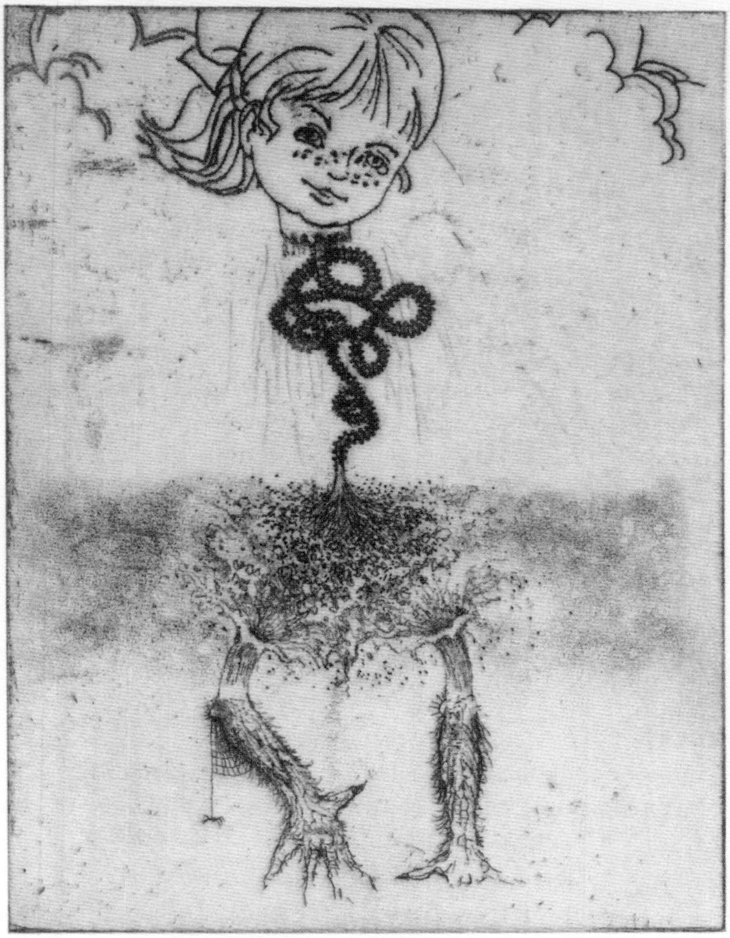

Jake and Dinos Chapman, 'Exquisite Corpse', etching on paper, 2000.

This etching is one of a series of 20 based on a surrealist game. The artists drew components of nightmarish bodies in turn. The grotesque comic-horror results are typical of the Chapman brothers' explorations of the human body.

complemented and packaged by the striking black, white and red cover art.

The other distinctive feature of Gothic over the last two decades is an apparently contrary retreat into textuality in which books, readers and writers are routinely Gothicised. The arcane, cursed or dangerous book has always been a recurring feature of Gothic fiction, but in the twenty-first century it has become an increasingly dominant motif. It cannot be a coincidence that this marks a moment in history at which the developed world's relationship with the book itself is undergoing an intense shift in the light of developing information technologies. In twenty-first-century Gothic, nostalgia for the book as object combines with fear concerning information itself: in a reprise of the biblical story of the Fall – a story given particularly Gothic inflection through the Promethean narrative of Mary Shelley's *Frankenstein* (1818) – the search for knowledge often results in a tale of exile and traumatic loss. For Michel Foucault, famously, knowledge is power, and the Gothicisation of books engages with an underlying concern with the way that, in the twenty-first century, power is bound up with information. Significantly, however, the thematic concern with books as objects often coincides with an emphasis on Gothic visual aesthetics. Whether in their cover art or their metafictional conceits, contemporary Gothic novels are vividly self-aware of their status as books. As such they speak to the ascendance of an age in which information has become the ultimate commodity.

Gothic in the Information Age

Digital and communications technologies are transforming the everyday landscape of people's lives in the twenty-first century, in all but the most isolated traditional communities. The profound shift in how information is shared and organised has led to the popular designation of the current period as the 'Information Age', suggesting that the preceding 'Industrial Age' is giving way to a new epoch. As with all paradigm shifts, it is difficult to date a beginning precisely. The change began in the late 1940s and early 1950s, in the wake of wartime developments in computer technology by the United States government, and developed gradually over the second half of the twentieth century, as computer systems became faster and more powerful. Crucially, however, it is not just the invention of computers, but what Krishan Kumar calls 'the explosive convergence of the computer with telecommunications' that brought about social change (1995: 10). The ability of modern technology not only to store and process information, but also to communicate it globally and virtually instantaneously began to affect economics, politics and social organisation. In his influential book *The Third Wave* (1980), Alvin Toffler identified the Information Age with 'post-industrial' or 'super-industrial' society, warning that in the face of 'the deepest social upheaval and creative restructuring of all time', 'humanity faces a quantum leap forward' (1981: 23).

The invention of the World Wide Web by Tim Berners-Lee in 1989–90 is often identified as a tipping point – a pivotal moment at which significant changes in everyday practices and attitudes began to take place among the general population of the West. By the year 2000 personal or home computing and mobile telecommunications had become a fact of life for a high proportion of individuals living in late capitalist societies. Email and mobile phones increasingly governed how people were communicating, with the launch of social networking sites such as MySpace in 2003, Facebook in 2004 and Twitter in 2006 accentuating this process. Finally, while e-book technology had been around for some decades (Project Gutenberg, the digital library, for example, was founded in 1971), the invention of electronic paper in the late 1990s led to the commercial development of e-readers. Pioneered by Sony in 2004 and the Amazon Kindle in 2007, they were to have a significant effect upon the publishing industry.

As a result of these rapid technological developments, the early twenty-first century is marked by fundamental changes in how information is conveyed, processed and organised. The effects, both positive and negative, on the everyday lives of individuals have been far-reaching. The internet facilitates global communities and grassroots protest; it also enables corporations and governments to compile information about individuals and gives anonymous users the opportunity to bully and abuse without redress. The lifestyle of individuals in the developed world is changing as many increasingly choose to shop, study, read newspapers, access pornography and find romantic partners online. The production and marketing of books, films, television and other cultural products is marked by what Henry Jenkins calls 'convergence culture', in which items are branded and promoted across multiple platforms and fan audiences increasingly participate in the production of meaning (Jenkins 2006).

Most significantly for the purposes of this essay, the book as traditionally conceived is under threat. Gothic novels can now be consumed on e-readers or tablets as easily as in paperback, and are as likely to be bought from an online retailer as from a traditional bookshop; archives are gradually being digitised; the accessibility of the world wide web means that obscure or previously overlooked authors can find readerships; new entertainment formats from apps to videogames compete with books for attention. Our reading habits are in the process of radical transformation and, while predictions of the traditional book's demise seem over-exaggerated, Western readers' relationship with the book is undergoing a profound renegotiation.

This renegotiation is one that the Gothic appears particularly well placed to navigate. Gothic fiction has always been markedly self-conscious about its written properties, and is frequently preoccupied with books and reading. In the earliest Gothic novels, these are almost invariably manuscripts – unique documents that are, while not quite anachronistic, rather different from the Gothic novel itself, which was mass produced via the printing press and widely circulated through libraries. These manuscripts are often secret or missing; they may be cursed or otherwise dangerous; they provide crucial information, or fail to do so; they draw attention to their own written qualities through fragmentation, unreliable narrators and embedded narratives.

The first Gothic novel, Horace Walpole's *The Castle of Otranto*, purported to be a medieval document discovered and translated, rather than composed, by its actual author's fictitious proxy. Found manuscripts abounded in the fiction of Ann Radcliffe and her imitators, and were parodied as a laundry list by Jane Austen in *Northanger Abbey* (1818). Shelley's *Frankenstein* and Emily Brontë's *Wuthering Heights* (1847) famously contain three levels of embedded narrative or tales-within-tales, while Charles Maturin's *Melmoth the Wanderer* (1820) goes further with four. Wilkie Collins's *The Woman in White* (1859–60) and Bram Stoker's *Dracula* (1897) are compiled from documents supposedly written by the novels' characters. Ghost stories by M R James, such as 'Canon Alberic's Scrapbook' (1895) and 'The Tractate Middoth' (1911), attach supernatural events to mysterious and portentous volumes that are best left undisturbed. Meanwhile H P Lovecraft's early twentieth-century invention of the 'Necronomicon', a fictional book supposedly containing lore regarding the Old Ones (a race of terrifying primordial beings), has spilled out into popular mythology and urban legend.

Later twentieth-century Gothic fiction maintained this fascination with dangerous books, from the monastic murders intended to suppress knowledge of Aristotle's missing work on comedy in Umberto Eco's *The Name of the Rose* (1980) to the search for copies of a demonological manuscript in Arturo Pérez-Reverte's *The Club Dumas* (1993), filmed by Roman Polanski in 1999 as *The Ninth Gate*. The postmodern interest in fictional self-consciousness or metafiction found a ready correspondence in the Gothic; indeed, as Neil McRobert argues, in contemporary Gothic texts, postmodern, self-reflexive fictional techniques are frequently used as a means of horror in themselves: 'self-consciousness has itself been "Gothicised," emerging as a new source and expression of fear' (2013: 44).

Contemporary Gothic's response to a digitised world is not only manifested in fiction. In the late twentieth century, the genre rapidly found a home in new media. Videogames such as *Alone in the Dark* (1992–2008), *Tomb Raider* (1996–2013), *Silent Hill* (1999–2012) and *American McGee's Alice* (2000, 2011) reworked Gothic narrative tropes and aesthetics. A closer appropriation of the literary, metafictional qualities of Gothic, however, can be found in Shelley Jackson's seminal hypertext fiction *Patchwork Girl* (1995). Hypertext fiction makes use of the computer's capacity for multiple links within a single document to create complex non-linear narrative. Here the reader's choice of which links to click on determines the shape, and sometimes the outcome, of the story.

In *Patchwork Girl* Jackson fuses form and content to particularly powerful effect. Taking the episode from Mary Shelley's *Frankenstein* in which Victor creates the female monster, Jackson splices chunks of the original text with her own, rewritten narrative, in which the destruction of the female monster is faked to enable her independence. Jackson simultaneously performs a similar manoeuvre with Mary Shelley's journal, where it is revealed that Mary Shelley

Frankenstein, iPad app by Dave Morris, published by Profile Books, 2012.

Dave Morris's interactive interpretation of *Frankenstein* (2012) is designed as an app and retells the story with the reader as Frankenstein's companion.

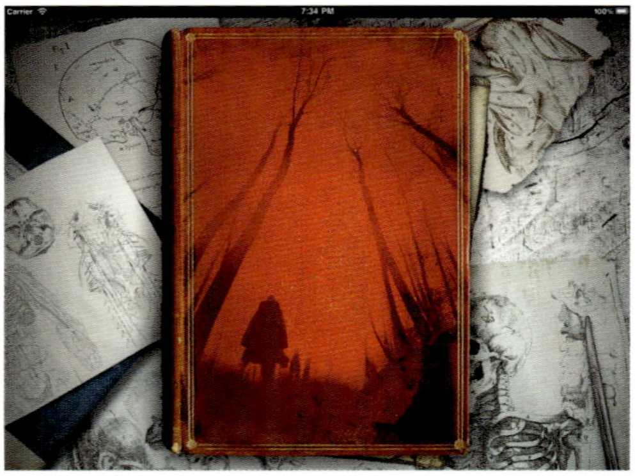

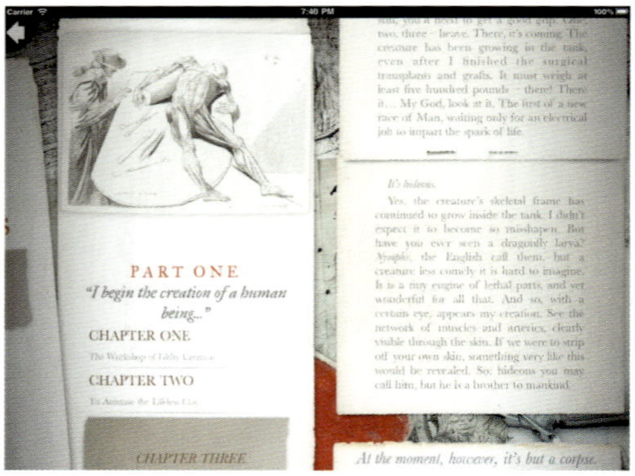

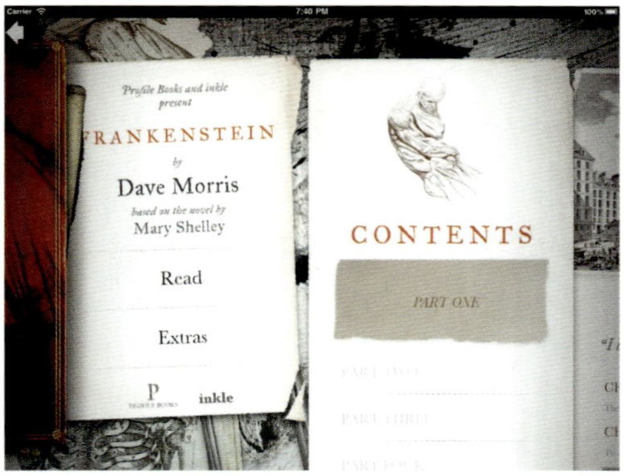

creates a female monster of her own and develops a relationship with her very different to that of Victor and his creature in the original novel. A further section of the narrative creates a 'Graveyard' of body parts, recounting the stories of the different women who make up the female monster's body; yet another interweaves parts of L Frank Baum's *The Patchwork Girl of Oz* (1913) with feminist theory, including Elaine Showalter on quilting history and Donna Haraway's 'The Cyborg Manifesto' (1991). The result is a multi-layered, multi-directional text composed of multiple scraps of writing and multiple narrative pathways. The choice of hyperlinks enables the body of the text and the monster to be stitched together in ways more or less unique to each reader. Moreover, in its disruption of conventional, hierarchical, linear narrative, the text enacts the decentralised, feminist form of consciousness that it describes.

Patchwork Girl was initially heralded as ushering in a new kind of literature, but in retrospect it has more in common with the traditional print book than first appears. As Paul Hackman suggests, '*Patchwork Girl* presents print as the remediated companion to, rather than the opponent of or a precursor to, hypertext' (2011: 105). *Patchwork Girl* offers an iteration of themes found in Gothic print texts. The meanings of form and content are closely allied, but this represents another elaboration of Gothic text in a new medium, rather than a threat to the Gothic novel. Hypertext has not continued to flourish as a medium, but its effects have continued to influence the Gothic novel – nowhere more so than in Mark Z Danielewski's seminal *House of Leaves* (2000), without which it is almost impossible to discuss twenty-first-century Gothic fiction.

Shelley Jackson,
Patchwork Girl, 1995.

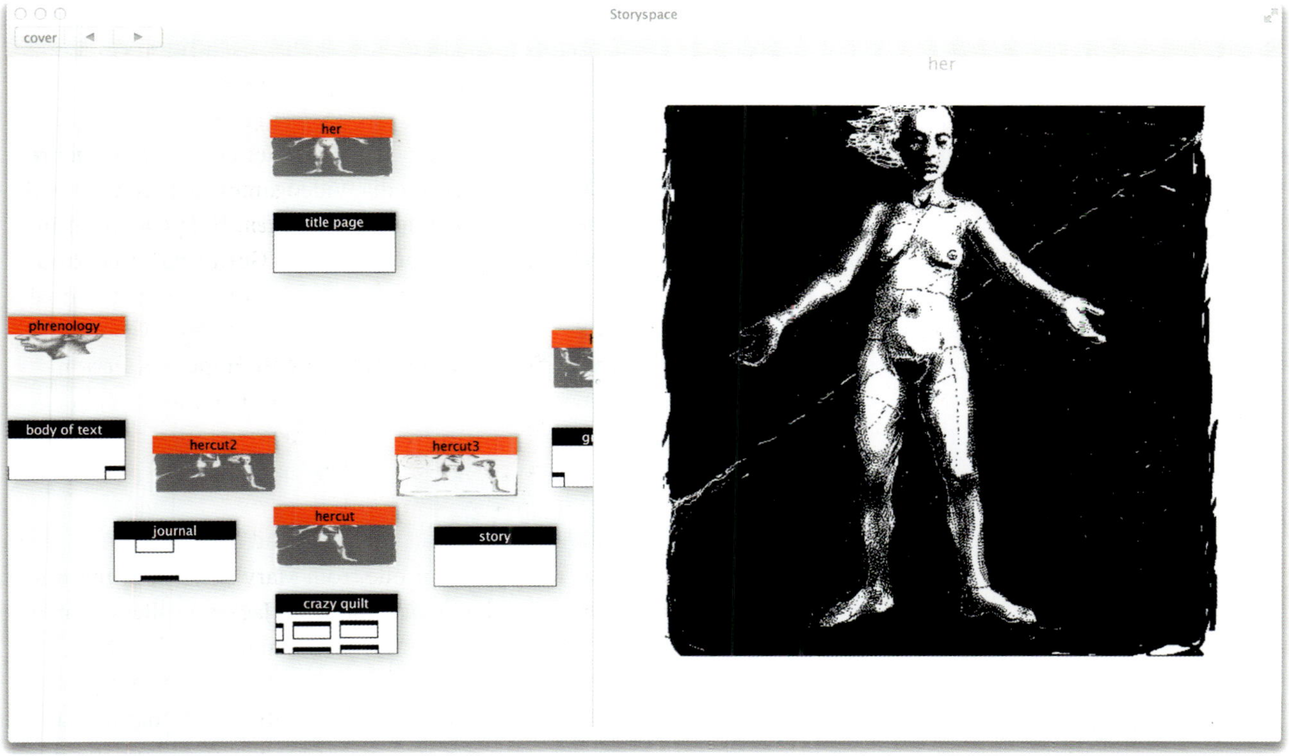

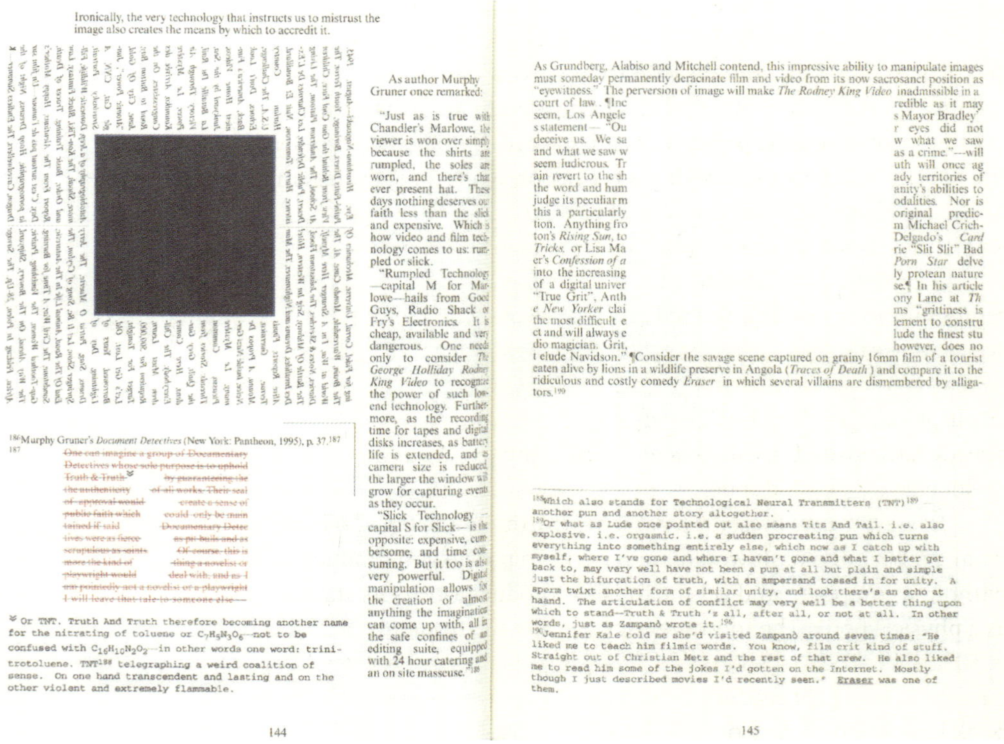

Ironically, the very technology that instructs us to mistrust the image also creates the means by which to accredit it.

As author Murphy Gruner once remarked:

"Just as is true with Chandler's Marlowe, the viewer is won over simply because the shirts are rumpled, the soles are worn, and there's that ever present hat. These days nothing deserves our faith less than the slick and expensive. Which is how video and film technology comes to us: rumpled or slick.

"Rumpled Technology —capital M for Marlowe—hails from Good Guys, Radio Shack or Fry's Electronics. It is cheap, available and very dangerous. One needs only to consider *The George Holliday Rodney King Video* to recognize the power of such low-end technology. Furthermore, as the recording time for tapes and digital disks increases, as battery life is extended, and as camera size is reduced, the larger the window will grow for capturing events as they occur.

"Slick Technology —capital S for Slick— is the opposite: expensive, cumbersome, and time consuming. But it too is also very powerful. Digital manipulation allows for the creation of almost anything the imagination can come up with, all in the safe confines of an editing suite, equipped with 24 hour catering and an on site masseuse."[186]

[186]Murphy Gruner's *Document Detectives* (New York: Pantheon, 1995), p. 37.[187]

[187] ~~One can imagine a group of Documentary Detectives whose sole purpose is to uphold Truth & Truth~~ ≫ ~~by guaranteeing the the authenticity of all works. Their seal of approval would create a sense of public faith which could only be maintained if said Documentary Detectives were as fierce as pit bulls and as scrupulous as saints. Of course this is more the kind of thing a novelist or playwright would deal with, and as I am pointedly not a novelist or a playwright I will leave that tale to someone else—~~

≫ Or TNT. Truth And Truth therefore becoming another name for the nitrating of toluene or $C_7H_5N_3O_6$—not to be confused with $C_{16}H_{10}N_2O_2$—in other words one word: trinitrotoluene. TNT[188] telegraphing a weird coalition of sense. On one hand transcendent and lasting and on the other violent and extremely flammable.

144

As Grundberg, Alabiso and Mitchell contend, this impressive ability to manipulate images must someday permanently deracinate film and video from its now sacrosanct position as "eyewitness." The perversion of image will make *The Rodney King Video* inadmissible in a court of law. ¶Incredible as it may seem, Los Angeles Mayor Bradley's statement— "Our eyes did not deceive us. We saw what we saw and what we saw was a crime."—will seem ludicrous. Truth will once again revert to the shady territories of the word and humanity's abilities to judge its peculiar modalities. Nor is this a particularly original prediction. Anything from Michael Crichton's *Rising Sun*, to Delgado's *Card Tricks*, or Lisa Marie "Slit Slit" Bader's *Confession of a Porn Star* delve into the increasingly protean nature of a digital universe.¶ In his article "True Grit", Anthony Lane at *The New Yorker* claims "grittiness is the most difficult element to construct and will always elude the finest studio magician. Grit, however, does not elude Navidson." ¶Consider the savage scene captured on grainy 16mm film of a tourist eaten alive by lions in a wildlife preserve in Angola (*Traces of Death*) and compare it to the ridiculous and costly comedy *Eraser* in which several villains are dismembered by alligators.[199]

[188]Which also stands for Technological Neural Transmitters (TNT)[189] — another pun and another story altogether.

[189]Or what as Lude once pointed out also means Tits And Tail. i.e. also explosive. i.e. orgasmic. i.e. a sudden procreating pun which turns everything into something entirely else, which now as I catch up with myself, where I've gone and where I haven't gone and what I better get back to, may very well have not been a pun at all but plain and simple just the bifurcation of truth, with an ampersand tossed in for unity. A sperm twixt another form of similar unity, and look there's an echo at haand. The articulation of conflict may very well be a better thing upon which to stand—Truth & Truth 'z all, after all, or not at all. In other words, just as Zampanò wrote it.[196]

[196]Jennifer Kale told me she'd visited Zampanò around seven times: "He liked me to teach him filmic words. You know, film crit kind of stuff. Straight out of Christian Metz and the rest of that crew. He also liked me to read him some of the jokes I'd gotten on the Internet. Mostly though I just described movies I'd recently seen." Eraser was one of them.

145

Mark Z. Danielewski, *House of Leaves*, 2000.

An unconventional haunted house novel in which the text itself is haunted and unstable.

Metafictions

If Gothic has always had a metafictional cast, then in *House of Leaves* this reaches its apotheosis. Danielewski's wildly ambitious, fiendishly complex novel allegedly took him ten years to write and quickly gained a cult following. The central narrative follows a photojournalist called Will Navidson. He moves to suburbia with his young family, only to find a mysterious labyrinth opening up in his otherwise ordinary house. Navidson films his experiences, and the resulting footage becomes the subject of an extended critical exegesis by a blind critic called Zampanò. On Zampanò's death his manuscript passes to a young LA tattooist and drug addict called Johnny Truant, who attempts to make sense of what he reads, his own story playing out in the footnotes and margins. An appendix contains the story of Johnny's mother Pelafina, who is confined to a lunatic asylum.

A masterpiece of metafiction, the novel contains not only these embedded narratives in which the characters read and comment on each other's story, but also footnotes referencing real and fictional critical works, multiple appendices, fake letters and photographs, and sections written in braille, musical notation or code. Most dramatically of all, Danielewski employs typographic play inspired by concrete poetry, which aims to exploit the material properties of the book by requiring the reader physically to manipulate the text, for example reading passages in a mirror or turning the book upside down. Danielewski recreates his fictional labyrinth inside the physical artefact of the book, so that the title, *House of Leaves*, refers not only to the family home the text describes, but also to the pages, or leaves, of the volume itself.

Danielewski's novel is firmly located in the Gothic tradition. It is at heart a haunted house story, while its nested narratives, fragmentary texts and unreliable narrators recall the found manuscripts of eighteenth- and early nineteenth-century Gothic. Yet the work is also the product of a digital age. Danielewski typeset the book himself on a 300 MHz G3 processor, while an early version of the novel was published online, appearing self-reflexively as an artefact in the published novel. The highlighting of the word 'house' in blue and 'minotaur' in red recalls digital hyperlinks. Blue represents an active link and red an inactive one: the house is an active network, always pointing elsewhere, while the minotaur is a dead end. The phrase '~~what I'm remembering now~~' (2001: 518) appears in purple, suggesting a link already visited – but as the reader cannot already have visited it, this creates an uncanny feeling of memory under erasure that is duplicated by the strike-through.

House of Leaves presents a paradox, worthy of the paradoxes of its metaphysical plot. It would not have been possible to produce without a computer, and yet the finished product asserts its status as a physical book. The footnotes that require the reader to flick back and forth between pages, the shadow images seen through the paper and the necessity of reading some sections upside down make the book impossible to read on an e-reader. It resists translation into other media, too. Danielewski insists that the book is unfilmable and that he will never sell the rights, presenting it as a kind of manifesto for books in the computer age:

> Books are remarkable constructions with enormous possibilities. We may be using a 300 MHz G3 to finish the layout of my book, but to get from the first page to the last takes impossible seconds. Not a second but *seconds*. And yet you can pick up a book – even an encyclopedia – and get from one to a thousand in much less than that. You can even access several pages at the same time. And you can carry this magical creation with you, write in it, and never need to hunt down conversion software to find out what you wrote and read years ago. But somehow the analogue powers of these wonderful bundles of paper have been forgotten. Somewhere along the way, all its possibilities were denied. (Danielewski, no date: online)

House of Leaves had its equivalents in other media. In cinema, 'found footage' became the equivalent of the 'found manuscript'. Although not the first example of the genre, the phenomenal box-office success of Daniel Myrick and Eduardo Sanchez's *The Blair Witch Project* (1999) popularised the trend. The film purports to be edited together from film footage shot by three students in search of the truth behind a piece of local folklore; they had subsequently disappeared without explanation. The documentary feel was achieved by recreating the film's premise as closely as possible in reality: its actors were not told what was going to happen, and were deliberately scared silly by the directors while camping in the woods. At least some of their filmed terror, therefore, was real.

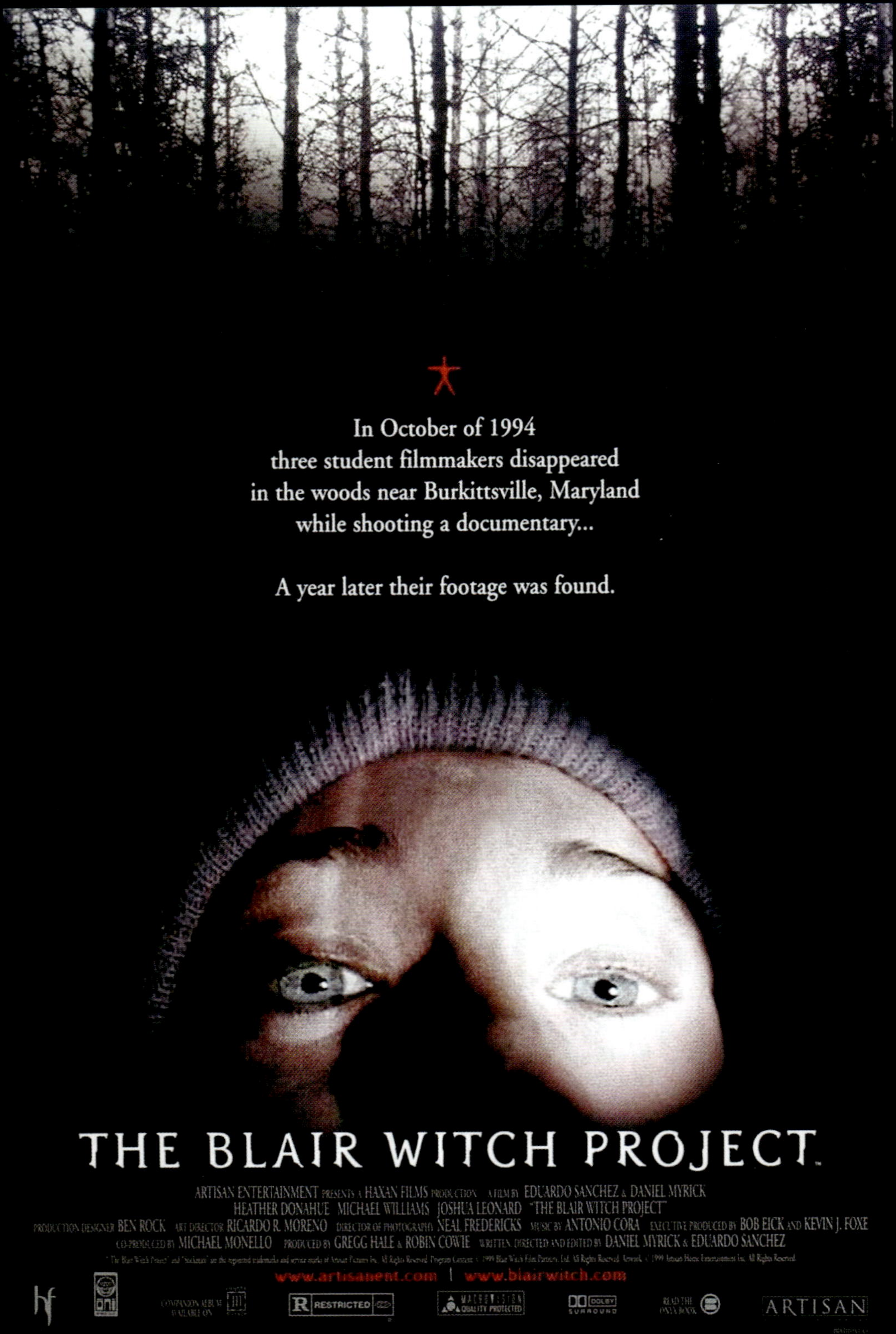
In October of 1994
three student filmmakers disappeared
in the woods near Burkittsville, Maryland
while shooting a documentary...
A year later their footage was found.
THE BLAIR WITCH PROJECT
ARTISAN ENTERTAINMENT PRESENTS A HAXAN FILMS PRODUCTION A FILM BY EDUARDO SANCHEZ & DANIEL MYRICK
HEATHER DONAHUE MICHAEL WILLIAMS JOSHUA LEONARD "THE BLAIR WITCH PROJECT"
PRODUCTION DESIGNER BEN ROCK ART DIRECTOR RICARDO R. MORENO DIRECTOR OF PHOTOGRAPHY NEAL FREDERICKS MUSIC BY ANTONIO CORA EXECUTIVE PRODUCED BY BOB EICK AND KEVIN J. FOXE
CO-PRODUCED BY MICHAEL MONELLO PRODUCED BY GREGG HALE & ROBIN COWIE WRITTEN, DIRECTED AND EDITED BY DANIEL MYRICK & EDUARDO SANCHEZ
www.artisanent.com | www.blairwitch.com
R RESTRICTED
DOLBY SURROUND
ARTISAN

OPPOSITE:
Poster for *The Blair Witch Project*, 1999.

'Found footage' soon became a staple of twenty-first-century horror cinema, with notable titles including *Cloverfield* (dir. Matt Reeves, 2008), *Diary of the Dead* (dir. George A Romero, 2008) and the extraordinarily popular *Paranormal Activity* franchise (dir. various, 2007). The format proved readily exportable and found international variants in the Spanish *REC* (dir. Jaume Balagueró and Paco Plaza, 2007) and its sequels and the Norwegian *Troll Hunter* (dir. André Øvredal, 2010). Elsewhere, Japanese horror film *Ringu* (dir. Hideo Nakata, 1998), based on the novel by Kôji Suzuki, translated the cursed book to the cursed videotape. Anyone viewing the tape is doomed to die unless they can persuade another person to watch it, the curse operating via a kind of visual contagion.

Books as Artefacts

Despite the popularity of these attempts to transfer the 'found manuscript' and 'cursed book' motifs to other media, however, it is in fiction that they have had most resonance. In the twenty-first century's increasingly digital world, Gothic writing is increasingly preoccupied with the book as artefact. Robert Mighall identifies Victorian Gothic as preoccupied with 'anachronistic vestiges': relics of a less enlightened time that re-emerge to trouble the present and its sense of its own modernity (1999: 18). In the ghost stories of M R James, these anachronistic vestiges sometimes take the form of books: rare manuscripts discovered by antiquarians who get more than they bargained for. James, no advocate of modernity himself, takes an almost gleeful pleasure in confirming ancient superstition.

Developments in printing technologies may have made the idea of the unique manuscript increasingly obsolete in late nineteenth- and early twentieth-century Britain (in Bram Stoker's *Dracula*, after all, Mina uses the 'manifold' function on her typewriter to produce multiple copies of the manuscript account of the Crew of Light's pursuit of the vampire). Books themselves, however, were not anachronisms; they were still the dominant means of recording and transmitting knowledge. In the twenty-first century, by contrast, the printed word is increasingly superseded by digital forms, and the book itself frequently invested with nostalgia. Publishing houses seek to inspire consumers' sentimental desire for the book as artefact with retro covers and specially commissioned illustrations, exemplified by beautifully produced hardback series such as 'Clothbound Classics' (Penguin) and 'Leatherbound Classic Collection' (Barnes and Noble), and reflected in the Folio Society's expansion from mail order only into prestige retail outlets. Why buy a space-consuming book when you can fit countless computer files on an e-reader or tablet? The answer is that the book is a sensory object, one in which the look and feel enhance the appreciation of what is within. Of course, this celebration of the pleasures of the book is far from unique to Gothic writing: it has influenced publishers in every genre. Nevertheless Gothic fiction, with its traditions of discovered manuscripts and cursed books, is particularly well suited to this trend and engages with it intra-diegetically – that is, within the narrative itself – as well as purely as a marketing device.

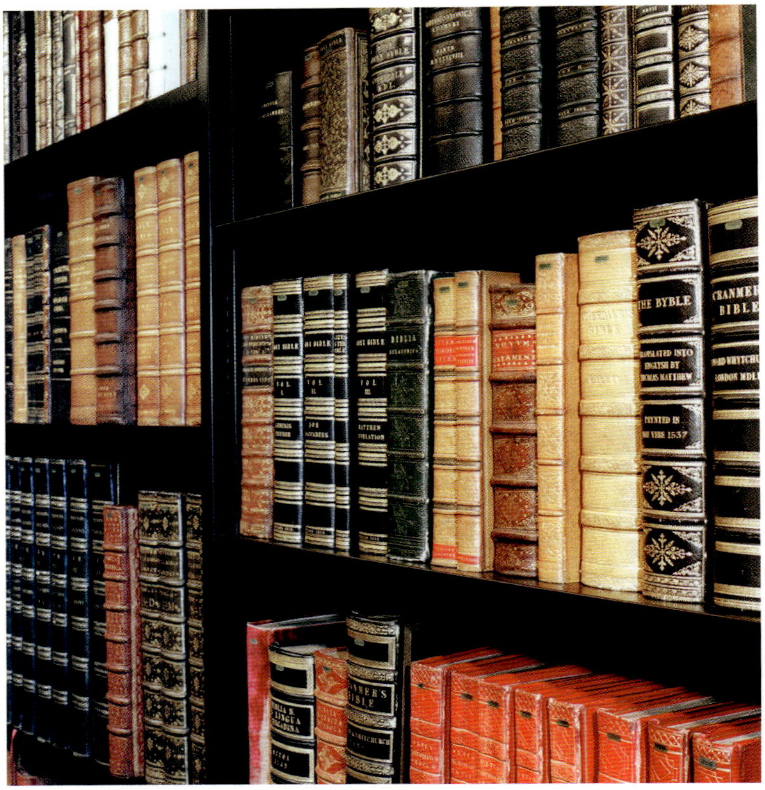

The King's Library at the British Library, London. The book as artefact.

Gothic novels in the twenty-first century make rich use of the book as artefact, both materially and thematically. The phenomenal international success of Dan Brown's blockbuster *The Da Vinci Code* (2003) inspired a trend for academic thrillers, in which historians and literary scholars pursue occult mysteries. In Brown's novel an academic and a police cryptographer pursue the secret of the Holy Grail through a series of artefacts that, once interpreted correctly, reveal coded clues to the Grail's whereabouts. Although Brown is more interested in objects and paintings than manuscripts, subsequent contributions to this sub-genre tend to emphasise research into apparently cursed or otherwise mysterious books – and in doing so they become increasingly Gothic.

In Kate Mosse's *Labyrinth* (2005), the books in question originally belonged to the heretical sect of the Cathars and, again, lead to the Holy Grail. A book containing a secret map in Elizabeth Kostova's *The Historian* (2005) reveals Dracula's present-day whereabouts, and it is Dracula himself – or his librarian minions – who is killing off historians. In Deborah Harkness's *A Discovery of Witches* (2011), a visiting research professor at Oxford calls up a supposedly missing alchemical manuscript from the Bodleian Library that reveals the origins of witches, vampires and demons. In these novels ancient books become a source of terror and danger, power and desire, but also of an oddly comforting link to the past. Through the process of reading, the protagonist uncovers the secrets of the past and in doing so, also discovers the secrets of her own identity. The past is generally as oppressive, cruel and bloody as might conventionally be expected from a Gothic novel, but the protagonist's literary excavations cause her to become rooted in history in a way that is satisfying and reassuring.

There are plenty of variations on the theme of the Gothicised book in other styles and genres, too. In Bret Easton Ellis's fake memoir *Lunar Park* (2005), the dangerous book is the author's own notorious *American Psycho* (1991), which escapes the bounds of fiction to haunt a fictional version of its author. Similarly, in Jeremy Dyson's *The Haunted Book* (2012), an apparently autobiographical frame narrative by 'Jeremy Dyson' presents its narrator as simultaneously nostalgic for and haunted by the ghost anthologies of his childhood:

> One collection I owned, *Stranger than Fiction: 50 True Tales of Terror*, filled me with an irrational fear. It might have been the cowled skeleton embossed into the front (the book had long since lost its dustjacket). Or it might have been to do with the contents themselves. Either way, on a dark, windy night, or when I was alone in the house – even in my early teens – I would place that book in another room before I went to sleep. (2012: 16)

'Dyson' accepts a commission to write a book of ghost stories based on a series of 'true' accounts gathered by a journalist who is mysteriously reluctant to write the book himself. He explicitly sees the project as a chance for his rational adult self to recapture his childhood wonder towards the supernatural, implicitly inviting a haunting from a lost child self (although this child figure is later revealed to have an alternative meaning). The determinedly rational 'Dyson', increasingly spooked by the process of research and writing, happens half-way through upon another book which suddenly takes over his narrative in a kind of literary possession – only to be possessed in turn by another, older book, and then another, in a game of infinite recession. The writer loses control over his creation; direction and linear progress are lost in an overwhelming accumulation of dreadful anecdotes. What is more, the haunting is deadly: one of the books is dedicated 'To the memory of U. REEDER'; this foreshadows a dramatic twist at the end in which what seems to have been happening for the book's first 300 or so pages is radically undercut.

Historical readers can be haunted too. In Jo Baker's ghost story *The Telling* (2008), reading is not absolutely prohibited, but given an incendiary quality by Chartist politics; it is, appropriately enough, Milton's *Paradise Lost* that offers its young nineteenth-century heroine unbearable temptation and knowledge. In *Florence and Giles* (2010), John Harding's rewriting of Henry James's *The Turn of the Screw* (1898), the child protagonist is forbidden to learn to read, but teaches herself from the Gothic novels which she finds in Blithe House's neglected library, and whose flavours colour her narration of events. After reading Ann Radcliffe, she casts herself as imprisoned heroine; as she reads Edgar Allan Poe, her narration becomes increasingly unstable.

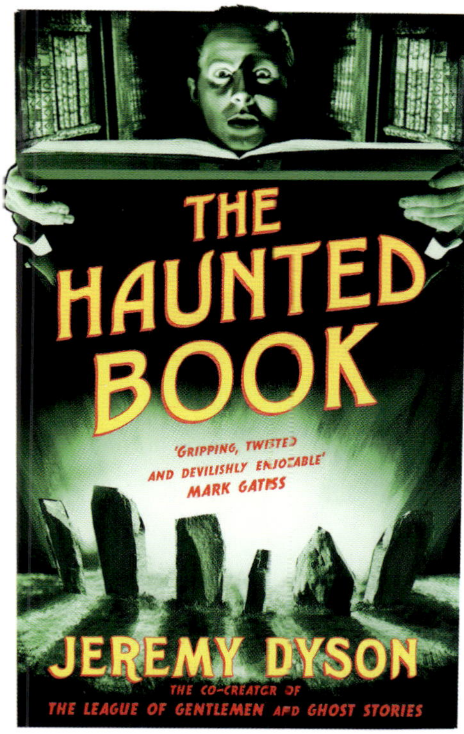

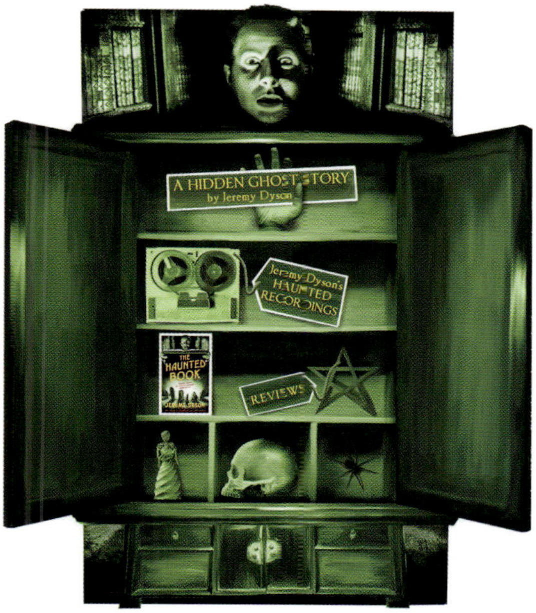

The interactive front cover of Jeremy Dyson's, *The Haunted Book*, 2012, in which an animated sequence is revealed on scanning with an app.

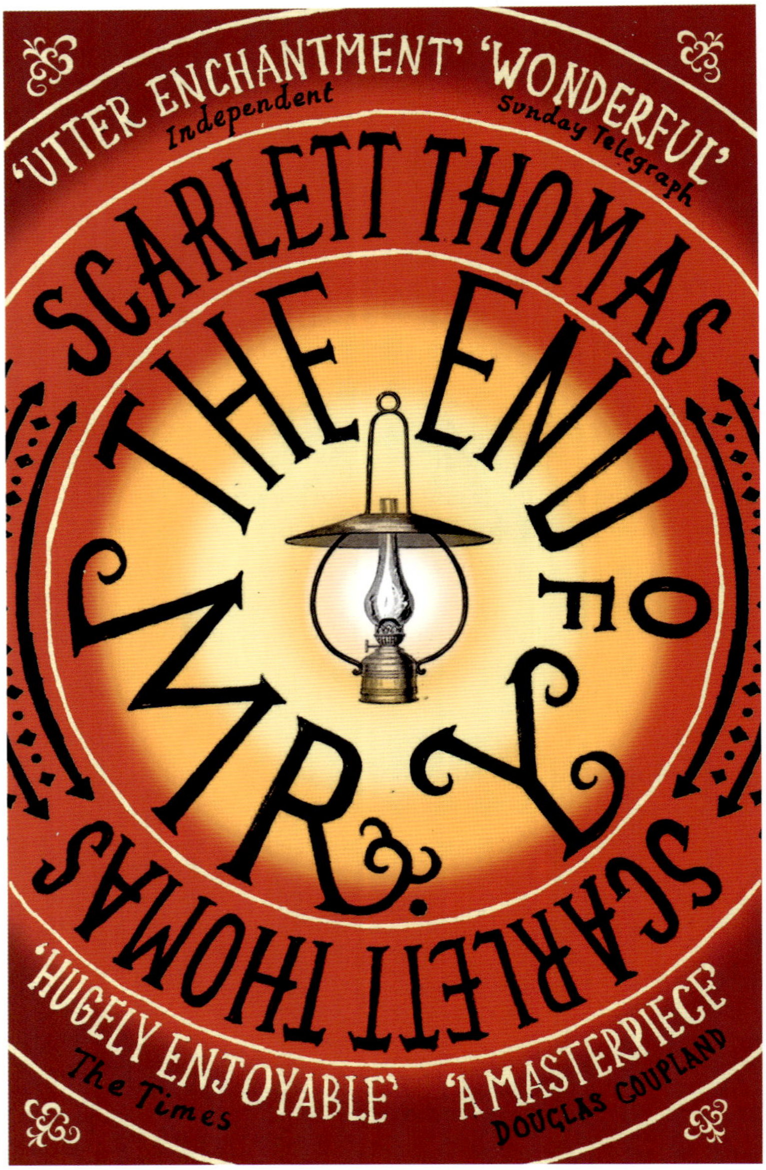

Front cover of Scarlett Thomas, *The End of Mr Y*, 2006.

The 'cursed book' plot has become familiar enough to spawn its own caricature. *The Book with No Name* (2007), by Anonymous, unfolds as a parodically baroque Western set somewhere on the Mexican-United States border and sends up the cliché in a riot of Tarantinian violence, the book itself becoming a deadly weapon. Natasha Mostert's *Season of the Witch* (2007) offers a slight variation, in that the forbidden book is a digital diary hacked by the protagonist. Here the object of nostalgia is not a physical book, but a mental 'memory palace' that reasserts the powers of the human mind in a world of digital archives and networks.

A book that synthesises many of these trends is Scarlett Thomas's *The End of Mr Y* (2006), the first-person account of a PhD student named Ariel Manto who discovers a copy of a missing, and supposedly cursed, nineteenth-century novel in a second-hand bookshop. As everyone who has read this novel has mysteriously disappeared (including her PhD supervisor), reading is figured as a forbidden activity in which the reader, faced with the embedded narrative, is invited to share. Like the anti-dedication at the beginning of *House of Leaves*, 'This is not for you', the novel sets up a prohibition automatically transgressed by the act of turning the page (Danielewski, 2001: ix). The book becomes commensurate with the Gothic castle or haunted house, a forbidden space that nevertheless must be entered in order for narrative to begin.

In *The End of Mr Y*, the forbidden space of the book is doubled with a labyrinthine and intermittently Gothicised space called the troposphere, in which the subject inhabits, and travels between, other people's minds. The embedded narrative describes Mr Y's discovery of a potion concocted according to homeopathic principles that enables access to this mysterious realm. Ariel is unable to resist the temptation to recreate and ingest the potion and finds herself falling – the trajectory is horizontal, but the verb is deliberate – into a black tunnel. Here the earliest forms of writing give way to hieroglyphics, then alphabets and numerals, equations of increasing complexity and finally binary code: 'millions and millions of 0s and 1s waterfalling down the walls around me' (2008: 195). The troposphere in *The End of Mr Y* is constructed out of information. As information systems become more complex, so does the troposphere: in Mr Y's nineteenth-century account of the same experience, the tunnel ends shortly after Newton's F=ma. Moreover the physical appearance of the troposphere is determined by the user's consciousness, and thus by the media that structure their understanding of the world. For Ariel, the troposphere looks disconcertingly like a videogame.

The troposphere functions in the novel like a hypertext. At any given point, the protagonist can choose to jump to adjacent minds and, depending on their choices, create a different route through what the novel later calls 'MindSpace' (2008: 310). *The End of Mr Y* is nominally a linear narrative, but the troposphere works to disrupt that, with the conclusion circling backwards through time to show Ariel and Adam in the Garden of Eden. The book's curse is, in fact, that of the original sin of eating from the tree of knowledge. The Gothic protagonist's often perplexing desire to enter the house, or turn the page, is explicated as the human impulse towards a 'fortunate fall'.

Marketing Gothic Fiction

The End of Mr Y does not only feature a cursed book and embedded narrative; it also appeared in a striking red jacket with black-edged pages. The novel's cover forms a self-conscious citation of the book as artefact, exploiting the novel's central device as a marketing strategy. Similarly, Dyson's *The Haunted Book* comes with an interactive cover, in which scanning with a particular app triggers an animated sequence of metal doors opening, leading to further material.

A book's look and feel are, of course, carefully designed by the publisher. Yet in the case of many twenty-first-century Gothic novels, they are foregrounded to such a degree that they become an intrinsic part of a book's meaning. As Glennis Byron writes of Carlos

Ruiz Zafón's international bestseller *La sombra del viento* (2001), which was translated as *The Shadow of the Wind* in 2004, 'the expanded understanding of what Gothic might be in the twenty-first century [may well be] defined as much by marketing strategies as by academic discourse' (Byron 2012: 371). She describes how *The Shadow of the Wind* was initially marketed as a 'thriller' or historical fiction. Once placed in the international market, however, it was increasingly presented as Gothic in promotional material and reviews, to the extent that by 2007 Zafón was himself referring to the novel as Gothic in interviews.

Perhaps the most extreme example of the marketing of the Gothic book as artefact is J J Abrams and Doug Dorst's *S.* (2013), which returns to the influence of *House of Leaves*. A shrink-wrapped slipcase contains the simulacrum of a battered library book, heavily annotated in different coloured pens by two separate readers. The novel, *The Ship of Theseus,* tells one story while the annotations tell another – that of two students pursuing (inevitably) an academic mystery surrounding the fictional book's author, V M Straka. Inserted between the pages are postcards, letters, newspaper clippings and other documents that enhance the story. Abrams (better known as the show-runner for a string of American TV shows including *Alias* and *Lost*, as well as the director tasked with reviving *Star Wars* and *Star Trek* as movie franchises) told the *New Yorker* that:

> It's intended to be a celebration of the analog, of the physical object. In this moment of e-mails, and texting, and everything moving into the cloud, in an intangible way, it's intentionally tangible. We wanted to include things you can actually hold in your hand: postcards, Xeroxes, legal-pad pages, pages from the school newspaper, a map on a napkin. (Rothman 2013: online)

Mark Lawson in the *Guardian* noted that 'Although an electronic edition has been released, the book should clearly be experienced in its physical form, which is one of the most staggering feats of book production I have ever seen' (2013: online). Unlike *House of Leaves,* however, the academic tone of *S.* is not entirely convincing. Eric and Jen read *The Ship of Theseus* more like fans, searching for clues, than literary critics interpreting a text. The book's tangibility becomes its *raison d'être,* and its fake layers provide only a simulacrum of depth.

The appeal of the book as object has also been richly explored in children's fiction of the new millennium. *A Series of Unfortunate Events* (1999–2006) by Lemony Snicket, a.k.a. Daniel Handler, consciously deployed metafictional devices, most notably that of an intrusive, omniscient author-narrator ('Lemony Snicket' himself). 'If you are interested in stories with happy endings', *The Bad Beginning* opens, 'you would be better off reading some other book. In this book, not only is there no happy ending, but there is no happy beginning and very few happy things in the middle' (Snicket 1999: 1). However, the books were also embellished with black and white illustrations, fake embossed interior covers and bookplates, and deliberately slurred typefaces. More than simply illustrated books, these were books that drew attention to their status *as* books.

This technique became increasingly heightened in children's publishing as the twenty-first century progressed. A recognisable Gothic aesthetic became evident in the design and marketing of children's books, from cover art to interior illustrations. This aesthetic drew on a heady cocktail of influences, including the mid-twentieth-century illustrations of Charles Addams, Edward Gorey and Ronald Searle, the graphic novel art of Dave McKean and the film production aesthetics of Tim Burton, Henry Selick and Rick Heinrichs. The children's book as Gothic object reached its apotheosis in Chris Riddell's *Goth Girl and the Ghost of a Mouse* (2013). An extremely funny parody of adult Gothic novels, it references everything from Samuel Taylor Coleridge's *The Rime of the Ancient Mariner* (1798) to Robert Stevenson's *Mary Poppins* (1964). The volume is lavishly illustrated and embellished with a silver-embossed inner cover, place-marker ribbon and pull-out 'secret' book.

The exploitation of a Gothic aesthetic has also resonated with a rise in the number of Gothic titles pitched towards children and young adults, and a growing perception of Gothic as pedagogically beneficial. As Chloe Buckley argues, 'In current mass market children's fiction, Gothic dominates and reviewers lavish praise on anything deemed "deliciously scary"' (2014: 254). She goes on to explain that contemporary writers and critics 'project onto childhood a delight in fear, while simultaneously also needing that fear to serve a pastoral, maturational function', in which the scary book enables children to navigate trauma successfully, thus preserving an understanding of children's literature as serving a pedagogical purpose (2012: 261).

Gothic children's fiction indulges the nostalgic desires of the adult: children's books are frequently purchased and read by adults, whether parents, educators or simply fans. Ever since J K Rowling's *Harry Potter* sequence (1997–2007) famously attracted a dual child and adult readership, the publishing industry has openly acknowledged and exploited the crossover appeal of children's books. The self-awareness of contemporary Gothic children's fiction plays into adult nostalgia for the magical encounters with books experienced in childhood, and constructs a lost, original experience of fear in the manner described by Jeremy Dyson above.

Nowhere is the importance of Gothic aesthetics more evident than in the children's writing of Neil Gaiman. Also a widely admired adult novelist, Gaiman began his career writing comics, including the celebrated *The Sandman* (1989–96); as a result his fans are particularly receptive towards collaboration with illustrators and comics artists. Gaiman's work includes two picture books with a Gothic sensibility, the content of which challenges conventional age-categorisations of children's publishing. The first, *The Wolves in the Walls* (2003), is a frankly terrifying picture book in which wolves can be heard scratching in the walls of an ordinary family house before emerging to evict the inhabitants and go on the rampage. It is illustrated in a haunting mixture of line drawing and photo-collage by Gaiman's long-time collaborator Dave McKean.

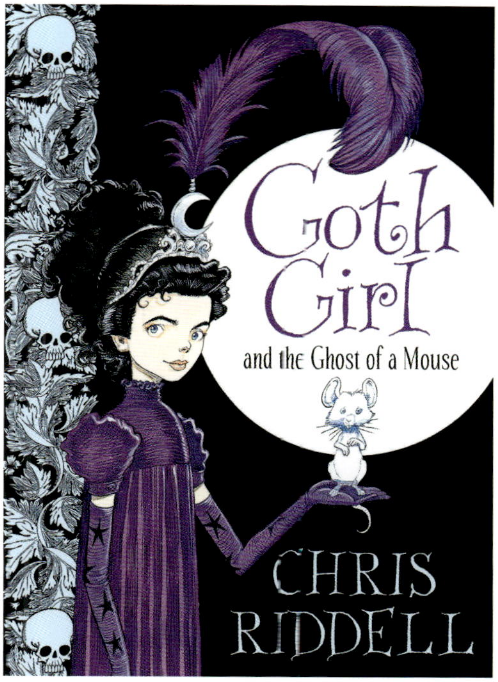

Front cover of Chris Riddell, *Goth Girl and the Ghost of a Mouse*, 2013. *Goth Girl* cleverly pastiches classic Gothic literature.

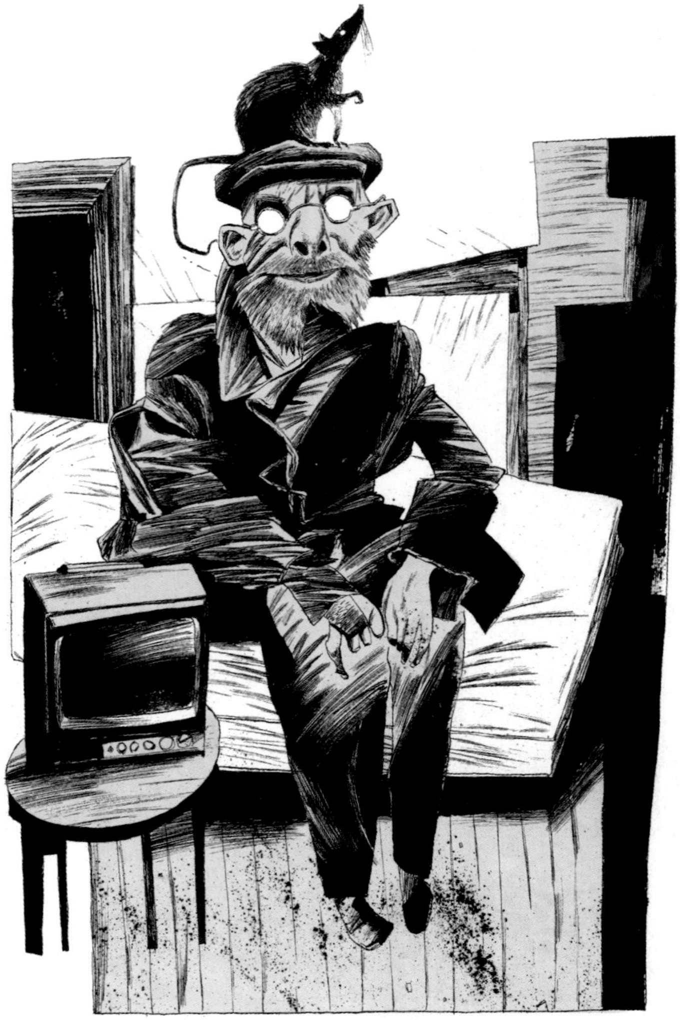

Original artwork for *Coraline* by Dave McKean, 2002.

The second example of Gaiman's Gothic picture books, *The Dangerous Alphabet* (2009), illustrated by Gris Grimly, directly recalls Edward Gorey's macabre alphabet primer *The Gashlycrumb Tinies* (1963). Like its predecessor, *The Dangerous Alphabet* exploits the tension between the morbidity of the content and the infantilism of the form, with an added self-conscious nod and wink to a presumed Goth audience. As a result it is difficult to say exactly what age the work is aimed at; it is perhaps best viewed as a faux-naïve picture book for adult readers. Nostalgia is combined with a playfully desecrational impulse that refuses to fix childhood as a static zone of putative innocence, constructing it rather as a mobile space of spoiled or imperfect knowledge. Gaiman puns wildly on the phonetic sound of the letters and disrupts the alphabet to preserve the rhyme scheme, thus also disrupting any serious pedagogical purpose while preserving the playfulness of the text. As the two children journey in search of treasure through the alphabet and the sewers simultaneously, the process of acquiring knowledge itself is Gothicised. Here binaries of innocence and knowledge, child and adult are challenged and subverted.

Simultaneously, Gothic presentation and design have become increasingly important in the marketing of 'classic' novels. The iconic

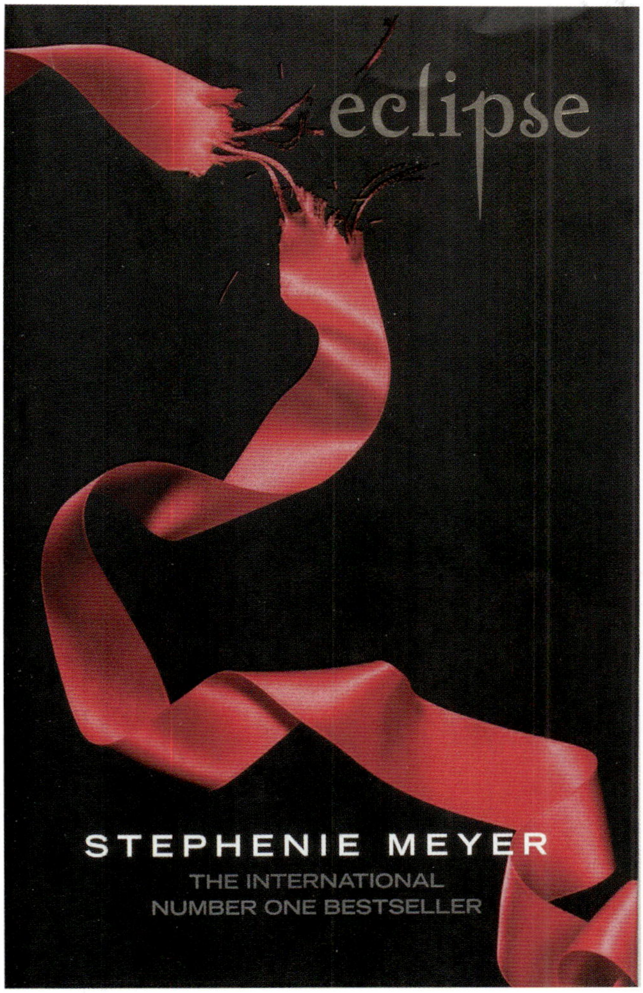

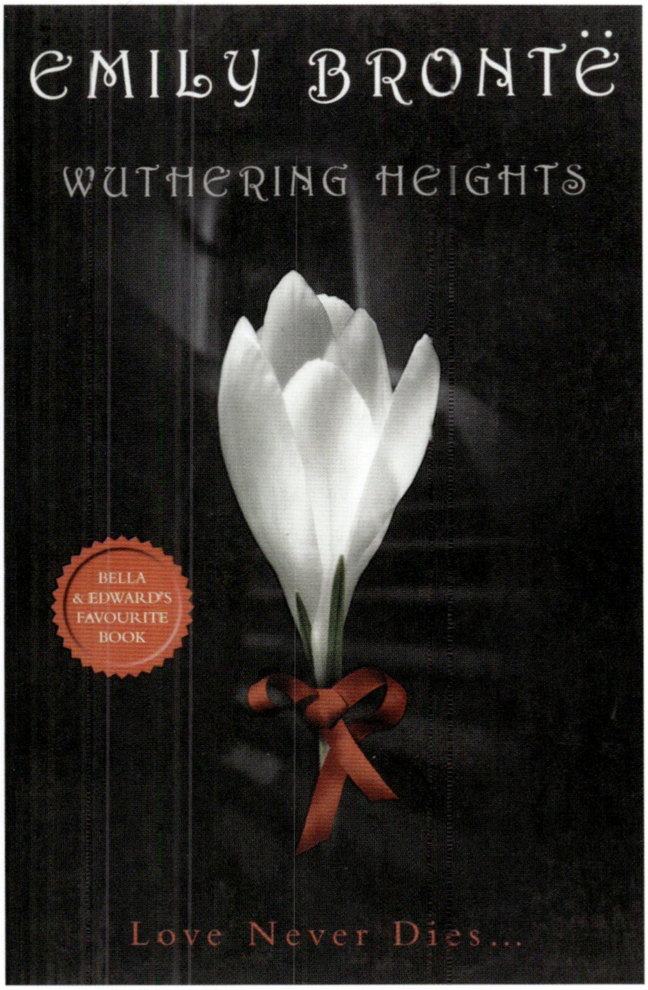

ABOVE LEFT:
Front cover of Stephenie Meyer, *Eclipse*, 2007.

ABOVE RIGHT:
Front cover of a HarperCollins edition of *Wuthering Heights* by Emily Brontë, 2009.

covers of Stephenie Meyer's vampire romance saga *Twilight*, with their single red and white symbol on a black background (or, in a special 2010 Christmas edition, a white background and red-edged pages), were imitated widely in cognate teen fiction such as the 2009 reissue of L J Smith's *The Vampire Diaries: The Awakening* (1991). However, *Twilight*'s cover art was also adapted by HarperCollins in 2009–10 for reissues of *Jane Eyre*, *Wuthering Heights* and *Tess of the d'Urbervilles* – and in the United States for *Pride and Prejudice*, *Sense and Sensibility*, *Romeo and Juliet* and *The Scarlet Letter*.

The marketing campaigns for these books explicitly pitched them towards the vast *Twilight* audience: *Wuthering Heights* bore a sticker advertising it as 'Bella and Edward's favourite book'. (*Twilight* fans will recognise this as misdirection, as the couple argue about the novel, which Bella loves but Edward detests.) In practice, response to the marketing strategy was divided; many commentators commended the strategy for encouraging teenagers to read classic literature, while others declared that Emily Brontë would be turning in her grave. It was enormously successful nevertheless, with sales of *Wuthering Heights* increasing from 8,500 a year to 34,000 in the wake of the reissue. Elsewhere, classic Gothic novels were revisioned

OPPOSITE:
Front cover of Seth Grahame-Smith, *Pride and Prejudice and Zombies*, 2009.

as graphic novels, pop-up books and even, in the 'Babylit Primer' range by Jennifer Adams and Alison Oliver, toddler board books, including *Dracula: A Babylit Counting Primer* (2012), *Wuthering Heights: A Babylit Weather Primer* (2013) and *Sherlock Holmes in the Hound of the Baskervilles: A Babylit Sounds Primer* (2013).

Do-It-Yourself Gothic

If the exploitation of Gothic aesthetics in packaging and constructing books as objects could be regarded as cynical commercialism, then the strongly DIY impulse that accompanies it in contemporary culture enables fans and readers to take control of narratives and shape them to their own ends. The rise of fan fiction, or fanfic, emerged in response to cult films and TV programmes such as *Star Trek* in the later twentieth century, but achieved critical mass once it migrated online.

Fan fiction takes characters and settings from its favourite texts and uses them to tell new stories. Slash fiction, a particularly popular variant, creates erotic pairings between two characters who are not paired in the original text, usually two men; the name derives from the forward slash in pairings such as 'Kirk/Spock'. Notoriously, E L James's fanfic version of *Twilight*, published on the web, became the erotic bestseller *Fifty Shades of Grey* (2011). For Henry Jenkins, fans are 'textual poachers' or 'rogue readers' – autonomous and critically engaged subjects who appropriate scraps and fragments of culturally legitimated narratives creatively to fashion new meanings (1992). In his recent book *Convergence Culture: Where Old and New Media Collide* (2006), Jenkins demonstrates how fan opinions and practices increasingly shape the production and marketing of texts.

Seth Grahame-Smith's *Pride and Prejudice and Zombies* (2009), written to commission for Quirk Books and swiftly turned into a franchise of similar titles, bears many of the hallmarks of fan fiction. Taking on the popular musical concept of the 'mash-up', in which two generically distinct tracks are mixed together to create a new one, it functions retrospectively to introduce horror conventions to classic realist and romantic fiction. The conceit operates on the basis of incongruity, of splicing together two apparently incompatible discourses. Done for sensational and comic effect, the novel's effectiveness depends on its faithful adherence to the generic conventions of the two texts it sutures. It does not, therefore, achieve any great insights into either classic fiction or horror.

Pride and Prejudice and Zombies constitutes an extreme and debased version of Alexandra Warwick's contention that 'contemporary culture *wants* to have trauma, it is induced, predicted and enacted, even when it is not actually present' (Warwick 2007: 11). Jane Austen's *Pride and Prejudice* (1813) is not a text free from suffering and distress; however, after several decades of popular film and television adaptations, it has become perceived as the quintessential cosy costume drama, the archetypal drawing-room romance. Mashing it up with zombie fiction responds to the perceived nostalgia of Austenites by subjecting their sacred cow to ritual desecration, substituting a nostalgic view of the past with a Gothic one founded in the idea of undead return.

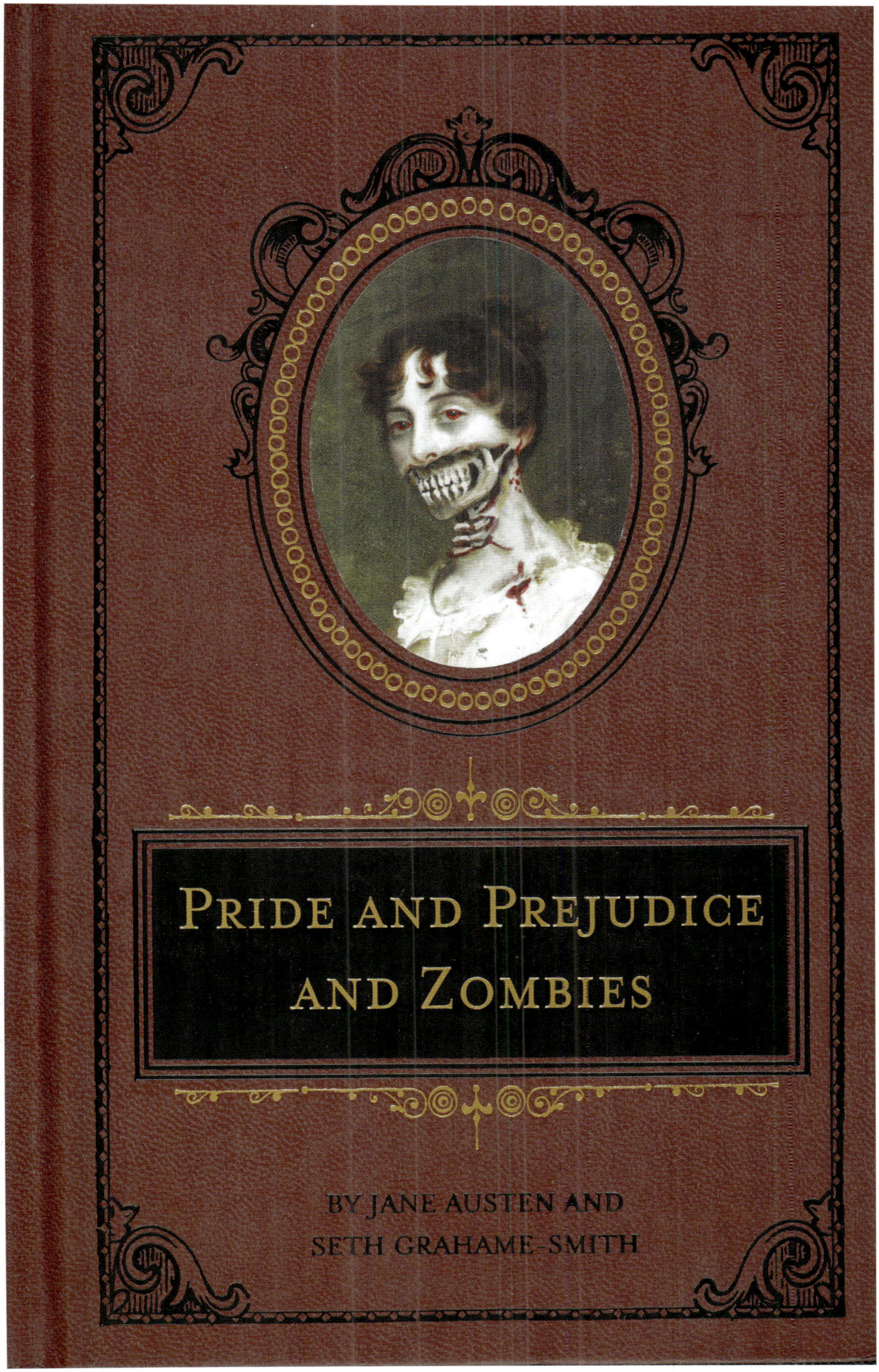
PRIDE AND PREJUDICE
AND ZOMBIES
BY JANE AUSTEN AND
SETH GRAHAME-SMITH

This attitude to the book can also be recognised in the contemporary cultural phenomenon of Steampunk. Just as Goth subculture in the 1980s drew on literary and cinematic precedents to fashion a spectacular visual style, Steampunk too first emerged as a literary genre. By the twenty-first century, however, it was established as a fully fledged subculture with its own communities and events. The term 'Steampunk' tropes on the late twentieth-century science fiction sub-genre Cyberpunk, but has more in common with nineteenth-century science fiction, since it imagines a future based on nineteenth-century science. In K W Jeter's *Infernal Devices* (1987), a brilliant watchmaker creates clockwork human automata. *The Difference Engine* (1990), by William Gibson and Bruce Sterling, describes an alternative nineteenth century in which Charles Babbage has succeeded in building a mechanical computer, creating a steam-powered digital revolution. *The League of Extraordinary Gentlemen* (1999–2012), the comics sequence of Alan Moore and Kevin O'Neill, imagines the heroes of nineteenth-century popular fiction, such as Allan Quatermain, Jekyll and Hyde, Captain Nemo, Mina Murray and the Invisible Man, as co-existing in a single fictional-historical universe. Much Steampunk fiction retains the Gothic sensibility of the nineteenth-century science fiction by which it is inspired. However, this sensibility is often more evident in the visual complexity and chiaroscuro of its fictional worlds than in its narrative trajectories. Steampunk is often Gothic in its patchwork assemblage of scraps and fragments of the Gothicised past, but more so in its evocation of a world of gas lamps and grime, palaces of crystal and cast iron, and top hats, goggles and corsets.

Both Goth subculture and Steampunk are notable for their conversion of literature to lifestyle: the living out of narrative themes and aesthetic motifs through everyday practices, from dress and home décor to social events. In the twenty-first century this has spread beyond subculture to inform a range of commodities – from mass-produced Hallowe'en sweets and toys to the *haute couture* of fashion designers such as Alexander McQueen, John Galliano and Riccardo Tisci, both for their own labels and for major fashion houses such as Dior and Givenchy. Such proliferation of Gothic commodities informs one of the cherished practices of Steampunk subculture: 'retro-fitting', or customising pieces of current technology to look Victorian. Laptops are set in lovingly carved wooden cases or made over to look like typewriters, while e-readers are bound in artificially aged, embossed leather. The object retains its function, but acquires a patina of 'pastness', a fake historicity.

Drawing on the twenty-first-century renewal of interest in handicrafts, Steampunk retro-fitting asserts the value of the individual and hand-made over the mass-produced corporate design of Apple and Dell. In doing so, it returns to the Arts and Crafts Gothic championed in the nineteenth century by John Ruskin and William Morris, which found a celebration of creative craftsmanship and spiritual community in medieval Gothic architecture. As Jeff Vandermeer argues, 'The parallel couldn't be more obvious: Steampunks seek to reject the conformity of the modern, soulless featureless design of technology – and all that implies – while embracing the inventiveness and tech origins of machines' (2011: 99).

Steampunk fashion is likewise driven by the production of a character; participants will devise a name and narrative to go along with their look. The sartorial style brings together a mash-up of Victorian and other vintage styles with science fiction accessories, for example cogs, clockwork, goggles and parasols that transform into weapons and other ingenious gadgets. Victorian styles are not replicated with historical accuracy, but are deliberately subjected to bricolage (top hats with brass goggles, military uniforms embellished with leather straps and brass cogs to create a 'robot' arm, or corsets and crinolines as outerwear) to create a fantastic aura.

Steampunk embodies well the characteristic ambivalence of twenty-first-century Gothic. It expresses nostalgia for a world before the Information Age, while simultaneously celebrating scientific and technological progress. In doing so it reflects a new balance between two opposing models of Gothic: one that repudiates the oppressive past in the service of enlightened modernity, and one that reflects nostalgically on the imaginative riches of former eras. Nowhere is this more strongly evident than in those aspects of twenty-first-century Gothic that highlight the new models of participation and convergence encouraged by digital culture. Gothic readers have always been implicated by the text, not only consuming but also consumed by its wonders, its pleasures and its terrors. In the participatory culture of the early twenty-first century, however, they are active in constructing its meanings, whether through hypertext, lifestyle practices, fanfic or retro-fitting. The DIY aesthetic is visible in found footage film and in the scribbled annotations in the margins of *S.*: even where produced and marketed by big corporations, contemporary Gothic seeks the illusion of the hand-made. The sinister threat of the book as artefact goes hand in hand with the pleasure of the book as object. In such ambivalence lies Gothic's continuing power to signify and its enduring vitality at the dawn of the Information Age.

Further Reading

Beville, Maria 2009. *Gothic-postmodernism: Voicing the Terrors of Postmodernity* (Amsterdam: Rodopi). Beville proposes a new genre, Gothic-postmodernism, suggesting that Gothic and postmodernism are linked through their focus on sublime terror and unrepresentability. She discusses a number of late twentieth- and early twenty-first-century novels.

Cherry, Brigid, Peter Howells and Caroline Ruddell (eds) 2010. *Twenty-first Century Gothic* (Newcastle: Cambridge Scholars Press). A diverse collection of essays on Gothic in contemporary culture, from anime to music videos.

Olson, Danel 2011. *21st-century Gothic: Great Gothic Novels Since 2000* (Lanham, MD: Scarecrow Press). An anthology of 53 essays on Gothic works published between 2000 and 2010.

Spooner, Catherine 2006. *Contemporary Gothic* (London: Reaktion). An accessible critical examination of the proliferation of Gothic themes across the spectrum of contemporary culture, from literature and film to art, fashion and advertising.

Watkiss, Joanne 2012. *Gothic Contemporaries: The Haunted Text* (Cardiff: University of Wales Press). A critical examination of the motif of haunting in a selection of twenty-first-century novels, with an emphasis on metafiction.

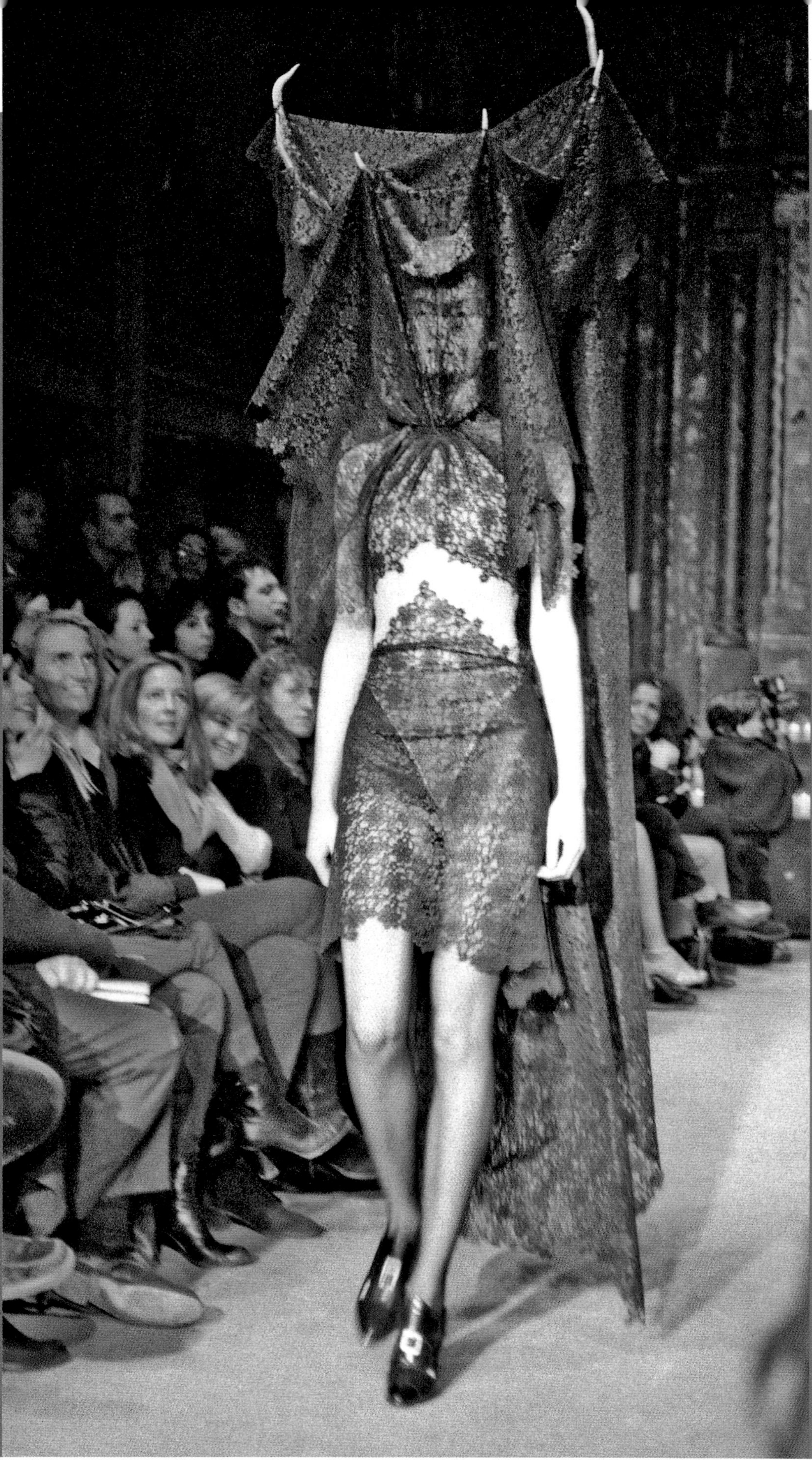

Black lace dress worn with veil and antlers, Alexander McQueen *Dante* collection, autumn/winter 1996. Now in the collection of Daphne Guinness.

From the Crypt: Alexander McQueen

Alexander McQueen was a visionary designer who brought Gothic influences into couture. This black lace dress is part of his autumn/winter 1996 *Dante* collection, shown for the first time in Christ Church, Spitalfields. The collection was inspired in part by Dante Alighieri's *Divine Comedy*, with medieval touches such as a hooded falcon on the arm of a model, but also included the influence of high Victoriana in lilac silk corsetry with black lace overlay, evoking the elaborate conventions of mourning. Some models wore clothing printed with photographs of the Vietnam War by Don McCullin, and a plastic skeleton sat in the front row among the journalists. McQueen said that he had drawn inspiration for the collection not only from death, but from the presence of death in life. The eclecticism of the various motifs used in the show mirrors Gothic literature's plundering of earlier sources to create the new.

Lee Alexander McQueen was born in Lewisham, south London, in 1969 and started his fashion career as a Savile Row apprentice. He studied for a MA in Fashion at Central St Martin's; his final degree show in 1992 was entitled *Jack the Ripper Stalks His Victims* and included locks of McQueen's own hair sewn into clear plastic pockets inside each garment, in imitation of nineteenth-century mourning jewellery. The Ripper murders were a subject McQueen returned to several times – in the location for the *Dante* show (Christ Church is located next to the Ten Bells pub, associated with the Ripper victims Annie Chapman and Mary Kelly), and in the title of his autumn/winter 2009 collection, *The Horn of Plenty*, named after another pub allegedly frequented by Mary Kelly.

McQueen drew direct inspiration from Gothic literary motifs and especially from Gothic film throughout his career, basing collections on *The Birds* (spring/summer 1995), *The Hunger* (spring/summer 1996), and *The Shining* (*The Overlook*, autumn/winter 1999). He blended dark fairy tales with the work of Tim Burton for his show *Supercalifragilisticexpialidocious* (autumn/winter 2002), and set the catwalk show for *Voss* (spring/summer 2002) in a glass box on a lunatic asylum-styled set. He also used the darker side of the natural world as a recurrent theme in his work: the antlers worn with this particular dress re-emerged in his autumn/winter 2006 collection *Widows of Culloden*, this time in white, worn with a white lace dress and veil. Birds of prey also feature in multiple collections, most notably in *Voss* where a model wore a headdress of taxidermied hawks that appeared to be attacking her – a direct reference to Alfred Hitchcock's *The Birds* (1963). Fresh flowers were sewn to a dress in *Sarabande* (spring/summer 2007), McQueen stating that 'Things rot. It was all about decay. I used flowers because they die'. By finding beauty in death, decay and savagery, McQueen embraced the Gothic sensibility.

TANYA KIRK

Photographing Goths:
Martin Parr at the Whitby Goth Weekend

Oh, why did I ever go to Whitby?
With the return of the Whitby Goth Weekend (or 'WGW') in the spring and autumn of each year, there is barely a newspaper published across the country that does not contain a photoshoot of some of the festival's more spectacularly dressed participants. What started out in 1994 as a small, informal meeting of some forty Goth penpals in the town made famous by its appearance in Bram Stoker's *Dracula* has become a large-scale, biannual music and fashion event.

The Goth subculture that the WGW celebrates first emerged in the late 1970s in the wake of the rapidly diminishing punk scene. Leaving behind the guitar-led noise of punk, early pioneers of what would become the Goth sound – Joy Division, Siouxsie and the Banshees, UK Decay – placed an emphasis on driving rhythms, distinctive vocals and lyrics that veered towards the dark and lugubrious subject-matter of Gothic fiction and film. In 1979 the British Goth band Bauhaus brought all of these elements together and released what has come to be regarded as the first Gothic rock record: 'Bela Lugosi's Dead', Goth music's equivalent, perhaps, to Walpole's *Otranto*. By referencing the demise of the most famous film incarnation of Dracula, Bauhaus – and, by extension, the Goth scene – flaunted its literary influences and credentials for all to see. Beyond Bauhaus, Stoker's famous creation provided a great deal of material for songwriters, as well as a wealth of visual cues for those wishing to adopt a more theatrical sartorial look. Other key inspirations for Goth music and fashion included Edgar Allan Poe's melancholic stories, and the stagey excesses of British Hammer Horror films.

The look and style that the early Goth scene fostered has fared much better than its musical counterpart. Although bands like The Sisters of Mercy and The Cult, having attained mass appeal in the mid-1980s, continue to perform to this day, the heyday of Goth music seems to have passed. Goth subculture, by contrast, has retained and even strengthened its stronghold, becoming a global fashion statement that encompasses a vast array of styles, from Victoriana and Lolita to fetish and Steampunk. The relations between these various elements are not, themselves, uncontroversial. Twice a year, however, these and other sub-groupings of Goth converge on a small corner of north Yorkshire to celebrate at the WGW the music, fashion and lifestyle of all things alternative and dark.

In a series of photographs of the April 2014 Whitby Goth Weekend commissioned specially for the British Library's *Terror and Wonder* exhibition, the award-winning British photographer Martin Parr captures the diversity, energy and inclusiveness of a sub-cultural scene that, several decades after its first appearance, continues to thrive. While Bela Lugosi may, indeed, be dead, Goth certainly is not: like a vampire, zombie or other undead thing, Goth defiantly returns to life, continuously reinventing itself with the same force and energy as that which drives literary manifestations of the Gothic imagination.

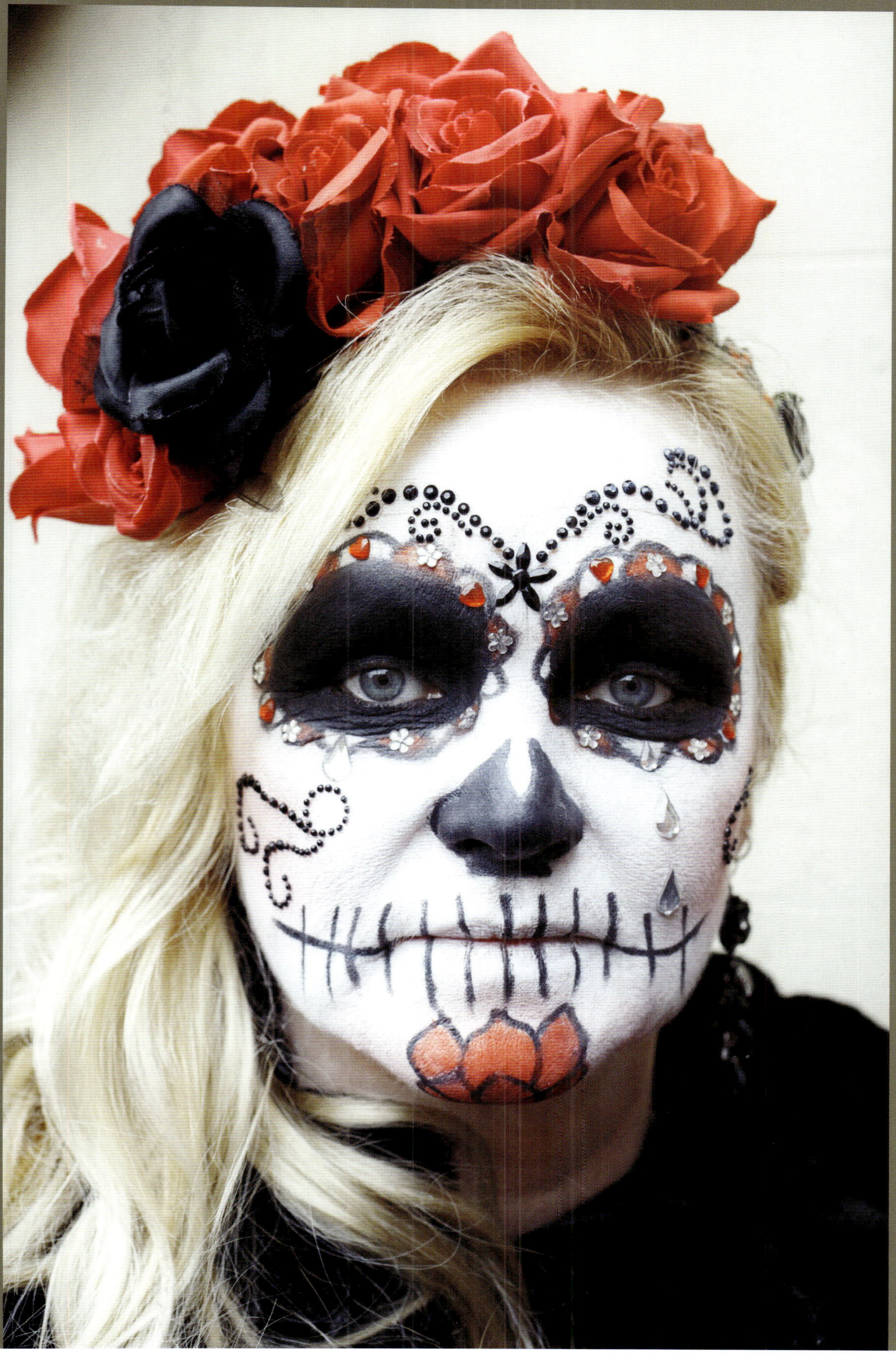

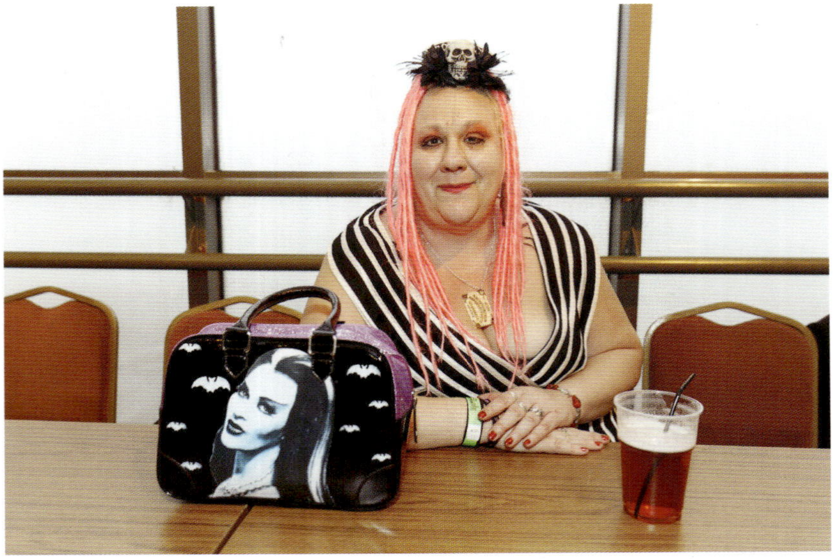

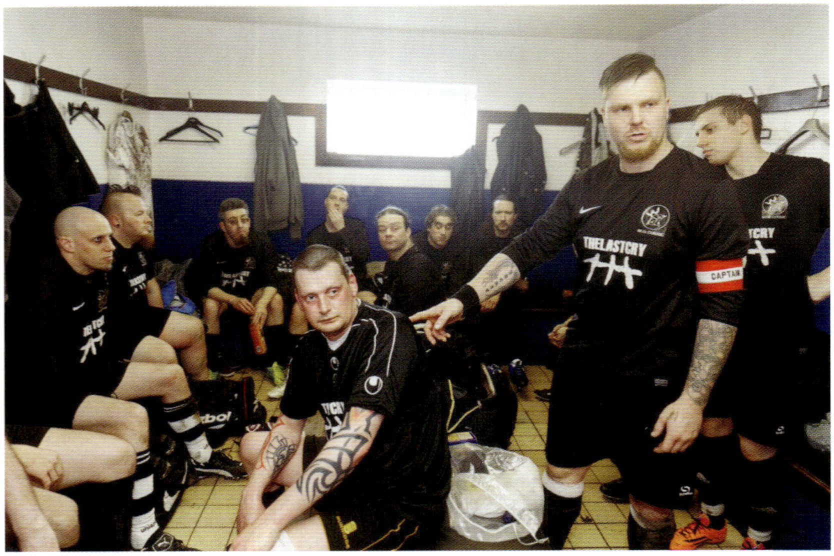
THELASTCRY
CAPTAIN

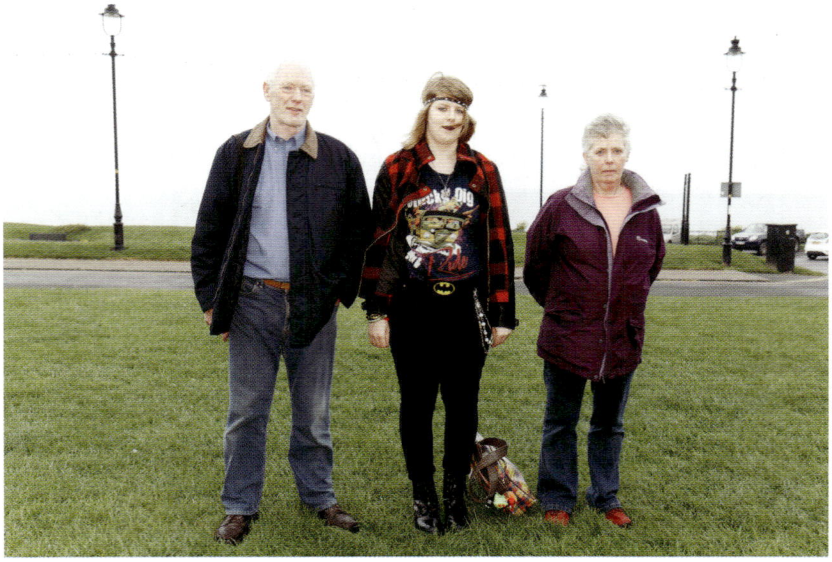

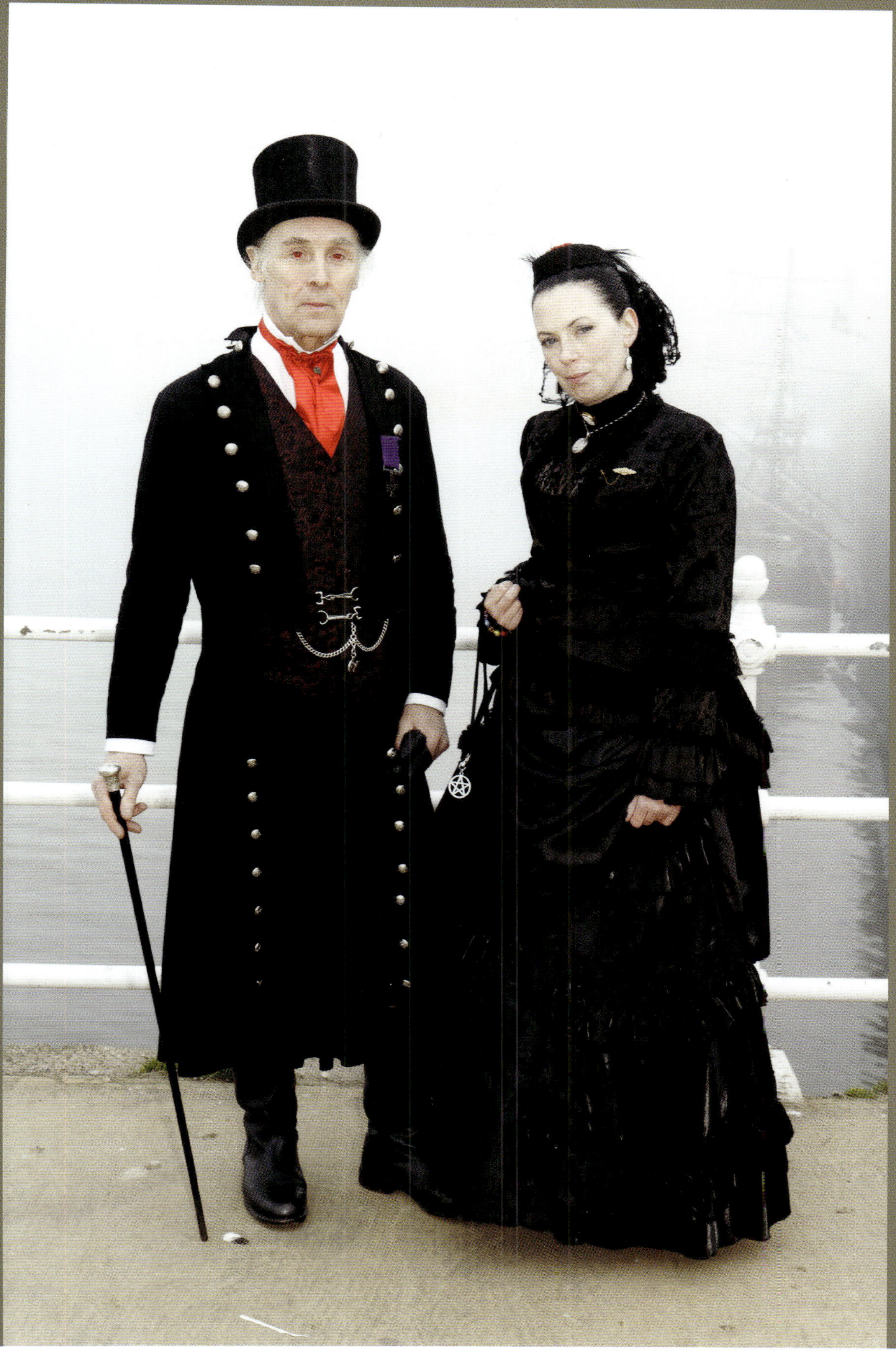

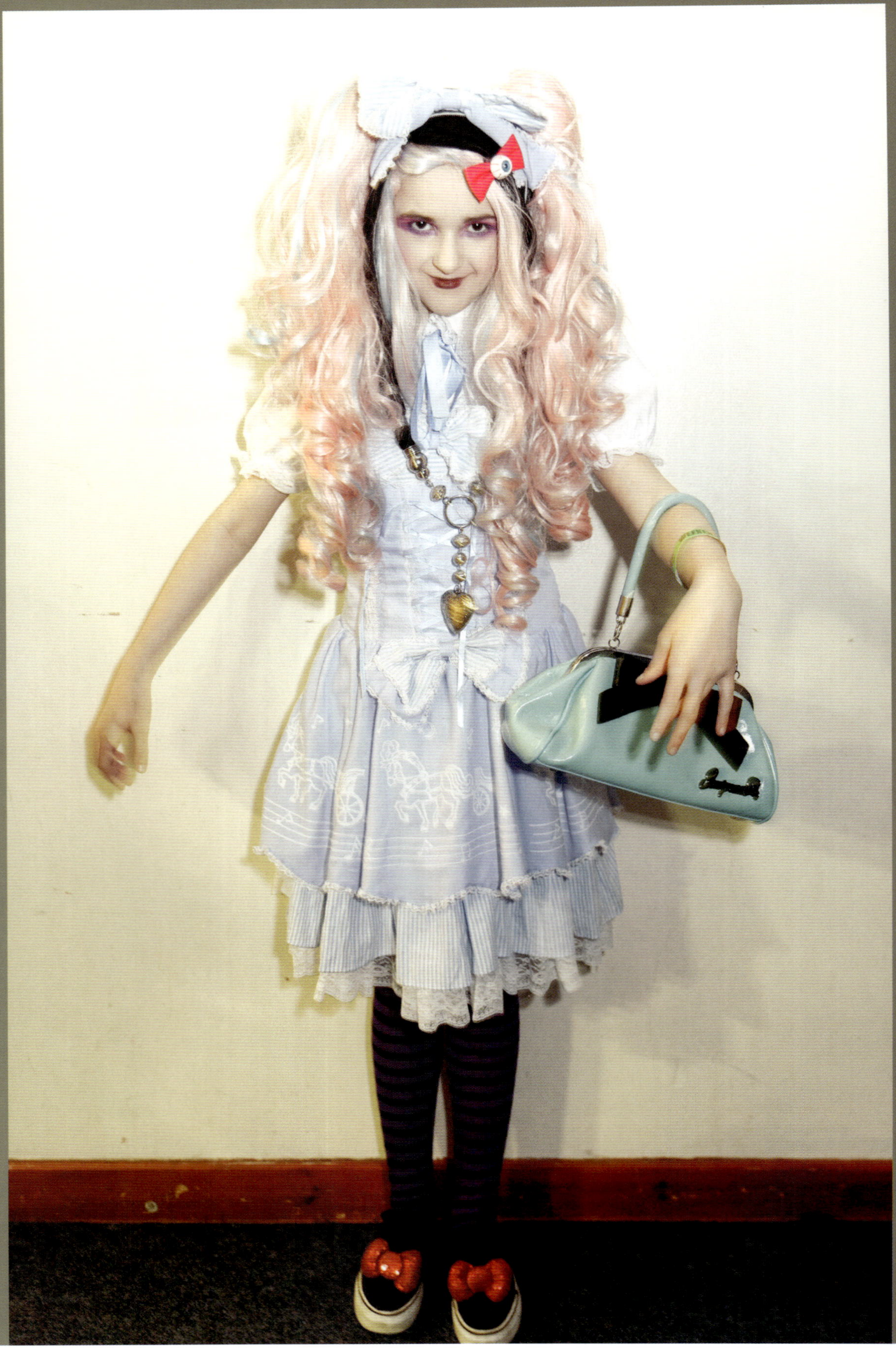

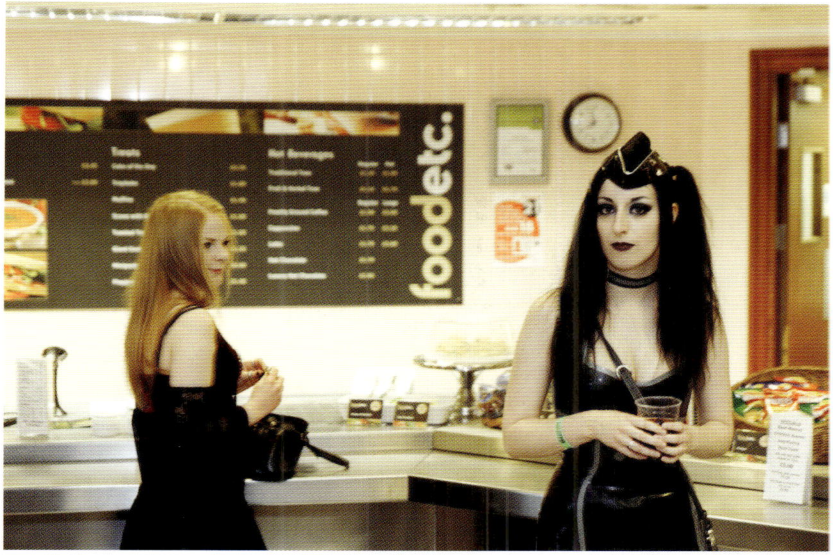
foodetc.

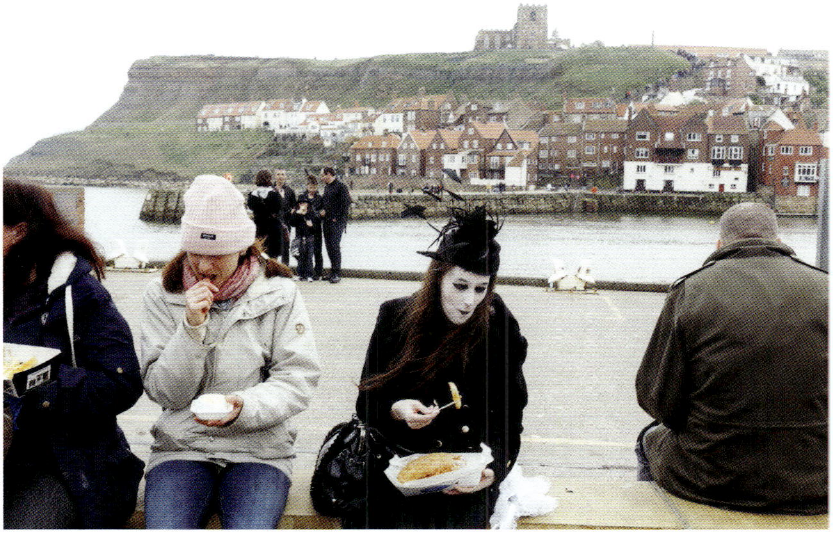

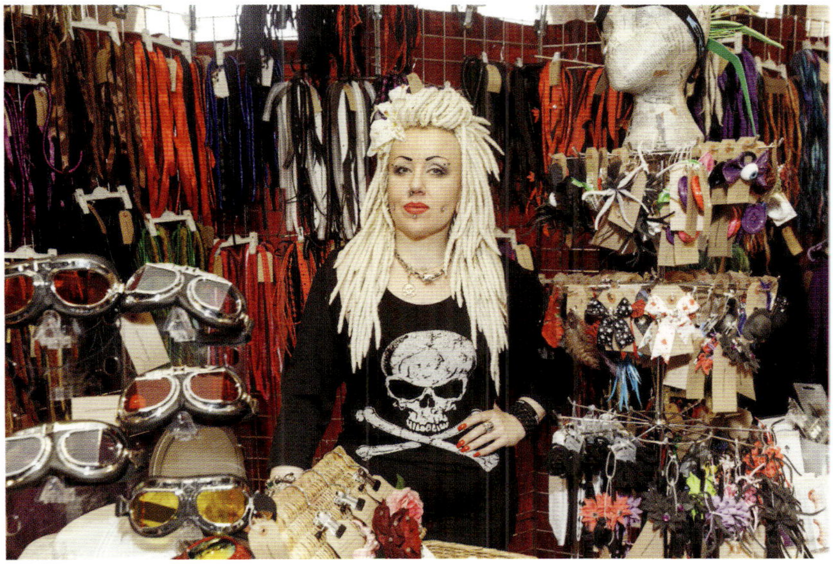

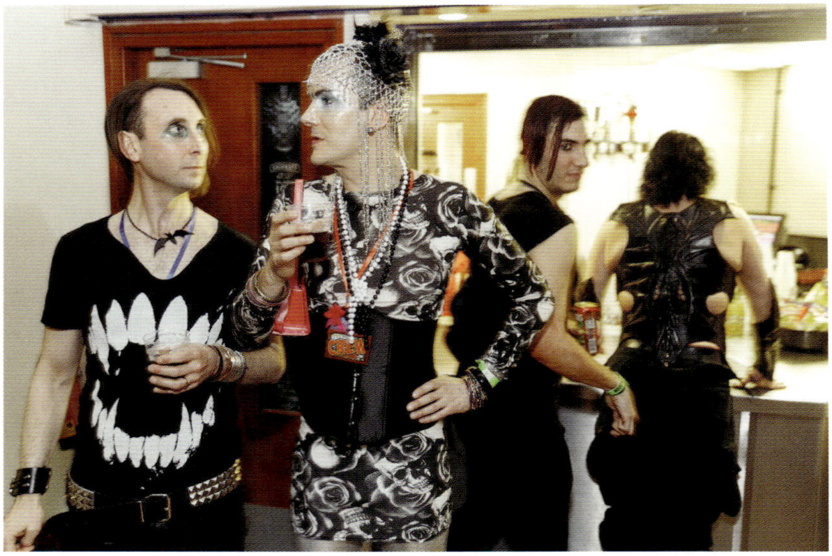

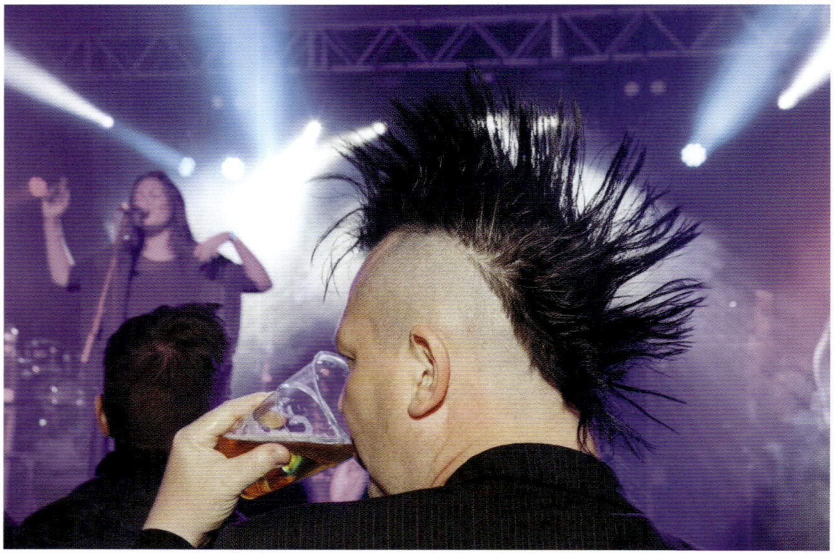

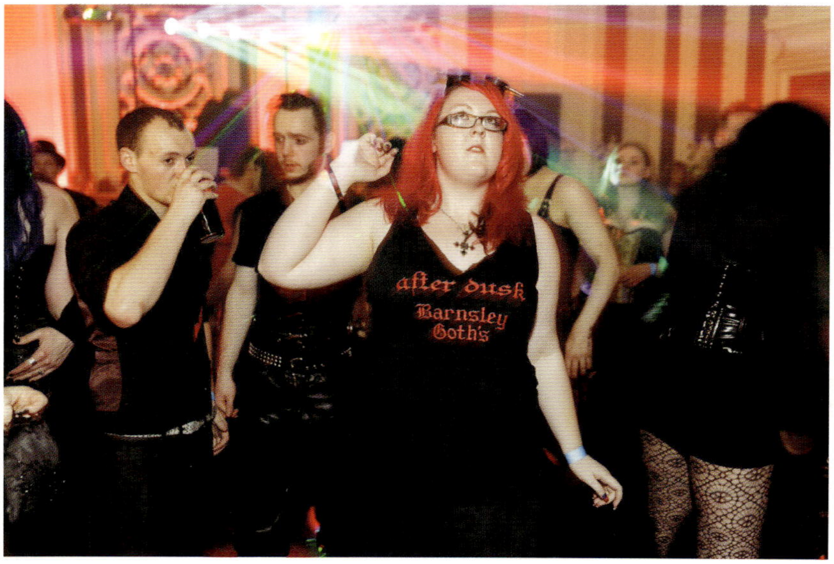
after dusk
Barnsley
Goth's

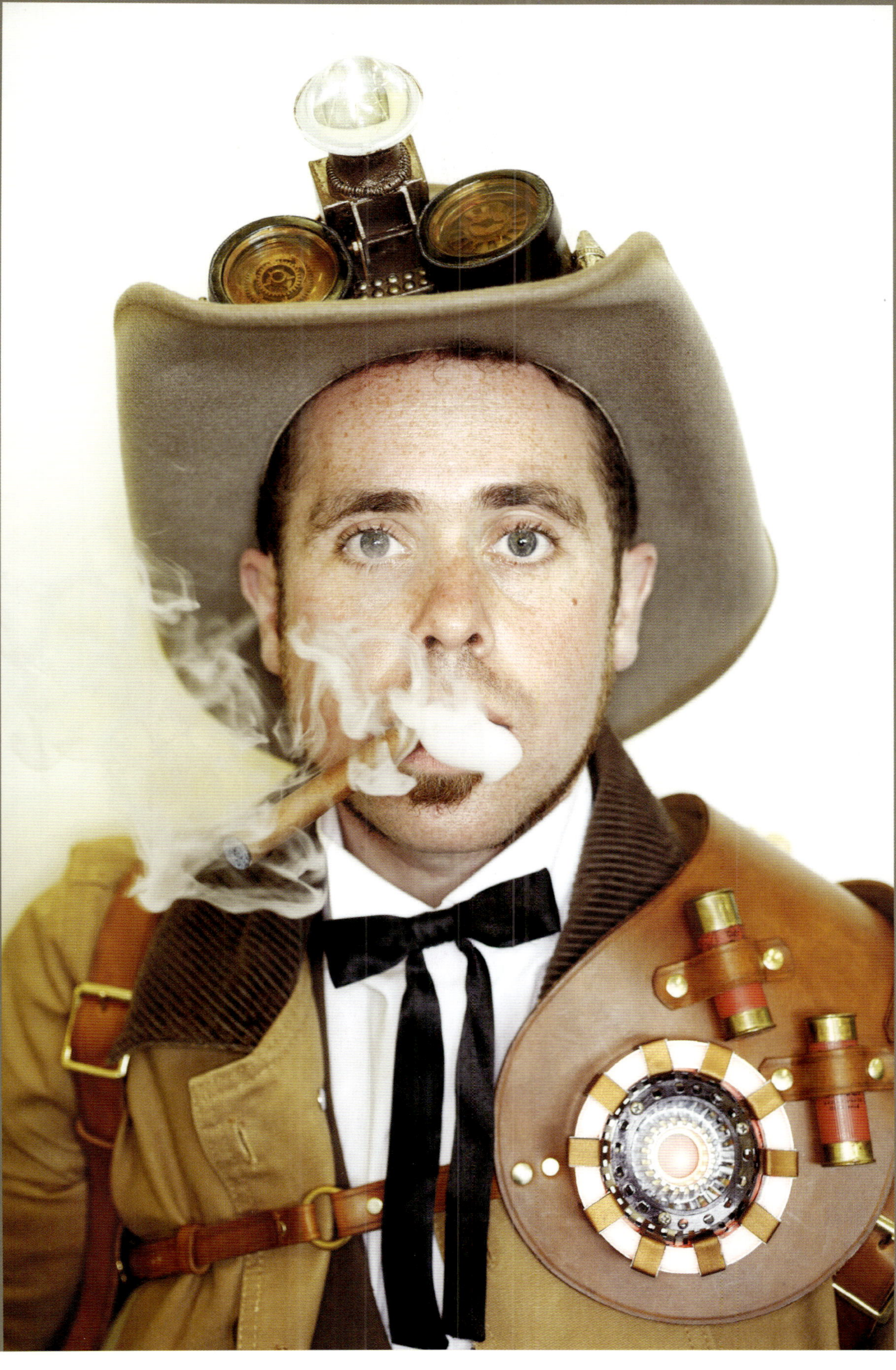

Bibliography

Introduction

Anon. 1797 'On the Titles of Modern Novels', *Monthly Magazine and British Register, for 1797. From July to December, Inclusive*, IV: 347–9.

Clery, E J 2002. 'The Genesis of "Gothic" Fiction' in Jerrold E Hogle (ed), *The Cambridge Companion to Gothic Fiction* (Cambridge: Cambridge University Press), pp. 21–39.

Clery, E J and Robert Miles (eds) 2000. *Gothic Documents: A Sourcebook, 1700–1820* (Manchester: Manchester University Press).

Colley, Linda 1992. *Britons: Forging the Nation, 1707–1837* (New Haven: Yale University Press).

De Quincey, Thomas 2000. *The Works of Thomas De Quincey, Vol. II: Confessions of an English Opium-Eater, 1821–1856*, ed by Grevel Lindop (London: Pickering & Chatto).

Drake, Nathan 1798. *Literary Hours: or, Sketches Critical and Narrative* (London)

___ (1804). *Literary Hours: or, Sketches, Critical, Narrative, and Poetical. Volume III* (London).

Groom, Nick 2012. *The Gothic: A Very Short Introduction* (Oxford: Oxford University Press).

Johnson, Samuel 1765. *The Plays of William Shakespeare, in Eight Volumes, with the Corrections and Illustrations of Various Commentators; To Which are Added Notes by Sam. Johnson* (London).

Kliger, Samuel 1952. *The Goths in England: A Study in Seventeenth and Eighteenth Century Thought* (Cambridge, Mass: Harvard University Press).

Lee, Sophia 2000. *The Recess; or, A Tale of Other Times*, ed by April Aliston (Lexington: University of Kentucky Press).

Lewis, W S (ed) 1937–83. *The Yale Edition of Horace Walpole's Correspondence*, 42 vols (New Haven: Yale University Press).

Longueil, Alfred E 1923. 'The Word "Gothic" in Eighteenth Century Criticism', *Modern Language Notes*, 38.8: 453–60.

Montagu, Elizabeth Robinson 1769. *An Essay on the Writings and Genius of Shakespear* [sic]. *Compared with the Greek and French Dramatic Poets* (London).

Morley, Henry (ed) 1887. *Tales of Terror and Wonder* (London: George Routledge and Sons).

Oxford English Dictionary Online <http://www.oed.com.ezproxy.stir.ac.uk/> [accessed 21 January 2014].

Pope, Alexander (ed) 1725. *The Works of Shakespear* [*sic*]. *In Six Volumes. Collated and Corrected by the Former Editions. By Mr. Pope* (London).

Reeve, Clara 2003. *The Old English Baron*, ed by James Trainer, with introduction and notes by James Watt (Oxford: Oxford University Press).

Sabor, Peter (ed) 1987. *Horace Walpole: The Critical Heritage* (Abingdon: Routledge).

Scott, Sir Walter 1824. 'Prefatory Memoir to Mrs Ann Radcliffe' in *The Novels of Mrs Ann Radcliffe [. . .]. To Which is Prefixed, a Memoir of the Life of the Author*, Novelists' Library, vol. x (London: Hurst, Robinson, and Co.,), pp. i–xxxix.

Thomson, Douglass H (ed) 2010. *Tales of Wonder* by Matthew Gregory Lewis (Peterborough, Ont.: Broadview).

Walpole, Horace 1779. *A Letter to the Editor of the Miscellanies of Thomas Chatterton* (Strawberry Hill).

Walpole, Horace 2003. *The Castle of Otranto: A Gothic Story* and *The Mysterious Mother: A Tragedy*, ed by Frederick S Frank (Peterborough, Ont.: Broadview).

Chapter 1

Andrews, Malcolm 1989. *The Search for the Picturesque: Landscape, Aesthetics and Tourism in Britain, 1660–1800* (Aldershot: Scolar Press).

Anon. 1722. *The Comical Pilgrim; or, Travels of a Cynick Philosopher, thro' the most Wicked Parts of the World, namely, England, Wales, Scotland, Ireland, and Holland* (London).

Ascham, Roger 1570. *The Scholemaster or Plaine and Perfite Way of Teachyng Children, to Vnderstand, Write, and Speake, the Latin Tong* (London).

Bartell, Edmund Jun. 1804. *Hints for Picturesque Improvements in Ornamental Cottages, and*

Their Scenery: including some Observations on the Labourer and His Cottage (London: Architectural Library).

Blair, Robert 1743. *The Grave. A Poem* (London).

Chris Brooks 1999. *The Gothic Revival* (London: Phaidon).

The Builder's Dictionary: or, Gentleman and Architect's Companion 1734. 2 vols [unpaginated] (London).

Burke, Edmund 1990. *A Philosophical Enquiry into the Origin of Our Ideas of the Sublime and Beautiful*, ed by Adam Phillips (Oxford: Oxford University Press).

Camden, William 1701. *Camden's Britannia Abridg'd; with Improvements, and Continuations, to this Present Time*, 2 vols (London).

___ 1722. *Britannia: or A Chorographical Description of Great Britain and Ireland, together with the Adjacent Islands*, 2 vols (London).

Claudian 1963. Trans by Maurice Platnauer, 2 vols, Loeb Classical Library (Cambridge, MA: Harvard University Press).

Davenant, Charles 1701. *Essays Upon I. The Ballance of Power. II. The Right of Making War, Peace, and Alliances. III. Universal Monarchy* (London).

Defoe, Daniel 1706. *Jure Divino: A Satyr* (London).

Denham, John 1709. *Coopers-Hill A Poem* (London).

Duncan, Daniel (trans) 1706. *Wholesome Advice against the Abuse of Hot Liquors, Particularly of Coffee, Chocolate, Tea, Brandy, and Strong Waters* (London).

Gibbon, Edward 1994. *The History of the Decline and Fall of the Roman Empire*, ed David Womersley, 3 vols (Harmondsworth: Penguin).

Gough, Richard 1768. *Anecdotes of British Topography* (London).

Green, Dennis H 2007. 'Linguistic and Literary Traces of the Ostrogoths' in Samuel Barnish and Federico Marazzi (eds), *The Ostrogoths from the Migration Period to the Sixth Century: An Ethnographic Perspective* (Woodbridge: Boydell and Brewer), pp. 387–416.

Groom, Nick 2008. 'Romantic Poetry and Antiquity' in James Chandler and Maureen McLane (eds), *The Cambridge Companion to British Romantic Poetry* (Cambridge: Cambridge University Press), pp. 35–52.

___ 2012. *The Gothic: A Very Short Introduction* (Oxford: Oxford University Press).

Hebron, Stephen 2006. *The Romantics and the British Landscape* (London: British Library).

Hurd, Richard 1762. *Letters on Chivalry and Romance* (London).

Innes, Thomas 1729. *A Critical Essay on the Ancient Inhabitants of the Northern Parts of Britain, or Scotland*, 2 vols [continuously paginated] (London).

Johnson, Samuel (ed) 1765. *The Plays of William Shakespeare*, 8 vols (London).

Jordanes 1915. *The Gothic History*, ed and trans by Charles Christopher Mierow (Princeton: Princeton University Press).

Kidd, Colin 1999. *British Identities before Nationalism: Ethnicity and Nationhood in the Atlantic World, 1600–1800* (Cambridge: Cambridge University Press).

Langley, Batty 1747. *Gothic Architecture, Improved by Rules and Proportions* (London).

Leslie, Charles 1739. *Masonry: A Poem* (Edinburgh).

Lewis, W S (ed) 1937–83. *The Yale Edition of Horace Walpole's Correspondence*, 42 vols (New Haven: Yale University Press).

Lonsdale, Roger (ed) 1969. *The Poems of Gray, Collins and Goldsmith* (London: Longman).

MacDowall, Andrew Lord Bankton 1747. *An Essay upon Feudal Holdings, Superiorities, and Hereditary Jurisdictions, in Scotland* (London).

Marcellinus, Ammianus 1986. *The Later Roman Empire (A.D. 354–378)*, trans by Walter Hamilton, ed Andrew Wallace-Hadrill (Harmondsworth: Penguin).

Musset, Lucien 1975. *The Germanic Invasions: The Making of Europe AD 400–600*, trans by Edward and Columba James (London: Paul Elek).

Newbery, John 1762. *The Art of Poetry on a New Plan*, rev by Oliver Goldsmith, 2 vols (London).

Percy, Thomas 1765. *Reliques of Ancient English Poetry*, ed Nick Groom, 3 vols (London and Bristol: Routledge/Thoemmes Press, 1996).

Piozzi, Hester Lynch 1786. *Anecdotes of the Late Samuel Johnson, LL.D. during the Last Twenty Years of His Life* (London).

Pope, Alexander 1984. *The Poems of Alexander Pope*, ed John Butt (London: Methuen).

Pott, Joseph Holden 1782. *An Essay on Landscape Painting* (London).

Sowerby, Robin 2012. 'The Goths in History and Pre-Gothic Gothic' in David Punter (ed), *A New Companion to the Gothic* (Chichester: Wiley-Blackwell), pp. 25–37.

Temple, William 1720. *The Works of Sir William Temple, Bart.*, 2 vols (London).

Thomson, James 1736. *Works of Mr. Thomson*, 2 vols (London).

Thompson, E A 1948. *A History of Attila and the Huns* (Oxford: Clarendon Press).

Turner, Sharon 1799–1805. *The History of the Anglo-Saxons, from Their First Appearance above the Elbe, to the Death of Egbert*, 4 vols (London: Cadell and Davies).

Virgil 1998. *The Aeneid*, trans by C Day Lewis, ed Jasper Griffin (Oxford: Oxford University Press).

Verstegan, Richard 1605. *A Restitution of Decayed Intelligence* (Antwerp).

Walpole, Horace 1762–3. *Anecdotes of Painting in England; with Some Account of the Principal Artists; and Incidental Notes on Other Arts*, 4 vols (Twickenham).

Warton, Thomas 1762. *Observations on The Fairie Queene of Spenser*, 2 vols, 2nd edn (London).

Webb, John 1725. *A Vindication of Stone-Henge Restored: in Which the Orders and Rules of Architecture Observed by the Ancient Romans, are Discussed*, 2nd edn (London).

West, Gilbert 1732. *Stowe, The Gardens of the Right Honourable Richard Lord Viscount Cobham* (London).

Chapter 2

Aikin, John and Anna Laetitia 1773. *Miscellaneous Pieces in Prose* (London).

Becket, Andrew 1789. 'Review of *The Castles of Athlin and Dunbayne*', *Monthly Review*, N.S. 3 (December) 91.

Coleridge, Samuel Taylor 1797. 'Review of *The Monk*', *Critical Review* (19 February) 194–200.

Beckford, William 1786. *An Arabian Tale, from an Unpublished Manuscript: With Notes Critical and Explanatory* (London).

Blackstone, William 1765–9. *Commentaries on the Laws of England*, 4 vols (Oxford: Clarendon Press).

Burke, Edmund 1757. *A Philosophical Enquiry into the Origin of Our Ideas of the Sublime and Beautiful* (London).

Byron, Lord George Gordon 1809. *English Bards and Scotch Reviewers* (London: Cawthorn).

Drake, Nathan 1798. *Literary Hours: Or, Sketches Critical and Narrative* (London).

Lewis, W S (ed) 1937–83. *The Yale Edition of Horace Walpole's Correspondence*, 42 vols (New Haven: Yale University Press).

Lewis, Matthew Gregory 1796. *The Monk, A Romance*, 3rd edn, copy annotated by Lewis, held in the British Library. BL: C.28. b 4–6.

Radcliffe, Ann 1794. *The Mysteries of Udolpho, A Romance, Interspersed with Some Pieces of Poetry*, 4 vols (London).

____. 1826. 'On the Supernatural in Poetry', *New Monthly Magazine and Literary Journal*, 16.1 (January), pp. 145–52.

Reeve, Clara 1778. *The Old English Baron: A Gothic Story* (London).

Rhodes, Ebenezer 1824. *Peak Scenery; or, The Derbyshire Tourist* (London: Longman, Hurst, Rees, Orme, Brown and Green).

Sabor, Peter (ed) 1987. *Horace Walpole: The Critical Heritage* (Abingdon: Routledge).

Walpole, Horace 2003. *The Castle of Otranto, A Gothic Story* and *The Mysterious Mother*, ed by Frederick S Frank (Peterborough, Ont.: Broadview).

Walpole, Horace 1765. *The Castle of Otranto, A Gothic Story*, 2nd edn (London).

Chapter 3

Anon. 1872. *Handbook to the Prince Consort National Memorial* (London: John Murray).

Austen, Jane 1995. *Northanger Abbey*, ed by Marilyn Butler (London: Penguin).

Barrow, Logie 1986. *Independent Spirits: Spiritualism and English Plebians, 1850–1910* (London: Routledge).

Carlyle, Thomas 1829. 'Anticipation; or, an Hundred Years Hence', *Edinburgh Review*, 49.98 (June) 439–59.

Collins, Wilkie 1990. *Basil*, ed by Dorothy Goldman (Oxford: World's Classics).

De Quincey, Thomas 1971. *Confessions of an English Opium Eater*, ed by Alethea Hayter (Harmondsworth: Penguin).

Dickens, Charles 2000. *The Old Curiosity Shop*, ed by Norman Page (London: Penguin).

___ 2003. *Bleak House*, ed by Nicola Bradbury (London: Penguin).

___ 1850. 'Old Lamps for New Ones', *Household Words* 1.5 (June) 265–7.

Eastlake, Charles L 1970. *A History of the Gothic Revival* (Leicester: Leicester University Press).

Hamilton, W R 1836. *Letters from W R Hamilton to the Earl of Elgin, on the New Houses of Parliament* (London: John Weale).

Himmelfarb, Gertrude. 1984. *The Idea of Poverty* (London: Faber and Faber).

Hobsbawm, Eric. 1997. *The Age of Capital 1848–1875* (London: Abacus).

Jenkyns, Richard 1991. *Dignity and Decadence* (London: HarperCollins 1991).

Justyne, William 1865. *Guide to Highgate Cemetery* (London: J Moore).

Lyell, Charles 1997. *The Principles of Geology* (London: Penguin).

Mansel, H L 1863. 'Sensation Novels', *Quarterly Review* 113.226 (April) 481–514.

Marx, Karl 1990. *Capital, Volume 1*, trans by Ben Fowkes (London: Penguin).

Miles, Robert 2002. 'The 1790s: the Effulgence of Gothic' in Jerrold E Hogle (ed) *The Cambridge Companion to Gothic Fiction* (Cambridge: Cambridge University Press), pp. 41–62.

Oppenheim, Janet 1985. *The Other World: Spiritualism and Psychical Research in England 1850–1914* (Cambridge: Cambridge University Press).

Owen, Alex 1989. *The Darkened Room: Women, Power and Spiritualism in Late Victorian England* (London: Virago).

Pugin, A W N 1853. *An Apology for the Revival of Christian Architecture in England* (London: John Weale).

___ 1898 *Contrasts* (Edinburgh: John Grant).

Reynolds, G W M *The Mysteries of London* http://www.victorianlondon.org [accessed 10 December 2013].

Ruskin, John 1959. *The Lamp of Beauty*, ed by Joan Evans (Oxford: Phaidon).

___ 1854. Letter, *The Times*, 25 May 1854, p. 7.

___ 1880. Letter to *The Builder*, 9 December 1854, in *Arrows of the Chace* (Kent: George Allen), vol 2, pp. 254–6.

Schor, Esther 1994. *Bearing the Dead: The British Culture of Mourning from the Enlightenment to Victoria* (Princeton: Princeton University Press).

Sue, Eugène 1845. *The Mysteries of Paris* (London: Chapman Hall).

Chapter 4

Booth, Charles 1902. *Life and Labour of the People of London* (London: Macmillan).

Booth, William 1890. *In Darkest England and the Way Out* (New York and London: Funk and Wagnalls).

Curtis, L Perry Jr 2001. *Jack the Ripper and the London Press* (New Haven, CT: Yale University Press).

Doyle, Arthur Conan 1981. 'The Hound of the Baskervilles' in *The Complete Sherlock Holmes* (Harmondsworth: Penguin), pp. 667–766.

Hurley, Kelly 2002. 'British Gothic Fiction, 1885–1930' in Jerrold E Hogle (ed), *The Cambridge Companion to Gothic Fiction* (Cambridge: Cambridge University Press), pp. 189–207.

Kipling, Rudyard 1891. 'The Mark of the Beast' in *Life's Handicap: Being Stories of Mine Own People* (London: Macmillan), pp. 240–58.

___ 2007a. 'My Own True Ghost Story' in *The Phantom Rickshaw and Other Ghost Stories* (Fairfield, CT: 1st World Library), pp. 35–44.

___2007b. 'The Phantom Rickshaw' in *The Phantom Rickshaw and Other Ghost Stories* (Fairfield, CT: 1st World Library), pp. 7–34.

___ 2007. 'The Strange Ride of Morrowbie Jukes' in *The Phantom Rickshaw and Other Ghost Stories* (Fairfield, CT: 1st World Library), pp. 45–72.

Lankester, Edwin Ray 1880. *Degeneration: A Chapter in Darwinism* (London: Macmillan).

Machen, Arthur 2006. *The Great God Pan* and *The Hill of Dreams* (New York: Dover).

Marryat, Florence 2010. *The Blood of the Vampire*, ed by Greta Depledge (Brighton: Victorian Secrets).

Mearns, Andrew 1883. *The Bitter Cry of Outcast London: An Inquiry into the Condition of the Abject Poor* (London: James Clarke).

Nordau, Max 1895. *Degeneration* (New York: Appleton Language).

Punter, David 1996. *The Literature of Terror*, vol 2 (London and New York: Longman).

Stevenson, Robert Louis 1984. *Dr Jekyll and Mr Hyde and Other Stories*, ed by Jenni Calder (Harmondsworth: Penguin).

Stoker, Bram 1996. *Dracula*, ed and intro by Maud Ellmann (Oxford: Oxford University Press).

Walkowitz, Judith R 1992. *City of Dreadful Delight: Narratives of Sexual Danger in Late-Victorian London* (London: Virago).

Wells, H G 2000. *The Island of Doctor Moreau*, ed by Brian Aldiss (London: Everyman).

Wilde, Oscar 1985. *The Picture of Dorian Gray*, ed by Peter Ackroyd (Harmondsworth: Penguin).

Chapter 5

Auerbach, Nina 1995. *Our Vampires, Ourselves* (Chicago and London: University of Chicago Press).

Barker, Clive 1986. *The Hellbound Heart* (London: HarperCollins).

Blackwood, Algernon 1910. 'The Windigo', in Basil Davenport (ed) *Ghostly Tales to Be Told* (London: Faber and Faber), pp. 21–77.

Bouzereau, Laurent (dir.) 2000. *All about The Birds* (Universal Studios Home Video) [on DVD].

Bowen, Elizabeth 1999. 'The Demon Lover', Angus Wilson (ed), *The Collected Stories of Elizabeth Bowen* (London: Vintage), pp.661–6.

Carter, Angela 1979a. *The Bloody Chamber and Other Stories* (Harmondsworth: Penguin).

___ 1979b. *The Sadeian Woman: An Exercise in Cultural History* (London: Virago).

Clover, Carol J 1992. *Men, Women and Chainsaws: Gender in the Modern Horror Film* (London: British Film Institute).

Conan Doyle, Arthur 1922. *The Coming of the Fairies* (London: Hodder and Stoughton).

Du Maurier, Daphne 1992. *Rebecca* (London: Arrow Books).

___ 2004. *The Birds and Other Stories* (London: Virago).

Freud, Sigmund (1919) 1990. 'The "Uncanny"' in Albert Dickson (ed), *The Penguin Freud Library, Vol 14, Art and Literature* (Harmondsworth: Penguin), pp. 335–76.

Giles, Dennis 1984. 'Conditions of Pleasure in Horror Cinema' in Barry Keith Grant (ed), *Planks of Reason: Essays in the Horror Film* (Metuchen, NJ: Scarecrow Press), pp. 38–52.

Hill, Susan 1998. *The Woman in Black* (London: Vintage Books).

James, Henry (1907–9) 1986. *The Aspern Papers* and *The Turn of the Screw* (Harmondsworth: Penguin).

James, M R 1987. '"Oh, Whistle, and I'll Come to You, My Lad"', in Michael Cox (ed), *'Casting the Runes' and Other Ghost Stories* (Oxford and New York: Oxford University Press), pp. 57–77.

Kitchener, Richard F (ed) 1988. *The World View of Contemporary Physics: Does the World Need a New Metaphysics?* (Albany: State University of New York).

Lurie, Alison 1992. *The Language of Clothes* (London: Bloomsbury).

Madoff, Mark S 1989. 'Inside, Outside and the Gothic Locked-Room Mystery', Kenneth W Graham (ed), *Gothic Fictions: Prohibition/Transgression* (New York: AMS), pp. 49–62.

Martin, Sara 2002. 'Gothic Scholars Don't Wear Black: Gothic Studies and Gothic Sub-culture' in *Gothic Studies* 4.1: 28–43.

McGrath, Patrick 1988. 'The Angel' in *Blood and Water* (Harmondsworth: Penguin), pp. 1–16.

___ 1989. *The Grotesque* (Harmondsworth: Penguin).

___ 1994. *Dr Haggard's Disease* (Harmondsworth: Penguin).

Moers, Ellen 1976. *Literary Women* (London: Women's Press).

Moretti, Franco 1983. *Signs Taken for Wonders: Essays in the Sociology of Literary Forms* (London: Verso).

Twitchell, James B 1985. *Dreadful Pleasures: An Anatomy of Modern Horror* (New York and Oxford: Oxford University Press).

Wall Hinds, Elizabeth Jane 1992. 'The Devil Sings the Blues: Heavy Metal, Gothic Fiction and "Postmodern" Discourse', *Journal of Popular Culture*, 26.3: 151–64.

Wharton, Edith 1973. 'Introduction', in William R. Tyler (ed), *The Ghost Stories of Edith Wharton* (London: Virago, 1996), pp. vii–x.

Wheatley, Helen 2006. *Gothic Television* (Manchester and New York: Manchester University Press).

Chapter 6

Botting, Fred 2002. 'Aftergothic: Consumption, Machines and Black Holes', in Jerrold E Hogle (ed), *The Cambridge Companion to Gothic Fiction* (Cambridge: Cambridge University Press), pp. 277–300.

Buckley, Chloe 2014. 'Gothic and the Child Reader, 1850–Present', in Glennis Byron and Dale Townshend (eds), *The Gothic World* (Oxford: Routledge), pp. 254–63.

Byron, Glennis 2012. 'Global Gothic', in David Punter (ed), *A New Companion to the Gothic* (Oxford: Blackwell), pp. 369–78.

Danielewski, Mark Z 2001. *House of Leaves* (London: Doubleday).

___ [no date]. 'A Conversation with Mark Danielewski', <http://www.randomhouse.com/boldtype/0400/danielewski/interview.html> [accessed 11 January 2014].

Dyson, Jeremy 2012. *The Haunted Book* (Edinburgh: Canongate).

Hackman, Paul 2011. '"I Am a Double Agent": Shelley Jackson's *Patchwork Girl* and the Persistence of Print in the Age of Hypertext', *Contemporary Literature*, 52.1: 84–107.

Jenkins, Henry 2006. *Convergence Culture: Where Old and New Media Collide* (New York: New York University Press).

Kumar, Krishan 1995. *From Post-Industrial to Post-Modern Society: New Theories of the Contemporary World* (Oxford: Blackwell).

Lawson, Mark 2013. 'S. by JJ Abrams and Doug Dorst – review', *The Guardian*, 13 November, <http://www.theguardian.com/books/2013/nov/13/s-jj-abrams-doug-dorst-review> [accessed 11 January 2014].

McRobert, Neil 2013. *The New Labyrinth: Reading, Writing and Textuality in Contemporary Gothic Fiction* (unpublished PhD thesis: University of Stirling).

Mighall, Robert 1999. *A Geography of Victorian Gothic Fiction: Mapping History's Nightmares* (Oxford: Oxford University Press).

Rothman, Joshua 2013. 'The Story of "S": Talking With J. J. Abrams and Doug Dorst', *The New Yorker*, 23 November 2013, <http://www.newyorker.com/online/blogs/books/2013/11/the-story-of-s-talking-with-jj-abrams-and-doug-dorst.html> [accessed 11 January 2014].

Snicket, Lemony 2001. *A Series of Unfortunate Events. 1: The Bad Beginning* (London: Egmont Books).

Thomas, Scarlett 2008. *The End of Mr Y* (Edinburgh: Canongate).

Toffler, Alvin 1981. *The Third Wave* (London: Pan Macmillan).

Vandermeer, Jeff, with S J Chambers 2011. *The Steampunk Bible* (New York: Abrams Image).

Warwick, Alexandra 2007. 'Feeling Gothicky', *Gothic Studies* 9.1: 5–15.

Illustration Credits

2 Universal/The Kobal Collection; **20** Courtesy of the Lewis Walpole Library, Yale University; **21** © The Trustees of the British Museum; **23** Courtesy of the Lewis Walpole Library, Yale University; **27, 30, 34** © The Trustees of the British Museum; **55** © National Portrait Gallery, London; **56** CSG CIC Glasgow Museums and Libraries Collections; **63** Courtesy of the Lewis Walpole Library, Yale University; **69** © The Trustees of the British Museum; **73** Courtesy of the Lewis Walpole Library, Yale University; **77** © Tate, London 2014; **79** © National Portrait Gallery, London; **84** Photograph Courtesy of The National Gallery of Ireland; **86** © Tate, London 2014; **92** The Bodleian Library, University of Oxford; **96, 98, 112** © The Trustees of the British Museum; **113** V&A Images; **119** Science & Society Picture Library; **134** The National Archives; **141** Courtesy Royal Armouries; **142, 143, 144** BFI National Archives; **150** Prana-Film/The Kobal Collection; **152** 20th Century Fox/The Kobal Collection; **163** BFI National Archives; **154** Universal/The Kobal Collection; **155** Paule Saviano/Lebrecht Music & Arts/Alamy; **159** Science & Society Picture Library; **161 top** © 1973 Studiocanal Films Ltd/The Kobal Collection; **161 below** Universal/The Kobal Collection; **163** BFI National Archive; **167** BFI National Archives; **169** Selznick/United Artists/The Kobal Collection; **173** Hammer Film Productions/The Kobal Collection; **175** © Clive Barker; **176** Reproduced with permission of Senate House Library, University of London; **181** © Jim Kay. Published by Walker Books, courtesy www.alisoneldred.com; **182** BFI National Archive; **183** Laurel Entertainment/The Kobal Collection; **185** Photo Steve White, © Jake and Dinos Chapman/White Cube; **188** Courtesy Profile Books; **189** © Shelley Jackson, courtesy Eastgate; **191** Artisan Pics/The Kobal Collection; **195, 196** Courtesy Canongate; **200** © Dave McKean; **204** Getty Images; **208–15** © Martin Parr/Magnumphotos.

Index

Figures in *italic* refer to pages on which illustrations appear.